A TOUCHSTONE BOOK
PUBLISHED BY SIMON & SCHUSTER INC.
NEW YORK LONDON TORONTO SYDNEY TOKYO

THE PULITZER PRIZES

VOLUME 1, 1987

EDITED BY
KENDALL J. WILLS

Designed by Bonni Leon
Manufactured in the United States of America

10 9 8 7 6 5 4 3 2 1
10 9 8 7 6 5 4 3 2 1 Pbk.

ISSN 0896-2197

ISBN 0-671-65956-1
     0-671-64466-1 Pbk.

The editor is grateful to the following for permission to reprint:

Introductory essay on public service reporting, by Andrew Schneider and Matthew Brelis. Used by permission of Andrew Schneider and Matthew Brelis.
"Pilots on drugs—doctors can't report them," by Andrew Schneider, in The Pittsburgh Press, *September 21, 1986, page 1. Reprinted with permission of* The Pittsburgh Press.
"Anatomy of a system that didn't work," by Andrew Schneider and Matthew Brelis, in The Pittsburgh Press, *October 12, 1986, page 1. Reprinted with permission of* The Pittsburgh Press.
"Top air doctor OKs pilots at risk," by Andrew Schneider and Matthew Brelis, in The Pittsburgh Press, *November 16, 1986, page 1. Reprinted with permission of* The Pittsburgh Press.
"Pilots' secret cocaine treatment called bad medicine," by Andrew Schneider, in The Pittsburgh Press, *December 4, 1986, page 1. Reprinted with permission of* The Pittsburgh Press.
"Air crews fly through customs because they're called 'low-risk,' " by Andrew Schneider, in The Pittsburgh Press, *December 21, 1986, page 1. Reprinted with permission of* The Pittsburgh Press.

Pulitzer Prize nominating letter, by Dale Allen, Editor, of the Akron Beacon Journal. *Reprinted with permission of the* Akron Beacon Journal.
"The Goodyear War," by staff members of the Akron Beacon Journal, *November 30, 1986, pages 1, B1–8. Reprinted with permission of the* Akron Beacon Journal.
"Pulitzer Prize belongs to all at Beacon Journal," by Doug Oplinger, in the Akron Beacon Journal. *Reprinted with permission of the* Akron Beacon Journal.

Pulitzer Prize nominating letter written for Mr. Woestendiek by Eugene Roberts, Executive Editor, The Philadelphia Inquirer. *Used by permission of* The Philadelphia Inquirer.
Introductory essay on investigative reporting, by John Woestendiek. Used by permission of John Woestendiek.
"Evidence of innocence: Doubt cast on a murder case," by John Woestendiek, in The Philadelphia Inquirer, *April 20, 1986, page 1-A. Reprinted with permission of* The Philadelphia Inquirer.

(continued at back of book)

ACKNOWLEDGMENTS

I owe enormous gratitude for this project to Deborah J. Bergman, my editor at Simon & Schuster, who found promise in an idea and patiently guided me through the process of turning it into a book. I would also like to thank the following people, who helped in a variety of ways to make this anthology possible: Peggy Piaskoski, Robert D. Stang, Joanne Kenen, Paul F. Linn, Robin Kuzen, my brothers, Michael and Robert, and, most of all, my parents, Sherilyn L. Wills and Robert H. Wills.

To Louis G. Nierstheimer

CONTENTS

INTRODUCTION

Featured in these pages are the latest members of journalism's most exclusive, yet unofficial, club—that special group of people who share the honor of having their names forever linked with the phrase "Pulitzer Prize winner."

As American journalism's most prestigious awards, the Pulitzer Prizes have been synonymous with the best in the business for nearly 70 years.

Until now, though, the year's award-winning articles, photographs and editorial cartoons have never been collected in a single publication. It is my hope that this volume, in addition to paying tribute to the winners, will become a long-term record of some of the best journalism of the year and expand the audience of any individual contribution beyond its usual circulation to national readership.

Editors and reporters can find practical lessons in these articles, and aspiring journalists may study them and learn from the reporting and writing techniques. Those outside the journalism profession will discover that the Pulitzer-winning selections are a good read and remain timely even as the stories continue to unfold.

Since the earliest of times, mankind has had a passion to record the events of the day. Yet what constitutes "news," and the methods of gathering it, continue to change. Today, history is recorded instantly in words and photographic images, and the meaning and consequences of each day's events are given immediate analysis. Journalists are already researching, reporting and writing articles that will be chosen as the outstanding Pulitzer Prize-winning works next year.

Modern journalism is also, by nature, ephemeral. Today's headlines are quickly discarded as tomorrow's news steals our attention. This volume offers an opportunity to step back, briefly, to note some of the major events of our time and to celebrate outstanding achievement in one of the oldest professions.

Although this is the first complete collection of the 1987 Pulitzer Prizes in journalism, the book represents neither a beginning nor an end. The Pulitzer Prizes, established by a grant from Joseph Pulitzer and administered by Columbia University, were first awarded in 1917, and the Pulitzer Prize Board has conferred hundreds of awards since then. This collection of photographs, editorial cartoons and writings is the first in what will be a series of annual anthologies.

Only the journalism categories are included in the anthology, because many of the Pulitzer Prizes in the arts and literature categories are printed elsewhere. The pieces published here are reproduced in their entirety and represent a solid sample of each winner's work—a sample that should satisfy even readers with the most hearty appetite for journalism.

The Pulitzer Prizes includes articles, photographs and cartoons that will appeal not only to journalists and news buffs but to anyone with an interest in the compelling issues that confront Americans today and that will likely command our attention for years to come. Consider, for example, *The Pittsburgh Press*'s uncovering of the dangers posed by airline pilots who abuse drugs and alcohol, and the bureaucratic mess that prevents officials from grounding them.

Or relive the detailed saga of a takeover battle started by an international financier who wanted to gain control of a Midwestern city's largest employer, which wanted no part of the deal. The *Akron Beacon Journal* recounts how Akron, Ohio, was gripped by The Goodyear Tire & Rubber Company's costly fight to thwart Sir James Goldsmith's hostile takeover attempt.

Coverage of other current events also earned newspapers Pulitzer Prizes. This year, *The Philadelphia Inquirer* won three awards, two for its coverage of injustice in the courts, including John Woestendiek's articles that helped free a man wrongly convicted of murder, and a third for a feature story by Steve Twomey about the excitement and danger aboard an aircraft carrier.

The Miami Herald won for its early coverage of the Iran-contra affair, while *The New York Times* won two awards, for its staff's investigation into the causes of the explosion of the space shuttle Challenger and for its report, by Alex S. Jones, of the bickering within a powerful family that led to the sale of a media empire.

The *Los Angeles Times* also won two prizes, for Michael Parks's reporting from South Africa under increasingly restrictive conditions, and for Richard Eder's authoritative book reviews. The "Bloom County" cartoons, drawn by Berke Breathed, earned an award for *The Washington Post,* as did the political and social commentary of Charles Krauthammer.

For its award, the *Chicago Tribune* explained to its readers the medical promise and the limits of gene therapy, and Jonathan Freedman's editorials campaigning for reform of United States immigration laws won the editorial writing award for *The Tribune* of San Diego.

Finally, two photography prizes were awarded this year. Kim Komenich of the *San Francisco Examiner* recorded the fall of President Ferdinand E. Marcos of the Philippines and the rise of his successor, Corazon C. Aquino, while David Peterson of *The Des Moines Register* captured the anguish of Iowa farmers whose dreams had been shattered by economic devastation.

I have not tried to critique the winning works; that is left to the reader. Each chapter is introduced by the winner's description of the story behind the story—or the story behind the photos or cartoons, as the case may be. These accounts provide fascinating background to some of the most important journalism of the year and give insight into how the journalists turned their work into prize winners. The winning selections are followed by biographical sketches of the contributors, who, after all, the book is really about.

Kendall J. Wills
New York City
April 1987

THE PULITZER PRIZES

PULITZER PRIZE BOARD

1987 SPECIAL CITATION

The Pulitzer Prize Board issues a special citation to Joseph Pulitzer Jr., the grandson of the founder of the Pulitzer Prizes, "for his extraordinary services to American journalism and letters during his 31 years as chairman of the Pulitzer Prize Board and for his accomplishments as an editor and publisher."

ONE

FLYING HIGH—PILOTS ON DRUGS

1987 WINNER IN THE PUBLIC SERVICE CATEGORY

"For a distinguished example of meritorious public service by a newspaper through the use of its journalistic resources . . . a gold medal."

The Pittsburgh Press
Andrew Schneider
Matthew Brelis

Each day Americans who use air travel place their lives in the hands of flight crews, some of whom suffer from dangerous medical problems and serious drug addictions. *The Pittsburgh Press* documents flaws in the federal system that is supposed to guard against these risks.

Our immersion into the medical world of the Federal Aviation Administration began with an anguished call from a physician. The doctor said he was frustrated at his inability to stop an airline copilot who was being treated for a near-fatal cocaine overdose from leaving the intensive care unit and climbing back into the cockpit of a passenger jet.

Patient confidentiality prevented the doctor or his hospital administration from notifying the pilot's airline or the FAA about the airman's chronic drug problem. The pilot's body was scarred with track marks, indicating years of drug use. Interviews with his family and friends confirmed that the young man had a long history of drug abuse.

It was difficult to understand why FAA records for the pilot, including medical reports, showed no indication of drug use during any of the medical examinations that are required by the agency every six months.

Subsequent interviews across the country with more than 100 aviation medical examiners presented an even more puzzling picture. These doctors, who are authorized by the FAA to perform the physical exams, agreed that their examinations can rarely detect drug or alcohol abuse, because the FAA does not mandate the testing of blood or urine.

In addition, we found that aviation safety authorities have long criticized the FAA for its refusal to compare the names of licensed pilots to the National Driver's Registry, which lists all motorists whose licenses have been revoked or suspended for driving while intoxicated.

We obtained documents showing that when the inspector general's office at the Department of Transportation cross-checked the pilots' names with the registry, it found that more than 16,000 had lost their driving privileges for driving while intoxicated—something the FAA was supposed to know but did not.

We also discovered that the agency even closed its eyes to specific reports from law enforcement officials on the continuing criminal drinking problem of a pilot who later crashed a twin-engine plane into a Tennessee mountainside. Pathologists said the alcohol level in the pilot's blood at the time of the crash was four times the FAA's permissible limit.

Next, we learned that a helicopter pilot who had a heart condition documented as potentially fatal was able to get his FAA medical certificate reissued—a necessary condition for flying—despite the objection of the agency's own doctors.

Our misgivings about the agency's system grew when we learned that the same pilot flew his helicopter into a ravine in California, killing himself and his passenger. The National Transportation Safety Board said the pilot's heart failure led to the crash.

We pursued the history of the pilot's medical certification and found that it was the federal air surgeon himself, Dr. Frank Austin, who ignored warnings from seven other doctors, including cardiac specialists, that the pilot's heart was so severely damaged that he could not fly safely.

We obtained and evaluated FAA reports on the medical certification of more than 2,500 pilots, as well as medical records of hundreds of others, and what we saw was an alarming pattern of the flight surgeon repeatedly overruling the recommendations of the agency's own panel of doctors.

Through further documentation and interviews with dozens of doctors, including medical directors of the major airlines, we confirmed that more than 250 commercial airline pilots and copilots with potentially fatal or instantly debilitating medical conditions were allowed, by Austin, to return to the cockpit.

The FAA's medical regulations require that pilots found to be using drugs be grounded permanently. But despite repeated petitions by medical authorities to have the FAA treat drug abuse like alcoholism, by which pilots would be allowed to fly again once they had been rehabilitated from the disease, the agency refused. As a result, much of the treatment for drug abuse was done secretively.

We interviewed officials at dozens of drug treatment centers across the country and found that scores of airline pilots had received or were receiving clandestine treatment for cocaine abuse. Some of these clinics were delivering dangerously substandard care, and several doctors feared that some pilots had returned to flying while still addicted.

Moreover, by following tips from several pilots and flight attendants, we were able to show how crews on international flights pass by customs inspections and could easily bring drugs into the country. Security officials at a dozen major airports and at United States Customs entry points told how virtually anyone in an airline uniform could pass through security points unchecked.

Our articles resulted in several reforms: Federal Air Surgeon Frank Austin was removed from office; the National Driver's Registry is now cross-checked with lists of licensed pilots; more extensive FAA medical exams are being developed; and methods to tighten airport and customs security are being evaluated.

—Matthew Brelis and Andrew Schneider
The Pittsburgh Press

PILOTS ON DRUGS— DOCTORS CAN'T REPORT THEM

SUNDAY, SEPTEMBER 21, 1986

BY ANDREW SCHNEIDER

Doctors and nurses at six Pittsburgh area hospitals say they have treated members of USAir flight crews for cocaine overdoses but are forbidden by law from reporting the potential safety hazards to officials who could prevent the personnel from flying.

The most recent incident occurred shortly before midnight on Sept. 10, when Chris Ganas, a 30-year-old USAir pilot, blue-faced and near death from a cocaine overdose, was brought by friends to the parking lot of Mercy Hospital. "He wasn't breathing and was far more dead than alive," said a doctor.

A doctor and a nurse used a rubber bag-mask to force air into Ganas's dormant lungs as others loaded him onto a stretcher for the short race to the treatment room. Within moments, two IVs were started and a tube was inserted to help him breathe. Doctors and nurses crowded around him, administering a stream of drugs to lower his out-of-control heart rate and blood pressure and to try to counter the massive amount of cocaine that was destroying his lungs, heart and central nervous system.

To the amazement of everyone, Ganas survived, even though, as one doctor put it, his blood and urine samples showed "a level and collection of drugs that I thought nobody could live through." In fact, 33 hours later, over the objections of his physicians, Ganas removed the tubes and sensors connected to his body and left the hospital.

Some medical personnel at Mercy and other hospitals say they are angry, frustrated and terrified that the legal roadblocks of patient confidentiality—which they willingly adhere to under other circumstances—prevent them from officially reporting pilots' drug abuse to the appropriate safety authorities.

"It doesn't make any sense at all. We are required by state law to report all gunshots, stab wounds and child abuse to the police, and seizures and a dozen other problems to DMV (Department of Motor Vehicles), but when we have a pilot carrying a deadly level of cocaine, we've got no one we can legally notify to decide whether this guy should be flying," says Karen Congelio, clinical supervisor of Mercy's Emergency Department.

While neither Ms. Congelio nor any other nurses or physicians at Mercy would confirm that the patient was Ganas, other information obtained by The Pittsburgh Press shows Ganas was admitted that night near death from an overdose of cocaine and other drugs.

A USAir official would not discuss the case beyond saying that Ganas has not flown since Sept. 7 and that he was taken off flight status after the question of his drug abuse was raised by The Pittsburgh Press. Ganas could not be reached for comment. His father, Chris Sr., a highly respected senior USAir pilot, said he has no idea where his son is.

The Federal Aviation Administration says no commercial airline accident has ever been attributed to drug abuse by crew members. But cocaine use by flight crew members creates a safety hazard that could be devastating, say the experts who are treating USAir employees for drug abuse on an individual basis and also under contract to the airline.

"Cocaine presents a tremendous euphoria, a feeling of tranquility and wellness and well-being and that can be dangerous, especially for pilots," said Rick Hatfield, executive director of Brighton Woods Treatment Center, North Side.

"Say they get an abort order or have to get out of the path of another flight. If you're feeling falsely comfortable and secure, you're not going to react to that danger in the way you should."

Sharon Eakes, director of therapy at Gateway Rehabilitation Center in Beaver County, shares the concern.

"Using cocaine in a plane poses life-threatening situations. Heavy users can have heart arrhythmia and grand mal seizures. If a pilot has a seizure you've got a problem," she said.

Even without a medical crisis, she said the risks remain significant: "The cocaine takes away any sensation of discomfort. You feel all powerful, like you can do anything. You feel like you can do anything better. Of course, you can't."

Coke addicts who are between doses of the drug, she said, "are real lethargic, really depressed, paranoid. They're not sleeping, not eating. If you get caught up in a cycle like that, you've got trouble. If you're a pilot, responsible for a few hundred people, you're dangerous."

Physicians and nurses at area hospitals say they have become more aware of flight personnel receiving treatment for drug-related problems in the past few months. But the medical personnel say they aren't certain whether the number of cases is increasing or that the publicity surrounding the ongoing grand jury investigation of USAir employees' involvement with cocaine has made these cases more noticeable.

The grand jury has been hearing testimony from USAir employees for the past two months. It is unclear whether the investigation is centered on cocaine use or trafficking. To date, more than a half-dozen witnesses have been questioned and at least three have been granted immunity.

Few details are available about the USAir investigation because grand juries operate in secrecy and only the witnesses themselves are permitted to discuss their testimony.

As the biggest hub for the nation's sixth busiest airline, Pittsburgh has more than 7,000 USAir employees. Almost 600 USAir flights each day land and depart from Greater Pitt.

Although physicians and nurses at only six of the area's 36 hospitals were interviewed by The Pittsburgh Press, 23 cases of flight crew drug abuse were quickly recalled by emergency room staffs at Mercy, St. Clair, Presbyterian-University, Allegheny General, North Hills Passavant and Forbes Regional.

In addition, personnel at all six hospitals said they treated numerous cases of drug abuse or dependence among non-flight employees such as mechanics, baggage personnel and reservation clerks.

In those cases dealing with flight crews, 20 of the incidents involved cocaine overdoses, two were heroin reactions and one dealt with valium and alcohol. In 18 of the 19 cases where medical personnel could recall the patient's employer, the airline was USAir. The other was TWA.

The mixture of pilots, co-pilots, engineers and flight attendants differed from hospital to hospital, but the total showed 12 cockpit crewmembers and 11 cabin crew.

"We're seeing more flight attendants at Forbes Metro but at

(Forbes) Regional the percentage of pilots is higher," said Dr. Philip Phillips, chairman of the emergency departments at Forbes Health Systems.

All the doctors and nurses interviewed, while asserting the importance of patient confidentiality, expressed great frustration at being unable to keep drug-impaired airline crewmembers from climbing back into the cockpit of a passenger jet.

"The law puts doctors and nurses in an unbearable position where we are being forced to turn our backs on what may be a genuine threat to public safety. We're in the business of saving lives and we have a moral responsibility to do what is right, but the laws block our way," said Dr. Paul Paris, the co-director of Presby's Emergency Department.

"We need a law that allows us to report serious, debilitating, medical conditions in those cases where an individual is employed in a position where he or she is responsible for the lives of others, and flight crews clearly hold the lives of hundreds in their hands."

Many pilots share the doctors' concerns.

"In the old days, booze was the biggest problem in the cockpit, and while it presented some personality problems and led to some good brawls, I never had to worry about the guy in the second seat (co-pilot) flipping out," said a senior USAir pilot who asked that his name not be used. "Now, on some of my flights, I'm so worried about what the cokehead sitting next to me might do at 34,000 (feet) that I'm terrified to leave the flight deck, even to go to the head."

Even rehabilitation clinics where flight personnel are treated for drug abuse are prohibited from informing the airline unless the employee gives them permission to release the information. Both Ms. Eakes of Gateway and Hatfield of Brighton Woods said permission is granted in most cases, but not all.

"Clearly there is a need for a reporting mechanism and protection against liability for medical personnel who use that mechanism in cases such as this. Existing state and federal statutes prohibit the disclosure of such information, even if—as in the case of an airline pilot—withholding the information may risk catastrophe," said James Redmond, executive vice president of the Hospital Association of Pennsylvania.

Pennsylvania law specifies that patient information can only be released to government officials "exclusively for the purpose of obtaining benefits due the patient as a result of his drug or alcohol abuse or dependency."

Federal law forbids the use of any medical record or information to initiate or substantiate criminal charges "or to conduct any investigation of a patient."

All the medical personnel interviewed stressed they had no desire to become criminal investigators.

"Our overriding concern is the safety of the public, not enforcement of drug laws. We are physicians and nurses, not cops and we don't want to be," says AGH's Dr. Kim Zaiser. "But how can laws insist we take definitive, specific actions in cases of child abuse and seizures when we are forbidden from doing anything when we suspect that a patient's condition may cost the lives of hundreds?"

Doctors at St. Clair and Forbes and nurses at Mercy, Passavant and AGH privately admitted that in a handful of serious cases they violated the law and notified authorities of the problems. However, all expressed uncertainty that anything was done to ensure that the patient received the proper treatment.

"I'd do it again," said a nurse at Passavant. "I couldn't sleep for three nights worrying whether that cokehead we treated would drive his plane into the side of a mountain with 300 people aboard. Finally, I just called the airline and told them and it became their problem."

Most of the emergency department supervisors questioned said that while they couldn't openly encourage a doctor or nurse on their staff to violate the law, they would support their action.

"Remember, we're talking about safety and not enforcement. We're talking about the safety of lots of people and I would back my people all the way and let the legal chips fall later on," said Dr. Richard DiIlio, chairman of St. Clair's Emergency Department.

Across town at Forbes, Dr. Phillips echoed those views. "It's a moral and ethical decision that each individual must make. We know we're risking ourselves to liability but we have a social obligation to the community we serve. Not only do we fly on these aircraft, but they're over our communities around-the-clock. I'd back my staff to the hilt if that was the only way to ground someone who was a potential hazard, but we wouldn't have to do this if there was a law allowing us to report a problem to an FAA physician or if someone else was watching."

Many doctors agree the laws governing their actions do not acknowledge the severity of the cocaine problem.

"The law clearly has not kept up to the changes in our society. Cocaine is a problem today. It took years for the laws to catch up with alcohol and drunken driving. I'm afraid it may take years to catch up with the special dangers of cocaine, and I'm afraid it's time we may not have," said Dr. David Mosienko, chairman of the Emergency Department at Canonsburg General Hospital.

While private physicians and nurses are prohibited from reporting drug abuse, 7,000 FAA-certified physicians who conduct extensive, mandatory flight physicals on the nation's 500,000 air crewmembers are required to report any suspected or proven substance abuse.

"But it's pure luck if we can prove cocaine use because there is nothing in the examination that will help us detect it. Unless they come in with powder on their nose, there's not much we can do," said a flight examiner from Philadelphia.

The lengthy examinations are required every six months for commercial pilots and yearly for other flight personnel, but screening or testing for drug use or abuse is not permitted, said Dr. John Jordan, the FAA's deputy federal air surgeon.

"There are ongoing discussions in this agency over the issue of drug testing for pilots and it's a very controversial matter. But, for the time being, only FAA personnel, in safety-related jobs such as flight controllers and inspectors, will be required to undergo drug screening. It will be a while before a decision is made on the airline pilots," Jordan said.

Dr. Gerald Pifer, an orthopedic specialist at AGH who has also served for years as an FAA medical examiner, said the drug screening of pilots is needed.

"It is common knowledge that someone under the influence of drugs is not going to be able to properly control an aircraft in the same manner as someone free of drugs. With pilots, screening goes beyond invasion of patient privacy. We're not dealing with someone who chooses to destroy his own life with drugs, but perhaps the 350 lives of the people aboard his aircraft. The controls must be tightened as much as possible," Pifer said.

Jordan acknowledged that with the exception of Virginia, which in 1979 passed a law protecting physicians who report impaired pilots, doctors and nurses throughout the country may face liability from violating patient confidentiality laws.

"It could be a great help if the (civilian) medical profession were permitted to report impaired flight crewmembers to responsible safety authorities, but we understand the confidentiality problems they face. I hope it will change some day," Jordan says.

(Press staff writer Mary Pat Flaherty contributed to this report.)

ANATOMY OF A SYSTEM THAT DIDN'T WORK

SUNDAY, OCTOBER 12, 1986

BY ANDREW SCHNEIDER AND MATTHEW BRELIS

Charles Joseph Hvizdak loved to fly and liked to drink. The combination may have led to his fiery death on a Tennessee mountainside.

Safety investigators say the government's system designed to identify alcohol or drug impaired pilots should have kept Hvizdak out of the cockpit.

Hvizdak had 7,500 flying hours when he burned to death soon after dawn Feb. 22, trapped in the wreckage of a flaming, twin-engine Beech 18, halfway up Pack Mountain, 3½ miles northeast of Copperhill, Tenn.

The Federal Aviation Administration pathologist in Oklahoma City reports that tests of the 36-year-old pilot's blood showed an alcohol level of .158, nearly four times the FAA permissible level of .04.

"It may be a very significant factor in the crash," a technician at the FAA's Forensic Toxicology Research Unit said. But the fact that Hvizdak drank heavily should have been no surprise to the FAA.

Seventeen months earlier, Robert Jambois, the assistant city attorney for Kenosha, Wis., stormed out of a courtroom where Hvizdak was being arraigned for his seventh driving-while-intoxicated conviction, and began what ultimately was a futile effort to get the FAA to take action on an obviously impaired pilot.

"The evidence showed that an intoxicated driver flipped his van after hitting a parked car at a hundred miles an hour and his only ID was a commercial pilot's license," Jambois says. "I couldn't believe that anyone with such a long record of DWIs could still be licensed to fly, so I called the FAA."

The accident that fueled Jambois' anger occurred on a quiet, residential street, just minutes after Kenosha's 175 taverns closed at 2 a.m. Police officer Louis Perri arrived at the scene to find a large crowd peering into the windows of an overturned van.

"The doors were jammed shut from the crash," Perri said, and Hvizdak, unhurt, was trapped in the rear of the van, "like a goldfish in a bowl." Although Hvizdak "had a blood-alcohol level of .25, two and a half times Wisconsin's legal limit for intoxication, he was walking normally. Most people would be flat on their backs," Perri said.

Jambois' efforts to notify the FAA took more than a simple phone call. His first try was to the FAA's closest office, in Milwaukee. "They said they weren't the office that handles that and I should call Oklahoma City," he said.

Someone at the FAA's Aviation Record's Center in Oklahoma told him, "We don't do anything about cases like that, call the Chicago office," he recalled.

At the FAA's Great Lake's Regional Office in Chicago, Jambois finally connected with an investigator who said he'd come to Kenosha. "A week later, he showed up and took our records on the case and those of the DA. I thought Hvizdak's flying days were over."

That wasn't the case, even though the K-Airways pilot was jailed, awaiting trial. Hvizdak was freed from detention on a work-release program that allowed him to fly whenever K-Airways needed him, which was frequently, according to Paul Ericson, the charter company president.

Jambois contacted the FAA investigator in October and again in December and was told each time that there were "more pressing demands."

K-Airways also had pressing demands: "We cannot operate without a pilot, with the specialized aircraft that we operate," Ericson wrote to the Kenosha district attorney, appealing for Hvizdak's occasional release.

"The airline's Beech 18 tail-dragger, a WWII vintage aircraft, with its tail wheel and double rudders, was a bitch to control on landings and takeoffs and Chuck was the only guy around who could handle it," said one mechanic at the Kenosha Municipal Airport.

Ericson says Hvizdak's time in a work-release program didn't matter.

"We knew he wasn't drinking (in jail), and what better control could there be? I don't give a good damn what they say, he was not dependent on alcohol," he said.

Others who knew him told federal safety investigators that Hvizdak would drink heavily two or three nights a week.

Hvizdak's alcohol problem should have been detected without Jambois' intervention. The FAA claims its medical examination system can detect pilots with drug and alcohol problems.

But the 6-foot-tall, blond-haired, brown-eyed pilot had gone through at least a decade of annual FAA medical exams, the last one on April 9, 1985, while he was still in jail.

However, a check of his medical certificates dating back to 1977, showed none of the FAA-approved medical examiners reported any suspicions of an alcohol problem. This was further compounded by the fact that Hvizdak repeatedly lied on his medical application denying that he had traffic convictions or an "excessive drinking habit."

Hvizdak underwent court-ordered alcohol assessment by the Drug and Alcohol Council of Kenosha County in September 1981 and January 1985. Both times the agency reported that the pilot used alcohol irresponsibly and suspected an alcohol dependency.

The Marine Corps Vietnam veteran was divorced twice. The second marriage, to a commercial airline pilot whom he met in flight school, ended in 1979 because of Hvizdak's drinking, his former wife told investigators.

Although the FAA medical examiners are informed that marital problems can be a sign of excessive drinking, his divorces were apparently overlooked.

Flying was his love. At 17, Hvizdak was working on airplanes; at 25, he was learning to fly, and a year later, he had his first pilot's license. He joined K-Airways in 1983.

But a three-page rap sheet of driving offenses documents his penchant for fast driving and hard drinking.

"He would go out on Saturday night, have a few beers, get behind the wheel and drive like a fool. He drew cops like flies," said Ericson.

In January 1980, Hvizdak's driver's license was revoked after a conviction for leaving the scene of an accident. In the next four years he racked up 20 other violations, including seven convictions for driving while his license was revoked, two speeding offenses, one citation for reckless driving and seven for driving while intoxicated.

Ericson said he fired Hvizdak in early 1985 for drinking, but re-hired him two days later. Hvizdak worked at K-Airways until he died.

In the three days before his death, Hvizdak flew a lot, beginning with a long, night flight to Shreveport, La., on Feb 19.

The next day, he was grounded by bad weather in Peoria, Ill. before returning home. On Feb. 21, a round-trip to Romeo, Mich. Around 6 that evening, Hvizdak hailed a cab and headed to town.

He spent the last night of his life at Friar's Lounge in Kenosha drinking bottled beer at $1.25 a pop. Two shifts of barmaids told safety investigators that Hvizdak drank several beers in the quiet tavern which draws an older crowd, many of them supervisors from the nearby American Motors plant, where Hvizdak's air charter company got most of its business. He fell asleep several times at the end of the long bar before leaving at midnight.

An hour later, James Vannoy, manager of K-Airways, paged Hvizdak for a flight.

By 2 a.m., he was airborne to Milwaukee to pick up three large pieces of machinery for a rush flight to Atlanta.

At 3:10 a.m., after eating a sandwich at Gen. Mitchell Field in Milwaukee, he took off, the 600 pounds of steel firmly secured in the back of the plane. Soon he was at his assigned altitude of 11,000 feet.

With the exception of dozing at the bar, it had been more than 18 hours since Hvizdak had had any sleep, and a long night lay ahead.

As with all of the thousands of other aircraft sharing the skies, supervision of Hvizdak's flight was passed from one air traffic control center to another as he flew south.

At 4:45 a.m., he acknowledged instructions from Indianapolis (ATC) Center to "squawk and ident," to identify himself to the controller watching the blip marking his plane as it crawled across the radar screen.

"Okay. There you go," Hvizdak radioed back, but it was the last communication he made.

Indianapolis Center called several more times, but Hvizdak did not respond. ATC knew the Beech 18 was still flying, its path traced on radar.

At 5:25 a.m., Indianapolis Control turned reponsibility for the aircraft over to Atlanta Control, and warned that the flight was "NORDO," no radio.

"He just calls when he wants to go," the Indianapolis controller said.

For 45 minutes, Hvizdak failed to talk to any of the controllers.

At 6:21 a.m., one of the score of pulsing radar screens in the darkened Atlanta Control showed that Hvizdak had dropped below his assigned altitude.

Six minutes and 45 seconds later, he disappeared from the screen at 2,900 feet, hidden from radar by the tall Appalachian Mountains.

About the same time, two hunters saw the plane slowly break out of the low clouds that obscured the mountain tops and head in the direction of Pack Mountain.

Moments later, the Beech 18 sliced steeply through the tree tops, clipped its right wing and slammed deep into the soft ground among the poplar and hickory. It burst into flames. Only the engines and a portion of the wings remained.

The National Transportation Safety Board is expected to release soon its findings on the cause of the crash. But Safety Board Chairman Jim Burnett is angry about what he already knows.

"It never should have happened," he said. "Even in a case as blatant as this one, with this much exposure, the FAA was unable to identify a problem. To make it worse, when they finally got a call from the city attorney, who said this pilot has been released from jail to go fly, it wasn't given priority treatment by the FAA.

"At this time it's not clear to me whether this was the individual assessment of the person (FAA investigator) who was working or whether it represents a generic attitude of the FAA, or FAA policies, to downplay reports of this type. I hope it's the former, but it's not a good sign."

Things could have been worse, Burnett said. "He could have been flying passengers, the airline was authorized by the FAA to do that."

TOP AIR DOCTOR OKS PILOTS AT RISK

FAA STAFF, PHYSICIANS CITE DANGER TO PUBLIC

SUNDAY, NOVEMBER 16, 1986

BY ANDREW SCHNEIDER AND MATTHEW BRELIS

More than 250 professional pilots or co-pilots once grounded by potentially fatal or debilitating medical conditions have been returned to the cockpit by Dr. Frank Austin Jr., the federal air surgeon, often over the objections of the Federal Aviation Administration's leading medical consultants and staff.

As the federal air surgeon, Austin is the final authority in virtually all appeals of medical decisions made by the 7,000 FAA-approved aviation medical examiners, who perform mandatory flight physicals for each of the nation's 700,049 pilots.

Doctors familiar with the cases handled by Austin characterize the decisions of the nation's top aviation medicine official as dangerous, reckless and a serious threat to safety that may endanger the lives of thousands.

"We cannot wait for a major catastrophe, for an airliner crash that might be medically related to one of his decisions," said Dr. Lawrence Marinelli, medical chairman of the Air Transport Association, a group that represents the airlines.

"We can't sacrifice 200 or 300 people just to prove that Frank (Austin) is wrong. His argument is that everything is working fine, so he's right. That argument just won't hold water forever," says Marinelli, who is also medical adviser to TWA.

Austin, federal air surgeon since Oct. 1, 1984, admits that he often ignores the panel of FAA medical consultants, whom he acknowledges are leading specialists in their fields, but defends his practice by saying the pilots in question have not died.

But one did.

"I exercised my professional opinion," Austin said. "I applied my own judgment, and I certified those people. They haven't died or crashed. Except O'Brien."

Joseph O'Brien was piloting a helicopter with one passenger when it crashed Aug. 3 in a California ravine. A National Transportation Safety Board investigator said O'Brien suffered a heart attack shortly before the helicopter crashed.

"I stand by my actions and do so proudly," said Austin. "I've put a lot of pilots back in the air who have been locked out of the cockpit for years and their safety record shows it was a safe decision.

"I have to take the rap for these cases. If I certify them, people will yell that they're going to crash. If I don't, then it's charged that the (FAA) is unfair to the pilots," said Austin.

Austin's actions have erupted into a rapidly expanding controversy, an emotional tug-of-war, with the air surgeon and hundreds of unemployable pilots who want to return to work facing off against airline doctors and medical experts who fear they're not safe to fly.

The 62-year-old air surgeon is revered by pilots whose wings were clipped in the past by decisions of other doctors, grounding some of them for as long as a decade. Airborne again, these pilots herald Austin's policies as long overdue and without need of defense. They are proud to call him one of their own—a pilot who understands the ecstasy and pressures of flying and has a more realistic view of safety.

At the other end of the emotional gamut is the trepidation voiced by doctors hired by the FAA for their expertise who express astonishment at Austin's medical decisions. It is not only the number of pilots that Austin has let fly again that gravely concerns the air surgeon's critics, but also the severity of the pilots' medical ailments. From crop duster to test pilot to 747 captain, pilots have been put back in the air by Austin.

According to government documents the cases include:

• A USAir pilot with bypasses on three of the arteries of his heart and a transplanted plastic heart valve.

• A 37-year-old pilot for People Express who had six bypass grafts, two of which show strong clinical indications of becoming clogged.

• A Western Airlines pilot who had two heart bypass operations, an artificial valve transplant and "greatly diminished blood flow" in critical areas.

• A 53-year-old United co-pilot with a heart attack that produced extensive damage to the crucial organ and "presents a significant chance" for future heart attacks.

• A 37-year-old Republic co-pilot with severe diabetes, which must be controlled with daily insulin injections, and several other serious complications which could lead to a sudden coma.

• A 57-year-old American Airlines pilot with a heart attack and a triple bypass who has had unexplained episodes of loss of consciousness.

In all of the cases, Austin was ruling on pilots who had applied for a special issuance—an exemption the FAA allows if a pilot can prove that his medical condition is less serious than the diagnosis which automatically grounded him. Grounding is mandatory if one or more of nine specific medical conditions are present. These conditions include a medical history or clinical diagnosis of alcoholism, diabetes requiring medication for control, drug dependency, epilepsy, heart attack, coronary heart disease, personality disorder, psychosis, or unexplained loss of consciousness.

While the infirmities are as varied as the pilots Austin has recertified for flight, most of these nine disorders can strike the pilot without warning. This sudden incapacitation could leave pilots unable to operate their aircraft and result in a crash.

"Austin's playing the odds that his decisions won't catch up with him, but people may die because of it. Those of us who know what he's doing are scared to death that one of Austin's personal decisions will fly a planeload of passengers into the ground," said Dr. Harry Gibbons, FAA's former chief of medical research.

Austin, a 30-year Navy officer who began his aviation medical career as a flight surgeon in Korea, had a rapid and dramatic impact on the air surgeon's office. With military bluntness, he attacked what he perceived to be a major problem with the agency's "crawling pace" of acting on requests for medical certification.

Most of the country's 700,049 aviators are in good health. It is only a fraction of this group, about 2,000 a year, who have medical problems so severe that they must be evaluated by the federal surgeon.

Federal records show that in 1985 Austin granted 994 exemptions, or special issuances, to pilots with illnesses that would normally disqualify them from flying. That represented 75.1 percent of all exemptions requested. A year earlier, under former air surgeon Dr. Homer Reighard, 584 special issuances were written, or 46.7 percent of those requested.

The largest number was for third-class, or private, pilots. Issuances in that category jumped by 70 percent—from 352 under Reighard to 598 in Austin's first year.

TESTING IS REDUCED

Word rapidly spread among grounded pilots, especially those with heart problems, that there was a relaxation of the medical requirements which kept them out of the cockpit. Many of the extensive, expensive and invasive cardiology tests were no longer required.

"I reduced the number of tests, just got rid of them," Austin said with pride, a Texas twang still in his voice. "Stress tests cost $400, thalium scans, $600; MUGA tests $400 . . . Come on, some physicians have said to demand all these tests is malpractice."

The Pittsburgh Press reviewed the medical reports on 284 cardiac cases that were evaluated by the specialists. In a third of the cases, the doctors thought the pilot healthy enough to return to flying, in another third the hazard to safety was classified as moderate, but in the remaining third, the doctors ruled that the risk of sudden incapacitation, the loss of the ability to safely fly, was high. Twenty-five cases were pending a decision, awaiting additional information.

However, government records showed that in 77 of the cases where the specialists ruled that the potential danger was moderate to high, Austin nevertheless issued the certificate allowing the pilot back into the cockpit. In 19 of the 77 cases, there was total agreement among the specialists that the risks were extremely high, yet Austin allowed them to fly.

"Having someone who hasn't put a stethoscope on a patient's chest for years overruling the recommendations of the leading clinical specialists in the country is just not good medicine. Austin's actions are

endangering the passengers that fly with these pilots, the pilots themselves, the people on the ground and other aviators sharing the
same air space," said Gibbons, the former FAA chief of medical re
search.

In 47 other cases, where the consulting physicians strongly recommended that the pilot be granted only a second- or third-class certificate, the records show that Austin upgraded them to a higher flying
status. There were numerous cases where the consultants said the pilot
could fly only if specific tests were ordered to monitor any deterioration
of already potentially hazardous medical conditions. In at least 12 of
these cases, Austin issued the certificate with no request for testing
and in 17 others, the amount of testing requested was drastically
reduced.

"They were calling for tests that were expensive and that I felt
unnecessary, and wouldn't tell us anything we didn't already know,
so in some cases, I just didn't ask for them," Austin says.

Consultants familiar with the process will look for negative aspects
in a medical file, Austin said. "They look for all the things that will
enable them to say 'disqualified.' If I've gotten a big (medical) documentation that says that this and this are bad—and that's usually
what I get—I'll go through it and look for the favorable," Austin
said.

While his willingness to shun the advice of some of the nation's
leading cardiologists has confounded his medical colleagues, there is
genuine fear among the doctors and staff about another large group of
pilots recertified under Austin.

In at least 126 cases, mostly involving heart conditions, he acted
without consulting the specialists.

"It was bad enough that Austin was ignoring our recommendations
on who was safe to fly, but what was really frightening us was that he
was ruling on scores of cases that neither we, nor his staff, ever saw,"
said Dr. Myrvin Ellestad, who served 12 years as an FAA medical
consultant. "God only knows who he approved to fly."

"In my last year on the panel, I guess Austin ignored our decisions
and recommendations more than 100 times in cases that we felt the
risks were too high. There may be a lot more that I don't know about
but I'm sure there are a lot of sick pilots flying because of Austin's

actions," says Ellestad, chief of cardiology at Memorial Medical Center in Long Beach, Calif.

Former air surgeon Reighard said, "I couldn't properly function without the consultants.

"Not only would it be politically unwise for a single individual to make these crucial decisions but there is no way that a non-cardiologist, like myself, could safely and accurately rule on risks and benefits to safety in a rapidly changing medical arena where we had to evaluate advances like heart valves, bypasses, new drugs and the like," Reighard said.

"These people are on the cutting edge of advancements in their fields. The guidance we need to make the best decisions on safety cannot come from physicians in ivory towers or medical administrators but from doctors with day-to-day hands-on experience with patients and that's what we had with our panel of consultants."

PANEL ABOLISHED

Within weeks of taking office, Austin met with his medical consultants and heated arguments began. The first battle was over the way the physicians presented their recommendations. Austin told them to stop recommending recertification or denial for the pilots they reviewed, but rather to present their evaluations as they do in the military, in terms of the risk each pilot posed to the public safety. Then he would decide who flew.

"They took great exception to this and told me to stuff it. They essentially told me that I was incompetent to make these sorts of determinations and I had better sit down and listen to them," Austin recalled with a chuckle.

Nevertheless, at the next bimonthly consultants' meeting, the specialists began reporting their findings in degrees of risk, but that was the last meeting for most of them for almost a year. Austin abolished the panel and began handling the cases himself.

"The panel was contributing to the backlog. They were a big part of the problem," said Austin, adding that there were nearly 1,400 special issuance cases pending when he took office.

"If they denied certification before, they would deny them again. I felt this panel was entrenched and unbending in its thinking and I didn't agree with them and there's nothing in the regulations that says

I have to agree with them. I exercised my authority as federal air surgeon and certified these pilots because I thought they were fit to fly," Austin said.

As unprecedented as Austin's actions were, by working without the panel of consultants, he cleared hundreds of cases during his first several months on the job.

Austin takes pride in pointing out that the number of special issuances nearly doubled from 1984 to 1985. In fact, he gave his staff a letter of appreciation for reducing that backlog of cases by 80 percent in his first six months.

One of Austin's goals is to speed up the qualification system. Under previous administrations, pilots who applied for special issuance were often caught in a bureaucratic merry-go-round. The FAA required medical information that was no older than six months. But by the time a pilot had gone to his AME (aviation medical examiner), the AME had forwarded the information to Oklahoma City and it had been sent to Washington, the information was no longer valid and new tests had to be conducted.

"I tried to put a stop to that," Austin said. "If I need fresh data, I'll call up the (pilot's) doctor and talk to him."

Not ordering new tests is "an unacceptable practice," said Dr. Richard Masters, medical director of the 49,000-member Air Line Pilot's Association. "Talking to someone doesn't update the evaluation. What good would it do for you to talk to me if I hadn't done a stress test on (the patient) since 1985?"

Austin said that lawyers were helpful in whittling down the backlog.

They often would walk into his office with brief cases filled with appeals and an hour later Austin would give his staff a pile of fresh certificates to issue.

"I did that because I thought the people were qualified," Austin said. "Any lawyer that represents a client can come in and see us. I've seen dozens of them."

One Washington lawyer, Mark McDermott, a former attorney for the FAA, said he handled more than 60 cases during Austin's first year and the air surgeon said the arrangement helped expedite the certification process.

"McDermott or some other lawyer would bring me a full medical summary of what other medical experts said the status of the pilot's health was. If I concurred that the pilot should fly, then I issued a Telex or call to Oklahoma City and had Dr. (Audie) Davis (manager of the FAA's aeromedical certification branch) issue the certificate," Austin said.

But Austin's solo certification system and his direct dealings with lawyers ended after about a year because of "a fire storm of criticism" from airline medical directors, consultants and some of his staff, he said.

"They're accusing me of everything. Of having pilots buying me meals or giving money to get their ticket and that's just absurd. I just see things different than they do and they try to slander me. I've done nothing wrong," Austin said angrily.

Airline doctors held repeated meetings with Austin, his boss, Anthony Broderick, associate administrator for aviation standards, and FAA Administrator U.S. Navy Adm. Donald Engen. The senior FAA officials repeatedly supported Austin's actions, even when the airline doctors presented specific cases of what they called "dangerous and reckless decisions."

With little enthusiasm, Austin said, he reconvened the panel, and stopped dealing privately with lawyers.

No longer having the easy access to Austin "is bad for the system," said McDermott. "I'm in favor of anything that makes the system more efficient. Some cases are clear cut enough that they can be decided without too much consternation."

McDermott said he refuses to represent more than 40 percent of the pilots who come to him for help and sees no threat to safety with the ones he does represent. "If I thought there was any problem I wouldn't present their cases," he said.

PILOTS COME CALLING

Lawyers were not the only individuals to get private audiences with Austin. Pilots could call and make appointments.

"My staff has cautioned me numerous times that they don't like to see the pilots come into the office because it biases their decision and that it is a risk that when you see somebody and see how healthy they are," he said.

While Austin denies a sick pilot can walk into his office and come out with a special issuance to fly, he issued certificates immediately after meeting with some pilots.

"My wife called and got an appointment and we flew down to Washington," said Anthony Benvenuto, a People Express pilot, recalling his visit to Austin's office on the third floor of the FAA Building on Independence Avenue in Washington.

"He was as cordial as you could imagine. He's got a lot of practicality. It's like you're talking with a regular person."

The pilot's meeting with Austin ended his 20-month wait for recertification following heart surgery.

"He gave me a second-class medical (certificate) on the spot," Benvenuto recalled.

"As we were leaving I said, 'Do you know I fly captain?' and he said 'Okay, okay, we'll talk about first-class in a year.' "

A year later, Benvenuto got his first-class ticket.

"I pray for us, and I pray for Dr. Austin," said Benvenuto.

Although he has since reinstated the consulting panel of specialists, Austin's relations with the airline doctors and specialists did not improve.

"He finally reinstated the panel but it didn't help us very much because he didn't pay attention to their recommendations anyway," said Marinelli.

Austin continued to ignore many of the recommendations.

Government records show a Delta pilot with two heart attacks and "significant coronary disease" was rated as a high risk by the panel but certified by Austin. An Eastern pilot with extensive scarring and disease of the heart and bypasses that were becoming clogged was approved the same month. A Republic co-pilot with severe diabetes was also approved, even though FAA regulations forbid certification of aviators with diabetes serious enough to need insulin to prevent shock.

There is great concern and agreement among aviation medicine experts about the dangers of a pilot in a diabetic coma in the cockpit.

"Diabetic coma or insulin shock is very insidious. They're wide awake. Their eyes are open. They look like they're consciously doing something, meanwhile, they're actually out of it. They don't slump over and grab their chest like with a heart attack so the guy next to him knows that something's wrong and can grab the control. With a diabetic reaction, it can be so subtle that the guy in the next seat might not know something is wrong until his partner flies into a mountain," said Marinelli.

Austin said he thought the diabetic pilot, who must take insulin injections twice a day, presented "no risk."

"His company wanted him back. Republic sent me a letter and said they would monitor him, so I certified him," he said.

"Certification of medically dependent diabetics is medically irresponsible," said ALPA's Masters. "Republic doesn't have a regular medical department so I can't imagine how they'd monitor him."

Officials at Northwest Airlines, which merged with Republic in August, said Friday they were unable to find anyone who knew about the case. "But we're still looking," said a spokesman.

Seven other pilots—second- and third-class aviators with diabetes —also were certified by Austin.

He defended his actions, citing a recently completed AMA study on aviation medical certification standards. "They said that diabetics on oral medication should be allowed to fly, so I certified them," he said.

However, most of the certificates were granted before the panel issued its report. In at least three cases, the type of stringent monitoring recommended by the AMA was not required on the certificates Austin issued.

The tension over Austin's action is increasing. Earlier this year, American Airlines found itself embroiled in a bitter union arbitration hearing over a pilot that Austin certified and the airline found too dangerous to fly. Arguments were completed last month and a ruling is expected shortly.

In August, after the O'Brien crash, Dr. Ellestad, a senior consultant to the FAA and one of the nation's leading cardiologists, resigned. In his letter of resignation, Ellestad told Austin "you are certifying cardiacs of all classes that I consider unfit to fly.

"If you proceed with your present policies, I believe it will only be a matter of time before we lose a 747 full of passengers due to a sudden cardiac event in the cockpit," he wrote.

O'BRIEN CASE CITED

A heart attack in the cockpit of a Bell Jet Ranger is believed to be the cause of the crash which killed O'Brien, as reported in The Pittsburgh Press last month.

In 1984, an aviation medical examiner and FAA doctors said O'Brien's heart was too diseased to let him continue flying. The pilot appealed the decision to the FAA in Oklahoma City, but was unsuccessful. He then took his case to Washington where a team of medical consultants reviewed his case and concurred that he was an unsafe risk.

In January 1985—a year after O'Brien's AME denied him a medical certificate—Austin issued one to O'Brien with several restrictions. On May 5 of this year, however, Austin ordered those restrictions lifted.

Austin said he issued the certificate with no exemptions because O'Brien's record seemed to show him to be healthy.

"O'Brien may not have been candid with me," Austin said. "He may have had an event (heart attack) and he didn't tell us about it. I was dealing without total information."

Austin said that until the investigation is complete, blame of O'Brien's death and that of the passenger, Joseph Foster, should not be assigned.

"Thank God only two people died, but we can't operate that way," said Marinelli.

"We can't say, 'It's okay, there weren't very many people killed.' You know, like the lower the number of dead, the better that Frank (Austin) is doing. That's no way to run any airline."

Concern over Austin's decision making brought together airline officials and the pilots' union—recently bitterly divided by labor negotiations and strikes—in an unusual alliance.

"Labor-management agreements have historically respected corporate and labor trust in the decision making of the federal air surgeon," said ALPA's Masters. "Austin's decisions have undermined that trust. And now we can't accept (Austin's) decisions whether they are favorable or unfavorable."

At United, Medical Director Dr. Gary Kohn, agreed:

"Austin's actions take away some of the information we used to count on. It used to be that FAA issuing a first-class medical certificate was a well-thought-out, conservative approach to aviation medicine. Our experience over the last two years means that we have to rely more closely on our own evaluation of a specific case because the FAA certification practices are not always logically apparent to us."

Pan American's Dr. John McCann said that he is concerned about some of his pilots who Austin certified.

"His actions have given us some heartburn. At times he's been a great help in getting some of our airmen back to work that we felt did not pose undue risk. But he's made some blunders in some cases in terms of his assessment, but we believe we have been able to catch them and it becomes our decision whether they fly."

"We're up to our necks handling the day-to-day alligators that are snapping at us all the time, we just don't have the time to inspect every action the FAA takes," said Dr. Robert Wicks Jr., medical director for American Airlines. "We've got to assume that they are doing things properly. In fact we have to count on it, it's their responsibility."

TWA's Marinelli discovered Austin had certified a 54-year-old pilot who suffered from problems of inadequate blood flow to the brain, resulting in symptoms similar to stroke, such as paralysis and slurred speech.

"He was certified and got a special issuance but he needed a current medical (exam) and he came to me for the medical," Marinelli recalled. "When I saw him, I didn't think he was fit to fly so I refused to give him the certificate and sent him back to Frank. In the meantime, the pilot decided to go into retirement. A week or two later he got a ticket (certificate) from Frank. He called me and said he got his medical back and asked if he could go back to work. I examined him again and he had the same problem and I refused to let him fly." The pilot retired, but the experience left Marinelli shaken.

"Frank sent him back to us twice and that man never should have been certified in the first place."

The list of high-risk pilots certified by Austin encompasses all the major airlines, documents show. American, United and Pan Am led the way and several pilots for USAir, Delta and Eastern also received special issuances.

Officials at airlines that have medical departments have identified many of the individuals involved and in most cases say they have succeeded in keeping the pilots out of the cockpit. But that's caused a labor-management conflict.

The contract that ALPA members have with every major airline except People Express and American says that the standards set by the air carrier cannot be more stringent than those established by the FAA.

This policy already has led to legal battles between some pilots and their airlines. Airline doctors say more are expected.

Austin said that any conflict is the result of labor agreements with airlines and unions, and not the fault of his office. "The FAA sets minimum standards and the airlines can apply more stringent standards if they wish. But if they negotiate that away, they have to deal with it."

Some doctors and FAA staff members express concern that carriers without medical departments may not know the actual physical conditions of their pilots.

"For every case that we, United and American, argue with Frank (Austin) about, there might be a hundred others with the same conditions that are already flying because the other airlines accept the FAA's decision and don't know they might have a potentially dangerous pilot flying," said Marinelli.

Dr. Robert Poole, the medical consultant for both USAir and the agency, agreed.

"Without a full-time medical department there is no real way for an airline to tightly control the health of its pilots. We must rely too much on the FAA's system."

Poole said he knows of two or three of the high-risk pilots that Austin certified, but was surprised at a dozen others that had been given the okay.

"I don't know whether they are still flying with USAir, but I'm going to find out," the doctor said. "I am as concerned as everyone else is but I don't think that USAir or the other airlines can do anything about what the air surgeon is doing. The regulations are on his side."

One airline doctor supports Austin.

"We work very closely with the FAA and we have no bone to pick with the federal air surgeon. I know there have been some cases where pilots have gotten special issuances, but I couldn't tell you how many because we don't keep track of them," said Dr. David Millett, medical director of Eastern.

But in March, the Air Transport Association notified its members of Austin's increasing number of special issuances and advised them to be alert.

Pilots who have been recertified say the FAA knows more about their medical condition than that of other pilots, making them safer to fly with than pilots who do not submit to regular testing.

"The medical directors for airlines are shocked about this (increase in special issuances)," said United pilot Joseph Tringali, who returned to flying in July after a 5½-year layoff which included being denied a special issuance by Reighard in 1983.

"They feel things are being shoved down their throats. It is a complete 180-degree reversal. Once they realize Dr. Austin is making guys like me tow the line and go through exams, they may calm down."

Yet Austin said he is not planning on changing.

"I took a pay cut to come here, but the job needs me.

"I am not experimenting with the public safety. My critics are wrong. They are the doomsayers of the world. If they wait long enough, someone will make a bad landing and some people might die. But what is the alternative? Not to certify anyone?"

PILOTS' SECRET COCAINE TREATMENT CALLED BAD MEDICINE

CLANDESTINE PRACTICE BRANDED A THREAT TO PASSENGERS, POSSIBLE FEDERAL VIOLATION

THURSDAY, DECEMBER 4, 1986

BY ANDREW SCHNEIDER

Secret treatment of cocaine-dependent pilots is bad medicine, endangers airline safety and may be a violation of federal law, punishable by enormous fines or the loss of an airline's right to fly, aviation medical experts say.

The Pittsburgh Press reported Sunday that a survey of 17 clinics across the country found that more than 69 pilots had been treated for cocaine addiction without the knowledge of the Federal Aviation Administration.

"Any pilot who conceals the fact he's been treated for drug addiction, or any other serious medical problem, is in clear violation of FAA regulations the very first time he gets back into the cockpit," said Dr. Barton Pakull, FAA's chief psychiatrist.

"But beyond violating the regulations, it's bad medicine. It's just far too dangerous to allow people treated for cocaine, alcohol or any other type of drug abuse to fly without the FAA first determining that their rehabilitation was complete, their aftercare appropriate and a psychological evaluation completed to ensure that the brain was not damaged by the drugs."

Almost all of the clinics contacted said they did not do the extensive testing needed to confirm brain damage. Some said they would run the tests but only if there were clinical signs of possible trouble. Pakull insists that testing for possible brain damage must be done on all cases of serious addiction, regardless of the substance.

"The refusal or failure of these clinics to notify the FAA or the airlines may not be illegal, but it sure is reprehensible."

Nevertheless, almost all the clinic directors and rehabilitation specialists interviewed cited patient confidentiality as the reason they did not and would not notify the FAA or the airlines about a pilot under treatment.

"Baloney, it has nothing to do with patient confidentiality. Refusing to tell the FAA or the airlines is a vivid example of the gluteus maximus syndrome. They're covering their butt so they don't get sued, it has very little to do with medicine," said Dr. Joseph Pursch, a senior FAA psychiatric consultant who has treated a dozen pilots for cocaine use at his California clinic.

Dr. Jon Jordan, FAA's deputy federal air surgeon, said any medical professional who has knowledge that a pilot is using his (medical) certificate and isn't qualified for it "is running a hell of a risk as far as liability is concerned.

"They worry about getting sued by their patient for disclosure of confidential information. But that's nothing compared to the liability they'd face if they didn't advise the agency and their patient was responsible for some kind of catastrophic accident," Jordan said.

However, while Jordan said he sympathizes with the argument that the naming of patients might drive away pilots who need treatment, he said "the secrecy is not good for the long-term rehabilitation of the pilots nor our overall concerns with aviation safety."

Pilots demand the secrecy. They insist that if the FAA finds out they have a drug problem, they'll never fly again. The agency's rules list drug dependency as one of nine potentially serious medical conditions for which a pilot can be grounded.

"We don't have any choice, we have to follow the regulations as they are written today. We cannot re-certify pilots with a history of drug dependency unless they apply for a special issuance, and as of this date, nobody has," said Dr. William Hark, manager of FAA's aeromedical standards branch.

FAA records show that only three cocaine-using pilots have received special permission to fly again after rehabilitation. However, the certification for all three was based on treatment for accompanying alcoholism. The Air Line Pilots' Association, which represents 47,000 pilots from 46 airlines, last week issued a strong statement about the need to identify and get treatment for pilots with drug problems.

"ALPA has taken a very strong position that we cannot and will not condone the clandestine management of drug treatment cases because it can lead to inadequate treatment and management and does not provide for careful monitoring of the success or failure of the pilot's rehabilitation," said Dr. Richard Masters, the union's medical director.

"In the area of substance abuse, secrecy is the great enemy of air safety and every effort must be made to bring the problem into the open," he said.

Some doctors said they agonize about keeping the officials in the dark.

"I agree that we have an absolute obligation to the safety of the public and it's not an easy decision to keep this problem from the airlines or the FAA, but, in reality, it is the patient's decision," said Dr. Michael Healy, medical director of the Baylor Parkside Lodge in Denton, Texas.

"Look, we're faced with pilots who have their career on the line. They juggle their vacation time so they can get a month off without their airline catching on. They truly believe that if the FAA finds out, they'll never fly again. I would be more willing to notify the FAA if the agency had a more open and progressive attitude of treating cocaine addiction as the disease it is."

Across the country, at Seaborne Hospital in Dover, N.H., the professional staff also battles with the issue of confidentiality.

"This is a very tough position to be in. We're bound by our ethics and our professional commitment toward anonymity. We would do everything in our power to convince a patient to allow us to notify the FAA or his employer. We understand their fear over losing their job but without their permission, we can't discuss it with anyone," said Bud Charest, the hospital administrator.

"I am a white-knuckle flyer and believe me, I fully share the public's concern about the health of a man in the air, five miles up, with 300 people in his care. That's a legitimate concern, but there's another side of the coin. If that pilot had an abuse problem, admitted it, received the proper treatment and follow-up and is abstaining, he's a hell of a lot safer asset in that cockpit than the guy who's a heavy social drinker, or uses a couple of lines of coke now and then.

"Remember, a recovering addict is a far safer risk than someone who hasn't admitted a problem. So if we're faced with the choice of treating someone without their employer's or the FAA's knowledge, or not treating them at all, then damn it, we'll treat them."

Some clinic directors acknowledged they were working with representatives of the airlines of the cocaine-addicted pilot, but none would discuss it on the record. However, several admitted they know that secret medical treatment of pilots is against FAA regulations.

"The airline has the responsibility to ensure that its pilots have valid and properly obtained medical certificates. If we discover that this is not the case, and that the airlines have knowledge of it, the FAA can and will take action against the carrier," said Richard Stafford, a senior FAA spokesman.

AIR CREWS FLY THROUGH CUSTOMS BECAUSE THEY'RE CALLED 'LOW-RISK'

SUNDAY, DECEMBER 21, 1986

BY ANDREW SCHNEIDER

MIAMI—Almost all of the passengers from the 128 overseas flights arriving at Miami International Airport each day fight for position at one of the 26 U.S. Customs inspection stations. Their bags—and sometimes their person—are poked, prodded and examined. Airline personnel line up at a counter reserved for them.

Inspectors search for those who match the often-changing psychological or physiological profile of the drug smuggler "and things that just don't look right," says Prospero Ellis, head of the "rovers," a highly trained team of undercover customs inspectors.

Every day, about 700 flight crew members and 9,000 inbound international passengers pass through the sprawling, tightly guarded customs inspection center on the first floor of the airport.

Crews from Eastern flights from Haiti, the Dominican Republic and elsewhere in the Caribbean; Pan Am flights from South America; Avianca crews off flights from Colombia, pass through without even the most superficial check of their baggage, none pausing more than a few seconds to sign a customs declaration.

"Pilots and stews are like everyone else—they carry drugs for money but most of the time we don't check them because we think they're a low-risk group," Ellis says. "So we let them come in five or 10 times without being checked, and then we grab and really shake them hard. We tell them it's just to keep them honest."

An inspector working the flight crew counter watches the last of a stream of airline employees walk toward the main door.

"They're the ones that should be checked more closely because they know the system and how to get around it. Even when the flights from Bogota come in, we never check them. If they're in uniform, we just sign them out and move them through," he says, shaking his head.

"With hundreds coming through every day, I'm not sure what else we can do, but if we don't stop them, who else will?"

Customs' open door for flight crews worries some investigators, but they say that only a small percentage of those trafficking in drugs try to smuggle them through customs. The vast majority of narcotics brought into the country are shipped as cargo.

Out on Miami International's 5 square miles of runways, parking and cargo areas, members of the Customs Service's Contraband Enforcement Team swarm over baggage and cargo from the international flights that land every few minutes.

On a ramp at mid-terminal, CET Inspectors Jim Engleman and Jack Brooks work a flight that just came in from Haiti. They grab random boxes, bags or suitcases flowing down a conveyor belt and squeeze the sides of the containers, sniffing for the telltale acrid scent of cocaine. They poke a small tool into the hollow rattan tubing of wicker baskets being loaded on baggage carts. Nothing, but they keep looking.

A half-hour later and across the runway, in a cargo warehouse, the pair—armed with .357 Magnum handguns and carrying a 22-pound bag of power drills, wrenches and pry bars—poke long, thin, steel probes with a jagged collection tip into narrow cardboard boxes filled with flowers from South America.

"Perishables are prime hiding places for coke because the dealers know we can't keep flowers, frozen fish or anything else that will spoil around long enough for a thorough inspection, so they load them up with drugs," says Brooks.

With so few inspectors and so much cargo, "it takes a lot of luck to find it even if we know the favorite hiding places," says Engleman.

Last month, they got lucky. On the morning of Nov. 27, Brooks and another partner stuck a probe into one of 2,500 boxes of carnations being unloaded at Avianca's warehouse, and they found 293 pounds of cocaine. The Colombian airline was fined $4.7 million.

In the past year, the team found 7,269 pounds of cocaine and 14,134 pounds of marijuana, and arrested 72 people.

Much of the drugs they don't intercept end up in the hundreds of single-story windowless concrete warehouses that house South American and Caribbean import-export firms that border the airport.

In places such as these, drug agents say, most airline crews trafficking in drugs make their pickups to carry north.

A little more than a mile west of the airport, a block off 72nd Street, a DEA agent peers through the dark-tinted windows of his van. Using binoculars, he watches the front of a warehouse crowded among a score of others.

"There aren't enough dump trucks in all of Miami to haul away all the coke that's probably in those buildings," he says.

Within 30 minutes, only four people leave the building. Two are in airline uniforms—a co-pilot and a flight attendant. The young, dark-haired pilot gets into a rental car with Broward County tags. "He's going back to the airport at Fort Lauderdale," the drug agent says.

A few moments later the flight attendant gets into a waiting Yellow Cab. Both crew members carry identical boxes, marked "Stereo Special."

"They're either having a hell of a sale on stereos or they give great discounts to airline personnel," the agent says, "but lots of their customers leave here carrying the same boxes, head straight for the airport and get on planes heading north. I don't have X-ray vision, so I can't tell you there are drugs in those boxes, but I'll bet you my rowboat that there's nothing in there that plays real music."

Twelve minutes later, the cab drops the flight attendant off in front of the airport. She hurries past security, straps her "stereo" onto her luggage cart and boards a jet headed for Boston.

"We'll get her. Not today, but we'll get her, the guys running that warehuse and the people she's delivering the junk to in Boston," the agent says. "There are a lot of cops looking at drugs and airports."

Secreted among the thousands of tourists, business people and foreign visitors who pack the half-mile-long terminal are scores of undercover investigators from the DEA, the FBI, U.S. Customs, the Border Patrol, Immigration and Naturalization, and a half dozen other special local, state and federal teams or task forces.

With all these investigators crammed into the airport, there are the inevitable stories of the narcotics agent who spends a week shadowing a suspicious-looking Latin who is hanging around the terminal clutching a paper sack containing a white teddy bear to his chest. But when the guns are finally drawn, it turns out that the man he was following was an investigator from another agency and the teddy bear concealed his two-way radio.

Nevertheless, a lot of significant drug seizures and arrests are made at the airport.

"A flight coming in from Bogota may have as many as 50 mules (carriers) on that one plane. We know they have coke on their body, in their body or in their baggage. They know we know it, so it becomes almost a contest to see how many of them will get past us," Matthews says.

It is the fact that so many traditional couriers are getting stopped that is forcing some organizations to use members of airline crews, says a customs investigator who recently returned from South America.

"It was no big deal for the Colombians to get stewardesses or pilots who were carrying small bags (of coke) for themselves or their friends for free to switch to muling kilos for big bucks. They're paying them more (than the average courier) because they're more reliable, and they know where they can find them if they screw up," says the investigator.

"The guys flying prop-jobs loaded with coke into dirt strips in the 'Glades understand the risks they're taking, but I don't think the flyboys in the jumbo jets shuttling between Miami and L.A. really know what they've gotten into."

Thirty miles north of Miami, at Fort Lauderdale International Airport, Det. Glenn Topping and his partner, Bill Barnes, prowl the terminal for the organized crime unit of the Broward County Sheriff's Department. They echo many of the customs investigator's views.

"These dealers will write off a courier and a kilo in a heartbeat— they expect to lose a lot—but if they've got a shipment going to an important customer and they've got to deliver, they'll pay a little more money to a pilot or a flight attendant to ensure it gets there," says Barnes.

Topping says the trafficking is viewed as a game or an adventure by some. "Someone stops them in the airport and says 'If you want to make $2,000 real quick, wait in your hotel room and someone will call you.' They think it's a lark, but once they mule the first load, they can't get out of it."

Barnes says some of the flight crews are too naive to be involved in trafficking.

"They really don't understand that if they lose a shipment or talk too much to the wrong person, they can wind up very dead. . . . The South Americans who are supplying the coke don't play games. If they have a problem, they kill it."

Back at Miami International, the evening supervisor of Metro-Dade's airport team, Lt. Joe McGillivray, sips at a small cup of black Cuban coffee sold from a dozen stands that dot the terminal.

"Everyone says that we shouldn't worry about pilots because they make too much money to run drugs. But some of them use drugs, and nobody with a heavy drug habit makes enough money to support it without outside money. If you don't have enough guts to sell it, then your only choice is to transport it, and that's why we're worried about these flight crews."

TWO

THE GOODYEAR WAR

1987 WINNER IN THE GENERAL NEWS REPORTING CATEGORY

"For a distinguished example of reporting within a newspaper's area of circulation that meets the daily challenges of journalism such as spot news reporting or consistent beat coverage . . ."

Akron Beacon Journal
Staff

When Sir James Michael Goldsmith set his sights on the Goodyear Tire & Rubber Company as a possible takeover target, the company fought the deal at every turn. The *Akron Beacon Journal* recounts the bitter fight and tallies the losses to both Goldsmith and Goodyear.

In the fall of 1986, Sir James Michael Goldsmith, a flamboyant British-French financial buccaneer who had made his fortune buying, reorganizing and selling giant corporations, decided to take a run at the Goodyear Tire & Rubber Company.

For much of this century, Goodyear has been at the center of Akron's economic and political life as the city's largest employer. In a region where a steady decline in manufacturing had caused many thousands of people to lose their jobs, the thriving company symbolized hopes for a brighter economic future. Many in Akron feared that a successful takeover of Goodyear would be catastrophic, portending a breakup of the company that would be an economic blow to the community on the scale of a major natural disaster.

For the *Beacon Journal,* it was the biggest story in a generation and as difficult a challenge as the newspaper had ever faced.

The story was unfolding behind closed doors at the Goodyear headquarters building and on stages far away in Washington, New York and London. The complex and frequently obscure battle for Goodyear was fought by pinstriped warriors who spoke an arcane financial patois.

The staff of the *Beacon Journal* responded with a remarkable effort, producing literally hundreds of stories explaining the Goodyear war in all of its dimensions and, in the process, providing readers with unique insights into the takeover frenzy that is currently shaking the foundations of corporate America.

Beacon Journal reporters worked 20-hour days for weeks to provide powerful day-to-day coverage of the Goodyear struggle from the halls of Congress to Wall Street boardrooms. Working under intense deadline pressures, the paper's relatively small corps of reporters regularly

scooped journalistic giants and the more experienced members of the national financial press.

There was also a steady stream of analytical pieces that explored the economic roots and social consequences of the war.

The coverage was brought alive with strong graphics and powerful photography.

The stories were filled with people. There was Wall Street whiz kid Jeffrey Berenson, who proposed Goodyear as a target with the prospect of millions in fees twinkling in his eye. And there was Steve Seigfried, a Goodyear worker who had lost three previous jobs during the steady decline of Akron's tire manufacturing industry.

There was Goldsmith, who saw himself as a crusader battling to revitalize the American economic system brought low by the selfish interests of entrenched corporate managers. And there was Goodyear chairman Robert Mercer, the defender of a corporation made vulnerable, in his view, by the marketplace victories that were supposed to define success.

"Who the hell are you?" asked Representative John F. Seiberling, Democrat of Ohio and the grandson of Goodyear's founder, in a confrontation with Goldsmith at a congressional hearing. "I am a potential bringer of change," Goldsmith told *Beacon Journal* reporters in an exclusive interview.

As Mercer and Goldsmith struggled, the *Beacon Journal* also produced stories defining the economic and public policy issues reflected in the Goodyear war. Economists argued whether raiders like Goldsmith were truly beneficial to American business, while regulatory experts pondered the social utility of arbitrageurs who were earning immense profits in takeover struggles, and religious leaders discussed the ethical issues associated with takeovers.

In addition to its exhaustive news coverage, the *Beacon Journal* reached out to provide a forum for public opinion during the struggle, publishing hundreds of letters from concerned readers. And the *Beacon Journal*'s editorial board provided perspective and opinion on the battle with a barrage of editorials, cartoons and columns.

In the end, Goldsmith did not win control. Goodyear bought the raider out and the company remained in the hands of local managers.

But it was a costly victory. Thousands of Goodyear workers are

losing their jobs. The company's managers have been forced to abandon their plans for growth through diversification. Instead, they have redefined Goodyear's future in terms that Goldsmith himself suggested.

On November 30, 1986, just nine days after the end of the battle, the *Beacon Journal* produced an exhaustive eight-page reconstruction of the struggle. In the days before its publication, seven reporters and editors worked more than 500 hours interviewing the players, drawing on many other sources. In addition, artists, photographers and copy editors contributed hundreds of hours to the effort.

The story they produced was the capstone of an extraordinary endeavor. The *Beacon Journal* had answered a remarkably difficult journalistic challenge and, in the process, had set a new high standard for coverage of business and economic issues by general interest newspapers.

—Dale Allen, Editor
Akron Beacon Journal

THE GOODYEAR WAR

HARD TO TELL THE WINNER FROM THE LOSER

SUNDAY, NOVEMBER 30, 1986

Early in September a tall, powerful-looking man of middle age with a bald pate and a refined international accent met in New York City with two young American investment bankers.

The middle-aged man was Sir James Michael Goldsmith, a flamboyant British-French financial buccaneer who had made his fortune buying, reorganizing and selling giant corporations. Goldsmith was shopping for a new company.

The Americans—Jeffrey Berenson and Denis Kelly of Merrill Lynch —had been working with Goldsmith for some time. If he bought with their help, Merrill Lynch could make $100 million or more and become a superstar in the takeover craze sweeping American business.

That day, Goldsmith decided. The target would be Goodyear.

Goldsmith and his advisers calculated that, like a piece of real estate, the giant tire company could be subdivided and sold in pieces for a vast profit.

If all went well, within a few weeks Goldsmith would buy enough Goodyear stock to control the Goodyear blimp and all it stood for: an 88-year-old institution with 133,000 employees in 28 countries.

Goodyear and Akron fought back with intensity and conviction, and in the end, Goldsmith did not win.

But it was a costly victory. Thousands of Goodyear workers, including more than 700 in Akron, will lose their jobs. The company's managers were forced to abandon their long-term plans of growth through diversification. Instead, they have redefined Goodyear's future in terms that Goldsmith himself suggested.

And what kind of win is it when Goldsmith, the loser, goes home with profits of $94 million plus $37 million in expenses—all from Goodyear's war chest?

If Goldsmith is gone, his shadow will remain, leaving Akron less certain in its hopes for a future that glittered with promise just 10 weeks before.

A chronicle of the Goodyear war follows.

WEEK I

SATURDAY, SEPT. 13—THE GOODYEAR AIRDOCK, CLOSED TO THE PUBLIC FOR MORE THAN 50 YEARS, IS OPENED TO KICK OFF THE 1986 UNITED WAY CAMPAIGN IN SUMMIT COUNTY.

The sun seemed to be shining on Akron as it had few times in recent history.

At a few minutes past 11 a.m., the 600-ton iron doors of the Goodyear Airdock began sliding apart ever so slowly.

Hearts pounded as fast as the Akron Symphony Orchestra's timpani drums rising to the first crescendo of the theme from *2001: A Space Odyssey*.

Men and women cried.

It was a day to remember where you were.

Steve Seigfried, a Goodyear Aerospace employee, had worked until 11:30 the night before inside the airdock, preparing it for the United Way party. He stayed home on Saturday. He already had heard the orchestra practice *2001* at least a dozen times, anyway.

William Newkirk, Goodyear's vice president for public relations, carefully chose his position inside the airdock—next to a golf cart, where retired Goodyear chairman and chief executive officer Edwin J. Thomas and his wife were seated. He wanted to ensure the older couple's safety "from any gusts of people," Newkirk said.

Rufus Johnson wanted to be at the airdock that morning. But Saturdays are working days for Johnson, a janitor at the Goodyear barbershop. It didn't matter that almost all of the shop's customers would be at the airdock. A working day is a working day.

Donald Walsh, the vice president and resident manager of Akron's Merrill Lynch Pierce Fenner & Smith brokerage, drove to Columbus in the morning with his wife and two sons. They had decided to spend the weekend visiting Walsh's parents.

John Seiberling, the congressman from Akron, started the day at his residence in Washington, D.C., about a mile from Capitol Hill. Even though it was a Saturday, Seiberling went to his House office, anyway, "to clean out the 'in basket,' " he said.

Mark Blitstein, Goodyear's director of investor relations, decided not to bother fighting the crowd at the airdock. Besides, he had company. His parents had flown in from New York to visit and celebrate Blitstein's 35th birthday on Sunday. "They really came to see my 11-month-old son," Blitstein said with a laugh.

Robert Mercer was front-row center as the first beam of late-morning sunlight cut into the cavernous building.

The view was inspiring.

"When those doors started to open, it was tough not to get hit right here," Mercer said, tapping his chest with his fist.

Mercer is the chairman and chief executive officer of Goodyear. Though he took no credit on stage that morning, it was his idea to offer the airdock as a launching pad for the United Way campaign. He had been the United Way chairman the previous year. "He knew you need a big send-off to get the campaign going," said Howard Flood, chairman and chief executive officer of the First National Bank of Ohio and Mercer's successor as United Way chairman.

But nobody had anticipated how big this day would be.

The first cautious predictions of the turnout were in the 20,000 range.

Then Goodyear officials giddily suggested as many as 100,000 would show up. That figure was later inflated to 150,000. And still that was on the short side.

When the day was done, United Way officials boasted that as many as 300,000 people had visited—or at least had attempted to visit—the airdock. Even dignitaries like Sen. John Glenn and Cleveland Mayor George Voinovich got stuck in unexpected traffic jams and missed the ceremony.

Perhaps so many came because of what the blimps and the airdock represent to the community.

When the airdock was constructed in 1929, more than 52,000 people worked in Akron's rubber mills. During World War II, the number of jobs swelled to more than 80,000. As late as 1965, the rubber industry still employed more than 40,000 people in the Akron area. Twenty years later, that figure has been cut almost in half. And the paring continues.

Despite the slumping tire industry, the Goodyear blimps have remained aloft. And even though they are no longer based here, they still serve as aerial ambassadors from the city where some 300 blimps were built.

The blimp and the airdock also represent a tether to the future. The show on the weekend of Sept. 13 was not only for the community—it was put on to impress officials from the U.S. Navy as well. At stake was a $193 million military contract, which could put as many as 600 people back to work building blimps in the airdock again.

But probably many people came out just because it was a beautiful day—and for the opportunity to finally see the inside of this building that is so large, legend has it, that clouds used to form inside and rain down on the blimp builders.

Whatever the reason, Mercer was thrilled they came.

"It was a mob scene," he said. "And a beautifully behaved mob. I don't know where else you'd get a crowd that size in one place in such a short time and not have a problem—fights, pickpockets, drunkenness—all the bad stuff. Absolutely none of that. It was an incredible day for the community. And of course, the day was flawless. Not a cloud in the sky."

At least not that anybody could see. Yet as Akron and Goodyear celebrated this glorious day, a whirlwind of economic change was beginning to stir on the horizon.

The storm soon would blow unfamiliar forces—corporate raiders, arbitrageurs, junk bond dealers—into the Akron area. Soon, Goodyear and the community would be introduced, in Mercer's words, "to a new and not very pretty world."

During the next 10 weeks, Goodyear and Akron would be drawn together again—but this time they would huddle in the fear that their long relationship could be lost. And people with diverse backgrounds such as Steve Seigfried, Rufus Johnson, Donald Walsh and Robert Mercer would find their lives interlocked in a way they might never have expected.

Six days after the airdock reopened—on Sept. 19, 1986—Sir James Goldsmith bought his first 66,000 shares of Goodyear stock.

WEEK II

THURSDAY, SEPT. 25—REPRESENTATIVES OF SIR JAMES GOLD-SMITH PURCHASE 1.7 MILLION SHARES OF GOODYEAR STOCK WORTH $56.3 MILLION.

"I am a potential bringer of change," Goldsmith would warn Akron in the weeks to come.

Goldsmith views himself as a corporate Robin Hood. He takes money locked up by corporate bureaucracy and gives it to its rightful owners—the shareholders.

In the process, he has amassed a fortune estimated at close to $1 billion.

But for many in Akron, whether the change he promised would be good or bad became a secondary issue. For them, his hedonistic life-style seemed more important than his economic philosophy.

Details of Goldsmith's private life are sketchy—because he likes it that way—but sensational.

He grew up in his father's luxury hotels. His ambition was evident early. At age 7, little Jimmy informed his parents that he did not need to learn to read and write. He would be rich enough some day to hire someone to read to him.

He quit school at age 16 and supported himself for a while by gambling. He honed his nerve—nerve that would later serve him well when making billion-dollar deals—in many of Europe's finest casinos.

In 1954, at age 20, Goldsmith created his first sensation. He eloped with 17-year-old Maria Isabel Patino, daughter of a Brazilian tin magnate. She was four months pregnant. Goldsmith once said he rather enjoyed the notoriety he received for defying his wealthy wife's parents.

The marriage ended tragically. His wife died giving birth to a daughter, Isabel. He won a custody battle with his wife's parents for the child.

He since has married twice again, each time openly living with his wife in one country and a mistress in another. He has five other children. He had a son, Manes, and a daughter, Alix, by his second wife, Ginette. While he was married to his second wife, he also had a daughter, Jemima, and a son, Zacharias, with his mistress, Lady

Annabel Birley. Goldsmith married Lady Annabel in 1978. They had another son, Benjamin.

Goldsmith once demonstrated his domestic agility by taking both families on vacation, housing one at each end of the island of Sardinia and boating back and forth.

"Anybody who can pull off that can't be all bad," a Virginia insurance commissioner and church elder said in 1984 when he was confronted with Goldsmith's blatant infidelity during a hearing concerning Goldsmith's takeover bid of the Continental Group.

Goldsmith currently keeps a mistress, French reporter Laura Boulay de la Meurthe, at his town house in New York City. Lady Annabel and their children live at Goldsmith's London home. He also owns a home in Paris that once belonged to songwriter Cole Porter.

Perhaps even more intriguing than Goldsmith's love life is his mercurial personality. One associate described him as a manic-depressive who visits fascist countries when he gets overly depressed. A former employee says Goldsmith is prone to temper tantrums. "His temperament is more like a woman's than a man's," the former employee told Fortune magazine. "He's up and down all the time."

Goldsmith also is said to be paranoid about the press and rubber products.

He believes that Soviet agents have infiltrated the Western press. He once offered $75,000 for the best investigative story on the Soviet Union's influence on the Western media. He filed 63 lawsuits against the British magazine Private Eye, which linked him to a conspiracy to obstruct justice in a murder case. He won an apology, but the scandalous court case damaged his reputation in England, probably costing him a position in the government.

To combat what he sees as the press's socialistic bias, he has become a publisher, using his French magazine L'Express to espouse his right-wing ideology. He is so prominent within the right wing, he was invited to chair the annual dinner of a conservative think tank in Washington, whose keynote speaker was President Ronald Reagan.

Geoffrey Wansell, a London journalist who is writing a biography of Goldsmith, confirmed the tycoon's fear of rubber bands. Goldsmith reportedly once refused to board a plane because he spotted a rubber band in the aisle.

"I think he certainly does not much like rubber bands," Wansell said. "That's the truth. He is in some ways a superstitious man and I don't think it's exclusively rubber bands.

"I think there are certain other rubber things he doesn't much care for, except of course, naturally, tires. He's clearly fascinated by them. He's not terribly keen on . . . some strange rubber things. He's not a man who has rubber in his office. He wouldn't have, like, a pencil eraser or that kind of thing."

But Goldsmith has not allowed his fears and diversions to get in the way of business.

Though he came from wealth, his fortune was self-made.

He built a grocery conglomerate in Europe, then dismantled it to concentrate on dealings in the United States, where he found the deregulated corporate environment more to his liking. To avoid U.S. taxes, though, he controlled his empire through shell corporations spread from the tiny Cayman Islands to Liechtenstein.

With a large appetite for corporate acquisitions, Goldsmith found that a feast awaited him in America.

He swallowed companies like Diamond International and Crown Zellerbach, spit out the unwanted parts while fattening his net worth by several hundred million dollars. With Crown Zellerbach, he ingested without ill effect a dreaded poison pill—a corporate device designed to make takeovers unprofitable by permitting shareholders in the target company to buy stock in the acquiring company at a sharp discount from market prices.

Next on the menu was Goodyear.

By late September, he had taken another bite out of Goodyear.

And still no one knew he was even sitting at the table.

WEEK III

TUESDAY, SEPT. 30—GALE L. GALLOWAY, MAVERICK GOODYEAR DIRECTOR AND CHIEF EXECUTIVE OF ITS CELERON CORP. PIPELINE SUBSIDIARY, RETIRES. GALLOWAY HAD WARNED GOODYEAR A YEAR EARLIER THAT IT WAS VULNERABLE TO A TAKEOVER.

If Sir James Goldsmith is an economic radical, Goodyear chairman and chief executive officer Robert Mercer seems to embody the corporate heartland.

He is a company man in a company town.

Mercer's 40-year career has been much like Goodyear's blimp—never flying too high, or too fast, but always moving forward at a steady pace.

After joining Goodyear as an assistant manager of hose sales, he advanced steadily through the ranks—manager of industrial products operations at Goodyear's Los Angeles plant in 1963; general manager of the plant in 1968; assistant to the president of Goodyear in 1972; president and chief executive officer of the subsidiary Kelly-Springfield Tire Co. in 1974; Goodyear executive vice president and a seat on the board of directors in 1976; president of Goodyear in 1978; chief operating officer in 1980; chief executive officer in 1982; and chairman of the board in 1983.

Mercer's personal life reflects his work.

He is wealthy—he makes about $1 million per year—but he doesn't flaunt it.

His life seems to emphasize family, hard work and loyalty.

As a child, he got in fights with kids who claimed that a Chevy was better than a Ford. Mercer's father was a Ford dealer.

He finished school after serving in the Navy in World War II. He graduated from Yale in 1947 with a degree in mechanical engineering.

His sport was baseball. He had a tryout with the Brooklyn Dodgers as an outfielder. Manager Chuck Dressen liked this skinny kid's spunk, but told him to come back when he gained 40 pounds. "I gained the 40 pounds," Mercer likes to relate, "but by that time I was 50 years old."

He has five children, all by the same wife. He has been married to Mae Mercer for 39 years. They have one home. It is in Akron.

His idea of a wild night on the town is a trip to Cleveland Stadium for an Indians game—and a hot dog with Stadium mustard, of course. The man drinks Ovaltine before he goes to bed.

He gives awards to Eagle Scouts. He serves on community boards, Akron Community Trust and the Akron Regional Development Board. He speaks to Rotary and Kiwanis clubs.

Personal quirks?

He likes sports cars, in particular his 1984 blue Corvette, which he drives to work every day. Why not something more expensive? He drives a Corvette because Goodyear has an exclusive contract to produce tires for the car.

Mercer is also something of a crusader when it comes to smoking and seat belts.

He stopped smoking about 12 years ago. Since then, he has become the leader in Goodyear's program to help employees kick the habit.

Mercer has been known to stop employees driving out of the company parking garage and remind them to fasten their seat belts. "You're valuable to this company and you're valuable to your family." Mercer once lectured to an executive who had not buckled up.

Such paternalism is reflective of a corporate culture that takes care of its own.

Mercer is only the sixth chairman of Goodyear in its 88-year history. All of them were products of a system that nurtured competitiveness and belief in the motto: "Protect Our Good Name."

Competitors refer to Goodyear as "Big Blue" out of respect and fear.

Mercer referred to the company's attitude about its position as the No. 1 tire maker in the world as a kind of "subtle arrogance"—pride without complacency.

Goodyear always has been the type of company that changed only on its own terms.

Goldsmith saw such an attitude as the corporate bureaucratic arrogance he wanted to destroy.

But for Mercer, Goodyear and all it stood for was worth preserving.

"(Goodyear) is his job 24 hours a day," Mrs. Mercer says. "He loves his job. He loves Goodyear."

He gives so much to his job that he once collapsed in his office and had to be hospitalized for stress.

Under Mercer's guidance, Goodyear acquired Celeron Corp. During the friendly takeover of Celeron, Mercer used the code name "Camel" to refer to the oil company.

By the first days of October 1986, Goodyear had acquired a code name, too. It was called "Patience Co." by Jeffrey Berenson, of Merrill Lynch, and Goldsmith. Patience seemed to fit both Goodyear and Mercer.

For example, the company was investing a billion dollars in building Celeron's crude oil pipeline from California to Texas that wasn't expected to generate profits for several years. And the company held on to Celeron even after slumping oil prices threatened to turn the "Camel" into an albatross.

And above all their personal differences, Mercer's patience may be the one attribute that distinguishes his business philosophy from that of the tempestuous Goldsmith.

But there was no time for patience now. Goldsmith was on the move. Mercer soon would have to act.

WEEK IV

TUESDAY, OCT. 7—THE FIRST RUMOR THAT GOODYEAR IS A TAKE-OVER TARGET SURFACES ON WALL STREET.

Goodyear stock was on the move.

On Oct. 7, it hit a 15-year high.

Hardly anyone on Wall Street knew who was behind the surge.

Jeffrey Berenson did.

A lead partner in Merrill Lynch's merger and acquisition group, the mysterious Berenson later would be identified as the real architect of Sir James Goldsmith's raid on goodyear.

Berenson in some ways typified a new breed of Wall Street investment banker who was changing the rules of takeover finance and reshaping corporate America in the process. He is youthful (although at age 36 he is a relative "veteran" of takeover fights), bright, aggressive and driven. Like most of his colleagues, he lives luxuriously, although more elegantly than most. He is a world traveler and natty dresser. His Park Avenue condominium is filled with fine art and antiques.

Unlike most of his colleagues, Berenson does not have a master's degree in business administration. He graduated magna cum laude from Princeton University with a bachelor's degree in romance languages, a background that some associates said may explain why he tends to be more reflective about his business than most of the young Wall Street hotshots.

As far as his feelings for Goodyear, Berenson confided to others that he believed the company had failed to provide an adequate return to its shareholders and thus was deserving of a raid. Berenson also was said to have discounted worries that a Goldsmith raid would devastate Akron or the company.

However, Berenson's feelings about Goodyear never became public.

"Among the many things I'm doing, Goodyear is but one," Beren-son said, explaining to a reporter why he would not grant an interview.

The attack on Goodyear was part of the spreading takeover fever on Wall Street. Almost daily, another of America's corporate giants was coming under siege. Investment bankers such as Berenson and arbitrageurs—the players who frequently are partners to successful raiders—were growing increasingly aggressive and daring.

As the Goodyear rumors were circulating, another takeover battle was ending that would dramatize the new power of corporate raiders and portend bad news for Goodyear.

Campeau Corp., a Canadian real estate firm, was in the process of a successful hostile takeover of the much bigger Allied Stores chain. Campeau's revolutionary weapon was a huge equity contribution, some $1 billion, from its investment banking firm, First Boston Corp. This was a departure from the usual takeover, in which a raider relied primarily on borrowings (often "junk bonds") to pay the costs of a tender offer for all or some of a target company's shares. The risk arbitrageurs, financial pros who invest in stocks of targeted companies, had to decide whether the potential reward of lining up with the raider offset the risk a deal would fall through.

In the Allied battle, the "arbs" saw little risk. With wealthy First Boston putting its own money into the deal, instead of simply underwriting securities others would buy, the arbs confidently gathered up Allied shares, eventually forcing the company to accept a takeover on Campeau's terms.

A month later, as the Goodyear takeover battle reached its climax, this new-found power of the raiders and arbs would be sapped almost overnight by a stunning event—an insider trading scandal centering on the most famous risk arbitrageur of all: Ivan F. Boesky. Arbs suddenly would begin bailing out of takeover stocks.

But that was later. In early October, Goldsmith, Berenson and associate Denis Kelly were confidently carrying out a strategy for acquiring Goodyear that was very similar to Campeau's in its takeover of Allied.

Under the plan, Merrill Lynch would become a Goldsmith partner, putting $1.9 billion of its own money into a tender offer for all

Goodyear shares. Goldsmith would finance the remainder of a tender offer with $2.6 billion in bank financing.

For the short term, Goldsmith was using $200 million in bank credit lines and some $230 million of his own and other partners' money to begin accumulating Goodyear shares. Later, Goldsmith would say he had $1 billion in investor money, outside of Merrill Lynch, earmarked for the takeover.

Merrill Lynch's commitment, and the additional support Goldsmith lined up from an old British ally, Hanson Trust, would leave no doubt that Goldsmith had the means to acquire Goodyear—a point Goodyear's advisers would make to Mercer as soon as Goldsmith's name surfaced.

Merrill Lynch had a lot riding on the outcome of the Goodyear-Goldsmith battle. The firm was getting $5 million up front to assist Goldsmith, but it would get much more, possibly $100 million or more in fees, if Goldsmith made the tender offer and succeeded in acquiring Goodyear.

In addition, the deal could catapult Merrill Lynch into the top rank of takeover finance, from its second-tier status below Goldman Sachs & Co., First Boston, Drexel Burnham Lambert Inc., Morgan Stanley and Salomon Brothers Inc.

For Berenson, a successful raid on Goodyear would enhance his growing reputation on Wall Street and bring new prestige to his associate, Kelly.

While the Goldsmith-Merrill Lynch pact was unknown to the investment world until the end of October, arbitrageurs in early October already had begun bidding up almost any rumored takeover stock with confidence, including Goodyear.

On the floor of the New York Stock Exchange, Christopher Bates said he had never seen such a frenzy in the three years he had overseen the trading of Goodyear stock. Each morning the traders would line up 10 or more deep waiting for the opening bell, and remain through the day, buying and selling Goodyear in front of Bates' narrow counter top.

Most of the buyers were arbitrageurs.

Bates, 30, is the grandson of a founding partner of the New York clearinghouse Robb, Peck, McCooey, whose subsidiary, RPM Specialist Corp., is one of about 55 companies that provide the "specialists" who referee all stock trades. Normally Bates handled Goodyear and four lesser-known stocks at his station in an anteroom of the exchange known as "the garage."

But now the Goodyear activity was so heavy Bates passed the other stocks to a colleague, and recruited another specialist, Fred Tramutola, to deal with the mob of traders bidding on Goodyear.

Bates was one of Goodyear's most important contacts with Wall Street, but there wasn't much he could tell the company. Bates knew Merrill Lynch was the heaviest buyer of Goodyear stock, but he said he didn't know who Merrill Lynch was buying for—nor should he, given the rules of the exchange against insider dealing.

Two weeks before the Goodyear takeover rumor became common knowledge on Wall Street, Goodyear knew something was awry.

The warning came to Mark Blitstein, Goodyear's link to Wall Street, in a flurry of phone calls—15 calls in 10 minutes to his office on the seventh floor of Goodyear headquarters.

On the morning of September 25, Merrill Lynch Capital Markets handled the sale of a huge block of Goodyear stock—1.7 million shares. One broker for Merrill Lynch sold the stock to another Merrill Lynch broker.

The broker selling the stock was acting on behalf of an institution. The other broker? According to the investors phoning Blitstein, the broker said he was acting on behalf of Goodyear.

Institutional investors holding large amounts of Goodyear stock wanted an explanation. Blitstein was dumbfounded. Goodyear, he was certain, was not buying its own shares. He would have known if the company planned a stock purchase costing $56 million.

Blitstein began to feel uneasy. Whoever bought those shares didn't want to be identified.

Blitstein found himself linked to this world of high finance via a circuitous route.

A native of New York, Blitstein, 35, came to Cleveland to study chemistry at Case Western Reserve University. He joined Goodyear's chemical division in 1977, but soon swapped his lab coat for a business suit after a variety of technical assignments. His field experience proved valuable in explaining Goodyear's diversification to Wall Street analysts and investors.

By the time the 1.7 million-share block of stock was purchased on

Sept. 25, Merrill Lynch already had purchased 116,000 shares on Goldsmith's behalf. But those earlier trades, made over the previous four sessions, were too small to be easily noticed.

When Blitstein learned about the first big purchase, he knew the implications could be profound—a raid might be under way. But Blitstein also knew there might be a less sinister explanation. The last thing he wanted to do was needlessly alarm his superiors, chief financial officer James Glass and chief executive Robert Mercer.

So before he sounded the alarm, Blitstein placed two calls. One was to company treasurer Oren Shaffer, who confirmed that Goodyear wasn't buying back stock.

Then a call to tire and auto industry analyst Harvey Heinbach, Blitstein's contact at Merrill Lynch, intensified Blitstein's concern.

Heinbach told Blitstein he wasn't permitted to comment on the transaction.

"My reaction at that point was, 'This is not a normal trade,' " Blitstein said.

Blitstein informed Glass and Mercer with hand-delivered memos. The note detailed what had transpired on Wall Street that morning and added Blitstein's impression that "somebody was up to no good."

For Blitstein, the subsequent days would be agonizingly uneventful. None of his contacts on the Street—investors, arbitrageurs, specialists, analysts—could name the buyer.

"Usually the name will surface somehow, especially a position that is that large," Blitstein said.

As Goldsmith's filing with the Securities and Exchange Commission later would show, the raider avoided detection through the first half of October as he gathered shares more slowly, limiting his individual purchases to smaller blocks of stock. Meanwhile, arbitrageurs became attracted to Goodyear stock by the mounting takeover rumors, making it that much harder for Blitstein to sort through the avalanche of trades in search of a raider.

Maybe the takeover rumor was unfounded after all, Blitstein thought at the time. Maybe, Blitstein surmised, a Wall Street "shark" might be at work, attempting to drive up the price of the stock by triggering a false rumor and selling out at a big profit.

A shark certainly would have been preferable to a raider, but in late September and early October, there was no way to know.

"We decided at that point that we would sit back and wait and see what happened."

Goldsmith, Blitstein said later, "allowed us to get into a sense of false security."

WEEK V

FRIDAY, OCT. 17—SIR JAMES GOLDSMITH MAKES HIS BIGGEST GOODYEAR PLAY YET AS HIS INTERESTS BUY 2.1 MILLION SHARES OF STOCK.

The waiting and watching ended abruptly on this day.

Returning from Japan that day, Goodyear chief executive Robert Mercer's plane stopped at Chicago O'Hare International Airport. Awaiting him was a message to call chief financial officer James Glass in Akron.

"What's up?" Mercer asked.

"I think we have a problem," Glass said.

"I'll be in in an hour," Mercer replied.

Glass was calling Mercer because the intensity of trading in Goodyear stock had reached a peak. There was another reason for the urgency but they didn't yet know it. Leading the buying was Goldsmith, whose representatives purchased 2.1 million shares this day, his first big play since Sept. 25.

The day before, 1.6 million shares of Goodyear stock had been traded. Glass had issued a public statement that the company couldn't "detect any pattern of accumulation" but his call to Mercer at the airport indicated he suspected trouble.

As Goodyear stock became the most active on the New York Stock Exchange, rumors about potential buyers were swirling. The first of several rumored suitors was GAF Corp., a chemical firm from Wayne, N.J. "That was the heavy street rumor," said Mark Blitstein, Goodyear liaison with Wall Street.

Was it a case of disinformation? "I don't think there was any disinformation," Blitstein said. He thought it was just Wall Street building a story.

Blitstein virtually was certain that Merrill Lynch Capital Markets had something to do with the heaving trading, but there was no raider in sight.

"At that point, all of the other arbs (arbitrageurs) had gotten into the feeding frenzy," Blitstein said, "and so it became more difficult to identify where the potential threat was."

Blitstein pursued what few leads he had. The same day Mercer returned from Japan, Blitstein flew to New York to meet with Christopher Bates, a floor trader on the stock exchange who specializes in Goodyear stock. "Those two weeks we noticed a consistent trading pattern," Blitstein said.

Leaving New York, Blitstein believed there was little doubt Goodyear was a target.

Back in Akron, Mercer summoned key executives to his office on Saturday, Oct. 18.

At the meeting, everyone agreed the evidence showed "that somebody was accumulating our stock," Blitstein said.

Mercer turned to Blitstein: "How confident are you that this thing (a raid) is going on?"

"About 95 percent," Blitstein said.

Mercer sounded the alarm.

"Let's notify (investment banking firm) Goldman Sachs and get the SWAT team together," he said.

The SWAT team had been created in July as part of a general takeover defense scheme.

Now it was time to put the plan into action.

The SWAT team's job was to identify the raider and fend him off.

Goodyear had known for many months that it was a potential target for a raid. The company had spoken with analysts in an effort to boost its stock price so it would be less of a target.

In July, Goodyear's board of directors also approved a "shareholder rights plan"—or "poison pill"—that was designed to scare off potential raiders.

Even William Newkirk's public relations staff went to a takeover camp in Maryland for four days in mid-July. "There was no sense of urgency or anything like that, it just seemed like the thing to do at the time," Newkirk said.

The SWAT team began meeting each morning, gathering around a long oval table in Mercer's fifth-floor "Mahogany Row" office.

A second nerve center was set up in an office on the seventh floor.

It was called the "war room." About a half dozen corporate and financial people would occupy the room at a given time.

The Goodyear defense team included some of the company's highest-ranking officials:

Oren Shaffer, vice president and treasurer; John Ross, assistant secretary; Frederick Myers, vice president, general counsel and secretary; Gary Wittkamper, another legal associate; and Mercer and Glass.

The SWAT team was advised by Tom Mindell, the investment banker from Goldman Sachs & Co. Goodyear also had assistance from Cahill Gordon & Reindel, a New York law firm, which in turn recommended hiring The Carter Organization, a proxy solicitation firm.

Deciding that the best defense was a good offense, Goodyear began adding the highest-priced talent in the takeover game to its defense team. The new players were accustomed to working for raiders rather than targets.

An important addition was the investment banking firm of Drexel Burnham Lambert Inc., which pioneered the use of high-risk "junk bonds" as a tool for raiders to take over companies.

In this case, Drexel meant Martin Siegel, a financial whiz kid specializing in mergers and acquisitions. Drexel and key executives, including Siegel, later would be subpoenaed in the federal government probe of insider trading violations on Wall Street. There is no apparent link between the subpoenas and Drexel's work for Goodyear.

After Goodyear hired Drexel, Drexel brought in New York attorney Joe Flom, one of Wall Street's best-known takeover artists.

The thinking was that if Goodyear didn't scoop up Flom and Siegel, they would end up in the enemy camp. Whoever the raider was, Mercer said, "we didn't want him to have Drexel and Flom.

"They knew what to say," he explained. "They knew the language (in meetings). Whether or not it was worth the money to pay them, I don't know. But I do know this: You'd be severely criticized if you went into this kind of battle without hiring the best people in the business to advise you."

The best people will cost Goodyear a minimum of several million dollars, company officials said.

And if nothing else, Goodyear executives had to feel relieved to learn that Drexel and Flom weren't already working for the still un-identified raider.

The Carter Organization was brought on board with one mission—identify the raider.

Carter is hired more often in corporate-control battles than any other company of its kind.

It specializes in scouting out the enemy. It used electronic services to monitor stock transactions.

From these transaction records, Carter hoped to spot patterns of trading that would lead to particular brokers and through them to the mysterious raider.

The Goodyear commission was big enough to prompt Carter owner Donald Carter to get involved personally in the search.

Carter's job involved as much art as science. Success would depend as much on the company's extensive contacts in Wall Street's back offices as on the official records.

"You can go just so far in the paper trail in trying to track down the investor," Carter said. "In the end, you need some corroboration."

Soon, the raider would be in sight.

WEEK VI

SATURDAY, OCT. 25—THE BEACON JOURNAL REPORTS THAT SIR JAMES GOLDSMITH MAY BE THE CORPORATE RAIDER WHO HAS TARGETED GOODYEAR FOR A TAKEOVER.

Wall Street sleuth Donald Carter did his job.

By Oct. 24, he had given Goodyear the raider's name.

Sir James Michael Goldsmith.

How certain was Carter that he had found his man?

"One hundred percent," he told Goodyear officials.

Mercer's first move was to turn to his lead investment bankers, Goldman Sachs.

"Does he (Goldsmith) have the money?" Mercer asked.

He does, Goldman Sachs' Tom Mindell replied.

Mercer wanted to know if Goldsmith could be stopped.

The answer was possibly, but at great cost.

To stop Goldsmith, Goodyear would be forced to sell two major subsidiaries, lay off thousands of workers and, in so doing, abandon a business strategy molded over decades.

Mercer's advisers presented him these bleak options:

• Buying back the stock that Goldsmith had purchased.

• Pushing the price of the stock too high for Goldsmith by selling subsidiaries, trimming operations and taking on debt.

• Finding a "white knight" who probably would take the same actions, but likely in a less brutal fashion.

"Unbelievable," Mercer said of the options.

Though the harshness of the alternatives was shocking, the possibility that Goodyear might face this day had been clear for some time.

"We recognized the pattern that targets fell into," Goodyear's Wall Street liaison Mark Blitstein said. "And I think we recognized some of the vulnerability that we had. And some of that vulnerability was almost necessary if we were going to achieve our long-term objectives.

"And if you're committed to a long-term strategy, you have to take the risk that somebody can come in and capitalize on that."

A key part of that strategy came in 1983, when the company launched an ambitious diversification program that took it into the oil, gas and pipeline business. This was Celeron Corp., Goodyear's biggest-ever non-tire venture. More than $1 billion was sunk into a pipeline project that wasn't expected to pay off for years.

Mercer saw Celeron as a key to Goodyear's future, a move that could help insulate the company from the dramatic ups and downs of the auto industry. Someday, Mercer wanted Celeron to provide as much as 25 percent of Goodyear's annual earnings.

But there was a competing pressure, one that emphasized results for stockholders. Goodyear needed to be able to convince investors that their stock was worth what company officials knew the assets were worth. Otherwise, their stock could be perceived as undervalued and the company could be targeted for takeover and profitable dismemberment.

"So your assets are undervalued. That's a nice thing to say," Mercer said. "And the market hasn't recognized it, so therefore you're doing something wrong because your stock is not where it's going to be. And immediately you're on the defensive: 'You guys are doing a lousy job for the shareholders and we want to enhance shareholder value.'

Now, who the hell can argue against enhancing shareholder value? So that's his program going in," Mercer said, referring to a raider.

Actually, Mercer believes any company, when scrutinized, is worth more broken up.

"This'll happen in any company you're looking at. I think it would happen in the case of Firestone even though (chief executive officer) John (Nevin) has sold off a lot and bought stock back in; the breakup value has got to be higher than the market," Mercer said. "It would be absolutely weird if it were the other way around."

But some critics believe Celeron was a costly mistake that tied up company assets and diluted earnings for all of Goodyear, in the end sowing the seeds of Goodyear's crisis.

"I think the diversification was poorly thought out and not in the best interests of the shareholders," said John Neff, manager of the Windsor Fund, a mutual fund in Valley Forge, Pa. "They were paying up for an oil position that the shareholder, when he bought the stock, had never figured on. He was buying a tire business and some of the other businesses. I think it was a dereliction of management. Goodyear never earned a very good return, and it was made worse with the Celeron thing."

The fund managed by Neff had a sizable holding of Goodyear stock but he sold it before the Celeron acquisition.

The glut in worldwide oil production this year put added strain on Goodyear's overall balance sheet. In the first quarter of this year, Goodyear posted a loss for only the third time in its history. It was attributable to write-downs of oil reserves.

But the questions of what might have been or should have been were moot at this point. Mercer needed to act, and to act, he needed a plan.

The plan came from Mercer's SWAT team and support troops as-sembled in the company's seventh-floor war room, where scenarios were tacked to the walls.

Some sheets contained financial information pertaining to the var-ious restructuring options.

Another chart listed potential white knights—companies that pos-sibly could rescue Goodyear and stave off the raider by offering to purchase Goodyear shares in a friendly transaction. The list was short, but had some of the most powerful corporate giants in the country, including Exxon Corp., Chevron Corp., the Sumitomo Group of Japan, and Chrysler Corp. None of the potential candidates was contacted by Goodyear, company officials said.

Still another chart diagramed Goldsmith's financial empire.

Goldsmith had his own battle team in New York City—a small group headed by Roland Franklin, a longtime adviser and head of Goldsmith's North American business operations. Franklin works out of Goldsmith's General Oriental holding company headquarters on Fifth Avenue.

The Goldsmith brain trust also included attorneys in the law firm of Weil, Gotschal & Manges, which has offices in New York and Washington. Among the firm's staff in Washington is Robert C. Odle Jr., who was the director of administration for Richard Nixon's Committee to Re-elect the President in 1972. Others were investment bankers, Jeffrey Berenson and Denis Kelly of Merrill Lynch.

Goldsmith's war room was Berenson's office on the 45th floor of the Merrill Lynch tower at 1 Liberty Plaza in lower Manhattan. There, Berenson directed a staff of about a dozen assistants who performed financial calculations and gathered data.

Goodyear also learned from Wall Street sources that Goldsmith might be picking up a powerful British ally—Hanson Trust, a company with billions of dollars in cash.

The rumor was that Hanson Trust, known to be looking for acquisitions, had just arranged a $4 billion or $5 billion line of credit. Blitstein said Goodyear was the only takeover target on the market that would have required that size investment.

On Friday, Oct. 24, Goodyear publicly acknowledged it might be the target of a corporate raider. Some 4.1 million shares of Goodyear stock changed hands that day, making it the second-most actively traded stock. The price hit $44 a share, another 15-year high.

Mercer sent a letter to his company's 13,000 Akron employees, promising that "we are not sitting idly by."

This heavy trading activity raises the very distinct possibility that someone is accumulating our stock," Mercer wrote. The company expected to know that someone's identity "very soon."

The public learned that the raider might be Goldsmith the next day, when the Beacon Journal quoted sources close to Goodyear identifying him.

The raider was in sight. The battle was near. Mercer sent chief financial officer James Glass and legal counsel Fredrick Myers to New York to meet Goldsmith on Monday, Oct. 27.

Mercer also sat down and talked with his wife, Mae.

"(He told me) 'It's going to be tough,' " she recalled. "He said, 'You're going to have to understand what's going to happen. I'll probably get some bad press because of Goldsmith's tactics.' And he said, 'I'm going to be a very busy guy.' "

WEEK VII

FRIDAY, OCT. 31—SIR JAMES GOLDSMITH FILES A REPORT WITH THE SECURITIES AND EXCHANGE COMMISSION DETAILING FINANCING FOR THE TAKEOVER OF GOODYEAR AND PLANS TO SELL NON-TIRE RELATED ASSETS.

As the warm breath of Indian summer eased the transition from October to November, the Akron community had just begun to comprehend what was going on at Goodyear.

City Councilman Robert Otterman proclaimed that the council had to do something to halt this man Goldsmith.

What? He wasn't sure. Just something. That kind of frustration was beginning to mount.

On Monday, trading in Goodyear stock reached an all-time high, with more than 12.7 million shares trading hands, the ninth highest volume day for any individual stock on the New York Stock Exchange. Many residents, including some Goodyear employees, sold their stock as the price reached $48.50 per share. There was an unfounded rumor that three Goodyear executives had been fired for selling stock.

"Some people sold before they found out for sure that Goldsmith was involved," a Goodyear executive said. "After that, it slowed down."

The North Hill United Methodist Church faced a similar dilemma. The church had received a gift of 100 shares of Goodyear stock the week before. The donor asked that the stock be used to help pay for the church's new roof.

Selling that stock at more than $48 a share was tempting.

"The roof is going to cost $150,000," North Hill pastor Robert Muffly said. "But we decided we wanted to be supportive of Goodyear. We didn't want to be part of this raider's attempt."

The church kept its stock.

That sort of attitude was spreading.

Nowhere was it any more evident than at the Goodyear barbershop.

Rufus Johnson, 51, is sort of a handyman at the barbershop. He isn't a Goodyear employee. The shop's owner, John Emery, is an independent contractor. But all of the shop's customers work for Goodyear. Johnson saw the pain in their faces every day. He decided to speak out on their behalf.

On Tuesday evening, chief executive officer Robert E. Mercer stopped by to get his hair cut—"typical corporate cut, a little off the sides," Emery said—and his shoes shined. Mercer was preparing for his first meeting with Goldsmith. The meeting would take place at Goldsmith's New York town house on Thursday at noon. Mercer talked with Emery and Johnson about the meeting.

Johnson spoke his mind.

"Mr. Mercer," he said simply, "it's Rambo time."

Mercer chuckled at the thought of Johnson—a wiry 5 feet 6 inches and 125 pounds—taking on a corporate giant like Goldsmith. But Mercer wasn't laughing at the fight he saw in Johnson's eyes.

Mercer repeated the story to several associates. "Rambo time" quickly became the catch phrase around the executive headquarters. Mercer's letter to Goodyear employees on Wednesday, Oct. 29, took that same get-tough attitude. He named Goldsmith for the first time as the raider. He pledged to use all of the company's resources "to stave off a hostile takeover." He condemned the flaws in the free-enterprise system that would allow foreigners to usurp America's industrial base.

Rufus Johnson wanted to be part of the fight.

He had never seen any of the *Rambo* movies, but he served in the Air Force for more than four years until he was injured in a jeep accident. "I'd like to speak to that Goldsmith myself," Johnson said. "I'd tell him what I think. Hey, this guy threatened my livelihood. I want my little piece of bread, too."

91

Johnson, who has six children and 12 grandchildren, has done cleaning and odd jobs at the barbershop for seven years. Before that, he worked at the meat market. Before that, in landscaping. His little piece of bread has never been too big, but he's proud of the way he's earned it.

He walks more than a mile every day to catch the bus to take him to his job. "He's always here at 6:30 in the morning," Emery said. "I remember one day last year the weather was so bad I just turned over in bed and went back to sleep. There wasn't any point in going in to work. But later I called the shop, and sure enough Rufus was there."

"I'm no different than the next guy," Johnson said. "I'd like to have a million dollars or a billion dollars. But not if I had to hurt people to get it. I'd rather have a million friends than a million dollars if I had to get it that way. People all smile when they see me. I'm not afraid to look anybody in the face.

Mercer consulted others besides Rufus Johnson before his first meeting with Goldsmith.

He telephoned Bill Creson, former chief executive at Crown Zellerbach Corp., which was successfully raided by Goldsmith. Creson predicted what he thought would happen, saying, "Your choices are kind of limited."

Goodyear aides funneled any data available on Goldsmith to Mercer, who devoured it, including *Goldenballs!*—a book about Goldsmith's libel suit against a satirical British magazine. It was Mercer who later repeated the passage from *Goldenballs!* about Goldsmith's paranoia of rubber bands.

Mercer even called former race car driver Jackie Stewart in Scotland to glean more information about his adversary.

"Jackie, do you know a guy named Sir James Goldsmith?" Mercer asked.

"Oh, you mean Jimmy," replied Stewart, who informed Mercer about Goldsmith's presence on the European social scene.

On Monday of the week, Mercer met in Washington with John S. R. Shad, chairman of the Securities and Exchange Commission. According to a Goodyear spokesman, Mercer asked if the SEC could do anything to block Goldsmith, but Shad indicated Goldsmith's actions appeared to be perfectly legal.

Mercer had planned to be in New York later that day ready to step into the first meeting between Goldsmith and Goodyear executives James Glass and Fredrick Myers, but travel delays caused by bad weather and a transportation mix-up in New York City caused him to arrive after the meeting had ended.

Still Mercer was able to gather intelligence from the two executives and draw on the knowledge of Wall Street advisers Joe Flom and Marty Siegel, who had worked with Goldsmith in the past.

Mercer also called his wife, Mae, from the airport on his way to New York to meet Goldsmith.

"We were at that point calling him Goldfinger because it read like a James Bond movie," Mrs. Mercer recalled. "So I said to him, 'Oh, by the way, when you meet Mr. Goldfinger, please be sure to tell him we have a son-in-law whose name happens to be James Bond. Gotcha.' "

So now Mercer had James Bond and Rambo on his side.

The Thursday meeting had been set up after Glass and Myers had returned from New York on Monday.

From the outset, there were overtones of psychological maneuvering by both sides.

Mercer agreed to meet Goldsmith at his town house because he said he wanted to learn more about him, to see him in his natural habitat. Goldsmith did not insist on the site, Mercer said.

However, he was careful not to let Goldsmith have too great a home turf advantage. Mercer said he had other important business to attend to, telling Goldsmith that the meeting could not last beyond 1:30 p.m. He did have another business meeting scheduled, but it wasn't related to Goodyear.

Mercer recalled that the meeting with Goldsmith went something like this:

Mercer arrived at Goldsmith's town house at 116 E. 80th St. shortly before noon. He knocked on a door that said 116. A stretch limousine was parked in front. A Goldsmith aide dressed in a business suit answered the door.

"Oh, you've got the wrong door," the aide said.

"This is 116, isn't it?" Mercer replied.

"Yes, but this is the butler's entrance," the aide said. "You've got to go next door."

Mercer walked 20 feet, knocked on a door that looked exactly like the one he just left. The same aide answered the door.

"What happened?" Mercer asked.

"I didn't want to bring you in through the kitchen," the aide replied.

Inside, Mercer found himself flanked by two 8-foot-high marble statues of nude women as he moved through the hallway until it opened into a three-story atrium.

"Sir James will greet you in the living room," the aide told Mercer.

The living room is on the second floor. Mercer began to climb the spiral staircase. More psychological warfare from Goldsmith, who was waiting at the top of the stairs. He extended his hand to Mercer when the Goodyear CEO was still two steps below him so that at 6 feet 3 inches, Goldsmith towered over his visitor.

They sat in the living room.

Goldsmith began to make small talk.

Mercer declined. "I really don't have all that much time," he said. "I think we ought to get on to our business discussion."

The butler announced that lunch was ready.

They moved to a dining room that reminded Mercer of a Hollywood set—a very long table with two places set at the far end. Goldsmith sat at the head of the table, Mercer to his right.

Above the fireplace behind Goldsmith's seat was a huge oil painting of another nude woman. Mercer noticed it as he took his seat, but was determined not to glance at it again. "The guy's not going to catch me looking at that oil painting," he thought.

The first course was served: salmon.

Several bottles of wine were nearby in buckets.

Goldsmith offered some to Mercer. He declined. "I don't like to drink at noon," Mercer told Goldsmith.

"Would you care for some water?" Goldsmith asked.

"That would be helpful," Mercer said.

"Fizzy or otherwise?" Goldsmith asked.

"Otherwise," Mercer replied.

Once the matter of the water was settled, the main course arrived: lamb chops and vegetables. Mercer took a lamb chop and some vegetables. Goldsmith, known for his voracious appetite, be it food or companies, loaded up his plate. He wolfed down the first plate of food, then filled it up again. Mercer declined seconds.

The talk turned to Goodyear. Goldsmith insisted that the company was losing its focus as a tire maker. Mercer disagreed, defending the company's diversifications.

Goldsmith eventually said Goodyear management could work together with him or else he'd put out a tender offer for all shares.

Irritated at what he perceived as Goldsmith's lack of knowledge of the industry, Mercer became uneasy. He thought to himself, "I've got a guy with 11½ percent of the company and the backing to buy it all. That's what you've got. And a guy who's willing to do it. Now how do you stop him?"

Mercer also was wary of Goldsmith's quick temper. "If I push him too far," Mercer recalled thinking, "it happens (Goldsmith makes a tender offer for all Goodyear's stock) just like that."

They agreed that they were not interested in accepting or paying "greenmail"—that is, Goldsmith selling his shares back to the company for a higher price than other shareholders could receive.

Mercer wanted to know why Goldsmith was attracted to Goodyear.

"Because you are on the list," Goldsmith said. "You're just one of many companies on the list."

Goldsmith refused to show Mercer "the list."

"All the companies that you've read about that are currently under attack or have been taken over are on this list," Goldsmith said. "You've been on it for some time."

Then Goldsmith reiterated his contention that Goodyear had lost its focus.

Mercer asked for specifics.

"What about your recent excursion into aerospace?" Goldsmith responded.

"My God, Mr. Goldsmith, we've had aerospace since 1911!" Mercer said.

Mercer said Goldsmith looked surprised. "You have?" Goldsmith said.

Mercer said he began to explain why Goodyear was involved in industries such as oil and chemicals but thought that Goldsmith was only half listening. Mercer was convinced that Goldsmith's only objective was to "buy Goodyear, break it up, and run away with the proceeds."

The meeting ended.

The next day, Goldsmith formally announced his interest in buying Goodyear in a report filed with the Securities and Exchange Commission.

In the report, Goldsmith revealed that he held 12,549,400 shares, or 11.5 percent of Goodyear's outstanding common stock. He said he was interested in making an offer for all of the company's stock, but also left open the possibility of selling his holdings.

The filing contained a copy of a one-page letter Goldsmith wrote to Mercer, summarizing their luncheon meeting. In the letter, Goldsmith said he and Mercer had agreed that his interest in the company would not be termed hostile but unsolicited. Goldsmith said they disagreed over the issue of diversification. He also said he was looking forward to meeting with Mercer again.

Goldsmith also said if he won control of Goodyear that he would sell all divisions unrelated to tire production, including Goodyear Aerospace, which employs 5,100 in Akron.

And now Akron knew what this takeover was about.

WEEK VIII

THURSDAY, NOV. 6—GOODYEAR'S AEROSPACE SUBSIDIARY IS PUT UP FOR SALE AS GOODYEAR MANAGERS UNVEIL A SERIES OF PLANNED DIVESTITURES AND CUTBACKS.

Steve Seigfried's hopes for a secure future were tied to his job at Goodyear Aerospace and in early November he was worried.

As he always does when he's anxious, Seigfried paced. He walked in a loop through the kitchen—where a radio on the table brought him Goodyear updates—to the living room and across the shag carpeting that covers the family room floor.

Around and around he went, with four yapping poodles and his daughter's Doberman named Freedom for company.

The future was on his mind. Frustration was on his face.

Seigfried, 59, had started as an electrician at Goodyear Aerospace two years before.

In his mind, Goodyear was "a class company" run by a man who cares about Akron and America. Seigfried doubted that Sir James Goldsmith, whom he had read about in the newspaper, had any such affinities.

After a blue-collar odyssey of plant closings and lost pensions, Seigfried had hoped his $14.30-an-hour Aerospace job would mean security at last.

"When I got this job, I felt sure it would be there (until I retired)," he recalled. "Now we're not so sure."

Seigfried had tried to live according to the "old school" teachings of his father, who worked 40 years at B.F. Goodrich. The lesson was a familiar one in Akron in the days when rubber companies flourished. It went: Get a job, stay with one company and reap the rewards of stability after retirement.

But the world changed. Sun Products Corp., where Seigfried had started as an 18-year-old stock boy, closed its Akron-area plant in 1974 and moved south. After 29 years of service, he was left without a pension.

The shock stripped him, his 53-year-old wife Betty Lou believed, of his easygoing nature.

But Seigfried tried again. There was General Tire for eight years before the plant closed. Then two years at Bearfoot Corp. shoe sole factory in Wadsworth, until the corporation went bankrupt.

And now Goodyear, threatened by a foreign investor. Goldsmith was anathema to Seigfried, a man who would never buy a foreign car and scours labels for products made in America. But what could he do?

"It's just one of those things," Seigfried said. "You wait and see what's going to happen."

Events, meanwhile, were happening faster than they could be digested. Tuesday was Election Day and important local races were to be decided. But their significance partially was eclipsed by the Goodyear story.

On Monday, Goodyear announced it would look for a buyer for its oil and gas subsidiary, Celeron Corp., to raise money for battle.

Meanwhile, it was revealed that Hanson Trust, a cash-rich British conglomerate, was behind Goldsmith, and that Merrill Lynch may have been responsible for bringing the idea of a raid on Goodyear to Goldsmith.

And Akron, like its largest employer, began to fight back.

Joan Lukich of Akron, whose family has more than 200 years of combined service with Goodyear, took to the streets of downtown in a sandwich board urging Akronites to buy the company's stock.

"United We'll Stand, Divided We'll Fall," was her message.

John E. Hagerman, the 37-year-old president of Ohio Machine & Mold Co., talked to his accountant in preparation for doing what he had never done before—becoming an activist on an issue.

"The only hesitation I possibly had is I've never done this before because I try to keep my name out of the public view," he said.

Hagerman, whose 50-employee company is a Goodyear supplier, was incensed after seeing newspaper reports that Merrill Lynch, where his firm had $130,000 invested, was in cahoots with Goldsmith.

"If you want to get to the root of the whole situation, (it is that) Merrill Lynch stands to make an enormous profit in a very short period of time," he said. "And they're hiding behind this banner that says, 'We believe in a free-enterprise system.' Well, I don't buy that. I think there's some moral ethics that should prevail.

"It's just something that is not right. I don't care what any MBA from Harvard and working on Wall Street tells me. It's just not right."

On Nov. 5, Hagerman sat down in his paneled office not from from Goodyear's airdock and composed a letter to Daniel Tully, Merrill Lynch's president in New York.

It read: "I am extremely disturbed by your company's effort to assist Sir James Goldsmith in his attempted takeover of the Goodyear Tire & Rubber Company. Your total lack of sensitivity to this company, their employees, and the many communities in this country is appalling.

"Your shameless greed leaves me with no alternative but to withdraw all of my funds from Merrill Lynch. Although $130,000 is only a drop in the bucket, hopefully many more people like myself will find your actions deplorable. You give new meaning to the word bullish—or is it 'bully-ish'?"

United Auto Workers Local 856 at Goodyear Aerospace already had withdrawn about $70,000 in union funds held by Merrill Lynch.

While union leaders were caucusing about other responses they could take, Goodyear chief executive officer Robert Mercer was preparing for his second meeting with Goldsmith at the Goodyear board's first meeting since the raider's identity became known.

The men had agreed that the second meeting would be held in a small apartment leased by Goodyear near the United Nations building in New York City.

Mercer and Goldsmith spoke by telephone before the meeting. Goldsmith made the point that arbitrageurs now held 22 million to 23 million shares of Goodyear stock—about one-fifth of the company. In the conversation, Mercer said Goldsmith pointed out, "We (meaning Mercer and Goldsmith) have to satisfy the arbs."

Goldsmith arrived at the apartment with Jeffrey Berenson and Denis Kelly of Merrill Lynch in the early evening, but Mercer didn't catch their names.

Mercer recalled that he was concentrating on Goldsmith.

Also in Goldsmith's party was attorney Dennis Block of the Weil, Gotschal & Manges firm, and Roland Franklin, an executive with one of Goldsmith's holding companies.

With Mercer at the meeting were attorney Joe Flom ("our attorney, which is also his attorney," Mercer thought, referring to Flom's past association with Goldsmith); investment bankers Tom Mindell of Goldman Sachs and Marty Siegel of Drexel Burnham; and Irv Snyderman, a Goodyear lawyer from the Cahill, Gordon & Reindel firm in New York.

No food was served.

"Anyone want a Diet Coke?" Mercer asked.

Mercer was the only participant who was a novice in the takeover game. He thought, "Here's a country boy from Ohio sitting here with this crowd—and they do this thing 24 hours a day."

To Mercer, it seemed like a meeting of old friends. "Everybody knew everybody," he recalled.

Mercer said the Merrill Lynch representatives never spoke during the meeting.

At the second meeting, Goldsmith read Mercer a letter that eventually was filed with the SEC.

It concerned a tender offer for all shares for $49 a share. Goldsmith said he was prepared to make the tender offer, but if Mercer planned to restructure, he would wait to see what the plan looked like, Mercer said.

According to Mercer, the meeting went like this:

Mercer told Goldsmith a restructuring would take two weeks to implement, but said he "could beat the $49-a-share price."

Mercer told Goldsmith he could sit back while Goodyear was restructured "or have a fight on his hands."

Goldsmith "looked a little bit confused" and said, "this is more than I can digest."

Goldsmith, chomping on a big cigar, asked if there was a room where his group could go to caucus.

Mercer offered them a small room. The five went in, closed the door and remained for more than an hour.

"This is too much for us to handle," Goldsmith said when the group finally emerged. "I'll have to sleep on it."

"Suit yourself," Mercer replied.

"I'll call you in the morning," Goldsmith said.

Mercer was not given a copy of the letter outlining the tender offer, nor was he shown the letter. "I had nothing I could take to the board," Mercer said.

Mercer later contended Goldsmith had no intention of making the tender offer at that point, but only wanted to set a price for arbitrageurs to bid to.

Asked about the meeting later, a member of the Goldsmith team confirmed that his group crammed into a small room for an extended time.

The Goldsmith source said they talked "about a lot of things that would have surprised them (Goodyear management) and about which they knew nothing."

The source, who asked not to be identified, said Mercer and Goldsmith behaved professionally toward each other.

"The relationship, while obviously cool in light of the circumstances, was quite cordial," the source said. "They had very open conversations about their respective views of Goodyear.

"Bob Mercer conducted himself in a fair and intelligent and reasonable manner—obviously, under great pressure. He's a man of integrity. He spoke his mind fairly. On the other hand, I don't think he discounted or demeaned Jimmy's position. Jimmy is also a man who speaks his mind openly and straightforward.

"They have, in some ways, similar styles of doing business. Jimmy's a much more flamboyant character than Bob Mercer. But I think they got along quite well."

The source said Mercer compared favorably with many of the chief executives he had watched in previous encounters.

"CEOs are not always guys who know how to handle themselves," the source said. "Some are bitter and petty and mean and vindictive, and I don't think Mercer was that way at all. I think he appreciated that Goodyear would be a different Goodyear no matter what happened.

"Whether he agreed or disagreed with the rules of the game, the fact of the matter was the game was being played—and so he was going to play it on a basis that was in the interest of his sharcholders, his employees and management, as he saw those interests."

When Goldsmith and his team departed, Mercer had dinner and flew back to Akron.

Goldsmith called Mercer Thursday, Nov. 6, and said he had decided not to put out the tender offer. He indicated he would wait two weeks, Mercer said.

However, Mercer said Goldsmith cautioned him not to pull "any dirty tricks"—such as issuing subordinated debentures (a form of debt).

"Look," Mercer recalled saying, "I'm too busy putting that whole restructuring program together to get involved in that sort of thing."

In the community, people of all ages were getting busy, too.

At Cuyahoga Falls High School, seniors in Problems of Democracy who were scheduled to discuss election results had questions about Goodyear and Goldsmith.

"Mrs. Kreiner, what do you think (Akron Mayor) Tom Sawyer (who had been elected Tuesday to Congress) will do about Goodyear?" a student asked teacher Sandie Kreiner, whose father worked 36 years at Goodyear.

"Well, Andy," she said, "why does Goodyear bother you?"

The rest of first period was devoted to the subject.

"The kids got real emotional because a lot of their parents work there, or their neighbors work there, or their friends or relatives had worked there in the past," she recalled. "There is an emotional attachment to Goodyear."

She felt it herself. She remembered, as a child, going to Goodyear Christmas parties, where all the employees' children got gifts.

"It was a rubber town," she said. "You could smell the reclaim in the air. And I used to complain about it, and my mother said one day, 'Sandra, don't complain. That means Akron is earning money.' "

This battle of Goodyear's, that had become Akron's, captivated these teen-agers. They began writing letters to senators, congressmen and even Merrill Lynch. They planned a Goodyear stock-buying drive at the school. One publicity poster portrayed Goldsmith with a tread mark across his balding head.

Several students invented the Goldbuster game. A student-drawn cartoon of Goldsmith was set behind a Goodyear GT Eagle tire and used as a target for Velcro darts. The cartoon showed Goldsmith with a fat head and a mean, red mouth.

"They couldn't relate to him at all," Mrs. Kreiner recalled. "He's outside their experience. And that was a common bond for them, too. What are our moral values? What are our ethical values? What have we grown up with? And why is he so different?

"They found him to be an amoral person. Some of them said immoral and then we decided in psychology class that he was simply amoral. He doesn't know what's good, what's bad."

The issues of good and bad were blurred by the uncertainty facing employees at Goodyear Aerospace—no matter what the outcome of the takeover battle.

On the morning of Thursday, Nov. 6, a crowd of several thousand people milled together on the chilly floor of the airdock.

But this time—unlike the Saturday nearly eight weeks earlier when tens of thousands of people streamed through—there were no brightly colored balloons in the air. And no one was smiling. These Aerospace workers had come to hear what many already suspected—the company, part of Goodyear since 1911, was for sale.

Aerospace chief executive officer Robert Clark, from a balcony some 50 feet above, broke the news in a voice that cracked more than once.

The workers applauded when he said that no layoff or pay cuts were foreseen.

"Teamwork is the name of the game," Clark said. "Hang in there. Please remember—GAC is a very good company because of our people. Whatever the outcome, nothing can detract from our strengths."

The same morning, Goodyear announced publicly that the Aerospace sale was part of a restructuring the company would undertake in an effort to get the company's stock above $50 a share in coming weeks to better Goldsmith's threatened $49 a share tender offer.

Many of the Aerospace workers who were at the airdock returned home later in the day to find an interview with Goldsmith—the first he had granted to the local newspaper—on the front page.

"All change is frightening, and I am a potential bringer of change,"Goldsmith said. "And people are worried by change. . . . I understand that, and I'm sorry about that."

He warned in the interview that Goodyear would be reshaped dramatically regardless of who won the takeover battle. And already the prophecy was coming true.

Seigfried, whose shift starts at 3:30 p.m., didn't hear Clark's morning speech. He heard the news over the radio in the kitchen of his rural Norton home and then, as he does every workday, sat down to the big noon meal that he calls dinner.

Mrs. Seigfried had prepared pork chops and macaroni and cheese "because it was the quickest thing I could get ready."

Shortly after he arrived at work, Seigfried went with other second-shift employees to the airdock floor, where he listened to Clark repeat the news to a much smaller group.

"Here we go again," Seigfried thought. "I could end up losing a job again."

On Friday, Akron radio stations WSLR and WKDD announced they would join with the University of Akron to gather 100,000 signatures on petitions supporting Goodyear. The petitions, to be circulated at Akron U's Saturday football game against Austin Peay at the Rubber Bowl, and at local malls, would be sent to elected officials "as high as we can go," WKDD news reporter Barbara Adams said.

Meanwhile, local politicians joined the fray. Some 50 mayors and township trustees met with county officials in a brainstorming session. The mood was urgent.

"Damage control is what we're about," said Summit County Councilman Mark Ravenscraft.

Ideas flowed from the meeting—a parade, a national caucus, a letter-writing campaign. In the end, nothing would take place as planned.

Friday was a dark day for Goodyear.

The solidarity of the company's public posture showed signs of cracking.

At an evening testimonial dinner for Congressman John Seiberling, Clark said he would like to punch a reporter who had been writing stories about the possibility of a sale of Aerospace to Martin Marietta Corp. of Bethesda, Md.

Clark called the reporter the next day to apologize.

Meanwhile, the company's stock price had dropped since the restructuring was announced the day before.

Mercer confirmed one of the community's biggest fears—there would be layoffs as part of the restructuring. Cuts would happen with or without Goldsmith at the helm.

"There will be some gut-wrenching decisions that all of us will have to make," Mercer wrote in a blunt and emotional letter to employees. "Some of us will be victims of those decisions. For none of us will the life ahead ever be quite the same."

There was on the horizon, Mercer wrote, "a new and not very pretty world in which we are now forced to operate."

WEEK IX

WEDNESDAY, NOV. 12—THE AKRON POLICE DEPARTMENT PULLS $272,470 IN INSURANCE MONEY FROM MERRILL LYNCH LOCAL OFFICE, THE THIRD AND LARGEST MAJOR WITHDRAWL IN THE WEEK.

It wasn't a very pretty November for Don Walsh, manager of the Akron office of Merrill Lynch Pierce Fenner & Smith.

Many in Akron perceived Merrill Lynch to be the evil ally of Sir James Goldsmith in his pursuit of Goodyear.

Suddenly Walsh was seen by many as a member of the enemy camp in a city where he lived and prospered.

As manager of 42 brokers, Walsh oversees a brokerage office that is by far Akron's largest, as well as one of Merrill Lynch's biggest nationwide.

Walsh's lifestyle reflects his status. A home in Bath Township, ownership of two dozen harness-racing horses, and close friendships with such sports celebrities as Atlanta Braves manager Chuck Tanner and former baseball pitching great Jim Palmer. Walsh himself had been quite a baseball player in the 1960s, when he was a pitching star at Arizona State University, where he was a teammate of future major leaguers such as Reggie Jackson and Rick Monday.

There is one anomaly to Walsh's fast-paced existence. For 6½ years —a long time by the standards of his transient business—Walsh has worked in Akron. It's his choice.

Raised in Massachusetts and Scottsdale, Ariz., with tours of duty for Merrill Lynch in Hawaii, Guam, Southern California and Chicago, Walsh has taken a liking to the easy pace, friendly faces and varied scenery of Northeast Ohio.

Walsh considers himself one of Akron's civic boosters. He talks proudly of the financial support his office gives the Ohio Ballet. His oldest son attends the University of Akron. Walsh does not rule out moving on to a more prestigious job for Merrill Lynch that would take him out of Akron, but he says he is in no hurry and has turned down several choice assignments.

Although retirement is a long way off for the 40-year-old executive, Walsh and his wife, Terry, have decided this is where they want to settle eventually.

But by the second week of November, Walsh's bucolic existence in the Akron area had been severely jolted. People protested outside his office. Clients withdrew funds.

It was all part of a concerted effort by Goodyear and the Akron community to rebuff the takeover attempt by Goldsmith.

Walsh had learned of the role Merrill Lynch was playing in the takeover a month earlier, not from his home office, but at a gas station. At about 6 p.m. on Oct. 14, Walsh pulled his cream-colored Mercedes 380SL sports car into the self-serve Sohio station in Akron's

Merriman Valley. He chatted briefly with another customer, a Beacon Journal business reporter with whom Walsh had spent lunches talking sports and the stock market, in that order. The two men talked about the Boston Red Sox's dramatic playoff victory against the California Angels two days earlier.

"By the way," the reporter asked Walsh as they parted, "did you know Merrill Lynch is rumored to be the big buyer of Goodyear?"

"No," an apparently surprised Walsh responded. "You'd know better than I would. We don't deal with that end of Merrill Lynch."

Later, Walsh acknowledged that the reporter's remark hit like "a lightning bolt."

"It dawned on me," Walsh said, "that if in fact Merrill Lynch Capital Markets was involved, some people would somehow tie in the local Merrill Lynch office."

Congressman John Seiberling made the connection, telling union leaders that they could show their displeasure with Merrill Lynch by withdrawing accounts.

Upon reading that comment in the newspaper Walsh called Seiberling in Washington.

"You shouldn't have said anything (about pulling money out)," Walsh said. "After all, you represent the workers of Merrill Lynch."

"Well, I represent the workers and the people all the time in this community who are at odds with each other over some particular issue," Seiberling replied. "And I have to decide what is the right position to take. What's the use of beating around the bush? The people are obviously incensed at Merrill Lynch and they want to do something about it. . . . What the heck did you expect?"

But the withdrawals from Merrill Lynch were just one of the many forms the protest was taking as Akron dug in its heels against Goldsmith.

Some were humorous.

A Goodyear Aerospace employee designed and distributed "Sir James in Trunk" automobile signs similar to the popular "Child on Board" signs.

A target with Goldsmith's face as the bull's-eye circulated around Goodyear, as did a ribald cartoon, depicting what the author thought Merrill Lynch's slogan "Bullish on Amerca" really meant.

"The humor helped break some of the tension," a Goodyear employee said.

The community was responding as well.

The Rev. Bill Seith of the Goodyear Heights United Methodist Church used a character called Merrill the Blue-Chip Bear in a sermon. "Merrill the Bear is trying to Lynch a great company like Goodyear," Seith said.

Area residents sent rubber bands to Goldsmith after a Beacon Journal columnist wrote about his paranoia of rubber bands and listed Goldsmith's home and work addresses.

Letters poured in to the Beacon Journal. The newspaper published two full pages of letters—mostly angry—on Wednesday, Nov. 12; two more pages on Nov. 14; and another page the next day.

Radio station WNIR sent tapes of calls from irate listeners to Goldsmith.

The Akron Area Auto Dealers Association bought 2,000 shares of Goodyear stock to demonstrate its support. Other individuals continued to buy lesser amounts. Union members were urged to purchase stock.

The petition drive begun the week before by the University of Akron and radion stations WSLR and WKDD was in full swing. Lola Brown, a Goodyear employee, collected 13,000 signatures. Denny Richards, another supporter, collected 2,000 signatures.

Richards said when he took the petitions to Babcox Publications, he was escorted throughout the building so that he could get the signature of every employee. At a Giant Eagle food store in Cuyahoga Falls, he said a line of 40 people waited to sign the petition. One man told him, "someone ought to assassinate Goldsmith."

One Akron woman, when she learned that an area mall prohibited the petition drive, organized an impromptu boycott of the mall's stores. She was ushered outside by mall security.

On Friday, Nov. 14, Seiberling accepted 36,531 signatures from the petition drive organizers at Akron U's Rhodes Arena. He promised to deliver every one to President Ronald Reagan—or at least to the President's chief of staff, former Merrill Lynch executive Donald Regan.

Much of the local protest was spontaneous, a natural reaction to the encroaching forces of economic change that Goldsmith represented.

But Goodyear helped promote the anti-takeover sentiment wherever it could.

The public relations battle is an integral part of any takeover war. The power of public relations was obvious in 1984, when raider T. Boone Pickens attempted to gain control of Phillips Petroleum in Bartlesville, Okla. One of every five workers in Bartlesville was employed by Phillips. The public outcry was swift and severe. Demonstrations, complete with high school bands, made the network news. "Boone Buster" T-shirts were the most popular item of clothing in the city. Ultimately, Pickens backed down—although he and partners left with an $89 million profit.

Since then, both raiders and targets have employed high-powered public relations firms.

In this fight, Goldsmith was represented by Kekst & Co. of New York. Goodyear brought in two firms with takeover experience—Dix & Eaton Inc. of Cleveland and Braun & Co. of New York—to assist its vice president of public relations, William Newkirk.

On the advice of the outsiders, Newkirk, a former journalist, was to be the company's sole spokesman. That was to avoid confusion, he said.

Newkirk said Goodyear's strategy was to take the offensive even though it felt it was being attacked.

Goodyear's most visible PR thrust was setting up a teleconference for political leaders in more than 30 other communities with Goodyear facilities.

While Akron Mayor Tom Sawyer was the on-screen star, it was clearly Goodyear's show.

The company paid for everything, from the $60,000 cost of the satellite network that connected the cities to Sawyer's makeup. Goodyear staff members even rewrote Sawyer's speech, after rejecting his original draft. (Sawyer said he and his advisers revised the final copy, inserting phrasing that would be more comfortable to his delivery.)

Sawyer, who had just been elected to replace the retiring Seiberling in Congress, added a couple of homey touches of his own. He took a picture of his family to the New York studio where the broadcast originated and placed it behind him on the set. He also had a United Way cup from Akron on the desk in front of him.

As Newkirk saw it, efforts like the teleconference were just clean PR. "We were not being manipulative," he said. "We were being opportunistic."

Goodyear loaned personnel to the Akron Regional Development Board and to the organizers of the petition drive to help promote community support of the company.

A Goodyear public relations person also helped organize the bus caravan to Washington for a congressional hearing on Nov. 18.

And there were more subtle devices. A copy of the book *Goldenballs!*, which contained many derogatory passages about Goldsmith, was forwarded to Akron area journalists. So were articles about Goldsmith's niece, Clio Goldsmith, who has done nude modeling and acting.

Goodyear also made sure the Beacon Journal knew that Goldsmith was going to have dinner with President Reagan on Nov. 18, another morsel for a community hungry for any reason to dislike this foreign invader.

Meanwhile, Goldsmith had launched his own quietly effective PR effort.

Goldsmith steadily leaked information about his discussions with Mercer in an apparent effort to put his bid in the best possible public light and made an energetic effort to win over Akron in a 30-minute telephone interview with the Beacon Journal. The interview came at a time when Mercer was unavailable to the press.

Goldsmith also called Tom Seese, an Ohio legislator and president of UAW Local 856 at Aerospace. Goldsmith told Seese that he likes to pay high wages because they result in high-quality workers. Goldsmith also accused Goodyear of trying to make him a "scapegoat."

By the ninth week of the takeover war, PR effort was expanded to Columbus, where Goodyear lobbyists arranged to have three anti-takeover proposals presented to the Ohio Senate Judiciary Committee.

Goldsmith hired Dennis Wojtanowski, a former legislative liaison for Gov. Richard F. Celeste, to lobby against the anti-takeover legislation that Goodyear was urging lawmakers to pass.

While the Goodyear and Goldsmith forces maneuvered, union leaders converged on Akron early in the week to grope for a meaningful response to the crisis.

They didn't find one. Instead, they got a quick lesson in takeover terminology.

United Rubber Workers International president Milan "Mike" Stone reflected later that for the third time in three years his union was watching a rubber company under attack by a raider.

In 1984, Stone watched as B.F. Goodrich paid Carl Icahn $7 million in greenmail profits. He also saw Uniroyal's own management liquidate the company in response to another raid by Icahn.

But at least this time, Stone said, the workers were able to lend the company some moral support.

Unfortunately, Stone said, it took a company like Goodyear that was "big enough" to call attention to a situation that affected his labor force and the communities in which they work and live.

While the unions fretted, Goodyear began in earnest the process of paring down.

An early retirement offer to employees was announced; the Europa blimp was retired and a high-technology tire-manufacturing laboratory in England was closed; and Goodyear announced that it was ending its long association with Formula One auto racing, which takes place mostly in Europe.

Officials from Martin Marietta toured Goodyear Aerospace facilities in Akron. Aerospace employees were asked to tidy their offices because other prospective buyers would be shopping at the plant.

It was clear that Goodyear had started the process Goldsmith had promised to carry out. The question was, who would complete the job?

WEEK X

TUESDAY, NOV. 18–A CONGRESSIONAL SUBCOMMITTEE QUESTIONS SIR JAMES GOLDSMITH AND GOODYEAR CHAIRMAN ROBERT MERCER DURING A HEARING ON THE ATTEMPTED TAKEOVER.

Little work was getting done at Goodyear's facilities in Akron this Tuesday morning. Wherever there was a radio, people huddled around.

The past few weeks had been frustrating for Goodyear employees.

It had been difficult to concentrate on work when the future of the company seemed so unsettled. What divisions would be sold? How many layoffs would there be?

"And what do you tell your children about Christmas when you don't even know if you're going to have a job in a couple of months?" the wife of one employee asked.

Everyone was protective of the job he had. Expense accounts were reported more accurately, fewer supplies were missing. Workers shunned the media, fearful that some comment might put them in a bad light.

Now all that anxiety reached a peak as they listened to the broadcast from Washington.

Goldsmith, the bogeyman in their nightmares the past few weeks, was testifying before Congress. Maybe this was the last chance to gun him down. It wouldn't be easy. He had a reputation of shooting fast from the lip.

Goodyear would be represented by Mercer, its chairman and CEO. But on this morning, the company had an even more ardent defender, a man who is linked more inexorably with Goodyear than any person alive—Congressman John Seiberling.

Seiberling had worked for Goodyear as a corporate lawyer for 17 years. His grandfather, F. A. Seiberling, founded the company. His grandfather had hired Paul Litchfield.

It was Seiberling, the representative from Akron, who arranged to have a House subcommittee return from adjournment to hold the hearing, and who persuaded six of his colleagues to return from their home states.

For Goodyear, the timing of the hearing was perfect.

It came just after the disclosure that arbitrageur Ivan Boesky had been caught trading on inside information and had been fined $50 million and forced to return another $50 million in profits.

The hearing also came right as the Goodyear-Goldsmith negotiations were reaching the end of a two-week period in which Mercer was to begin a major restructuring of the company.

Moreover, at the same time Goldsmith was being questioned on the federal front, Ohio legislators were studying five bills that would hamper corporate takeovers.

Goldsmith arrived at the Rayburn building in Washington in a cab. Before the confrontation with Seiberling, he encountered other members of the Akron community. Several busloads of Goodyear workers and retirees had made the trip to Washington. They wore their blue Goodyear caps.

"Listen to what I say before you destroy me," Goldsmith said to the Akron faithful as he pushed his way through their midst.

After opening remarks by Seiberling, Akron Mayor Tom Sawyer, Ohio Sens. John Glenn and Howard Metzenbaum and other members of Congress, Goldsmith finally stepped into the firing line.

He drew first. He aimed for the heart.

He invoked the name of Paul W. Litchfield, chief executive officer of Goodyear for 30 years. "He (Litchfield) defined Goodyear's job quite clearly," Goldsmith said. "It was, he said, 'to build better tires, cheaper, and sell them harder.'

"The current management of Goodyear forgot Mr. Litchfield's lesson. It strayed into industries about which it knew nothing, jeopardizing the very heart of Goodyear's business and the security of all those associated."

Goldsmith's elegant, if somewhat arrogant, testimony continued for 10 minutes, twice as long as the time allocated.

As Goldsmith talked, Seiberling said he could feel his blood pressure rising.

Maybe his anger was even more personal. Financiers like Goldsmith had wrested control of the company from his grandfather in 1921. Seiberling often recalls the long talks he had with his grandfather.

"I was brought up knowing that investment bankers were evil men because of the Dillon Read episode in which they squeezed him (F. A. Seiberling) out of Goodyear and took over control of the company. I was brought up on a tradition to have a low opinion of Wall Street and bankers, investment bankers. So, while I don't still have the generic view that they're all bad, I think it goes back into my early roots. The feeling of antagonism to bankers trying to take control of businesses is a very deep-seated feeling—not only in my personal life, but in many, many people."

And as Goldsmith went on, Seiberling became more incensed. "I was so shocked at the arrogance of this man, who admitted that he knew nothing about the tire industry, who admitted that Goodyear was the best-managed tire company in the industry, to come in here and suddenly denounce the management and say they had mismanaged the company—that they made investments they shouldn't have made and wasted stockholders' money."

Finally it was Seiberling's turn. He said he hadn't planned to ask the question that would follow. Probably it was just a spontaneous reaction to the remarks he had heard for the past few minutes, for the events that had unfolded in his district the past few weeks.

"Mr. Goldsmith," Seiberling began, "you were interviewed by the Akron Beacon Journal and in that interview you stated, 'I certainly don't pretend to know the tire business.' Now you are saying that you do know more about the tire business than those who have been in it for many years because you're deciding how Goodyear ought to operate.

"My question is: 'Who the hell are you?' "

The Goodyear partisans in the gallery clapped loudly. Even Goldsmith applauded the question with his usual aplomb.

And back home around the radios at Goodyear, a lot of cheering could be heard in the halls that had been so quiet before.

Seiberling's question touched an emotional chord, but perhaps the most significant development on Tuesday occurred after the subcommittee hearing when Goldsmith and Mercer met for lunch.

Until this point, they had addressed each other as "Mr. Mercer" and "Mr. Goldsmith." Privately, Mercer has boasted about the fact that he never referred to Goldsmith as "Sir James."

Now Goldsmith wanted to get more familiar. As Mercer related their meeting over lunch at the Hay-Adams Hotel:

"May I call you Bob?" Goldsmith asked.

"If we're going to be this intimate, I guess you should," Mercer said.

"Well, I'm Jimmy," Goldsmith continued.

Goldsmith admitted that he was bothered by the prospect of "scandalous" state legislation that would change the way companies in Ohio operate. He wanted to move things along.

"I can't wait until Friday like you've asked me to because if this (Ohio) legislation goes through tomorrow (Nov. 20)—and I'm told it will—I'll be guillotined," he said.

"I think you've put more stock in that than our law department has," Mercer said about the prospect of state legislation. "We see it as an impediment, but not as a show-stopper."

He perceived that Goldsmith was feeling the fatigue of the battle. The hearing, the state legislation, the press coverage, the reaction from the Akron community—all these blows had begun to wear down the towering financier.

Sensing this, Mercer made his move, maneuvering Goldsmith toward a buyout.

"You can't shoot down a blimp and get away with it," he told Goldsmith. "This is an institution. This isn't just a company you can come in and take over."

"I have to act," Goldsmith said, indicating that he was ready to make the $49-a-share tender offer that would bring him control of Goodyear.

"That's not necessary," Mercer responded. "We have a program that will be better for shareholders."

He stared at Goldsmith and pointed his finger.

"Can you be bought out?" Mercer asked.

"My mind is open," Goldsmith said. "I've left all my options open."

Mercer leaped at the opening.

"You get your team together tonight," he said. "I'll get my team together. Let's see what we can work out."

"I'm having dinner with your President tonight," Goldsmith said. "Care to join me?"

"No. But you give him my best," Mercer replied. "I've got other things to do."

Goldsmith's evening with Ronald Reagan came as a result of his chairing a banquet marking the 10th anniversary of the Ethics and Public Policy Center, a conservative think tank based in Washington.

Meanwhile, his people and Mercer's people negotiated. The aides, with the bosses absent, talked past midnight Tuesday.

Wednesday morning, Mercer went to New York to meet with his board of directors.

Some have questioned the board's role during the takeover ordeal, wondering if the directors were only peripherally involved in the decisions.

"We were kept closely apprised," board member Steven Minter of Cleveland contended. "I'm not going to comment on the process in detail. I will just say that from the time it was apparent there was what seemed to be extraordinary movement to the stock, we were apprised of it. We were kept informed all along the way. We had telephone conference calls and there was correspondence and material was sent to us. I talked often with the (Goodyear) office."

The board met throughout the day and late into the night. Wednesday evening, rumors that a deal had been struck circulated.

But the final agreement proved elusive.

Three times during the board meeting the deal almost collapsed because Goldsmith demanded an immediate decision from the board.

Mercer relayed a message to him that the board wouldn't rush its deliberation.

The messenger was attorney Joe Flom, who specializes in takeover cases. Mercer said Flom was instrumental in the negotiations: Three times Flom left the room to talk with Goldsmith by phone, to calm him down.

Mercer said Flom used "some pretty strong language" to temper Goldsmith. "He talked to him like a Dutch uncle."

About 2 a.m. Thursday, the deal was struck.

"We almost lost it. It was that close," Mercer said afterward.

Goodyear stock had dropped to about $42 a share just before the settlement. But Goldsmith would receive $49.50 a share for stock, giving him a profit of $94 million for 10 weeks' work.

Goodyear's other shareholders would not be so lucky, at least in the short term. They could receive $50 a share from the company, but only for a little more than 40 percent of their holdings.

Through the long contest, Mercer and Goldsmith had insisted they wanted nothing to do with "greenmail"—a company's buying back of a raider's stock for a higher price than that available to other shareholders.

But in the end, Goldsmith walked away with something that looked a lot like greenmail, even though he and Mercer insisted it wasn't.

"We said we weren't going to pay greenmail," Mercer said. "And when this whole thing was put together, I asked two investment bankers. I said, 'Is this greenmail? If it is, we're not going to do it,' And they said, 'No, it isn't.' "

A little comic relief delayed the announcement for a few hours. Mercer said Goldsmith's people couldn't locate all of his stock shares.

Finally, about noon Thursday, it was done.

"We sent that limey bastard home," Akron's Sawyer declared.

But at what price?

EPILOGUE

SATURDAY, NOV. 22—GOODYEAR CHIEF EXECUTIVE ROBERT MERCER SAYS THE COMPANY WILL ANNOUNCE LAYOFFS IN AKRON ON MONDAY.

It was a time to declare victory.

Funny, though, not many people felt like celebrating.

The Save Goodyear Rally, which was supposed to draw thousands to the Rubber Bowl on Saturday, Nov. 22, became the Victory Rally and was moved to the University of Akron's Rhodes Arena. Only 300 people showed up. Only 60 were on hand for the Victory Dance that night at the NECI Convention Center.

Still, those who came out tried to make the best of it.

"Save Goodyear" signs were amended to "We Saved Goodyear." Another large sign said, "You Can Count on Our Town When the Chips Are Down." "We Sent the Invader Packing" read another. Goodyear banners were hung from the balcony and an inflatable blimp balloon hovered near the podium.

Akron Mayor Tom Sawyer told the rally crowd he had been misquoted in Thursday's Beacon Journal when he referred to Goldsmith as "that limey bastard."

"I would never use language like that," Sawyer declared. "I said, 'We sent that slimy bastard back home!' "

Congressman John Seiberling received a standing ovation when he spoke. So did Goodyear chairman and chief executive officer Robert Mercer. However, Mercer's speech hardly sounded triumphant. He used words like "painful" and "walking wounded." He acknowledged that there would be further personnel cuts. The following week, Goodyear announced that at least 680 jobs would be lost in Akron. The sale of Goodyear Aerospace and the Celeron oil and gas pipeline subsidiary was pending.

If victory meant that Goodyear and Akron were still on the same team, then a victory it was. Akron still had Goodyear, Goodyear was still in control of people who believed in its credo: "Protect Our Good Name." But Akron will be losing jobs and Goodyear will be sacrificing much of its long-range growth potential.

Goldsmith looked like the clear winner, walking away with a $94 million profit. But in the aftermath, he sounded bitter about failing to gain control of a company many people doubted he really wanted. Goldsmith criticized the Ohio Legislature and accused Goodyear officials of marshaling a conspiracy of big business, big labor and big government against him.

So the lines between victory and defeat appeared blurry.

Equally unclear are the answers to large economic and ethical questions raised in the war and the mounting wave of similar takeover battles across America.

Goldsmith argued that he was acting in the best interests of Goodyear's owners and in the best interests of America's economic future by "unlocking" between $2 billion and $3 billion in shareholder assets that the company's managers had been sitting on.

Goodyear shareholders, except those who jumped in when the stock hit its peak price in the $47–$49-a-share range, appeared better off for the takeover fight.

Goodyear's stock had been languishing around $30 a share for years, Goldsmith pointed out. Thanks to his efforts, he added, Goodyear has agreed to pay investors $50 a share for 40 percent of its outstanding stock. The company and its investment bankers now say Goodyear is worth between $50 and $60 a share.

"You've kind of taken shareholders over the hoop," said Windsor Fund portfolio manager John Neff. "Goldsmith for better or worse has enforced a discipline they (Goodyear) should have enforced on themselves."

But Neff confessed to having "mixed emotions" about takeover fights.

"I think the discipline people like him force on management is constructive, but I do have a little qualm about seeing companies being stripped, good productive employees being laid off to save top management jobs. If they'd done the right things previously, they wouldn't have had to do the purge."

Goldsmith argued that the money Goodyear has agreed to pay its shareholders will be reinvested in other companies that would create more new jobs and faster economic growth for communities like Akron. That, as he sees it, is the magic of capitalism.

Many economists agree with Goldsmith's basic premise: that raiders frequently serve a useful economic purpose by freeing capital locked in companies that are only marginally profitable or dying.

But executives like Mercer ask other questions.

If a company remains constantly vulnerable to raids by pirates like Goldsmith, how will its managers be free to sacrifice short-term profits to make long-term investments that they believe are in the best interests of its shareholders and workers as well as the communities in which it does business?

Can American corporations prosper and grow in the face of the continuous stockmarket turmoil created by Goldsmith and his fellow raiders?

Such corporate complaints appear to be receiving an increasingly sympathetic hearing from congressional representatives worried about the economic decline of older manufacturing regions and the long-term competitiveness of American companies in international markets.

Apart from that large policy question, there are other interesting ethical and regulatory concerns raised by episodes like the Goodyear war.

Should companies like Goodyear pay money to raiders like Goldsmith to go away?

Morally and ethically, how can raiders like Goldsmith and those who help them on Wall Street justify the enormous profits they receive without having made any real investment in the corporations involved?

Ten weeks ago, the people of Akron probably thought little about questions such as those.

But if nothing else, the entire ordeal gave the community an education in the economics of the 1980s.

For 10 weeks, the butchers and bakers as well as the movers and shakers were discussing risk arbitrageurs, corporate raiders, greenmail, and so forth. "It's like a car wreck," said one local resident. "You can't know what it's like until you've been in one." The community had been hit head-on. It was still intact, but everything was not quite the same.

Rufus Johnson was back at work at the Goodyear barbershop. He was still full of fight. "Why should I be happy?" he said excitedly. "That man came in here, took our money, and left. He hurt a lot of people." A customer—a Goodyear employee—with a long face took a seat in the shop. Johnson pointed to the man. "Does he look happy?" Johnson asked.

Steve Seigfried still had his job at Goodyear Aerospace. But he didn't know who would own the company or for how long his services would be required. And for that matter, the Goodyear Airdock, which Seigfried had helped prepare for that grand celebration 10 weeks before, may soon not belong to Goodyear anymore.

Don Walsh said business was back to normal at Merrill Lynch's Akron office. He said he expected to pick up a "substantial" number of new accounts. "I didn't say, 'Thank God, it's over,' because it's not over," he said. "The development in our community is just beginning. Changes are going to take place. The bottom line is that myself as well as people I work with are anxious to be a part of that, a meaningful part of it."

William Newkirk said that for the first time since he has been at Goodyear, he probably will have to lay off somebody. He has been told that he will have to reduce his public relations staff of 69 by six. Newkirk said he hopes to eliminate four of those jobs through early retirement, but still he'll have to make at least two tough decisions.

Mark Blitstein went back to watching Goodyear's stock as the company prepares its restructuring plan and tries to get the value of its stock up to $50 a share. If shareholders perceive that Goldsmith got a better deal than they did, Blitstein will feel much of the heat.

Seiberling returned to Washington to finish closing his office. He will return to Akron on Dec. 12, retiring after 16 years in Congress. He said his role in keeping Goodyear out of Goldsmith's control will rank high among his legislative achievements. "I think they're (Goodyear) forced to do some of the things that Goldsmith would have done, but he wouldn't have stopped there. I think Goodyear would have been taken apart limb from limb."

Mercer was back to the business of restructuring the company to which he had devoted so much of his life. He mused that maybe Goodyear could restructure by raiding someone else. "That's how dumb this thing is. And we can do it. But that's not our culture. That's not the way we operate. That's not what we're in business for. People think the bottom line is everything. Well, I wish that were so. But we've got some social consciousness that is involved around here. If that's taking it away from the shareholder, then we've been taking it away from the shareholder for 88 years."

And James Goldsmith?

He flew to his offices in Paris last week, maybe to plot his next takeover.

Left behind was testimony to the enormous power of Goldsmith's brand of capitalism.

He had terrified Akron without once setting foot in the city.

This story was written by reporters Stuart Warner, Melissa Johnson, Larry Pantages and Rick Reiff. In addition, the following staff members contributed to the effort:

Reporters Francisco Badillo, Don Bandy, Katie Byard, Kathleen Byland, Mark Calvey, William Canterbury, Jim Carney, Patrick Cole, Mark Dawidziak, Jim Dettling, Bob Dyer, Diane Paparone Evans, John Funk, Greg Gardner, Peter Geiger, Laura Haferd, William Hershey, Robert Hoiles, John Kostrzewa, E. L. Langer, Steve Love, Marcia Myers, Charlene Nevada, Terry Oblander, Bill Osinski, Mary Grace Poidomani, Glenn Proctor, Yalinda Rhoden, Eric Sandstrom, Ron Shinn, Cristal Williams, and Bruce Winges, executive news editor.

THREE

EVIDENCE OF INNOCENCE AND DISORDER IN THE COURT

1987 WINNERS IN THE INVESTIGATIVE REPORTING CATEGORY

"For a distinguished example of investigative reporting within a newspaper's area of circulation by an individual or team, presented as a single article or series . . ."

The Philadelphia Inquirer
John Woestendiek
H. G. Bissinger
Daniel R. Biddle
Fredric N. Tulsky

EVIDENCE OF INNOCENCE

On January 27, 1987, Terence McCracken Jr. got out of prison, where he was serving a life sentence for murder. He hugged his girlfriend. He joyously greeted his family. And he grasped John Woestendiek's hand and said, with simple directness, "Thanks."*

At the time—around mid-April 1985—it was the last story I wanted to do.

I had just finished a story that questioned the conviction of a man who had spent 12 years in prison for a jailhouse killing in Philadelphia in 1973. The time I had invested in the story totaled six months. The impact: next to none.

But beyond that, the experience had been frustrating. When it comes right down to it, there is really no way, short of having seen the crime or been with the wrongly accused person when it occurred, to be certain of a person's innocence.

Conversely, when we send people to prison, or to their deaths, it is not because we are certain they committed the crime. It is because 12 people were pretty darn sure, convinced, in legal terminology, "beyond a reasonable doubt."

For me, the story I had just finished only reconfirmed what I had learned from five previous years of reporting on prisons and prisoners: Criminal justice is often a guessing game. And, in a way, it seemed that all I had done in the previous six months—despite the new witnesses I found and the questions I raised—was make an educated second guess.

Those things considered, I had decided to file away the pleas I was receiving in the mail from prisoners and wait a while before tackling another "innocent-man-in-prison" story. So it was with something far less than enthusiasm that I agreed to meet with the man who said on the phone that his son, convicted of murder, was innocent.

He walked into the office on that April day in 1985 wearing blue

* From nominating letter written by Eugene L. Roberts Jr., executive editor of *The Philadelphia Inquirer*

jeans, boots and a tight black T-shirt. He was tall, over six-foot-four, and his goatee and swooped-back hair were prematurely white. His name was Terence "Screw" McCracken and he was a former member of the Warlocks, perhaps Pennsylvania's most notorious motorcycle gang. Among the crimes for which its members have been convicted were assaults on two *Inquirer* reporters in the 1970s. The group, authorities say, still is suspected of being involved in the unsolved murders of several young women from Philadelphia's suburbs.

Coming from a former Warlock and a father, his claim, at first, was not entirely believable: He was, he said, at home with his son, Terence McCracken Jr., when the crime was committed.

I had heard that one—and variations of it—before. Most people in prison say that they are innocent. Most, despite what they or their parents might proclaim, are not.

But the elder McCracken, normally a man of few words, had more to say.

He told of his son signing for a registered letter about the time the crime occurred. He recounted how two other men, at one point, had been charged with the crime in addition to his son but later got off. He said those men had come close to admitting to him that they—not his son—had committed the crime. He questioned a gunshot residue test that a state police scientist had said in court proved that his son had fired a gun the day of the crime. He cast aspersions on the testimony of a self-proclaimed eyewitness.

My enthusiasm returned, and after some further research and a talk with my editor, we decided to pursue the story.

It had been more than two years since Terry McCracken Jr., an 18-year-old high school senior living in Collingdale, a blue-collar suburb of Philadelphia, was jailed for a March 18, 1983, robbery at Kelly's Deli and the killing of a 71-year-old customer. Six months after his arrest, he had been convicted of second-degree murder.

After reading the trial transcript, I met with McCracken in jail. He recounted how he had spent March 18. He agreed to write down and send me a minute-by-minute account. He sent the jailhouse diary he had been keeping on yellow legal pads since his arrest. We talked on the phone at least once a week, going over details. I asked if he would take a polygraph test. He said he would.

Meanwhile, I also made contact with William Verdekal, then lodged in the same jail as McCracken—Delaware County Prison. About three weeks after McCracken's arrest, Verdekal and his business partner, John Robert Turcotte, had been arrested in connection with another armed robbery in a community near Collingdale. The gun that police had seized from Turcotte was found through ballistics tests to be the one that killed David Johnston, the customer shot in Kelly's Deli.

Those men were charged with conspiring with McCracken to commit the Kelly's Deli robbery and killing, but after McCracken's conviction, the charges against them were dismissed. They were convicted of other robberies and sent to prison.

Verdekal and McCracken had become acquainted in prison, and Verdekal—swayed, he said, by a made-for-television movie about the murder conviction of an apparently innocent young man in Connecticut—had told McCracken he was willing to help him.

In our first prison interview, however, Verdekal was not forthcoming. He reiterated that he wanted to help, but said he was afraid of incriminating himself. He wanted assurances. I told him I could give him none. He said little of relevance, which was just as well, because guards refused to let me bring a pen and pad into the prison. Instead we chatted until our time ran out, and when I left, it was with the agreement that we would get together again.

In subsequent interviews—at Delaware County Prison and at state prisons at Graterford and Rockview—Verdekal opened up and told his full story. Turcotte committed the robbery and killing while he waited outside the delicatessen in his truck, Verdekal said. Neither man knew McCracken at the time, he added. Verdekal, too, consented to take a lie detector test.

To administer the tests to Verdekal and McCracken, *The Inquirer* retained William B. Anderson, chairman of the criminal justice department at West Chester State College, a former career agent with the Federal Bureau of Investigation and a past executive director of the Pennsylvania Crime Commission. In addition to those credentials, Anderson was a personal friend of the district attorney whose office had prosecuted McCracken. In one of our meetings, he admitted that he hoped the results of the tests would not reflect poorly on the district attorney.

Before the testing was to take place, I spent three weeks conducting research for Anderson's "control questions"—talking to friends and family of the two subjects to learn some embarrassing, little-known details about their lives. These questions were designed to throw the subjects off guard and to create a reaction against which Anderson could gauge the truthfulness of their responses to his more critical inquiries. The better the control questions, Anderson had told me, the more conclusive his tests would be.

Anderson, after administering the polygraph to Verdekal, said Verdekal was being truthful when he stated that he had not met Mc-Cracken until after the robbery, that McCracken had no part in the robbery and that Turcotte actually committed the robbery.

McCracken passed, too. No, he did not rob the store; no, he did not shoot Johnston; no, he did not know Verdekal until meeting him in prison. And no, he said—truthfully, according to Anderson—he had never in his life fired a handgun.

That conflicted with what a state police scientist had said at Mc-Cracken's trial. Repeatedly and without equivocation, that scientist said his test, conducted on the hands of McCracken the day of the crime, showed the presence of gunshot residue.

Because of the confusing nature of the gunshot residue testimony, because questions had been raised about it and because it—more than anything else—resulted in McCracken's conviction, according to jurors I had interviewed, I sought another expert. No one in the Philadelphia area, one local ballistics expert told me, was familiar with the method of testing that the state police scientist had used. The method had been developed only recently by a group of scientists that included Dr. Peter F. Jones of California.

After a telephone conversation with him, *The Inquirer* retained Jones to review the gunshot residue test report and the local scientist's testimony in court. Jones, in a report for *The Inquirer,* concluded that the local scientist had erred repeatedly in his testimony, that the particles on McCracken's hands were not necessarily gunshot residue and that they could have come from other sources in the environment, such as the car engine McCracken and a friend said they were working on the day of March 18. Jones subsequently appeared in court at one of several hearings on McCracken's request for a new trial.

While the work of the experts—Jones and Anderson—bolstered the contention that McCracken was innocent, the two-part series that appeared one year later was built upon more routine investigative reporting. It was more than 100 other interviews, court records, the help of two law enforcement officers who had private doubts about McCracken's guilt, and Verdekal's cooperation that made it possible to reconstruct not only what Terry McCracken did on that crucial day, but what Verdekal and Turcotte did as well.

The series appeared on April 21 and 22, 1986, under the title "Evidence of Innocence." On April 23, I reported that the assistant district attorney who successfully prosecuted McCracken had, according to sources, repeatedly expressed doubts about McCracken's guilt to his colleagues in the district attorney's office, but was instructed to proceed with the case. On April 24, I reported that Verdekal's wife confirmed Verdekal's account. "Terry McCracken is a victim," she said. On May 6, I reported that, in addition to Jones, five other forensic experts, including a supervisor at the FBI crime lab in Washington, said in interviews that based on the local police scientist's description of the particles found, there was no scientific basis to conclude that gunshot residue had been found on McCracken's hands.

In the summer of 1986, McCracken's family launched a petition drive. As winter approached, his friends, family and supporters demonstrated in front of the Delaware County Courthouse.

Officials in the Delaware County district attorney's office, while not denying the facts of the *Inquirer* stories, called them "one sided" and "an attempt to sell their papers by sensationalism." They said they remained convinced of McCracken's guilt and would continue to oppose his motion for a new trial.

But early in 1987, that motion was granted, and McCracken, his case assigned to a new judge, was subsequently freed on bail pending a new trial. Now 22, he lives with his parents and holds a part-time job as a telephone solicitor.

The district attorney's office, meanwhile, is attempting to reinstate the murder conviction and is appealing the order for a new trial, saying McCracken received a fair one the first time around.

"We should thank God that justice is determined by 12 citizens who hear the evidence and actually see the witnesses testify rather than determined by some vigilante approach of a newspaper printing what they want by some young, idealistic reporter," John A. Reilly, the Delaware County district attorney, wrote in a letter to one concerned constituent shortly after the articles appeared.

"I am sorry to hear that you are so upset," he continued. "However, I feel that there is no basis for this feeling. A jury of 12 citizens, after hearing all the evidence . . . found the defendant guilty beyond a reasonable doubt."

—John Woestendiek
The Philadelphia Inquirer

EVIDENCE OF INNOCENCE: DOUBT CAST ON A MURDER CASE

SUNDAY, APRIL 20, 1986

BY JOHN WOESTENDIEK

On March 18, 1983, David Johnston, 71, left his home in Collingdale and walked down the street to Kelly's Deli to get his daily paper and his daily number. Seconds after he walked in—shortly before 1:40 p.m.—he was shot and killed by a masked robber.

On that same cool and drizzly day, in that same small Delaware County town, Terence McCracken Jr., 18, was sent home from school with an eye infection and spent the day hanging around his neighborhood.

He worked on a neighbor's car, greeted the mailman and, later, watched with friends as police tried to track down a murderer. They were looking for a man in a red sweatshirt, much like the one McCracken was wearing under his blue demin jacket.

Before the day ended, Terry McCracken, apparently by virtue of the red sweatshirt, became a murder suspect. Three days later, he was arrested. And six months after that, based mainly on the testimony of one eyewitness and a test for gunshot residue, he was convicted of Johnston's murder.

Today, there is compelling evidence that McCracken, who faces a mandatory life sentence, did not commit the crime.

A six-month investigation by The Inquirer has raised basic questions about McCracken's guilt, and about some of the evidence and testimony used to convict him.

That investigation produced statements from another man—supported by a lie-detector test—who said that he was involved in the crime and that McCracken was not.

In addition:

•   At least three members of McCracken's family and two friends say they were with him either during or within two minutes of the time the crime was taking place at Kelly's Deli, seven-tenths of a mile from McCracken's home.

• A mailman had McCracken sign for a certified letter within minutes of—if not during—the robbery at Kelly's Deli, which began about 1:30 p.m. and lasted until about 1:38 p.m.

• A police scientist's conclusion, to which he testified in court, that gunshot residue was found on McCracken's hand was erroneous, according to a nationally known scientist who is credited with developing the test used to analyze residue on McCracken's hands.

• McCracken, in a polygraph test commissioned by The Inquirer, was determined to have given truthful answers when he said that he did not take part in the robbery or the killing, and that he had not fired a handgun—not that day, and not in his lifetime.

Moreover, The Inquirer's investigation indicates that it is mainly because of McCracken's conviction that the two men who, according to one of them, committed the crime have thus far gone unpunished.

Terry McCracken, who has been in jail for three years, was a senior at Academy Park High School when he was arrested March 21, 1983. He had planned to tour the country after his graduation, then join the Army. He had been, up until then, in only minor trouble with the law.

Still, to many of the blue-collar community of Collingdale, the news of his arrest came as little surprise.

McCracken is the son of Terence "Screw" McCracken, a former member of the Warlocks motorcycle gang whose reputation was widely known among Delaware County law enforcement authorities and whose poorly kept home on Pusey Avenue in Collingdale, later condemned by the borough, was considered by many a thorn in the community's side.

Primarily because of that, Terry McCracken was considered, in the private parlance of Collingdale police, an "NFG." The "N" stands for no; the "G" stands for good.

But within just two weeks, questions would begin to surface. First, while McCracken was behind bars, a robbery strikingly similar to the one at Kelly's Deli occurred at a beverage outlet in nearby Glenolden.

The following week, another similar robbery took place in Clifton Heights, leading to the arrest of two furniture deliverymen.

McCracken had been in jail 17 days when those two men—William

Vincent Verdekal and John Robert Turcotte—were arrested, minutes after the robbery of a Clifton Heights market on April 7, 1983.

The .38-caliber handgun police took from Turcotte that day was determined by ballistics tests to be the same gun that killed Johnston at Kelly's Deli in Collingdale.

When that fact—reported in the Delaware County Daily Times on April 15, 1983—made its way to the 6-by-9-foot jail cell Terry McCracken was in, he said, it was as if a bad dream had ended.

"I thought for sure I would be out that weekend," he said in an interview last year at Delaware County Prison, where he had been held since his arrest and where, pending a decision on his appeal for a new trial, he is still awaiting formal sentencing.

"I can understand why they arrested me. At the beginning I think maybe even I would have arrested me. But I can't understand, when they found the gun, why they didn't let me go," he said. "I thought that would clear everything up."

It didn't turn out that way.

Instead, Verdekal and Turcotte were charged along with McCracken with the holdup and killing at Kelly's Deli, and investigators set out to show that the three men had conspired to commit the crime.

McCracken went to trial first and, after a mistrial, was convicted Oct. 25, 1983, of second-degree murder, robbery and conspiracy.

The charges against Verdekal were dropped during his trial when Delaware County Judge Robert A. Wright ruled that there was no evidence to firmly link Verdekal to McCracken. After that, the district attorney's office dropped the prosecution against Turcotte but reserved the right to try him later.

Both Verdekal and Turcotte were convicted of other robberies and sent to prison—Turcotte with the knowledge that the Kelly's Deli charges could be renewed against him at any time, Verdekal in a somewhat less vulnerable position.

Delaware County District Attorney John A. Reilly says he believes all three men were involved in the crime, and he still hopes to bring Verdekal and Turcotte to trial.

Yet Verdekal, in four interviews held over six months at three different prisons, said that he played a role in the crime and that McCracken did not.

Verdekal said he went to the store briefly before the holdup, then waited in his leased white Mercedez-Benz truck outside the delicatessen as Turcotte committed the holdup. Then, he said, he drove Turcotte from the scene of the crime.

And, he said, the first time he ever met Terry McCracken Jr. was when he and Turcotte joined him as inmates of Delaware County Prison.

Verdekal's statements were supported by a lie-detector test administered to him on behalf of The Inquirer by a former FBI polygrapher.

The deliveryman said he was coming forward with the information "in order for me to rest, in order for me to sleep at night, to have a clear conscience. I can't live with seeing a kid 18 years old getting life in prison for something I know he didn't do."

In addition to Verdekal's statements, The Inquirer investigation revealed that:

• Ten people—including Verdekal and five other prison inmates—say Turcotte told them that he robbed Kelly's Deli, and shot Johnston accidentally. All 10 say he blamed it on having consumed large quantities of drugs and liquor that day.

• Turcotte, in a letter sent to Verdekal in prison, wrote, "All I can really say is that I'm sorry. I know if I told you about the gun or anything about what happen . . . it never would have happen. All I can say is you know I've never in my life been as drunk as I was that day."

• Turcotte, two lawyers involved in the case say, was at one point willing to plead guilty to the Kelly's Deli killing. In exchange, he wanted assurances that he would not get the death penalty, nor more than one life sentence for all the crimes of which he was then accused. No such assurances were given.

• Verdekal, also while awaiting trial, was willing to testify that Turcotte was the triggerman in the Kelly's Deli case and to give police information about other unsolved crimes in exchange for a lenient sentence, according to Verdekal and his attorney, Luke McLaughlin 3d. The district attorney's office turned down that offer, too, saying, according to McLaughlin, that if the information Verdekal could supply did not implicate McCracken, they were not interested.

• Two key pieces of evidence either disappeared or were destroyed by the time of McCracken's trial—the substance identified as gunshot residue, which, according to the police scientist's report, was destroyed during testing, and a sketch of the gunman made by a customer in the delicatessen, which officials in the distict attorney's office said was lost in the shuffle of pretrial paper work.

• There was disagreement among law enforcement officers investigating the Kelly's Deli case as to McCracken's involvement in it. One night, that disagreement almost led two investigators to come to blows. Some police officers involved in the investigation, though not willing to step forward publicly, say privately that they believe McCracken is innocent, and that Turcotte and Verdekal alone committed the crime.

• One of the customers in the store at the time of the holdup said in an interview that, although she never mentioned it to the authorities, she remembers thinking at a preliminary hearing attended by all three men that Turcotte more resembled the Kelly's Deli gunman than did McCracken. None of the customers or employees interviewed remember being shown pictures of Turcotte during the police investigation.

• Michael Aldridge, a former schoolmate of McCracken's and the only witness who identified him as being at the scene of the crime, originally told police that he did not recognize the man who fled the store. Three days later he told police it was McCracken. In subsequent court hearings, Aldridge further altered his account, and at one point he admitted on the witness stand that he had lied about certain aspects of his story to make it more believable.

Two acquaintances of Aldridge's say he has admitted in private conversations that he was not sure whom he saw fleeing the store, and that he identified the man as McCracken because police were insisting it was McCracken. Furthermore, Robert Brown, who was standing with Aldridge across the street from the deli at the time of the robbery, said in an interview that until police arrived, Aldridge gave no indication of having seen anything unusual at the store.

The Delaware County district attorney's office, informed of those findings, put little credence in them, and officials there said they remained convinced that McCracken is guilty, calling the case against him "among the strongest collection of circumstantial evidence against a defendant that we have ever had."

They discounted the statements from Verdekal and other prison inmates, saying that the veracity of jailhouse statements is questionable and that—though they had no proof of it—the inmates could have been theatened or intimidated by members of the Warlocks who are in prison.

March 18, 1983, was a dreary, cloudy Friday. Terry McCracken, as usual, slept as late as he could, then dragged himself out of bed to get ready for school. As he pulled on his clothes, his friend Tommy Akins drove up and honked his horn.

"I always picked him up in front of his house, and I always had to wait 10 or 15 minutes because he was usually still sleeping when I got there," Akins said. On the way to Academy Park High School, where McCracken was a senior and Akins a junior, Akins stopped at Kelly's. McCracken waited in the car while Akins ran in for his usual breakfast, a soda and cupcakes.

Because he'd missed the previous two days at school, McCracken checked in at the vice principal's office with a note from his stepmother. From there he was sent to the school nurse, Mary Panny, who, from across her desk, immediately saw that the eye infection that had kept him home had not cleared up. "You can't even keep them open," McCracken recalls her saying. The nurse sent McCracken home.

"If you know anything about conjunctivitis, or pinkeye, you notice it right away," Panny said in an interview. "It's not just bloodshot eyes, there's a discharge."

McCracken said he walked home in the rain, not quite a mile, and went back to bed, where he remained until about 11:30 a.m.

Shortly after noon, McCracken went to the home of a neighbor, Andrew Leicht, who was working on his car in front of his house. McCracken, whose family's phone had been disconnected, needed to call school to make arrangements for his English teacher to pick up a term paper due that day.

"He had told us that this paper was real important and that, if we couldn't be in class, to call him and he'd make arrangements to pick it up," McCracken said. His topic was the U.S. Marines.

McCracken called his school from Leicht's house. School secretary

Edith Chestnut remembers the call. It was about 12:30 p.m., she said. She paged English teacher Joseph Tortorelli over the public address system, spoke to him, then told McCracken that Tortorelli would drop by his house after school to pick up the report.

After the phone call, McCracken went back outside, where Leicht enlisted his help on his car.

"Terry didn't know a whole lot about cars," Leicht said in an interview. "I said, 'Why don't you give me a hand here and take off a few bolts, I'm in a rush.' He said 'all right' and he started undoing some bolts for me."

Leicht recalled that the intake manifold of his 1970 Chevelle was leaking and that he was working in the rain, rushing to install a temporary gasket he'd made out of cardboard so he could get to his job at a Radio Shack by 2 p.m.

At McCracken's trial, Leicht said he was with McCracken until shortly before 1 p.m. In the interview, he said he believed he was with McCracken until about 1:20 p.m., when he put his tools away and went inside to clean up for work, leaving his car running.

McCracken said that about 1:20, he left Leicht and went back to his own house. There, his father and stepmother were getting ready for a doctor's appointment. A friend from across the street, Vincent Cefaratti, was in the McCracken's living room watching television. And McCracken's brother Daryl, 17, and his brother's girlfriend, Clare Montanero, were quarreling. The dispute was over who would go to the store for cigarettes. McCracken volunteered.

Shortly after 1:25, McCracken said, he was on his way back from Larry's, a small corner grocery two blocks from his home, when he saw his mailman, Robert Vance.

Vance, in an interview, said that he told McCracken he had a certified letter for his father and that McCracken walked with him to his house. McCracken ran upstairs to tell his father he needed to sign for the letter. Terence McCracken Sr., who was in the bathroom, said he told his son to sign. "What the hell, we have the same name," he recalled in an interview.

No records are made of the times of delivery of certified letters, Vance said, but as he remembered it, the younger McCracken signed the receipt for the letter between 1 and 1:30 p.m.

McCracken, his brother and his parents, who were watching the clock because of the 2 p.m. doctor's appointment, said the mailman came at 1:30 p.m.

David Johnston, meanwhile, was well into his daily routine that Friday.

Johnston, retired from his job as a security guard at the Philadelphia Museum of Art, was a slightly built man with white hair, blue eyes and, neighbors recall, a meticulous appearance. After the death of his first wife, Johnston had remarried. About six years after that—in 1979—he and his wife moved from Philadelphia to Collingdale "because they thought it would be safer in the suburbs," said his stepdaughter, Connie Youkon of Philadelphia.

There, they lived a quiet life, for the most part keeping to themselves, occasionally going out for dinner and a movie, as long as it didn't interfere with a Phillies game on television. Johnston watched those regularly.

And every day, he walked to Kelly's Deli. He bought a newspaper and he played his state lottery number—the same one every day, according to Kelly's Deli employee Delores Bright—800, straight and in a box.

On March 18, Johnston, who had been suffering from ulcers, was walking a little more slowly than usual as he headed down Sharon Street to Kelly's Deli. It was wet outside, and he'd only recently completed a long hospital stay.

It was shortly after 1:30 p.m.

On March 18, 1983—like most every weekday morning—William V. Verdekal, 34, and John Robert Turcotte, 22, sat in a booth at Tony's Bar in Collingdale.

After going to a furniture warehouse in Bridgeport, N.J., and loading the day's deliveries into Verdekal's Mercedes-Benz truck, they generally went to Tony's to plan their delivery route.

That morning, though, Verdekal, an independent subcontractor, was calling customers to tell them his deliveries would be late because of the rain. "Nobody likes their furniture delivered in the rain," he said. Both men were drinking and had taken drugs that morning, Verdekal said in an interview late last year.

"Bob was drinking, and I know for a fact he was really gone on the meth, that and Jack Daniels in the bar," he said. "He came back and offered me some meth. I told him, 'No, I have some coke anyway.' "

Verdekal, who spent much of his late teens and 20s in prison for burglaries had picked Turcotte up hitchhiking one day in late 1982 and offered him a job. It was sometime after the busy 1982 Christmas season, he said, that they began committing robberies. While Verdekal maintains that he was the gunman in only one robbery—"it was a show-of-faith type thing"—he acknowledged that, generally, the planning and the profits were shared.

That morning in Tony's Bar, Verdekal was wearing cowboy-type clothes; Turcotte was wearing jeans and a bandanna, Verdekal said.

"Right around that time, the kids were wearing bandannas around their leg, and also around their neck. . . . In Bob's particular case he wore it most of the time because of the haircut he had. Sometimes he would just pull it down and wear it around his neck. I remember a time he said to me, 'Why not dress the way the kids dress here, they would never know,' which made sense, you know. Dress like a college kid and they'll think a college kid did it, dress in a suit, and they think a businessman did it. That was a diversion kind of thing."

Verdekal said he and Turcotte would steal clothing from various bars to wear during robberies. In his truck that day were a variety of jackets and sweaters, including a red sweatshirt, stolen earlier, he said, off a coat hook at Tony's. Also in the truck, Verdekal said, was a loaded .38-caliber revolver, which had been stolen in a house burglary and had been used in at least one previous robbery.

When they left the bar that day, Verdekal said, "I know he [Turcotte] was really stoned, and I was feeling pretty good myself." About 1:20 p.m., Verdekal said, he parked his truck across the street from Kelly's Deli and went inside.

Verdekal does not admit planning the Kelly's Deli robbery, or even discussing it beforehand. Nor does he admit that, when he walked into Kelly's that day, it was to "case" the store for a robbery, though the Delaware County district attorney's office, and others involved in the investigation, believe that to be the case.

At 1:23 p.m., Verdekal purchased a lottery ticket at Kelly's. While he was in the store, Edith Chestnut, the school secretary who had talked to Terry McCracken on the phone about an hour earlier, walked in. She knew Verdekal. Her brother is married to one of Verdekal's sisters.

They talked briefly, walked outside together and went their separate ways.

Verdekal said he returned to his truck. He said Turcotte checked the .38-caliber revolver, slid it into his pants, and got out of the truck. "He said, 'I'm going for cigarettes' . . . but I know he's going to rob the place at this point," Verdekal recounted.

Verdekal said he started the truck and drove a half block down the road. He parked, he said, but left the truck running. He sat there nervously as the windshield wipers slapped back and forth. The rain started coming down heavier, he remembered.

It was about 1:30 p.m.

Situated on Collingdale's main drag—MacDade Boulevard—Kelly's Deli was a small, family-operated store that did business mainly in lunchmeat and lottery tickets. By 1:30 p.m. that Friday, the lunchtime rush was waning and only two customers were inside.

Robert Murphy, a cashier for SEPTA, recalls that he stopped at Kelly's amid a heavy rain on his drive to the MacDade Mall. He parked in front of the store and went in for cigarettes. There was no line at the lottery machine, he said, so he decided to try his luck. Marie Fawns, whose mother, store owner Anna Dannelly, was in the back room, sold Murphy his lottery ticket.

The other customer, Catherine Laurie, was at the deli counter, where Delores Bright was filling her lunchmeat order.

It was then that the gunman entered.

"When he came in the store, I thought he was kidding," Bright said in an interview. "Kids used to do that all the time—walk in and say, 'This is a stickup.' And this guy had a sort of kidding look on his face—what you could see of his face."

The gunman's speech was later described by witnesses as slow and lethargic, perhaps slightly muffled by the bandanna that covered his face from the nose down. He wore blue jeans and boots, and the hood on his red sweatshirt was pulled over his head. Under the hood, he wore a dark-colored knit ski cap that covered most of his forehead. Virtually all that was visible were his hands and eyes. Two customers later described the gunman's eyes as "deep-set," but none noticed their color and none noticed any unusual redness or any discharge around them.

"This is a holdup. I'm not kidding, Lady," he said, waving his gun. "Everybody in the back."

As he herded Fawns, Bright, Murphy and Laurie toward the back of the store, he spotted Dannelly in the back room. "You too, Lady," he said. "I see you."

Fawns warned her mother, "Mom, he's got a gun. Do what he wants."

All five went inside the store's walk-in refrigerator, and Murphy, the victim of four previous robberies, quickly took steps to secure the door should the gunman try to enter.

The gunman returned to the front of the store and went to the cash register, only to be interrupted—five times—by more customers— first an elderly woman, then an employee from a local lumberyard, then a park guard, then Eugene Schoffield, the owner of a nearby tire store. The gunman could not put them in the refrigerator, which was being held shut by those already inside. So he ordered the first four to lie on the floor in the back room.

The fifth was David Johnston.

"We heard a shot and a man screaming, and I guess maybe another 15, 20, 30 seconds went by and it was all quiet," Richard P. Duffield, the lumberyard employee, later said in court.

Johnston was on the floor dying when yet another customer, Dudley Denison, approached Kelly's. He, like Duffield, his co-worker at Collingdale Millwork, was stopping for a sandwich to go.

Denison, in an interview, said he was reaching for the doorknob when the door to Kelly's opened and he came face to face with the masked gunman and his revolver. He put his hands in the air and backed up until he was in a parking lot on the side of the store. He placed his hands against the building.

The gunman ran behind him and along the side of the store, turning around once to point the gun at Denison. As soon as he was out of sight, Denison looked into the store, then ran to nearby Brennan's Bar.

"Somebody's been shot down at Kelly's," Harry Rudolph, a patron at Brennan's, remembers Denison saying. Rudolph ran to the delicatessen, and Denison followed, after telling the bartender to call police.

Police received that call at 1:39 p.m., less than a minute after getting another call from a woman who had heard the gunshot while standing on the street.

The shooting apparently occurred at 1:37 or 1:38.

At 1:40 p.m.—as a white Mercedes-Benz truck was winding its way toward Interstate 95—police arrived at Kelly's.

According to the driver of that truck, William Verdekal, John Robert Turcotte had not mentioned anything about his gun going off, and would not until the following Monday. At the time he said only, "I scored big. . . . I've got some money."

As paramedics arrived and tried in vain to save the life of David Johnston—the single bullet had been fired at point-blank range into his upper back and had exited through his neck—Verdekal's truck merged into the sparse, early afternoon traffic on Interstate 95. Turcotte, according to Verdekal, was counting money and talking about buying a car as they headed north to make their scheduled deliveries.

"Damn," Verdekal says he remembers Turcotte saying, "I have, like, $900 here."

Andrew Leicht's homemade cardboard gasket was doing the job. His Chevelle was still idling in front of his house when Leicht, cleaned up for work, glanced at a wall clock and came out his door. It was 1:40 p.m., he said, and Terry McCracken was standing on his front porch.

At most, this was three minutes after the shooting at Kelly's—seven-tenths of a mile away.

"I had looked at the clock right at the door, and I remember thinking, 'It's 20 till 2, I better get a move on.' I went outside, went toward the street, looked up and Terry was leaning up against his door," Leicht said in an interview.

"I said, 'Terry, I'll be home tonight about 8 o'clock, maybe a couple of minutes later; save some beer for me.' "

"Terry was the good one," said his father, now living in Upper Darby. "Daryl was the one who was continually getting in trouble. Terry had three or four little things, but he always had this sense about him that he never went overboard."

The home in which the McCrackens lived on the south side of Collingdale was, most neighbors agreed, an eyesore. In 1984, after McCracken's arrest, the house—where local teenagers frequently gathered to drink or just hang out—would be condemned by local health department officials, and, later, destroyed in a fire.

Most of McCracken's jailhouse diary is filled with memories of his neighborhood, along with details about his friends and his family, plans for the future, when he slept and what he ate in jail, who wrote him a letter and who paid him a visit.

"I have also learned that they finally found the real killer, but they still keep me," he wrote in April 1983. "My lawyer, John McDougall, tells me now they suspect me in a conspiracy. If this makes sense then I am a rather big moron."

In the hours after their April 7 arrest, John Robert Turcotte and William Verdekal were not cooperating with authorities at Clifton Heights police headquarters.

Verdekal, who had declined to talk with the arresting officers, was shackled to a chair in the hallway, where he was on the phone trying to reach his attorney, he recalled in an interview.

Turcotte was in a holding cell, where he had removed the brown sweater he was wearing—and had worn during the Westbrook market robbery, according to Verdekal—and had torn it up and tried to flush it down the toilet.

"He was being rowdy with them [the police]," Verdekal said. "When I first saw him was after he'd been pushing parts of the sweater down the commode. He was shackled feet and hands to the bars."

Later, after seizing the sweater for evidence, officers attempted to question Turcotte. Turcotte noticed that one of the officers had a Collingdale Police armpatch on his uniform.

According to police, he made this remark. "You're not going to pin that Collingdale murder on me."

That statement, the similarities in appearance between Turcotte and McCracken, and the similarities between Turcotte's gun and the one described by witnesses at the Kelly's Deli robbery, initially led investigators to suspect that Verdekal and Turcotte may have had a role in the Collingdale crime.

In the following week, on April 11, ballistics tests would show that

Turcotte's gun had killed Johnston, and other incriminating items—such as the lottery ticket purchased at Kelly's minutes before the killing—would be found in Verdekal's truck.

By then, Detective John Slowik of the Delaware County Criminal Investigations Division (CID) had gone to Bridgeport, N.J., to interview employees at Better Homes Delivery Inc., the warehouse out of which Verdekal and Turcotte worked.

Theorizing that McCracken might have worked with the two men, Slowik on April 8 asked managers of the warehouse about Verdekal's helpers. Because Verdekal was an independent subcontractor, the warehouse had no records of who worked for him. But they told the detective of a shabbily dressed young man, 18 or 19 years old, about 5 feet, 9 inches tall with sandy hair, Slowik would later testify. No one knew him by name.

Five days later, Slowik and another CID detective went to the warehouse with two photographs, both of Terry McCracken. The detectives took statements from the manager and assistant manager, both of whom said the picture resembled the young man whom they had never met or talked to but had seen working there.

With that, McCracken on April 27 was also charged with conspiracy to commit the Kelly's Deli murder and robbery, along with Verdekal and Turcotte.

In the weeks after their arrest, Turcotte and Verdekal were charged with other robberies. Verdekal was charged in April with the March robbery at Koban's Beverages in Glenolden. In May, Turcotte was charged with the robberies of two Delaware County gas stations in February—a Sunoco Station in Middletown Township and a BP station in Concord Township.

At the latter robbery, on February 25, 1983, a shot was fired into the floor of the gas station and tests on the recovered slug showed it was fired from the same gun that was later used at Kelly's—the first indication that the two men, in addition to having the gun after the Kelly's killing, also might have had it before.

By then, Verdekal was in touch with his attorney, Luke McLaughlin 3d of Norristown. He had met McLaughlin months earlier while making a delivery to his home, and the two had gotten together at Verdekal's request to discuss Verdekal's delivery business.

"His wife called me after he was arrested, and I went to talk to him down at Delaware County Prison," McLaughlin said in a recent interview. "We talked and we decided that it would be in his best interests to approach the district attorney and talk about a possible arrangement, whereby he would cooperate with the police in exchange for consideration at time of sentencing."

McLaughlin said he went to Delaware County in search of a deal. He spoke to John McKenna, head of the CID, then to a top official in the district attorney's office, he said.

"I was very circumspect, and I had to be vague to protect my client, but I told them that I believed we could help them. We believed that John Robert Turcotte had been pulling those robberies, and we believed he may have been the one who pulled the robbery at Kelly's delicatessen."

McLaughlin said he was told "unless Bill Verdekal was prepared to indicate that Terry McCracken was the triggerman at the Kelly's delicatessen robbery, that they didn't even want to talk to us."

McLaughlin said he later told authorities that his client was willing to take a polygraph test to support his statements, but "nothing ever came of it. They never reopened discussions or negotiations, although I went to the D.A.'s office on multiple occasions."

Verdekal admits that his prime goal at that point was saving himself, but he said that during the summer of 1983, as McCracken's trial drew near, he went as far as he could to help him.

"I had told my attorney Terry's not the one who did this. But there were no deals to be made," Verdekal said. "And you're not going to jump out, when they're asking for first-degree and the death penalty, and say, 'I'm the one who did it.' Nobody in their right mind would do that."

McLaughlin said that until McCracken's trial, he continued to seek a deal for Verdekal. Amid continued rejections from the district attorney's office, he said, he went to a state police detective, Thomas Ansel, who also requested that a polygraph test be administered to Verdekal. That request, too, was turned down by the district attorney's office.

Officials in the district attorney's office said they were not willing to give a lie-detector test to Verdekal because they did not believe he was telling the truth about his own involvement in the Kelly's Deli killing, and they were not willing to offer a deal because they felt he was the mastermind behind it.

According to sources close to the investigation, Ansel almost came to blows with McKenna one night at a Delaware County tavern. Ansel had been investigating a string of robberies he believed Turcotte and Verdekal had committed. Although Ansel declined to discuss the Kelly's case with The Inquirer, law enforcement sources said it was Ansel's belief that Verdekal and Turcotte were solely responsible for the killing and robbery. It was a shouting match over that point—whether McCracken should remain charged with the crime—that almost led Ansel and McKenna to blows, the sources said.

Two police sources close to the investigation said in interviews that they did not believe that McCracken was involved in the Kelly's Deli killing and robbery. Both, however, declined to be identified, saying they feared public comment would strain their working relationships with the CID.

Verdekal's attorney, McLaughlin, showed no such hesitation, however.

"From everything that I have seen, everything I have reviewed in the records and my conversations with various people, including Verdekal and Turcotte, I am as sure as I can be that Terry McCracken was not involved in the situation," McLaughlin said.

A CONVICTION FOR MURDER, THEN NEW CRACKS IN THE CASE

MONDAY, APRIL 21, 1986

BY JOHN WOESTENDIEK

On Oct. 18, 1983—a Tuesday exactly seven months after David Johnston was killed during a holdup at Kelly's Deli in Collingdale—Terry McCracken went to trial for murder.

His jurors in the Delaware County courtroom would hear six days of testimony.

They would hear from an eyewitness, who, though his testimony fluctuated, said he saw McCracken enter Kelly's Deli at the time of the March 18, 1983, robbery and flee the store less than 10 minutes later.

They would hear from a police scientist, who testified that tests had shown gunshot residue on one of McCracken's hands hours after Johnston, a 71-year-old retired security guard, was killed by a masked gunman at Kelly's.

They would hear from customers and employees of the small, family-owned delicatessen on MacDade Boulevard, several of whom, although they differed in the details of their descriptions, said that the gunman's clothing resembled what they were later shown of McCracken's.

And when the testimony was over, after just two hours of deliberations, they would pronounce McCracken—the 19-year-old son of Terence "Screw" McCracken, a one-time member of the Warlocks motorcyle gang—guilty of second-degree murder.

Today, as Terry McCracken, now 22, awaits formal sentencing to life in prison, an Inquirer investigation has uncovered evidence that suggests he did not commit the crime.

That evidence indicates that two other men were instead involved in the Kelly's Deli robbery—William Vincent Verdekal and John Robert Turcotte, who were arrested for a similar robbery 17 days after McCracken was jailed and who were found with the gun that killed Johnston.

Verdekal and Turcotte were charged, along with McCracken, with the holdup and killing at Kelly's. But after McCracken's conviction—and to a large extent because of it—the charges against them were dismissed.

Verdekal has since said in interviews with The Inquirer—and in statements supported by a polygraph test—that he waited outside the store in his truck as Turcotte committed the killing and that McCracken, whom he did not even know at the time, was not involved in the crime.

That information, and other findings that have come to light in a six-month Inquirer investigation, did not surface at the trial of Terry McCracken 2½ years ago.

As the trial started, McCracken, dressed in a suit and his hair neatly combed, sat with John McDougall, the attorney his father had hired for him. McDougall had represented his father, and other Warlocks, in the past. Sitting across from the defendant was the assistant district attorney assigned to prosecute the case, Howard J. "Bud" Gallagher.

The trial, before Judge Robert A. Wright in Delaware County Court, had originally begun Oct. 12, but a mistrial was declared after Michael Aldridge, the eyewitness, used the word *Warlocks* in his testimony. Wright ruled that the word was prejudicial, and a new jury had to be chosen.

Gallagher began by calling witnesses who had been in Kelly's Deli when the gunman entered, or had arrived at the store just before he fled.

They described the gunman as between 5 feet, 9 inches and 5 feet, 11 inches tall, 150 to 160 pounds. Most remembered a dark ski cap. Some said it was green, some said it was black, some said dark blue. The bandanna the robber wore over his face was variously described as light-colored, off-white, beige, red, paisley, blue and dark-colored. Some said the red hooded sweatshirt had no piping, others said it did.

McCracken's red hooded sweatshirt had white piping and a "Puma" insignia; none of the witnesses recalled the insignia.

The most specific description came from Robert Murphy, a SEPTA employee and five-time robbery victim. Murphy, one of two customers in the store when the robber entered, said the gunman wore a red hooded sweatshirt that was missing its drawstring, that he wore boots and that he carried the gun in his left hand.

Although it was not mentioned in court, Murphy had sketched for police a drawing of the masked gunman, he said in a recent interview.

Officials in the district attorney's office said in an interview that the drawing—which both they and Murphy say resembled McCracken— was lost sometime before the trial.

After Murphy's testimony, Catherine Laurie, the other customer, took the stand and told of a calm gunman with deep-set eyes. From the eyes, she said, he looked like John Hinckley. Laurie said he had never been shown any clothing by police.

Asked, "Other than the eyes being deep-set, did you make any other observation about the eyes?" she answered, "No." There was no mention from her—or any other witness—of the pinkeye that had led a school nurse to send McCracken home from school the morning of the murder.

Laurie was not asked in court whether McCracken resembled the gunman, nor did she offer her opinion—though by then she did have one.

It was at a pretrial hearing, Laurie said, attended by all three suspects, that she first saw John Robert Turcotte, who, like Terry McCracken, was about 5-foot-9 and 160 pounds, with sandy hair and a beard. "It's funny," she said in an interview, "but I remember thinking to myself that he looked more like the robber."

"It was the shape of his face and everything. . . . I said to myself, 'He looks more like the guy with the gun than McCracken.' " With the exception of her husband, she said, "I never mentioned that to anyone."

Also testifying on the opening day of the trial was Michael Aldridge, 20, a vocational-school student who lived in the neighborhood. By then, in statements to police and testimony at pretrial hearings, Aldridge had contradicted himself several times.

On the day of the robbery, about 3:15 p.m., Aldridge—the only witness who would identify McCracken as being at the scene of the crime—gave police this statement:

"I was on my way to Tire Kingdom [Tire World] and I saw The Boss [Eugene Schoffield] walk into this store [Kelly's]. The next thing

I noticed . . . was a guy with a red sweatshirt with a hood come out with a black hat. Wearing a black hat. It was a fitting type hat. A white guy. A little bigger than me. I think he was 19 or 25. He didn't have anything on his face at the time."

> QUESTION—*Did you notice any hair on his face?*
> ANSWER—*No.*
> Q.—*Is there anything you could add?*
> A.—*He ran to the back of the store. He was running in a running motion.*

At no point did he mention, as all of the witnesses in the store had mentioned, that the gunman was wearing a mask.

Three days later, on Monday, March 21, however, Aldridge told police it was Terry McCracken, whom he knew from school, he saw fleeing the store. He said he was on his way from—not to—Tire World, going to Kelly's Deli, and was about six houses away when he saw McCracken almost collide with a customer headed into the store and run to the back of the building with his hand concealed in the pocket of his sweatshirt, which he now specified had white trim.

This time, Aldridge said specifically that the gunman did not have a mask over his face when he saw him flee the store and almost run into the customer. The customer, Dudley Denison, said the gunman was wearing a mask.

Aldridge, in his second statement, said that he was going to Kelly's to get iced tea for Robert Brown, an employee at Tire World, and that he arrived before the police or paramedics.

On March 24, at an arraignment for McCracken, Aldridge gave basically the same story, but he said that he was standing in the middle of traffic and that, by the time he had a clear view, he could not see the gunman's face.

" . . . I didn't really look at the face when I first—when he first came out. . . . A red-like jacket and blue dungarees, that's all I noticed right then. . . . So then when the traffic was clear, I started to walk. And I looked up, and I seen Terry running to the back of the store . . . Terry McCracken."

McCracken's attorney, in an attempt to discredit Aldridge's testimony, argued at that hearing that, from the angle at which Aldridge was approaching the store, it was unlikely that he could have seen the fleeing gunman's face.

On April 8, Aldridge gave police a third statement, and a fourth account of what he had seen.

"Okay, Mike, why are you here today?" a detective asked him, according to that statement.

"To tell the truth of my story." Aldridge replied. In this statement, Aldridge said he was near Tire World when he saw McCracken— before the robbery—walking down the sidewalk toward Kelly's on the other side of MacDade Boulevard. He said they waved at each other, but didn't exchange words. He said he saw McCracken pull the hood of his sweatshirt over his head.

Aldridge told detectives he then went to Tire World, across the street and half a block away from Kelly's, and was standing out front, talking to Robert Brown, when he saw McCracken run out of the delicatessen. He said he went to the store after he saw ambulances arrive to see what had happened.

A month later, at McCracken's preliminary hearing, Aldridge repeated that account. But this time, he said that as McCracken was going into Kelly's, they called to each other from across the street, asking, "What's up?"

On Oct. 18, at McCracken's trial, McCracken's attorney sought to point out the discrepancies, and Aldridge said on the witness stand that he had lied about certain details in his earlier statements to police because he was scared:

QUESTION—*You weren't too afraid or scared to make up a story putting it {his vantage point} closer to Kelly's Deli to identify him, were you?*

ANSWER—*No sir.*

Q.— . . . *But you were afraid to say he was across the street?*

A.—*I thought it sounded better.*

Q.— . . . *So you decided what was right to say and what was not right to say.*

A.—*Yes.*

Q.—*And with him being charged with first-degree murder, you made up a story to what you would say to the world.*

A.—*Yes.*

Since McCracken's conviction, additional doubts have been raised about the veracity of Aldridge's statements to police and his testimony in court.

"I don't think there's any way he saw anything," said Robert Brown, the man Aldridge said he was standing with when he saw McCracken run from the store.

"Mike came up and we was talking, and five to 10 minutes passed, then all of a sudden I hear the cops start shooting toward Kelly's and Mike said, 'I'm going to see what happened.' I remember saying, 'Make sure the boss [Schoffield] is all right,' because he had just had a heart operation."

Although Aldridge testified that after seeing McCracken walking toward the store he watched the store for 15 minutes while talking to Brown, Brown said in an interview that Aldridge did not seem to be paying particular attention to Kelly's and did not indicate that he had seen anything unusual occur until after he saw that police had arrived.

Jody Hageman, a resident of Collingdale who described himself as a close friend of Aldridge's and whose house Aldridge visited during the three days after the Kelly's Deli killing, said, "Mike never told me he lied."

"He came over and said he'd been at CID [Delaware County Criminal Investigation Division] headquarters all night long," Hageman said in an interview, "but when I would try to bring up what happened, Mike would shuck the question or say, 'I'm not at liberty to say.' "

Two acquaintances of Aldridge's said in interviews that Aldridge admitted to them that he was unsure whether the person he saw fleeing the store was McCracken.

One of them, James Lannen of Secane, Delaware County, said, "He said that the cops had stuff on him, and that they thought it was McCracken and he just went along with them." It could not be determined what, if any, charges were pending against Aldridge at the time.

Glenn Severa of Collingdale, a close friend of McCracken's, said Aldridge made a similar comment to him: "He said, 'I'm really not sure if it was Terry or not, but we ain't gonna talk about that.' "

Aldridge did not return phone calls, but his father, Frank Aldridge, said on behalf of his son, "Michael never changed his story. They were just twisting his words around. He was sure then and he is sure now."

He said his son was afraid because of the reputation of McCracken's father. He added, "I really don't want to go into it any further; anything I say would just start stirring the whole thing up again."

In an interview in September, William H. Ryan, first assistant district attorney of Delaware County, said Aldridge "didn't want to get too heavily involved, he didn't want to show what he knew. . . . Again, I'm theorizing. So he says what comes to his mind in order to get the hell out. In the beginning he's vague or not forthcoming on the details for the same reasons he doesn't tell us who did it, and he's not real careful about choosing his words.

"But what motive does he have to lie?"

On the second day of McCracken's trial, prosecutor Gallagher presented evidence concerning residue removed from McCracken's hands the day of the robbery.

Robert E. Saunders, a criminalist for the state police at Lima, testified that an analysis he had conducted showed that while there were no powder burns on McCracken's hands, there were particles that contained lead. He identified those particles as gunshot residue.

Defense attorney McDougall objected to that conclusion, and later he would call his own expert, University of Pennsylvania chemist Gregory Farrington, who had been allowed to conduct his own tests on the samples, in Saunders' presence, and had found no particles containing lead.

In court, though, Farrington found himself at a disadvantage.

"The problem in the testimony was quite simple," he said in a recent interview. "Saunders stated unequivocally that lead was there. My difficulty was that I haven't done 200 analyses like he did and wasn't considered to have his expertise. On the other hand, I did not find lead."

The problem became more complex when Saunders testified that the incriminating particles he had found might have been destroyed in his testing.

"The whole thing is strange, and I don't think justice is working in this case," Farrington said. "I've always felt kind of personally responsible, but then when I think about it, I realize there wasn't anything more I could do because they were saying maybe the sample was destroyed in the tests. But it's bothered me ever since."

Most of the jurors said that although they were confused by the lengthy and complex gunshot-residue testimony, they felt it was the most incriminating evidence presented against McCracken. And Saunders, several jurors said, appeared more learned, more experienced and more confident than Farrington.

"The scientist from the state police was very convincing," one juror said. "It was like, absolutely, positively, without a doubt, in his many years of experience, this was gunshot residue. At one point, I specifically remember, he was asked directly, 'Could it be anything else?' He said, 'No.' "

But according to the scientist who developed the test Saunders used, Saunders was wrong.

"I conclude that the criminalist Saunders was definitely not justified in testifying that gunshot residue was found on the hand of Terence McCracken," scientist Peter F. Jones wrote in a report for The Inquirer. Jones was retained by The Inquirer to review Saunders' written report and courtroom testimony.

There are two accepted methods of detecting gunshot residue on a person's hands. The one used by Saunders, the newer and more conclusive of the two, makes use of a scanning electron microscope capable of X-ray analysis. It is used to detect the chemical elements that are in bullets and cartridge primers—lead, antimony, barium and copper —as well as their amounts, shapes and sizes.

Jones is credited with developing that technique.

Saunders, in outlining his background and expertise in court, cited the work done by Jones and his colleagues and said that his knowledge was derived in part from reading their published work. Additionally, he was trained in the method at the McCrone Institute in Chicago, whose instruction is also based on the work and reports of Jones and his colleagues.

Jones said that in his opinion, Saunders severely overstated what his test had found. Under the courtroom guidelines established by Jones and his colleagues for the U.S. Department of Justice, only particles containing barium or antimony, in addition to lead, can be considered gunshot residue, or "unique" to gunshot residue. Saunders found neither of those elements, according to his test report and testimony.

Less conclusive samples, which show certain elements of a certain shape that probably resulted from the firing of a gun, are considered "typical of" gunshot residue.

Finally, a sample is termed "consistent with" gunshot residue when it possibly was from a gunshot, but was equally likely to have come from occupational or environmental sources.

Two lead-containing particles were found on McCracken's hands. One of those also contained iron. According to Jones, the lead particle without iron should have been said to be "consistent with" gunshot residue.

The second particle, because there are so many environmental sources of iron, was not even strong enough to be considered "consistent with" gunshot residue, Jones said.

Saunders five times in his testimony stated unequivocally—and incorrectly, Jones said—that the particles he found were gunshot residue.

Jones said that Saunders twice incorrectly stated in court that there are no sources other than gunshot residue for similar lead particles.

And four times, Jones said, Saunders wrongly stated that the lead particles on McCracken's hand could not have resulted from working on an automobile.

Less than 40 minutes before the shooting, McCracken was working on a car engine with a friend and neighbor, Andrew Leicht, according to interviews with Leicht and his court testimony.

"Saunders incorrectly says that one could not get similar lead particles from batteries, auto exhaust, or from working on an automobile. . . . All of these sources can give lead particles," Jones said.

"Our report [for the Justice Department], which he repeatedly cites, clearly says that the particles that he found on the discs used to sample McCracken's hands are not unique to gunshot residue," Jones concluded.

On the third day of McCracken's trial, the prosecution concluded its case, presenting testimony it contended showed that McCracken knew William Vincent Verdekal, then 34, and John Robert Turcotte, then 22, before the killing.

But that link was fragile and would continue to erode.

Originally, detectives had interviewed two employees of Better Home Deliveries, the furniture warehouse out of which Verdekal worked as an independent deliveryman. The terminal manager, Michael Laterza, and assistant manager, John Pine, both said that the photographs of McCracken that detectives showed resembled a young man who had worked there.

Pine said he had seen the person about three or four times, while Laterza said he had seen him "maybe once."

Detectives also went to the Collingdale home of Verdekal's stepfather, Ralph Baylis, who by then had become familiar with McCracken's name through news accounts. He told them that he thought McCracken worked with Verdekal and that he once got a ride home from McCracken.

Continuing the efforts to link the three men, a detective on June 2, 1983, went to the home of Kenneth Thomson, also a subcontractor for Better Home Deliveries, who at the time was dating Verdekal's sister Sara.

Thomson said he was shown three pictures. He identified Verdekal, whom he knew, and Turcotte, whom he knew. He was then shown a photograph of McCracken, not unlike the ones he had seen in newspaper accounts of the Kelly's Deli case. Thomson correctly told the detective that the photo was of Terry McCracken and said, in addition, that it looked like a person who had once worked with Verdekal.

Two months later, Thomson, who by then had married Sara Verdekal, accompanied her on a visit to her brother in prison. Inside the jail, Verdekal pointed McCracken out to Thomson.

"At that point, I realized I probably made a mistake," Thomson said in an interview, blaming it on his assumption—based on what he had read in the newspapers and what detectives had told him— that the three men conspired to commit the crime.

"It never really entered my mind until it was put into my mind that he [McCracken] was one of the ones working with Bill," he said. "When they [detectives] are showing pictures and saying, 'This guy worked for Bill,' if they're telling me that, I believe them, even though I wasn't sure I'd seen him there," Thomson said. "It seemed like they were steering me into answering the way they wanted me to."

Detectives, at the insistence of the defense attorney, arranged a lineup for Thomson, Laterza and Pine before the trial. At that lineup, neither Pine nor Laterza could pick out McCracken, and Thomson told detectives that his earlier identification had been a mistake. He was never called to testify at the trial.

At the trial, Pine testified that the photos he had been shown of McCracken looked like the person he had seen in the warehouse. But, seeing McCracken in the courtroom, he could not identify him as that person.

Laterza, who was called to the stand but was dismissed by the prosecution without explanation before being asked whether he could identify McCracken, said in an interview, "If I remember right, I didn't remember McCracken at all. I couldn't pick him out of the lineup. So many people worked there I couldn't say who was who."

Verdekal said he had two other helpers who resembled McCracken, both in the color of their hair and the way they dressed. He said he believed that Pine was mistaking McCracken for one of them.

The statement of Ralph Baylis, Verdekal's stepfather, collapsed shortly after he took the witness stand.

Baylis had been questioned by police after the arrest of Verdekal and Turcotte.

"They wanted me to identify him [McCracken]," Baylis said in an interview. "They said somebody had seen him come out of the store. They tried to confuse me. After they told me about the robbery and all, I assumed he was the one who worked for Billy."

Baylis, in his statement to police, was quoted as saying that McCracken worked for Verdekal and that McCracken had once given him a ride home from King of Prussia. When he saw McCracken in court, though, he realized he was not the man he had been thinking of, Baylis said.

"So I told the judge the truth: I don't know the fellow."

McCracken's defense—that he was at home, seven-tenths of a mile from Kelly's Deli, when the killing occurred at 1:37 or 1:38 p.m.—primarily consisted of alibis from friends, neighbors and family.

In two days of defense testimony, McCracken's attorney, John

McDougall, also raised the possibility that Turcotte, not McCracken, committed the killing.

"Would a young man whose intention in the morning was to go to school . . . are you going to be asked to believe that somewhere, maybe 1:25 or 1:30, he said, 'Oh heck, nothing else to do, let me run down to Kelly's and rob the place.' "

McDougall pointed out that Turcotte—who had been arrested with the gun that killed Johnston and who was charged with robbing other places in much the same manner that Kelly's was robbed—bore a resemblance to McCracken.

"It's the defense contention," he concluded, "John Robert Turcotte is the robber and the killer and that he should be tried for those crimes."

On Oct. 25, 1983, the jury was excused at 2 p.m., and, after a lunch break, deliberations began.

Seven of the 12 jurors agreed to interviews under the condition that their names not be printed. Most said they found the testimony of state police criminalist Saunders convincing, and that witness Aldridge, despite his contradictions, also impressed them.

"It's hard to put into words," one juror said of Aldridge, "but he was very believable. . . . It seemed to be in line with human nature that he would be upset and confused and scared. And when he said, 'I talked it over with my father and now I'm going to tell the truth,' it was very moving. I thought at the time that I was the only one who believed him. I felt sympathy for him, rather than, 'this kid's a liar.' But it turned out all the other juror's felt the same thing I did."

The jurors said they were not particularly impressed by the testimony of family and friends. One friend from across the street, Vincent Cefaratti, said he was with McCracken until after 1:30 p.m. Another, Andrew Leicht, said that McCracken was helping him work on his car until about 1 p.m. and that he saw McCracken again before he left for work at 1:40 p.m. The jury said they both appeared nervous and inconsistent. And while mailman Robert Vance, who testified McCracken signed for a certified letter sometime between 1 and 1:30 p.m., seemed credible, they added, they still felt McCracken had time to commit the crime.

Despite the word *Warlock* having led to an earlier mistrial in Mc-

Cracken's case—and the judge's warning that any mention was considered prejudicial—two jurors said they were aware that the trial had some sort of a connection to motorcycle gangs.

One juror said that during the trial there were "murmurings that the family were Pagans or something," referring to another notorious motorcyle gang. "I wasn't aware of being consciously influenced by that, but . . . I know people can be subconsciously influenced. That was not discussed, but it was something that was kind of murmured."

Asked what he meant by "murmured," the juror said, "I heard somebody say something to the effect that the family was involved with motorcycle gangs." He was unable to elaborate.

Another juror said that going into the trial, he was familiar with the reputation of Screw McCracken and the Warlocks. He also said he knew that John McDougall "is a Warlock lawyer." He and other jurors said the issue of motorcycle gangs did not arise in their deliberations, however.

From the beginning of those deliberations, jurors said, there was no disagreement over whether McCracken was guilty, only over the degree of murder.

At 4:44 p.m.—after less than two hours of deliberation—the jury returned to the courtroom with its verdict.

The jury foreman was asked for the verdict on the charge of first-degree murder, which can result in either the death penalty or life in prison.

"Not guilty," the foreman said.

Cheers and cries of glee erupted from the family and supporters of McCracken in the courtroom. The judge called for order, and the foreman was asked for a verdict on the charge of second-degree murder, which carries a mandatory life sentence.

"Guilty," he said.

As some members of the crowd moaned, McCracken whispered "oh no," and put his head in his hands.

That night, McCracken was back at Delaware County Prison, and so was his attorney. John McDougall, who, shocked by a verdict he said he had not expected, put in a request to see inmate William Verdekal.

"Terry's attorney came to visit me the night that Terry got convicted," Verdekal said. "Here's a grown man in his 50s or 60s, and he's standing there crying, asking me to help. I mean real tears are rolling down his cheeks. I'm sure it wasn't any play to make me feel anything."

Since then, as McCracken has waited in Delaware County Prison, McDougall has submitted a series of motions and amended motions for a new trial.

He has said that Verdekal made comments that implicated him and exculpated McCracken. He has asserted that Aldridge was promised a reward for his testimony. He has said that he found five prison inmates who said Turcotte had admitted to them that he committed the killing. And, finally, in desperation, he has taken the stand himself during a hearing and has testified that Turcotte confessed to him.

According to McDougall—as well as Verdekal, his attorney, McCracken, McCracken's father and others—Turcotte, at a point at which he faced charges in connection with three other robberies, was willing to plead guilty to the Kelly's Deli killing in exchange for not receiving more than a life sentence.

"Bob [Turcotte] was calling a lot of people from prison," said David Grenfel, a brother-in-law of Verdekal's. "He tried to help. He told me everything and he called McDougall and told him everything. He called McCracken's father and said he was going to come forward, but the district attorney's office wouldn't let him."

Said Screw McCracken, "I've talked to Turcotte on the phone two or three times. He told me the whole thing was a fog and he can't even remember the guy's face. He said he was so messed up all he remembers is the gun going off. Turcotte told me himself it was him."

Verdekal has said in interviews that both he and Turcotte had been drinking and taking drugs on the day of the murder. Turcotte declined to be interviewed.

Both McDougall and Luke McLaughlin 3d, Verdekal's attorney, say Turcotte had stated that he would plead guilty to second-degree murder, make a statement about the killing and attest to it in a polygraph, provided he did not receive more than one life sentence for all the crimes with which he was charged.

Said McLaughlin: "It's my understanding that the D.A.'s response to that was that only if he pleaded guilty to murder one would they even talk to him.

"Why, when Turcotte was willing to plead guilty and clear the whole thing up, did they hang the death penalty over his head, then end up nol prossing the charges against him anyway?" McLaughlin asked. "If he's willing to do a life sentence, isn't that indication enough that he really did it?

"It is almost as if everything that was done—not letting Turcotte plead, refusing the polygraph examinations that were offered, nol prossing him so that they can still hang this charge over his head—all that seems to be an attempt to hide the truth, as opposed to get to it."

The Kelly's Deli charges against Turcotte were "nol prossed," or dismissed by the district attorney's office with prejudice, meaning that Turcotte can still be charged with and tried for the crime without creating double jeopardy.

Verdekal's legal situation is less clear. He was granted a demurrer by Judge Robert A. Wright, the same judge who had heard Mc-Cracken's case. Wright ruled during Verdekal's trial in February 1984 that with no testimony linking Verdekal to McCracken, there was insufficient evidence to let the case go to a jury. Normally, Verdekal could not be charged with the same crime again.

But the district attorney's office is appealing the demurrer in hopes of being able to prosecute Verdekal at a later date. State Superior Court has upheld the demurrer, ruling that it was appropriately granted. That decision is now being appealed in state Supreme Court.

Verdekal was sentenced to five to 10 years in prison for a March 28, 1983, robbery at Koban's Beverages Inc., in Glenolden. In October 1985, he was sentenced for the April 7 robbery at the Westbrook Market in Clifton Heights—the one that led to the arrest of him and Turcotte. He received six to 15 years for that, and was ordered to serve that term consecutively with the other sentence, making his total sentence 11 to 25 years.

It was after the Westbrook Market robbery that Verdekal and Turcotte became suspects in the Kelly's Deli killing. Detectives found in Verdekal's truck a lottery ticket purchased at Kelly's minutes before the killing, knit caps similar to the one the robber at Kelly's was described as wearing, a newspaper folded over to an article about the killing and, on Turcotte, the gun used to kill Johnston.

Turcotte agreed on Jan. 11, 1984, to plead guilty to four counts of robbery involving holdups at two gas stations and the Westbrook Market robbery. Each carried an eight-to-20-year sentence. He also pleaded guilty to one count of conspiracy in the Westbrook case, carrying a five-to-10-year sentence. While that could have meant a minimum of 37 years in prison, all the sentences were made concurrent, meaning Turcotte will have to serve one eight-to-20-year sentence and will be eligible for parole in 1991.

It was after that sentencing, McCracken's father said last month, that he talked to Turcotte a third time on the telephone.

"I talked to him right after he got sentenced. He said, 'Look, I gave it my best shot. This ain't easy. I'd be stupid to turn it down.' I had to agree with him. What do you do—say, 'No, I don't want eight to 20, give me life? ' "

Turcotte did not respond to four letters sent to the state prison in Huntington requesting interviews. The public defender who represented him, Stephen Leach, denied that Turcotte ever officially offered to plead guilty to the killing. The district attorney's office also said it received no such offer through either Leach or Turcotte.

"Turcotte never approached us, nor did his attorney," said Ryan, the first assistant district attorney, in September. "That was all from John [McDougall]. He was definitely talking to Turcotte out at the prison when he was visiting McCracken. John McDougall" Mc-Cracken's attorney, "could not ethically represent Turcotte's interest."

But, when Howard Gallagher, McCracken's prosecutor, was put on the stand April 11, 1984, during a hearing seeking a new trial, he said that the district attorney's office did discuss the possibility of such an offer with Turcotte's attorney prior to McCracken's trial.

"I spoke to Mr. Leach about that, but I told him that the office was taking that under advisement," Gallagher said. "We were considering it, but I specifically cautioned him that there was not an offer on behalf of the district attorney's office."

MCDOUGALL—I told you, did I not, that Turcotte was going to come in, plead guilty to murder and the robberies in return for a stipulated low sentence and no consecutive time for the robberies, is that not so?

GALLAGHER—*Yes.*

MCDOUGALL—. . . *A plea to murder and all the robberies in return for the one life sentence, was that not proferred from me?* . . .

GALLAGHER—*Yes.*

MCDOUGALL—*And did you relate that to your supervisors?*

GALLAGHER—*Yes, I did.*

MCDOUGALL—*Was that rejected?*

GALLAGHER—*Yes.*

On the stand, Gallagher also disclosed, under questioning, that Michael Aldridge had asked for a reward. "His exact words, as I recall them were, 'What about my reward?' I responded, I said, 'What reward?' He said, 'Captain McKenna [John McKenna, head of the Delaware County Criminal Investigation Division] promised me a reward.' "

In an interview, officials of the district attorney's office denied that a reward—though one was discussed—was promised.

As the post-trial hearings continued, McDougall continued to present new evidence. At one of those, he called Verdekal to the stand for the first time. Verdekal testified that he had never seen Terry Mc-Cracken before his arrest in April, and that McCracken had never worked for him or Turcotte.

Verdekal said at the hearing that he had information about the crime that "would have proven that Terence McCracken had nothing to do with it at all," and that Turcotte had committed the crime.

When pressed as to the source of his knowledge, Verdekal said Turcotte had told him so in prison. Verdekal did not, at that point, admit to a role in the crime. Verdekal, in interviews, said he was less than truthful at that hearing.

McDougall also presented five Delaware County Prison inmates who testified that Turcotte had admitted to them that he killed Johnston.

One of them, Raymond Davis, 25, testified that Turcotte had told him that McCracken was innocent and that it was he who had killed Johnston. "He told me he was surprised by the door opening. He said he turned around and there was an old man standing there and he fired the gun."

Another, David J. Sirulnik, said that while playing cards with him in prison, Turcotte said, "Isn't it a shame the person who is going to do the time on the murder charge is McCracken. . . . Those fools in Media have got the wrong man."

Later at the hearing, McDougall took the stand himself.

He testified that Turcotte had confessed to him that he was the one who shot Johnston during the robbery. "I remember the whole thing," McDougall quoted him as saying. "It was like a dream. I was so stoned, I can't remember the guy's face. The gun went off accidentally."

Officials in the Delaware County district attorney's office say that William Verdekal was lying. So, they say, were the inmates who said Turcotte admitted committing the crime. And they say they believe the reason is the Warlock connection.

Said Assistant District Attorney Dennis McAndrew, who is now fighting McCracken's motion for a new trial, "They were all prison people that he [Turcotte] had made these statements to, with the exception of John McDougall, who of course had represented bikers in the past. I say that not because I disbelieve, or any of us disbelieve John McDougall, but I say that because the perception of a person in prison . . . under those circumstances becomes one of fear—'What will he tell the other bikers and what will they do to me in prison?' "

Both Terry McCracken and William Verdekal passed polygraph examinations commissioned by The Inquirer.

The tests were administered by William B. Anderson, chairman of the criminal justice department at West Chester State College. Anderson is a former career agent in the FBI and past executive director of the Pennsylvania Crime Commission. While working for the FBI, he conducted hundreds of polygraph examinations.

On June 20, 1985, Anderson interviewed and tested McCracken at Delaware County Prison, asking six questions:

- "Did you have a gun in your hand March 18, 1983?
- "Are you the man who held up Kelly's Deli March 1983?
- "Did you shoot that old man in Kelly's Deli?
- "Have you ever shot a person with a gun?
- "Have you ever shot a handgun?
- "Did you ever know or work for Bill Verdekal prior to March 1983?"

To each question, McCracken answered "no," and, in each case, Anderson said, there was no evidence of any attempted deception. "It is my opinion McCracken was truthful when he denied the murder of March 18, 1983," Anderson concluded.

On July 22, 1985, Anderson interviewed and tested Verdekal at the State Correctional Institution at Rockview, near State College, Pa. Verdekal, Anderson noted in his report to The Inquirer, appeared eager to take the test.

"When questioned, he gave his motive for coming forward as 'justice and honor,' " Anderson said. He said Verdekal told him he "had nightmares when he reflected on the consequences to McCracken of this wrongful conviction.

"I've spent half my life in prison and know what it's like," Anderson quoted Verdekal as saying.

Verdekal was asked seven questions:
• "On the Kelly's Deli robbery day, did Turcotte wear a red sweatshirt with a hood and blue jeans?" Verdekal answered "yes."
• "Did Turcotte have the gun when he came out of Kelly's Deli that day?" Verdekal answered "yes."
• "Did Turcotte tell you the gun went off during the Kelly's Deli robbery?" Verdekal answered "yes." (Verdekal, in interviews with The Inquirer, maintained that he was not told about the gun being fired until the Monday after the robbery. Anderson pointed out that this question—unlike the previous two, which specifically pertained to the day of the robbery—did not contain a time element.)
• "Before the Kelly's Deli robbery did you ever meet or know Terry McCracken Jr.?" Verdekal answered "no."
• "Did Terry McCracken have any part in the Kelly's Deli robbery?" Verdekal answered "no."
• "Did Turcotte do the actual Kelly's Deli robbery?" Verdekal answered "yes."
• "Did you go in Kelly's Deli during the robbery?" Verdekal answered "no."

Anderson said that except for one question—the final one—Verdekal gave no indication of deception and that, in his opinion, Verdekal was telling the truth when he answered each of the others.

Anderson said the one indication of deception—when Verdekal answered "no" to whether he went into Kelly's during the robbery—

could relate to the fact that Verdekal went into the store before the robbery. Verdekal says he went in for a lottery ticket; investigators believe he was checking out the store as a robbery target.

In conjunction with the polygraphs, urine samples were taken from both men, analyses of which showed the presence of no drugs that would affect test results. In addition, both men received psychological evaluations that showed they were rational at the time of testing and sufficiently intelligent to properly comprehend the questions' meaning and results.

The Delaware County district attorney's office, after being told of the polygraph results, said the tests alone proved nothing.

"We would never hold anyone or let anyone go on the basis of a polygraph," said District Attorney John A. Reilly. "It's just a tool."

"Polygraphs are far from infallible," said Ryan. "The fact he [Anderson] got the results he did is not disquieting to us. It's not unusual."

Despite the reservations about polygraph tests expressed by Reilly and Ryan, the Delaware County district attorney's office did use them in their investigation of the Kelly's Deli killing.

Michael Aldridge, the witness who originally told police he did not know the man he saw running from Kelly's Deli after the shooting, was given a polygraph test during subsequent questioning by investigators. Officials in the district attorney's office said the test was used because John McKenna, head of the CID, "did not feel he [Aldridge] was being truthful."

McKenna, in an interview, said Aldridge passed all the questions except "do you know who did this? He failed that." McKenna said Aldridge responded "no" to that question.

When Aldridge was told he had failed that question—after the test —he said "McCracken did it," according to McKenna.

Asked whether Aldridge was given another test to confirm whether that statement was truthful, McKenna said, "After he clarified the answer, what would be the reason to go back and do it again? . . . There was only one question he failed on. Once he explains to you why he failed that, there's no reason to go back. He's clarified it."

• • •

"We are convinced beyond a reasonable doubt that Terry Mc-Cracken did it," Ryan said in the September interview. "We're convinced that Verdekal was running the show, with McCracken, Turcotte, and perhaps others we don't know about. But Verdekal was running a robbery ring here using young punks to help him out."

Of the actual shooting, Ryan said, "Our theory is that perhaps— we don't know—perhaps this guy [Johnston] gave him [McCracken] some grief and he panicked and shot the guy because he was scared."

Ryan said the prosecution's theory was that McCracken met Verdekal before the robbery, was given the gun, committed the robbery and killing, and then, before returning home, returned the gun and the money to Verdekal.

He added, "The investigation was done as a good investigation is supposed to be done. . . . We don't have any axes to grind. We drop cases against people we know committed crimes but we don't have sufficient evidence to convict them. We would have no reason to nail Terry McCracken just because his father is a stupid Warlock or an ex-Warlock. What do we care?"

Both Ryan and McKenna speculated that he may have committed the crime to impress his father.

"My father taught me a lot," McCracken said in an interview in a visiting room at Delaware County Prison. "I know he looks big and mean, but he's very smart. One thing he taught me was to always leave a person a man's way out. Like if you're arguing and a fight's about to start, always give the other person a chance to back down and still feel like a man.

"I don't think it's because of him that I'm in here," McCracken added. As he spoke, a mouse scurried out of an adjoining bathroom, along the bottom of the visiting room wall. McCracken glanced at it casually and continued.

"I guess the name McCracken was a hindrance. But I think that at first they honestly thought it was me. Then I think when they caught the other guys, they just didn't want to back down and look bad. But still I think things will get worked out."

"I don't want him to get his hopes up so much," Screw McCracken said in an interview. "His hopes go up and down like a roller coaster.

He knows he didn't do anything. He knows he shouldn't be there. And he still has this innocent hope that everything's gonna come out. He doesn't know it's probably going to take years of pounding to get everything to come out.

"It just doesn't make any sense. He was at home when this happened, and, I mean, who the hell is going to walk up the street, wave to a friend, and walk in and hold up a place in their own neighborhood —and then follow the cops around while they investigate?

"Everybody tries to tell me that he's in there because of me, that they wanted me, and this is the closest they could come to getting me, but I don't think that's it. I think it's the gunshot test. If it's proven that Terry didn't do this, what happens to their gunshot tests? If their gun tests are proven unreliable, how many people are in jail from this guy coming out and saying, 'Yeah, I'm positive.' "

Terry McCracken is still awaiting a ruling on his motion for a new trial. At least one more hearing is expected to be held before Judge Wright makes his decision—either to grant McCracken a new trial, or formally sentence him to the mandatory penalty of life in state prison.

"I try not to think about state prison," McCracken said. "I made it a point in my life that I won't be going to state prison. I plan to get out, and the first thing I plan to do is visit all my friends.

"All my friends now are getting into adult lives. Before, we were all kids. Now, they're getting married and having kids and getting jobs and all these things, and I can't touch any of it.

"You don't know what freedom means till you lose it."

DISORDER IN THE COURT

Rumors of conflicts of interest, rampant nepotism, petty politicking and inefficiency in the Philadelphia court system had circulated for years. But no one had tried before to substantiate those rumors. They turned out to be true, as *Inquirer* reporters discovered.

Don't do it. It will be a colossal waste of time.

That was the general reaction when word first filtered through the *Inquirer* newsroom in 1983 that two reporters had been assigned to investigate the Philadelphia court system. Too big, some reporters said. No one would talk about what really was going on, others said —at least not on the record.

It was hardly unusual for a newspaper to undertake such an investigation. Dozens of other papers had done court series in the past, invariably focusing on the sentencing patterns of judges. What made the *Inquirer* assignment so ambitious was its scope. Very few areas of the Philadelphia court system would be off-limits for *The Inquirer*'s investigation—except judges' sentencing patterns.

Instead, *The Inquirer* wanted to examine a system in which many of the people familiar with its workings commonly perceived that business was too often conducted not in open court but in back rooms, where lawyers and judges made secret deals, and that the court's administration catered to the politically powerful and winked cheerfully at mediocrity and misconduct.

And there was one other rule for the series: Everything would have to be directly attributed, either to a specific document or to an on-the-record quote. The use of blind sources would not be allowed.

Sounds wonderful, sang the newsroom chorus. The kind of thing that could set the stage for real reform, some said. And also impossible.

At the time of the project's inception, only two people shared any confidence that such a series could be successfully done. One was

Jonathan Neumann, the paper's projects editor and a winner of the Pulitzer Prize in 1978 with William K. Marimow for a series on police brutality. The other was Eugene L. Roberts Jr., the executive editor of the paper. In many ways, the project was a typical Roberts production, requiring enormous time and financial resources to be carried out —if it could be done at all. The amount of time seemed irrelevant to him. As metropolitan editor Steve Seplow said of him: "Gene Roberts doesn't think in months or years. He thinks in milleniums."

The project did not take quite that long. But it did take almost three years—from the very first interview, conducted in April 1983, to the very last one in January 1986—and involved the efforts of three reporters, H. G. Bissinger, Daniel R. Biddle and Fredric N. Tulsky. They interviewed more than 200 people, including half of the city's 120 judges. Weeks were spent in courtrooms just listening and observing. They reviewed thousands of documents and records. They also scrutinized payroll information from the city controller's office and the city personnel office, and internal memorandums from the district attorney's office that had never before been made public.

The *Inquirer* series "Disorder in the Court" was a herculean effort that clearly touched a nerve with the public. During the six days it ran, from January 26 through January 31, 1986, more than 200 readers called to congratulate the paper for its reporting and to relate their own experiences with a court system that in many ways had almost ceased to function.

But the naysayers who said the project could not be done were almost right.

Bissinger, Biddle and Tulsky, wrapped up in the pressure of working on something so massive and complicated, agreed on virtually nothing. They argued and squabbled but also propped each other up during those frequent occasions when it seemed as if the reporting would never end. Some projects, through a combination of skill and luck and good timing, fall neatly into place, seamless puzzles. This was not one of them.

During the course of reporting, dozens of wrong roads were taken, not because of bad instincts or inexperience, but because of the difficulty of proving in a particular case that something undue had actually happened. Dozens of leads went nowhere. Hundreds of hours spent in a musty, windowless room on the ninth floor of City Hall staring at page after page of court files did not result in a single printed word.

But inch by painstaking inch, a series began to develop. And it developed in the classic way that most investigative series ultimately become published—through hard work and the faith that enough leads would eventually develop into solidly documented case studies.

For the first several months, Bissinger and Biddle did nothing but conduct off-the-record interviews with lawyers intimately familiar with the court system. It was during those interviews that the series got a key and pivotal break: a complete willingness by Edward G. Rendell, the district attorney of Philadelphia at that time, to supply whatever help he could. Rendell gave the reporters free rein to talk to city prosecutors and made available many of the office's criminal files.

Following these interviews, Bissinger and Biddle then began to conduct on-the-record sessions with judges in the system. Both reporters felt that most judges would be inclined to defend the system, but something dramatically different happened. Many judges talked of the system not with pride, but with poignant despair over what was happening to it.

After a year, Bissinger and Biddle prepared a detailed memo on their progress for projects editor Neumann. The memo contained about 25 different examples of court system failures. Not all of these examples had been proven at that point, and some would never be, but the skeleton of a series was there.

According to the basic outline that developed, it was agreed that at least one part of the series would focus on judges conducting legal business behind closed doors, out of the public view. A part dealing with nepotism and patronage in the court would focus on judges hiring relatives for jobs. Another would deal with the impact of campaign contributions made by lawyers to judges.

Around the same time, the series received an enormous boost when Tulsky, sitting in court one day, saw something strange taking place. He watched a defense lawyer making an appeal to a judge for a new trial. That wasn't unusual, but the lawyer's argument was: He was asking for a new trial on the basis of his own incompetent counsel and the assertion that he had committed errors that even a first-year law student would not be inclined to make. Tulsky, himself in law school, knew something wasn't right.

After more than 50 interviews and a review of voluminous court documents, Tulsky tracked down 29 cases in Philadelphia in which some of the city's busiest and most prominent defense attorneys had made bids for new trials on the grounds that they had failed to take the most basic measures in defending their clients.

If they were telling the truth, they could be disciplined for gross neglect. If they were lying to help their clients, they also could be disciplined. Yet in none of the cases had any attorney been publicly disciplined for such testimony.

Any doubt about the series ended with the paper's computer study of campaign contributions from lawyers to judges. First, Bissinger and Biddle obtained copies of financial contributions for all Philadelphia judges' campaigns from 1979 through 1984. *The Inquirer* then commissioned a computer analysis of these records to determine the precise amounts of contributions made by lawyers to judges and when they were made. The paper then identified case after case in which lawyers, within a year of making a significant contribution to a judge, appeared in frong of that judge in court.

In the 55 Municipal Court cases identified by *The Inquirer* as having a significant campaign connection between the defense lawyer and the judge, 71 percent of the defendants won. The percentage of defense victories for all Municipal Court cases was only 35 percent.

It was in April 1985, two years after the project started, that the writing began in earnest. There were dozens of drafts, and under the direction of Neumann and Steve Lovelady, associate executive editor, special attention was given to making the writing as clear and lively as possible.

Finally, in January 1986, the impossible dream became a reality. "Disorder in the Court" ran on the front page of *The Inquirer* for six consecutive days and spurred dramatic action from those overseeing the court system.

The Pennsylvania Supreme Court, in an extraordinary step, seized administrative control of the beleaguered Philadelphia court system. The state attorney general's office began an investigation. A new rule was passed stating that a three-judge panel would review all claims of incompetent counsel made by lawyers for possible referral to the State Disciplinary Board. A judge was taken off a sex-crime case after he was quoted in the series as referring to a victim of a purported attempted rape as "coyote ugly."

"Disorder in the Court" generated hundreds of comments, and none of them seemed more flattering, or more gratifying, than a letter sent by Robert P. Casey, governor of Pennsylvania, to Bissinger, Biddle and Tulsky.

"*The Philadelphia Inquirer* has again shown itself to be one of the premier newspapers in the country and a true leader in investigative journalism," Casey wrote. "Your eye-opening series made our citizens aware of the desperate need for reform of the judicial system in Philadelphia."

—H. G. Bissinger, Daniel R. Biddle, Fredric N. Tulsky
The Philadelphia Inquirer

POLITICS AND PRIVATE DEALINGS BESET THE CITY'S JUSTICE SYSTEM

SUNDAY, JANUARY 26, 1986

BY H. G. BISSINGER AND DANIEL R. BIDDLE

Behind the scenes, Common Pleas Court Judge George J. Ivins privately agrees to take a case from a defense lawyer who is a longtime friend—and then sentences the lawyer's client, convicted of killing a young nurse in a car crash, to probation.

In another courtroom, on another day, Municipal Court Judge Joseph P. McCabe reduces bail for a murder defendant—without legal authority and without informing the prosecutor.

In yet another courtroom, Common Pleas Court Judge Lisa A. Richette sentences a convicted killer to prison—and then, after the victim's gratified family has left the scene, changes the sentence to probation.

In a fourth courtroom, Municipal Court Judge Arthur S. Kafrissen gets up from the bench at 10:45 a.m. and walks out for the day, leaving behind baffled witnesses, police officers and lawyers. It is, in the words of Clifford Williams, a disgusted witness, "complete chaos."

Day by day, this is the Philadelphia court system, where many judges and lawyers freely admit that, all too often, what is delivered is anything but justice.

It is a system in which many defense lawyers help finance judges' campaigns—and then try criminal cases before those judges. It is a system in which those same lawyers have remarkable success, with statistics showing that in Municipal Court, from 1979 to 1984, defense lawyers who had a role in judges' campaigns won 71 percent of their cases before those judges. By contrast, during the same years, only 35 percent of all Municipal Court defendants won their cases.

It is a system in which witnesses are sent to the wrong places by

173

incorrect subpoenas, and in which a judge dismisses a case because a witness isn't in the right courtroom.

It is a system in which defense lawyers get convictions overturned on the ground of their own incompetence by claiming they made errors that would shock a first-year law student.

It is a system in which the amount of money awarded in civil verdicts has skyrocketed and in which a person can win $143,500 for a broken toe suffered on the job.

It is a system in which hallways smell of urine, benches are carved with graffiti and stairways are missing railings.

And it is a system in which many judges feel overwhelmed, bereft of hope for improvement and wistful for other employment.

"I feel I am in the middle of a morass and it's getting worse. . . ." said Common Pleas Court Judge Francis A. Biunno. "I always walk around with the feeling 'I don't know what I'm doing.'. . . And I have been at this for 11 years."

After an exasperating day on the bench, Theodore A. McKee—one of the system's youngest and most idealistic judges—mused, "If I could make a living tooling leather or doing woodwork or teaching karate, I'd do it."

In a two-year investigation of Philadelphia's Municipal and Common Pleas Courts, The Inquirer interviewed more than 200 lawyers and judges. Many raised serious questions about the health of justice in America's fourth-largest city.

In addition, reporters pored over thousands of pages of court records, studied verdicts in tens of thousands of criminal and civil cases in Common Pleas Court over seven years, conducted computerized analyses of close to 5,000 judicial-campaign contributions and examined internal memos from several court agencies.

What The Inquirer examination found was a court system that is successfully functioning in many basic ways—despite an antiquated physical plant and a burdensome work overload. But at the same time, it is a system that has come to accept almost as routine a number of practices that on the face appear unethical, secretive or unfair to crime victims, witnesses and the public.

Among The Inquirer's findings:

• Court records show that judges have made crucial decisions—such as deciding to take a particular case or determining the length of a sentence—after private conversations with one side's lawyers. Some judges seemed to care little about the appearance of such contacts. Asked whether a prosecutor should have been present when the judge and a defense lawyer discussed reducing a sentence, Common Pleas Court Judge Bernard J. Avellino said, "I don't give a f——whether he's there or not."

• In some cases, judges have helped effect the release of dangerous criminals by changing sentences and reducing bail without informing the prosecutor—although law requires that a prosecutor be present for such actions. Some of those aided by the improper actions of judges were not petty criminals or first offenders: two were part of a group that police blame for five slayings in a war for the city's cocaine trade.

• Judges are elected, but their ability to win is not determined on the basis of merit or court experience. Judges and lawyers say that the large majority of candidates are elected on the basis of political or personal connections, ethnic background and money. When asked about his qualifications to become a judge, Common Pleas Court Judge Angelo A. Guarino put it this way: "There was a need for a guy like me to satisfy the party's needs at that time. Geographically I was well placed, and ethnically I was well placed. So they came." Judges and lawyers say also that local ward leaders have the biggest say in who gets elected and who does not. Common Pleas Court Judge James D. McCrudden bluntly described the burden of judicial candidates: "They have to bribe ward leaders."

• To finance this political support it is common for judicial candidates to accept hundreds and sometimes thousands of dollars in campaign contributions from lawyers who later practice before them. Records show dozens of instances in which, within months of election, judges have presided over cases involving lawyers who had donated to their campaigns. In more than a dozen instances, judges heard cases from lawyers who had served on their campaign committees, including some who had acted as committee chairman or treasurer. Judges rarely disclosed those political ties in court.

• In the courts' day-to-day administration, examples of nepotism and political patronage are rife. On a $55 million payroll that officials refuse to make public, at least 30 of the 120 Municipal and Common Pleas Court judges have relatives in court jobs. Other jobs go to kin of court administrators, ward leaders and elected officials—including relatives of City Council members who vote on the court's budget. None of this seems to trouble those in charge. Says Chief Deputy Court Administrator A. Joseph Teti: 'I'm just sorry that I can't get *more* of my family members on the court." He already has four.

• The routine workings of the system are beset by delays that cause enormous inconveniences to witnesses and jurors and result in hours or days of wasted time in the courtroom. Some judges estimate that they have spent as much as 25 percent of their courtroom hours in so-called "down time"—waiting for cases to be ready.

All in all, some of Philadelphia's most respected lawyers say, the Philadelphia court system is in a state of serious disrepair.

Stanford Shmukler, a criminal lawyer, said of the Common Pleas bench: "We do not have the highest-quality judiciary. . . . It has become a haven in many instances for political hacks."

In 1983, Marshall Bernstein, a well-known and highly regarded plaintiff attorney, called the Common Pleas civil system "a mess. It's a galloping nightmare." Now, Bernstein says, the court is striving to dispose of old cases and is having some success. But he adds, "We're still way, way behind. . . . There are still massive delays."

Said Common Pleas Court Judge Marvin Halbert, "Everything falls behind. . . . It's like p——ing in the ocean. . . . Am I deterring? Am I rehabilitating? Have I in any respect rehabilitated anyone? The only thing I know, I'm warehousing them. And I wonder 'What am I doing?' "

In the last few years, there have been improvements in the Philadelphia courts. Disposition rates are up in both the criminal and civil programs. And Common Pleas Court President Judge Edward J. Bradley was praised for his January 1984 appointment of highly respected Common Pleas Court Senior Judge Harry A. Takiff as the court's administrator.

Several programs in the court system have received nationwide attention. One is an arbitration program for the disposing of minor civil cases. The other is the court's felony waiver program, in which routine criminal cases are heard by judges without juries. These programs together account for the disposition of well over half the cases in the system.

But judges themselves warn against measuring the quality of the system by how many cases can be pushed through it.

"If you think this system can be called successful in its broadest sense, then you and I don't think alike," said Common Pleas Court Judge Kenneth S. Harris. "They will tell you it's better. They will tell you it's getting better because it's providing for more people on a given day. Query: Are you providing better justice for these people?"

Too often, says former District Attorney Edward G. Rendell, that justice is tainted by factors outside the courtroom—a private conversation, a friendly relationship, a political tie. Says Rendell: "There is infinitely too much screwing around with cases in City Hall."

A DAY WHEN JUSTICE IS STUCK ON HOLD

On a hot July morning, Judge McKee walked to the tiny chambers next to Courtroom 269 in City Hall. Ignoring the roar of the ancient air conditioner and the vibrations from the subway, oblivious to the scattered black smudges on the bright baby-blue walls, he hung up his suit coat and quietly buttoned his black judicial robe.

At 9:30 a.m., minutes before court was to open, McKee's court stenographer came into chambers with an urgent message: Somebody was coming to fix the emergency phone. Each courtroom has an emergency phone in the event of a serious problem, such as a judge's getting assaulted.

"Your emergency phone isn't working," the stenographer said.

"It hasn't worked since Jan. 2," McKee replied.

Moments later, McKee took the bench in Common Pleas Court, ready to dispense the day's justice. As it turned out, he spent the day juggling, cajoling, patching up one problem here, one problem there —all in the hope of trying at least *one* of the cases listed before him.

He would succeed in nothing.

Commonwealth vs. Anthony Crawford: Postponed. Officials had forgotten to transport Crawford from the detention center to the courthouse. *Commonwealth vs. Belinda McNeil:* Postponed. McNeil never showed up. *Commonwealth vs. Charles Guess:* Sent to another judge after McKee, during a pretrial conference, heard prejudicial evidence that forced him to remove himself from the case. Sentencing in *Commonwealth vs. Russell Bennett:* Postponed because of a discrepancy in Bennett's prior record. *Commonwealth vs. John Gingrich:* The case actually started, but the judge had to stop it when various factual issues could not be readily resolved.

The day ended as it had begun for Judge McKee: The five cases on his list remained pending.

"This," McKee said at one point, speaking to a once-packed courtroom that was now deserted, "is an absolute and total breakdown of the system."

ONE JUDGE'S QUEST FOR A FEW GOOD JURORS

In Courtroom 315, Common Pleas Court Judge Victor J. DiNubile Jr. tries to get a panel of prospective jurors so he can begin a trial. Few needs in the court system are so basic as assembling a jury. But the judge gets this response from the court administration: There are no prospective jurors left, because the court system has run out of them. The case will have to wait.

The next day, DiNubile tries to get a jury panel. He is told that, like an airplane on the runway, he is number nine in line.

An hour later, DiNubile negotiates with Jury Commissioner Nicholas Kozay Jr., sounding a little like a customer hoping to squeeze a break from a salesman.

"I start early. Does that count for anything?" DiNubile asks Kozay. "I'll take anything you give me. Normally I take 40 [potential jurors]. I'll take 30. I'll take anything."

The next day, DiNubile gets 34 prospective jurors, and a jury of six men and six women is selected by 12:45 p.m. Then, after lunch, the defendant elects to waive a jury and have his case heard only by a judge. The jury panel DiNubile has fought so hard to get is dismissed.

Says DiNubile: "There are days when I figure, 'What am I doing? What am I doing here?' "

DiNubile's father was a Common Pleas Court judge. Much to DiNubile's surprise one day, he saw his father's name on a list of judges taped to the wall of the tiny chambers office in the courtroom.

"It's got my father on it," said DiNubile. "He's been dead for three years."

HOMICIDE DAY: A WAITING GAME

By 10 a.m., almost 100 people had gathered in the hallway. You could hear the din of their anxious shuffling as they pressed against one another, not knowing where they would go next, if anywhere. Every few minutes, a court officer stuck his head outside the door and hurried several people inside, as if he were a doorman at some exclusive club.

He looked at a list and yelled out several names. Then his head popped back behind the double doors.

"What's going on?" someone asked.

"Twenty-one homicide cases," someone else said.

Courtroom 675. Homicide day.

Decisions regarding 21 homicide cases would be made in this Municipal courtroom, and ultimately it would be up to the judge to decide whether the evidence in each case was strong enough to be sent to trial in Common Pleas Court. The room was a whirlwind of snap-second action—testimony, bail hearings, legal arguments. In one courtroom with one judge.

The defense lawyers sat in the jury box of courtroom 675 like aging lions, slouched in wooden chairs and wearing their flappy raincoats, talking to one another in whispers, watching the proceedings with what many of them would call cynical disdain.

The judge in the courtroom that day, Joseph McCabe, a jowly, unsmiling man with an enormous bow tie sticking out from under his black robe, made it clear that no matter how many of these 21 homicide preliminary hearings got finished, win, lose, or draw, he was leaving the bench well before 5 p.m.

"We're not working beyond 2:30," he told an assistant district attorney. "If they overload the room, that's not my problem."

McCabe later explained that it was his standard procedure to hear cases for about five hours a day and return to his chambers to attend to paper work. Beyond such a time limit in the courtroom, he said, his temper could unravel with little provocation.

"You're faced with burnout," he said. "How much can you take, and really do justice?"

The double doors opened. More people came in and took seats under the bright, hot lights that made everyone look pale and timid. The double doors opened. More people left. The double doors opened.

Lawyers dressed in fur-trimmed wool coats marched in, talked to other lawyers and then walked out. The double doors opened. Defendants came in, peered around for the lawyers in the fur-trimmed coats who had marched in and marched out, and then they marched out, too. The double doors opened. A policeman in a shiny leather coat stuck his head through to see what was going on and then popped it back out. The double doors closed.

Harry Seay, a veteran criminal attorney, was among the waiting lawyers. After 3½ hours, he said: "Isn't this ridiculous!"

A defense lawyer named Daniel M. Preminger requested $25,000 bail for his client. The assistant district attorney argued for much higher. It went back and forth.

"What do you think this is, a tennis court?" McCabe finally snapped. "Every time I get a minute to think, someone thinks that's an occasion to make a speech." He set bail at $75,000. That ended court for the day.

Hearings were held in eight of the 21 cases scheduled for his courtroom that day, McCabe later said. Some of them did not go on because the prosecution wasn't ready. Or because a defense attorney was trying a case in another courtroom. One case was ready for a hearing, but McCabe did not get to it. In the meantime, numerous witnesses who had been subpoenaed never had the opportunity to say a single word and would have to return some other day. As for criminal lawyer Seay, he ended up sitting there without doing a single thing.

A few minutes after 2:30 p.m., McCabe adjourned Courtroom 675 for the day.

FOR ONE WITNESS, EIGHT WASTED MORNINGS

In a third-floor hallway, Michelle Swanson, a witness in a case, talked of the fear and dread of coming to City Hall to testify against her ex-husband in an assault case in which he had allegedly brandished a gun. She already had come to City Hall eight times, arriving as early as 8 in the morning, and waiting in court until 10:30 or 11 a.m. until being informed each time that the case had been postponed.

"I said I wouldn't come today," she explained. "I said [to her current husband], 'I'm not coming.' I've had it. He [the defendant] can postpone it, but I can't change my mind. Why can't I say, 'I don't want to come, let the son of a bitch stay in jail another month?' . . .

"Why can't they be more lenient with the witnesses and the people who go through this stuff?

"A lot of times I didn't want to be here because of the emotional stress. I hoped I would never have to look at that face again. I have nightmares about it."

IN MIDDLE OF A CASE, THE JUDGE WALKS OUT

Clifford Williams, a witness, was ready to testify at a preliminary hearing in a burglary case before Municipal Court Judge Arthur Kafrissen. He had the familiar witness jitters, not necessarily because of what he was going to say, but because he had just gotten a new job as a plumber and was concerned about missing work. Also, this was the third time he had been in court for the case.

The first witness, flown up from Arkansas at a cost to the prosecution of $620, testified. Then it was Williams' turn. But Kafrissen, according to those present, announced that he had a meeting to attend and left the bench about 10:45 a.m. Several days later, he told another judge that he had left the bench for a medical appointment.

Kafrissen rescheduled the case for two days later, forcing Williams to come to court again. But Williams said in an interview that his subpoena directed him to the wrong courtroom, in a different part of the city.

When he failed to show up in Kafrissen's courtroom, the defendant's lawyer asked that the case be discharged. Kafrissen granted the motion. The assistant district attorney, Wanda Foglia, said she asked the judge to reschedule the case because of the inconvenience Williams had been put through earlier in the week. But Kafrissen refused to change his mind.

Through a spokesman, Kafrissen declined to be interviewed.

"Every time I went down there I was prepared to testify," said Williams. "I can't keep taking time off from work. I wanted to see justice done, but I can't have it done at my expense. I can't afford it."

And he, like many others in the courtroom, said he was dumbfounded when Kafrissen walked out in the middle of the case at 10:45 a.m.

"You should have been there," Williams said. "It [was] complete chaos."

• • •

During the same week, Kafrissen left the bench again in the middle of a case, offering no explanation of where he was going, according to attorneys and witnesses present in the courtroom. During his absence of almost three hours, from 11:15 a.m. to approximately 2 p.m., a defendant in one case and a witness for the commonwealth in another case failed to return. In a third case, an employee with the Philadelphia School District waited in court roughly 6½ hours to give less than five minutes of testimony.

"We're there as commonwealth witnesses to do a job and fulfill our obligations," said the witness, who did not want to be identified, "and it's a little difficult for me to understand how someone who has a job can just say, 'That's it, I'll be back in three hours.'"

"If he had taken two minutes to talk to that courtroom, you would not have had a courtroom of angry people. I think that's what I was upset with, the lack of consideration. Treat us like human beings."

PRIVATELY, A WORD IN A FELON'S BEHALF

Every year in Philadelphia, thousands of witnesses are subpoenaed to appear in court to testify. They must testify, whether they like it or not, whether it might cause discomfort or pain or plain embarrassment. Those are the rules of law.

But Judge Kenneth Harris privately called another judge to avoid the kind of situation that average citizens face every day. In doing so, he avoided what he later acknowledged in an interview would have been the uncomfortable position of having to appear in *open* court in behalf of a convicted felon.

"Like it or not, nobody wants to be a witness to anything," Harris said.

In 1978, Harris, then a Municipal Court judge, privately called Common Pleas Court Judge Richard B. Klein to ask him to release a man on bail just after the man had been convicted of a shooting in connection with a drug deal.

According to an affidavit from Klein, Harris called and said he could vouch for the defendant, Anthony Devine, and his family because he had known them for a long time. Devine's lawyer was then Judge Harris' law clerk, Hugh Clark.

Klein's affidavit went on: "Judge Harris referred to the case, said it was his law clerk that tried the case, and advised me that he knew the family for a considerable period of time and felt sure that Anthony Devine would return for sentencing. He asked me to review the matter to see if I could set bail at a level that could be made by the Devines."

Harris made that phone call despite provisions in the the Code of Judicial Conduct that say a judge cannot "lend the prestige of his office to advance the private interests of others."

In this case, the defendant and his family had a lengthy history of criminal trouble. Devine's father, James "Sonny" Devan, had been found guilty of heroin-distribution charges in 1971 and sentenced to five years in federal prison.

In 1971, five years before becoming a judge, Harris himself was the lawyer who represented Sonny Devan at trial and was with him in court when he was sentenced.

The man that Judge Harris tried to help in 1978, Anthony "Ookie" Devine, had been convicted by Judge Klein of aggravated assault and a weapons charge for shooting Leroy Coleman over a heroin deal that had gone sour.

Trial testimony showed that Devine, then 19, had shot the man from point-blank range with a .357 magnum. At the time of the shooting, Devine was on probation for conspiracy to rape a 17-year-old girl. As a minor, Devine had been found delinquent for joining in the sawed-off-shotgun robbery of a laundry-truck driver, and for his admitted role, with three other youths, in forcing a 15-year-old boy to submit to anal and oral sodomy.

"All three convictions have involved serious injury or the potential for serious injury," probation-department investigator David Scotkin wrote in Devine's pre-sentence report. "The purpose of these crimes seem to be the benefit of the subject's life at the expense of others. One may conclude that he is becoming increasingly dangerous."

Klein refused Harris' request to set bail low enough to enable Devine to get out of jail. In an interview, Klein said he found Harris' call to be "unusual" but not something to get particularly upset over.

Ultimately, he sentenced Devine to 3½ to seven years in prison.

In an interview, Harris said that he had known the Devine family for a decade and that Devine's mother had asked him if he would testify in behalf of her son to help him get out on bail.

"I told her, 'Of course I would,' " Harris said. Instead of testifying under subpoena, however, Harris spoke to Judge Klein privately about the case.

"In viewing it now, I wish the hell I hadn't," the judge said in an interview. "I wish I had appeared pursuant to [a] subpoena and gotten it over with." No subpoenas were ever issued.

Harris said it had been his impression that Anthony Devine's prior record had involved "minor offenses." He said he had not been aware that it involved such charges as robbery and rape.

Harris said he did not believe that his knowledge of the father's drug record should have made any difference in vouching for the family to Judge Klein.

"Even though his father was convicted, the fact that a person has been arrested and convicted doesn't mean that it's a basis for denying bail to him or his family," Harris said.

He said he was reluctant to be subpoenaed and appear in open court, however, because of the possible appearance it might give.

After being paroled in 1983, Anthony Devine was indicted by a federal grand jury in February 1984 in connection with a drug-trafficking ring in North Philadelphia. He was convicted last year of two counts of heroin distribution and sentenced to five years in federal prison.

The family's contact with Judge Harris did not end with the judge's phone call to Klein in 1978. The same year, police arrested Anthony Devine on charges of carrying an illegal 9½-inch folding dagger. On Sept. 14, 1978, Harris granted a defense motion to suppress evidence against Devine and found him not guilty.

And in February 1983, Devine's father, James Devan, was arrested for alleddgedly carrying an unlicensed gun. Despite the fact that Judge Harris had previously served as Devan's attorney, he agreed to free Devan on his own recognizance, with no bail.

That same year, Harris made his second bid for election to a higher court and won. Now he is a Common Pleas Court judge.

TRYING A CASE FOR AN OLD FRIEND

Her name was Karen McNaughton.

She was a nurse, and a wife.

At 10 o'clock on the night of Oct. 21, 1981, she was driving her car on City Avenue to her job at Lankenau Hospital. She had been called in to assist with open-heart surgery.

Out of nowhere, a car sped past other vehicles in a terrifying blur. And then it swerved across the double yellow stripes into the wrong lane. There was the horrible scream of tires. And a deafening slam. And other drivers on the road that night knew instantly what had happened.

Karen McNaughton, at the age of 27, was dead, her blue Camaro backed up against a clump of trees, her body crushed and misshapen by the collision.

Her husband, Steven, remembers the uncontrollable grief after it happened. Later, after the case had made its way through the Philadelphia court system, he would feel another emotion: helplessness.

Craig Arno, the 16-year-old who killed Karen McNaughton with his car, was convicted of involuntary manslaughter and vehicular homicide.

When it came time to decide Arno's sentence, Common Pleas Court Judge George J. Ivins heard evidence that Arno had three juvenile criminal adjudications for burglary and theft. In addition, Arno had been stopped for speeding down City Avenue on a motorcycle seven months after the fatal accident. Police had to chase him for nearly three miles to stop him.

Ivins chose not to sentence Arno to jail. Instead, Arno was given five years' probation—and loss of his driver's license.

"You stand there and you see someone you love get mutilated . . . and the person who did it, he walks away," Steven McNaughton said later. "You put all the facts on the scales of justice, and he walks away."

But there was more to this case than what occurred in the courtroom. Judges are supposed to be assigned cases at random, to avoid any hint of impropriety, any suggestion that either side is able to pick the judge it wants. The Arno case had not been randomly assigned to Judge Ivins.

Instead, court record show, Ivins agreed to take the case after receiving a phone call from Arno's attorney, F. Emmett Fitzpatrick. Fitzpatrick, the former Philadelphia district attorney and a friend of Ivins', privately *asked* Ivins to take the case.

Before the case went to trial, two members of the district attorney's office agreed in private to let Ivins take the case. But both the victim's husband and mother say they were never told about the arrangement. And, they say, if they had known about it, they would have asked for another judge.

Karen McNaughton's relatives—like all other ordinary citizens who walk into City Hall—did not know the way the game of justice is sometimes played in Philadelphia.

On July 7, 1982, according to court records, a so-called in-camera (in-chambers) hearing was called by Ivins. Present at the session were defense attorney Fitzpatrick and Brian Rosenthal and Joseph Murray of the district attorney's office.

The main issue discussed at this session, the record shows, was how the case had gotten assigned to Ivins in the first place.

"About three months ago, two months ago, whenever it was, Emmett [Fitzpatrick] called and wanted to see me," Ivins said at the hearing. "He came over and asked me would I accept a case where there was a waiver [of a jury]."

According to state judicial rules, Ivins and Fitzpatrick had conducted what is legally known as an ex parte conversation—a discussion in which only one side in a case talks to the judge.

Ivins continued: "And at that point, Emmett advised me that it involved a killing by automobile, and I said, 'Look, I don't want to know any more about it. I'm satisfied to hear it [the case].' " He suggested Fitzpatrick get the prosecution's approval.

At that time, homicide cases were assigned through a calendar judge, Paul Ribner. Ribner said he randomly assigned cases to whoever was available, unless both sides agreed to waive a jury trial and try the case in front of a particular judge. Fitzpatrick asked that the case be assigned to Ivins, and the prosecution did not object—so Ribner assigned it to Ivins on July 1, 1982. But Ribner said later in an interview he did not know that Fitzpatrick had privately asked Ivins to take the case before it was officially assigned.

During the July 7 in-camera hearing, Ivins also described his long-standing friendship with Fitzpatrick.

"I've known Emmett for 30 years," the judge said. "We were quite close in the election of '74, when he was elected D.A. and I ran and was elected to the C.P. bench."

"I've had a very, very friendly feeling with respect to Emmett for a long time."

By the same token, said Ivins, he was friendly with several members of the district attorney's office, including Murray.

In an interview, Murray said he did not recall Ivins describing private contact with Fitzpatrick. He said he did not ask for a different judge because he trusted Ivins' integrity and believed, as many lawyers do, that Ivins tends to favor the prosecution. Rosenthal said the decision was Murray's and that he had not disagreed with it.

After Ivins established during the in-camera hearing that he would hear the case, records show, he asked the three lawyers not to say a word about any of this in public.

"I have an aversion . . . to discussing matters in newspapers," said Ivins. "I think some of these people get out of journalism school, having taken Journalism III, which is, 'Let's see if we can raise a rumor.' So, therefore, I'm merely going to say to both sides, if I accept this case—and assuming I do—I want no comments to anybody about this case in the newspaper; namely, that it's a neighbor of mine, or something. I don't want any of that."

Murray said the prosecution would abide by that. And so did Fitzpatrick.

When the Arno trial began, on July 19, 1982, Ivins disclosed that he had known Fitzpatrick for many years, that they had campaigned together in 1973, that Arno's mother worked in Municipal Court and that the judge and defendant lived in the same neighborhood.

Ivins did *not* disclose to those assembled, which included the victim's family, that he had taken the case only after Fitzpatrick had asked him to. Nor did he mention the in-camera hearing.

"This matter was assigned to me in the ordinary, routine course of events," he told those assembled in Courtroom 246 of City Hall. "I know nothing more about it than that."

In a non-jury trial, Ivins found Arno guilty. During a sentencing hearing on Jan. 25, 1983, Arno's mother testified that the accident had changed her son, that he had been punished enough. But prosecutors brought in evidence that Arno had been stopped twice for driving violations since the fatal accident. And the victim's husband related what Arno had said to him after the verdict.

"Walking out of the courtroom," Steven McNaughton testified, "he yelled the words *motherf——*."

In an interview, Steven McNaughton recalled his amazement at Arno's behavior. He also recalled how one of the judge's court officers had put a hand to McNaughton's shoulder minutes after Arno's probation sentence was announced and said quietly, "I'm sorry."

John DiDonato, the assistant district attorney at the sentencing, did not protest the sentence. He recalls a feeling of helplessness.

"I was seething," DiDonato said in an interview. "It was an insult to all the citizens of Philadelphia. It was saying to the victim's family, 'You waited to get justice. You did it the right way, and this is what you got for it.' "

As it turned out, Craig Arno was a bad probation risk. As terms of his probation, Arno had been ordered not to own or drive a car. But after his sentencing, Arno was stopped by police twice for speeding and driving without a license, insurance and proper car registration— all of which were probation violations. On May 1, 1985, two years after giving him his freedom, Ivins lifted Arno's probation and gave him the maximum sentence: 2½ to five years in prison. He is eligible for parole in October 1987.

Ivins would not comment on any aspects of the case.

Fitzpatrick, asked about his initial call to Ivins, said such requests were commonplace. He said he had made "dozens" of such calls to judges over the years. He said he mainly had wanted to make sure that Ivins was willing to try the case "on a waiver"—without a jury.

The phone call was proper, Fitzpatrick asserted, particularly in light of the fact that the case had been highly publicized, and also because the defendant lived near Ivins.

"It just makes common sense when you had the adverse publicity and the neighborhood involvement to ask in advance," Fitzpatrick said.

"It was the gentlemanly thing to do," he added.

But Karen McNaughton's husband sees it differently. On learning that Fitzpatrick had privately sought out Judge Ivins, Steven McNaughton used one word to describe his feelings:

"Disbelief."

PARTY AND FAMILY TIES SHAPE THE PAYROLL

WEDNESDAY, JANUARY 29, 1986

BY H. G. BISSINGER
AND DANIEL R. BIDDLE

As a supervisor in Common Pleas Court, Edward T. Halligan had a personnel problem, and he felt that the time had come to do something about it.

According to information he had received, an employee working for him in the court's pretrial-services unit, Curtis C. Carson 3d, had been habitually tardy and had been scheduling work for himself whenever he wanted.

But when Halligan scheduled a meeting with the employee in 1982 to discuss his performance, he ran into something unexpected: Carson's father.

Like his son, Curtis C. Carson Jr. works in the court system. He is a Common Pleas Court judge.

Halligan, in a memo written after the meeting, said he did not get to talk to Curtis Carson 3d at all. Instead, Halligan wrote, Judge Carson angrily told him to stop interfering with his son.

Halligan said in the memo that he suggested Judge Carson take his gripes to Halligan's boss, then Court Administrator David N. Savitt. The judge did so, and within hours Halligan got a call from Savitt. The court administrator's message to Halligan was simple: Let Carson's son work the schedule he wants.

And so, the young Carson was allowed to continue working his own hours. Savitt has confirmed that account.

Judge Carson is not the only elected official who has a relative on the court payroll. The Philadelphia court system is rife with examples of nepotism and political patronage.

Common Pleas Court officials say the payroll is not a matter of public record. "The public has never asked me for it," said President Judge Edward J. Bradley. And if someone asked, he said, "I wouldn't give it to them. . . . An employee has a certain amount of right to privacy. . . . It could be used for various wrong purposes, such as solicitation."

But copies of the Common Pleas and Municipal Courts' combined $55 million payrolls obtained from the city controller's office show that at least 30 of the 120 judges in the system—one in four—currently have relatives working for the courts. Many more previously have had kin in court jobs, or children hired into the court's summer-intern program.

Five top-level administrators in the court system have relatives on the payroll, as well, records show.

The Carson case demonstrates how nepotism can go beyond mere hiring. In an interview, Savitt paraphrased Judge Carson as having told him that supervisor Halligan's actions regarding the judge's son were "terrible and improper."

Savitt said that one of his reasons for letting the younger Carson work flexible hours was that "I knew Curtis Carson was a vociferous judge, and I wanted the court to run smoothly."

Several months later, the situation became moot when Curtis Carson 3d resigned. But he took another job on the court payroll—as a judicial assistant. The payroll shows he makes $20,979 a year.

His boss? His father, the judge.

The younger Carson declined to be interviewed. Judge Carson said he did not remember meeting with Halligan, but he said he saw nothing wrong with getting involved in his son's court job in any case. "Why shouldn't I?" he asked.

Carson also said he saw nothing wrong with the court's hiring judges' relatives. "I think the policy should be to pick the most qualified," Carson said. "If that happens to be a relative, fine."

A. Joseph Teti, the $61,505-a-year chief deputy administrator of Common Pleas Court—whose duties include overseeing the hiring process—has a daughter, a daughter-in-law, and two nephews in court jobs. The daughter-in-law, he points out, was hired long before she married his son. Teti says all are well-qualified and adds, "I'm just sorry I can't get more of my family members on the court."

The $25,000-a-year first deputy to Clerk of Quarter Sessions Edgar

C. Campbell Sr.—whose office is caretaker for hundreds of thousands of official criminal-case records—is the boss' son, Edgar C. Campbell Jr.

All of the judges and court officials interviewed described their relatives on the payroll as well-qualified and hard-working.

One judge said he once hired his daughter because he had been away from her for some time and wanted to get closer to her. Another said he hired his wife after she had lost her previous job.

The hiring practices of the court system are greatly affected also by political patronage. "The court system is a vast enterprise of patronage," said Common Pleas Court Judge Leon Katz. "It has tentacles that reach into the pocket of every taxpayer."

President Judge Bradley defends the hiring process. "I think we have, by and large, a good work force," he said in an interview. Noting that most of the court's jobs now require testing, Bradley said, "No matter who you are, if you flunk that test, you're not going to be hired."

Bradley acknowledged that some job-seekers could not be easily ignored. "I have to get a budget through City Council," he said. "Perhaps a councilman will recommend a relative for a job. I have to consider that."

Common Pleas Court Judge Savitt said that during his years as court administrator, from 1975 to 1983, he received an average of about one request a day from politicians and judges trying to get relatives or friends hired.

"There are frequent recommendations for jobs from people in politics or people in government," Savitt said in an interview. "The court operates not in a vacuum. A court administrator cannot tell a city councilman to go fly a kite. We depend on City Council for our budget."

While stressing that he tried to hire only qualified applicants, Savitt said of politicians' requests: "Some of these recommendations were for the highest-quality people. But some of them weren't."

THE PARTIES AND THEIR SWAY

Among those on the 2,441-person court payroll are relatives of Democratic and Republican Party leaders, relatives of former party leaders, relatives of ward leaders, relatives of current and former legislators and dozens of relatives of the parties' basic infantry: the committee person.

Longtime city Republican leader William A. Meehan had six relatives—all of them in-laws or spouses of in-laws—on the current payroll. Their annual salaries total $154,117. Meehan makes a distinction between the four relatives "I got hired" and two others who, he says, got court jobs without his help.

"I put enough other people's families on," Meehan said in an interview. "I can put some of mine on. They were four of the best [Republican] committeemen in Philadelphia! I'll show you the records if you don't believe me."

City Democratic Committee chairman Joseph F. Smith has a niece earning $14,013 on the Municipal Court payroll. She was hired Aug. 6, 1984, a little more than a year after Smith became party chairman. Ward 5 Democratic leader Peter J. Camiel, the former city Democratic chairman, has a brother working as a $20,978-a-year court officer in Common Pleas Court. Camiel's sister-in-law earns $31,574 as assistant chief court crier. Camiel says his son, a $22,242 jury-selection officer, got his job "on his own."

Ward 41 Democratic leader Nicholas P. Stampone's son earns $20,356 as a judge's personal aide.

The list goes on and on.

Former City Councilman Melvin J. Greenberg, a practicing lawyer, earns $28,313 as the Municipal Court's part-time solicitor. Former City Controller Thomas Gola's son is a $22,249 Common Pleas Court judicial aide.

Former state Rep. German Quiles (D., Phila.) is a $22,449 court officer in Municipal Court. So is former state Rep. Henry J. Giammarco (D., Phila).

Ward 58 Democratic leader Michael Stack's wife, former Board of Education member Felice Stack, is a $21,217 law clerk. Ward 1 Democratic leader James J. Tayoun's daughter was hired last April as a $13,714-a-year clerical assistant. She resigned Dec. 26.

With the exception of each judge's office staff, all court employees must pass standard tests to get hired. For a time, the court's administrative rules even included a pledge to hire, fire, promote and demote on a merit basis, unswayed by "political opinion or affiliation." Later that phrase was changed to "other non-merit factors."

But city political leaders talk as if political ties do influence the hiring process.

Republican leader Meehan, Democratic chairman Smith and former Democratic chairman David Glancey speak in candid terms about the court payrolls and how many jobs are filled through patronage.

In an interview, Glancey recalled how the system was explained to him—not by other politicians, he said, but by Judge Savitt, who as court administrator was in charge of hiring.

Savitt told him the hiring ratio: For every three jobs filled by the city Democratic committee, the Republicans got one job.

"It's almost as if it's a gentlemen's agreement . . . ," Glancey said. "It's not written anywhere."

Meehan said he started recommending party people for court jobs as a committeeman after graduating from college in 1948 and could not possibly estimate how many he had actually gotten hired.

The veteran Republican leader disagreed with Glancy's description of a 3-1 ratio, saying with a smile, "I ask for a lot." But he declined to put a figure on how many of his people actually are hired.

"You try to pick people who have done the best work [for the party]," Meehan said. "You try and reward everybody and let everybody feel if they do the job, they have a chance to be rewarded."

He contended that the rise of civil-service systems and government professionalism, over decades, has greatly reduced the parties' influence. Meehan said the judges themselves exercise internal patronage; a number of the court's job openings are filled by people who "come from a judge," he said.

"Could be a relative," Meehand said. "Could be a friend."

Democratic chairman Smith says the hiring of judges' relatives is "all done hush-hush-like," without the parties' involvement, and he doesn't like it. "I would rather see political patronage than I would nepotism," he said.

Smith insisted he had succeeded only in getting a few party-sponsored workers hired since he became the party's titular leader in 1983. He, too, said that much of the patronage system had given way to stricter hiring standards.

But Smith talked about the court payroll as if he were part of the hiring authority. "Now remember," he said, "those jobs don't come up every day. Unfortunately for me, not too many Democrats are leaving jobs." Thus, he explained, not enough spaces were available to be filled by *new* party-backed job applicants.

And he said that state legislators, City Council members and other politicians sometimes gave him headaches by going directly to the court's administration for patronage jobs. That can lead to one or another politician's getting an unfair share of jobs, Smith explained. "We like to lay the jobs around evenly," he said.

In some cases, city officeholders who help determine the court system's annual budget also try to have relatives hired. But they don't always like to talk about it.

In August 1977, the Common Pleas Court hired the daughter of City Councilman Joseph E. Coleman to work in public relations.

Coleman, who is now Council president, has said he did not try to use his influence to prompt the hiring of his daughter, who now earns $24,546 a year.

Court files contain a letter dated July 5, 1977, in which Coleman wrote to Savitt, "reminding you" of his daughter's job application.

"Please," the letter said, "let me hear from you on this matter soon."

She was hired six weeks later.

A JUDGE ENLISTS HIS WIFE AS AIDE

When Dveral Silberstein wasn't reappointed to the city Zoning Board after Mayor Goode took office, she needed a job. When her husband, Municipal Court Judge Alan K. Silberstein, could not dissuade his judicial aide from quitting, he had a $22,249-a-year opening for a personal aide on his staff.

So he hired his wife.

Judge Silberstein said his wife was eminently qualified for the job, with her experience on the Zoning Board. Before that, she had been a schoolteacher. He said the situation created no conflicts, but he said he could see how hiring a relative could lead to problems.

"It all depends on the relative and the person," Judge Silberstein said. "Obviously, you would have more control over a stranger. If there's a stranger, and they're not doing the job, you fire them. You may think twice about the relative."

Last November, Dveral Silberstein was reappointed to the Zoning Board, and she resigned from the court payroll.

JUDGE'S DAUGHTER BECOMES HIS SECRETARY

Given the size of the court's total work force—more than 2,000 people—President Judge Bradley believes that the number of judicial relatives on the payroll—less than 2 percent—is quite small. "I don't consider that an inordinate number," he said in an interview.

Common Pleas Court Judge William M. Marutani says any hiring of kin creates a public suspicion that someone has received special treatment.

"I don't think any judge should have any relatives on the payroll!" Marutani said loudly in an interview. "It is because you are a judge that you should be above suspicion."

Common Pleas Court Judge Lynne Abraham doesn't have any relatives on the payroll, either. "It always looks bad, even if they're competent," she said. "So I'd rather not do it."

Municipal Court Judge William Brady Jr. agrees.

"As a general rule," he said, "I shouldn't hire a close relative to be on my staff."

But he broke his own rule. In early 1984, his daughter, a graduate of the University of Pennsylvania, became his judicial secretary at a salary of $18,269. She stayed in the job 11 months before leaving for a school for designers in England, he said.

"I took the position I'd like to have her around me," Brady said in explaining why his daughter had taken the job. "I'd been away from her for a while. Obviously, it wasn't the best thing in the world."

Many other judges in the Philadelphia court system are not so contrite about nepotism.

Common Pleas Court Judge Eugene E. J. Maier said he would not be concerned about the appearance of having even a large number of relatives on the payroll. If the courts had only 100 employees, and his relative "were 100 out of 100, *that* might be something," Maier said.

"Do the people perform their jobs? Are they qualified properly? What difference does it make if they are related or not related?" Maier said.

His sister, Patricia C. Averill, was hired as a court computer-programs analyst at $25,313, before Maier, a former city commissioner, came onto the bench.

After Maier became a judge, his daughter, Elizabeth, was hired as a clerical assistant. She now earns $14,013. Maier said he had suggested that she apply for a court job and "probably" had asked President Judge Bradley to hire her.

Another Common Pleas Court judge with more than one relative working in the court system is Charles P. Mirarchi Jr. His relatives on the payroll now number eight: a sister, a daughter, two nieces, two nephews, a son-in-law and the son-in-law's brother. The yearly salaries of those employees total $198,801. Mirarchi has said he sees nothing wrong with having qualified relatives on the payroll.

The wife of Common Pleas Court Senior Judge John A. Geisz has been his secretary for eight years. When she was hired, she had had 10 years' legal experience at the U.S. attorney's office, and Geisz calls her the "best secretary" he's ever had. Geisz's son-in-law was his law clerk for a time before being hired by the district attorney's office about three years ago.

Geisz said that he also had tried to get his daughter to work in the court system but that she had refused. "I asked her to come work for me, but she wouldn't have anything to do with it."

Other judges with relatives on the payroll include Municipal Court President Joseph R. Glancey and Common Pleas Court Judge Alex Bonavitacola, who is a member of the state Judicial Inquiry and Review Board. Glancey's wife has been his secretary since 1980. Bonavitacola's wife was hired in April as a $19,731-a-year secretary.

In January 1978, Common Pleas Court Judge James R. Cavanaugh wrote to Judge Savitt. "I had my son resign a lucrative position as a busboy in a restaurant-bar because I thought the atmosphere was not good. I now feel responsible for obtaining substitute employment for him . . . Are there any part-time positions open for a college student . . . ?"

Cavanaugh's son was hired three weeks later as a temporary clerk. He later attended law school and rejoined the court last September as a $21,217-a-year law clerk. Judge Cavanaugh, who was elected to Superior Court in 1979, said in an interview that he did not recall writing the note but added that judges' relatives were hired "quite a bit" when he was on Common Pleas Court.

AFTER RESIGNATION, A NEW COURT JOB

One Common Pleas Court judge who no longer is on the bench, Paul A. Dandridge, did not use the system to hire his relatives. But through the system, he helped create a new job that he himself later filled almost immediately after his retirement.

While still on the bench in 1983, Dandridge served on a three-judge panel monitoring the city's compliance with a court order requiring the reduction of its prison population. As part of his duties, he regularly conducted hearings to determine whether anyone in the city's jails might be eligible for bail and therefore could be released.

On June 29, 1983, the three-judge panel agreed to appoint a paid bail master to hear these cases several times a month instead of having a judge do it.

Dandridge, according to an April 1983 memo, was consulted about the new post and helped decide how often hearings should be conducted.

On Aug. 1, 1983, Dandridge resigned from the bench at age 57 to go into private business.

On Aug. 17, 1983, the two remaining members of the three-judge panel, Eugene H. Clarke Jr. and Theodore Smith, appointed their former colleague Dandridge as the paid bail master.

Neither Clarke nor Smith felt there was anything improper about Dandridge's taking a job that he had been instrumental in setting up as a judge. "He didn't resign with the idea that he was going to be bail master," said Smith in an interview. "After he resigned, there came the question of a bail master. . . . I couldn't think, nor could he, of a more logical person for the job."

Dandridge did not answer numerous phone messages and declined a written request to be interviewed.

Since resigning as judge, Dandridge has gone into private business and heads a small company. His salary for the part-time job of bail master, according to President Judge Bradley, is about $20,000 a year.

INCOMPETENT COUNSEL: STAKING A CLAIM TO A NEW TRIAL

THURSDAY, JANUARY 30, 1986

BY FREDRIC N. TULSKY

In 1969, two men were stabbed, one fatally, during a fight in a Center City bar. Within weeks, Francis McFadden, then 33, was arrested on charges that included murder.

Eleven years and two trials later, McFadden went back into court, seeking a third trial by contending that his attorney in the second trial, Edward Reif, had not properly represented him.

Such last-ditch efforts by prisoners are commonplace, but in this case McFadden had a critical piece of extra help: Reif himself testified that he had committed a series of unjustifiable mistakes.

"I just did a bad job," he said, during a May 1980 hearing, of his failure to object to certain comments by the prosecutor, "something in retrospect, and when I reviewed the record . . . it's obvious that I did a bad job. That's the only explanation I can give."

Admissions of failure, once almost unheard of among defense lawyers, have in the last few years become a new legal weapon in Pennsylvania. Although no one knows for sure how many such cases there are, The Inquirer has studied 31 cases in the state in which defense attorneys have assisted in bids for new trials on the ground that they somehow had failed to take the most basic measures. The study focused on Philadelphia, where 29 of the cases originated.

Top law enforcement officials in Pennsylvania say the growing trend is a serious problem.

During one state Supreme Court argument last year, Chief Justice Robert N. C. Nix Jr. said that the frequency of such instances "has become alarming. Who would have thought that a lawyer would plead his own incompetence?"

Edward G. Rendell refers to such testimony as "the single most dangerous development" during his recently ended tenure as Philadelphia district attorney. "Our belief is that we are seeing trial counsel deliberately coming in and 'taking a dive' as a means of helping their clients," he said. Defense attorneys, he said, might err at the trial intentionally or later falsely testify that they have erred.

The cases involve some of the city's busiest and most experienced trial lawyers testifying that they had made errors that would be obvious to first-year law students. In some cases, judges have thrown out the new-trial bids by ruling that the attorneys' admissions were just not believable.

Over the last five years, veteran defense attorneys have admitted to neglecting to call potentially helpful witnesses to testify in first-degree murder cases; failing to interview potential witnesses; failing to protect their clients' right to appeal, either out of neglect or because they had not been paid to do so; and allowing conflicts of interest to stand in the way of giving their clients an adequate defense.

In one case, Vincent J. Ziccardi, the city's former chief public defender testified that he had counseled a client to lie in court. And in another, Timothy Crawford Jr., an experienced defense attorney, testified that he "forgot" to call his client to the witness stand in a first-degree murder case.

Four of the 31 cases examined by The Inquirer involved one lawyer, Reif, a former prosecutor and an attorney since 1957. Another lawyer, Adam O. Renfroe Jr., a former prosecutor and a lawyer since 1976, has been involved in three such cases since 1983. And four other lawyers have been involved in at least two such cases.

The spectacle of attorneys testifying to their own errors is so unorthodox that many legal experts outside the state, including top U.S. Justice Department officials, defense lawyers and judges, say they have never heard of such a case.

Retired U.S. Supreme Court Justice Potter Stewart, in an interview before his death in December, said, "In my experience on the Supreme Court . . . I don't remember ever having a lawyer come in and say he was ineffective in his representation of his client." After reviewing a summary of the cases examined by The Inquirer, Stewart said, "Based upon your findings in Philadelphia, I think it is a serious problem."

William Greenhalgh, a professor at Georgetown University and former chief of the American Bar Association's criminal justice section, said that the 31 cases from Pennsylvania were "tremendously significant. . . . It is an astronomic number of instances." Greenhalgh said he knew of no such occurrences elsewhere and added, "It may be a disease in the city of Philadelphia."

Some of the errors admitted to are clear violations of the state Code of Professional Responsibility, which governs the conduct of lawyers. But in no such case examined by The Inquirer has a lawyer in Pennsylvania been publicly disciplined for such admissions.

Officials of the state Disciplinary Board say such cases are seldom referred to the board. "The question," says John W. Herron, former chief disciplinary counsel of the board, "is how do we know about these cases? And the answer is, we generally don't."

Common Pleas Court Judge Edward J. Blake, who spends the bulk of his day hearing arguments for new trials, said he did not believe it was his job to refer allegations of lawyer misconduct to the state Disciplinary Board. "I find most lawyers, regardless of their relationship with the defendants, are professional men and women who tell the truth," he said.

But others take a far less benevolent view of this phenomenon. Rendell contends that defense attorneys admit to mistakes out of the hope that defendants who lose at trial may do better upon a second chance. Or, as he said, the defense attorneys are "trying to get two bites at the apple."

In fact, he said, assistant district attorneys have seen cases where defense attorneys appear to err deliberately during trial, opening the door for a second trial for their clients if they lose.

Said Deputy District Attorney Arnold Gordon: "What we are talking about is not honest error. We're talking about errors fundamental to a case done by an experienced attorney. Maybe, with an inexperienced attorney, if it is done one time, you can say that is honest error. But when an experienced attorney testifies that he didn't bother to call key alibi witnesses, he is either lying or he deliberately subverted the record."

Many defense attorneys say prosecutors exaggerate the problem. They contend that assistant district attorneys attack defense lawyers who acknowledge honest mistakes because such acknowledgment can jeopardize convictions.

And, they say, defendants too frequently are the victims of defense attorneys who fail their clients and then are unwilling to come into court and say so.

Even so, some veteran defense attorneys agree that in a small number of cases, defense lawyers distort their testimony in postconviction hearings in a way that helps their former clients. "Most defense lawyers don't believe they should ever lose," Ziccardi said. "So when they do lose, they are willing to say they were ineffective."

Some defense attorneys also say such testimony may help, rather than hurt, the reputations of the defense lawyers involved. "A client is only interested in getting back on the street," Ziccardi said. "If attorneys testify they were ineffective, prisoners will say, 'He's a stand-up guy, willing to come in.' "

Veteran defense attorney A. Charles Peruto Sr. says that a "minuscule" number of lawyers "have business that keeps them in court regularly because the word is around that they will help."

Whatever the motive, there seems little doubt that convicted criminals stand a far better chance of winning new trials when their trial lawyers admit to incompetence.

Judge Blake says he grants new trials in only about 3 percent of the cases he hears.

In contrast, of the cases examined by The Inquirer in which attorneys testified to having committed errors, defendants won new trials or other relief in nine of 30 instances, with one case still pending.

Prosecutors in such cities as Chicago, Los Angeles and New York say they have not experienced the phenomenon there. However, the problem appears not only in Philadelphia, but statewide.

"It happens here and has been a matter of concern to us," said Allegheny County prosecutor Robert Colville. "We see it as violating the spirit" of the state post-conviction hearing act, "which was designed to guarantee that defendants receive fair trials."

Claims of incompetent counsel almost always are brought by convicts facing long prison sentences. And instances of lawyers' admitting their own incompetence may be particularly numerous in Pennsylvania because state court decisions have made the testimony of a trial attorney critical for someone trying to win a new trial on such a ground.

Standards for testing whether an attorney has failed his client were set in 1978 by the Pennsylvania Supreme Court, which said the basic question was not whether the trial lawyer followed the best possible strategy, but whether there was some reasonable basis for the approach taken. If there was none, the courts then look to see if that was likely to have affected the outcome of the trial.

Under the standard, if the trial lawyer offers a justification for his actions, the defendant has serious problems in getting a new trial. On the other hand, if a lawyer testifies that he had no good reason for his actions, the defendant has a much improved chance of winning a new trial.

Such testimony, in fact, often puts the prosecutors in an ironic position. They are forced to staunchly defend the strategy chosen by their opponents.

Normally, a defendant seeking a new trial does not begin to attack his attorney's performance until all appeals have been exhausted. This usually is many years after the crime and the original trial.

Such time spans prompted Third U.S. Circuit Court Judge Arlin M. Adams to argue, in a 1984 dissent against considering a retrial for former Teamsters leader John J. Sullivan, who was convicted of murder in 1968:

"The panel's decision would appear to threaten the important principle of finality in criminal convictions obtained after full review of state courts. . . . Now, sixteen years after the crime, Sullivan will receive a new trial on the basis of an objection that was raised for the first time many years after the original trial and had not been made an issue on direct appeal."

THE DEFENSE CALLS NO WITNESSES

In the early morning hours of Nov. 14, 1980, a fight erupted outside the Cosmopolitan Club bar, 52d and Catharine Streets, that ended in the death of Curtis Warren Lyles, 29, of gunshot wounds to the neck, shoulder and knees.

Dwayne M. Hook, then 22, who himself had been shot in the knee during that fight, and a companion, Walter Shiver, then 25, were brought to trial before Common Pleas Court Judge Lisa A. Richette in November 1982.

The case against Hook and Shiver developed months after the incident when an eyewitness, Lydia Trapp, told police that the shooting had occurred after a dispute over drugs.

After the prosecution rested its case, Richette denied a request by the attorneys for Hook and Shiver to dismiss the charges. Even so, both Hook's attorney, Adam O. Renfroe Jr., and Shiver's attorney, Lewis S. Small, elected to rest their case without presenting any testimony. They then argued that their clients should be found not guilty.

Renfroe contended that Hook had shot Lyles in self-defense, but Richette disagreed: "The testimony of this young woman [Trapp], uncontradicted by you or anyone else, was that your client fired when that man was on the ground. How is that self-defense?"

After Richette's statement, both attorneys sought to reopen their case and present testimony, but the judge rejected that request.

Richette found Hook and Shiver guilty of voluntary manslaughter, conspiracy and possessing instruments of crime.

Within two months after the conviction, Hook fired Renfroe and hired Daniel M. Preminger. Preminger sought a new trial for Hook, arguing that Renfroe had not competently represented his client.

During two days of hearings in 1983, Preminger presented a series of witnesses who he contended could have helped Hook's case, had they been called.

One of those witnesses was Hook's physician, James A. Anthony, who testified that the gunshot that had hit Hook had shattered his leg, which would have made it "very difficult, extremely difficult" to get up from the ground, as Trapp had testified Hook had done.

Other witnesses testified that they saw Hook, after the shooting, being picked up off the ground and taken for medical care.

Ellen Ruth Hook, the defendant's mother, testified that she had spoken to these witnesses, and had given their names to Renfroe. She said that Renfroe had told her that if it became "necessary, he would get in touch with these people." She said she continued calling Renfroe before the trial, adding, "I could never understand why he never contacted any of these witnesses or he never wrote anything down that I told him."

During a third day of hearings, in November 1983, Renfroe appeared before Richette and explained that his fee for handling the case did not justify putting on a defense:

"Your honor, this matter basically molded down to a matter of economics, as far as I'm concerned. And I say that because there is an ethical problem here that we are supposed to present the best defense we could possibly present when you represent someone. It was my position because of the money problem that was involved . . . that with the limited amount of evidence that the commonwealth had to present, that without question it was my belief in the experience I have had and a number of cases that I have tried, I couldn't see how this case—how he could be found guilty. I still couldn't understand it, with all due respect to this court."

Renfroe, who according to testimony had been paid $2,000 by Hook's family to handle the case, added: "With all due respect, I will be very candid: I think, had I presented much more witnesses, many more witnesses, that without question it would have been a not-guilty case. I feel that I failed truly, I feel, in not presenting witnesses."

Renfroe testified that he never even interviewed the potential witnesses.

The state Code of Professional Responsibility forbids a lawyer from handling a matter without adequate preparation, and also from intentionally failing "to seek the lawful objectives of his client through reasonably available means."

Former state Disciplinary Board counsel Herron, when asked in hypothetical terms about an attorney who because of money problems fails to provide a full defense, responded, "The code requires an attorney to zealously represent his client. Nothing diminishes that duty, and certainly not economics."

In an interview, Richette said of the first trial: "It seems to me that when the defendant came in and documented all the things that Renfroe didn't do, it was clear that the defendant was denied his day in court."

Renfroe said recently of his defense, "If I was in the same situation, I might handle the trial the same way. They [the prosecutors] had one witness, who was not believable, not credible. The fact that there was no corroborating testimony led me to feel it was not necessary to bring in a lot of witnesses. I felt the judge would see there was a reasonable doubt and acquit" Hook.

At the close of the hearings in November 1983, Richette granted a new trial, not only to Hook but also to the co-defendant, Shiver, who had raised no questions about the competency of his own attorney. Explained Richette: "I can't separate one from the other. . . . They are both going to get new trials. That's it." Richette's decision on Shiver has since been overturned by the state Superior Court.

As for Hook, he had the right to seek a new judge, unfamiliar with the facts, to preside over his new trial. Instead, he said he wished to be retried before Richette, and she presided over a jury trial in November 1984. The state's star witness, Trapp, was unwilling to again testify, but her testimony from the first trial was read to the jury.

And despite the introduction of the evidence that never came out at the first trial, Hook was convicted again of voluntary manslaughter.

Attorney Preminger, in a recent interview, said there "should be a penalty if you are found ineffective. I am not talking about honest error. I am talking about mere sloth. If you can't show you tried to interview witnesses," he said, a punishment should be imposed.

NO SUBPOENAS, NO ALIBI TESTIMONY

On July 14, 1983, the day after Preminger began calling witnesses to show that Renfroe had ineffectively defended Hook, Preminger himself took the witness stand before Common Pleas Court Judge William Porter to testify about his own ineffectiveness in defending Wilfredo Carbonell in a September 1982 robbery trial.

Preminger, in answering questions from Carbonell's new attorney, A. Charles Peruto Sr., said he had failed to present five possible witnesses, all friends or relatives of Carbonell's who would have said they were with the defendant at the time of the robbery.

Prosecutors and defense lawyers agree that such alibis are seldom of value, particularly when the witnesses are friends or relatives of the defendant.

But the alibi witnesses in this case would have given compelling testimony for clearly remembering the night in question: They were with Carbonell, celebrating his birthday, at the time of the crime— the robbery of a bar.

Preminger testified that he had spoken to three of the witnesses, including Carbonell's wife, before trial, and that he was convinced they all were truthful. Even so, he testified, he never sought subpoenas to ensure their court appearance. He relied on Carbonell's wife to make certain that they appeared.

When they weren't in court when he needed them, he testified, he proceeded without them. He said there was no tactical reason for his decision.

Rather than seeking a delay to get the witnesses, Preminger said, "I considered the fact that Mr. Carbonell was incarcerated and wanted to get these matters over with." In addition, he said, he believed that the prosecution case was weak.

During a recent interview, Preminger said of his handling of the case: "I relied on the people to come in because they said they would. I made a mistake of assuming that they would keep their word. After 10 years as a defense attorney, that is not a bad record."

At the close of evidence at the hearing for a new trial, Assistant District Attorney Elliot Present urged Judge Porter to "be extremely suspicious" of the alibi witnesses, calling them "Johnny-come-latelies that have formulated an alibi."

Porter ordered a new trial for Carbonell, saying that Preminger had not provided an adequate defense. A pretrial hearing in the case is scheduled next month, more than five years after the armed robbery.

Six weeks before his testimony in the Carbonell case, Preminger was called to testify about his representation of another former client, John Lott, who had been sentenced to 10 years in prison after a December 1982 jury conviction of third-degree murder.

The incident involved the January 1982 shooting death of Larry Foster outside the Wilson Park housing project in South Philadelphia. Foster's companions that night identified Lott as one of three men who approached them and, ultimately, shot Foster.

At the December 1982 trial, Preminger called five alibi witnesses to testify that Lott could not have committed the slaying because they were with him that night, first at an Amway demonstration and then at a birthday celebration.

After presenting that evidence, Preminger rested his case. Never called by Preminger was Vincent Croft, a companion of Foster's, who had testified at a pretrial hearing that he knew Lott's voice, and that while he did not see the face of the killer, the voice that he heard was not Lott's.

When Preminger elected to rest his case, court records show, prosecutor John DiDonato put onto the record his concern: "I'm trying to prevent at some future time the defendant coming back and saying, 'I really wanted Mr. Croft to testify but my lawyer didn't call him.' "

As a result of DiDonato's concern, Lott stated in open court that he agreed with Preminger's decision to rest the case. Common Pleas Court Judge Samuel Lehrer advised Preminger that he would issue a bench warrant, to help him force Croft to appear in court, if Preminger desired. The trial then was recessed for the weekend, and the following Monday the trial was concluded. Preminger did not call Croft as a witness.

Six months after the conviction, after Robert M. Lipshutz had replaced Preminger as Lott's attorney, Preminger took the witness stand. He testified that after the trial had recessed for the weekend, Lott had called him and said that DiDonato's comments had "made him consider the question of whether or not he wanted to put Mr. Croft on, and that he had decided that he wanted Mr. Croft to go on."

However, Preminger testified, he was unable to reach Croft to ask him to testify.

Asked why he had not obtained a bench warrant, Preminger responded, "The truth of it is, I really can't remember why."

After hearing the post-trial evidence, Lehrer refused to grant a new trial, noting that Croft's full testimony could have damaged, rather than helped, Lott's case.

"In sum," Lehrer wrote in his opinion, "the failure to request a bench warrant for Croft had a reasonable basis designed to effectuate Lott's interest."

DiDonato's warning at trial is a measure that Pennsylvania prosecutors are turning to increasingly. Suddenly, prosecutors say, they find themselves having to protect defendants' rights or risk new trials later.

"We see defense lawyers who are losing a case resort to making intentional errors," said Allegheny County prosecutor Colville. "I have instructed my prosecutors to make sure that defendants' rights are protected, and if they see such errors taking place, to call them to the attention of the trial judge."

ATTORNEYS ACCUSED OF FALSE TESTIMONY

In several cases, the Philadelphia district attorney's office has accused attorneys in court papers of falsely testifying in an effort to overturn verdicts.

One such instance was the case in which Reif testified that he "did a bad job" in representing McFadden on murder charges.

McFadden had been convicted in connection with a Feb. 25, 1970, bar fight, in which Sheldon Frankel was stabbed to death and Gary Burdick was stabbed in the chest.

Two weeks after the fight, McFadden surrendered to police, accompanied by Reif, who later testified that he was a friend of the McFadden family. Reif was present as McFadden was placed in two police lineups before five people, including Burdick, who were in the bar at the time of the fight.

Burdick was the only one at the lineup to pick McFadden out. Others who had been in the bar that night made no identifications. Based on Burdick's identification, McFadden was arrested and charged with murder, assault and battery, aggravated assault and related charges.

In March 1971, McFadden—represented by lawyer A. Charles Peruto Sr.—was convicted by a jury before then-Common Pleas Court Judge James T. McDermott of second-degree murder and related charges, after Burdick had testified as the key prosecution witness.

After the conviction, McFadden hired Reif to take the case from Peruto.

Reif convinced a three-judge panel including McDermott that the judge had erred at trial by failing to properly instruct the jury on the lesser charge of voluntary manslaughter. In September 1972, 2½ years after the incident, the three-judge panel awarded McFadden a new trial.

On June 18, 1973, Reif represented McFadden in a one-week jury trial before then-Common Pleas Court Judge Joseph McGlynn, with the prosecution again relying largely on the testimony of Burdick. In addition, at this trial, the prosecution presented the testimony of Patricia Stewart, a barmaid who identified McFadden and said she had been afraid to testify at the first trial.

Stewart had failed to identify McFadden in the lineup after his arrest, but she testified during the second trial that she had remained quiet because of fear.

Reif presented a defense of mistaken identification, and he presented a witness who contradicted portions of Stewart's testimony.

The jury again convicted McFadden of second-degree murder and related charges. Reif represented McFadden throughout his post-trial motions, his sentencing to nine to 27 years' imprisonment and his appeal to the state Supreme Court.

In May 1979, almost six years after the second trial, McFadden filed a petition contending that Reif had poorly represented him.

Defense attorney Robert Simone was appointed to represent Mc-Fadden on this claim, and on May 21, 1980—more than 10 years after Sheldon Frankel was stabbed to death—Simone called Reif as a witness before Judge Blake.

Under Simone's questioning, Reif testified that he had made a series of errors, for no tactical reason.

Reif testified that William T. Cannon, the assistant district attorney, had assured him during the trial that the witnesses who had been unable to identify McFadden at the lineup would be brought into court, and that as a result he had "made a superficial attempt only" to locate the witnesses on his own.

He said he had relied, instead, on the prosecutor's assurances that the other witnesses would be made available, and he said he "felt that we had been shafted, in plain language," by the assistant district attorney.

He testified that even though those witnesses were not made available, he had made no effort to seek a delay, to give him time to find them, nor to call the matter to the judge's attention. Asked why not, Reif replied:

"Because I felt that it would be useless for me to bring it to the attention of Judge McGlynn. I felt that I would probably be criticized by Judge McGlynn for relying on Mr. Cannon instead of doing my own work, and I felt at this point it would be useless to put it on the record. . . . Actually, it was something I should have done myself, so it taught me a lesson. Unfortunately it was an expensive lesson for Mr. McFadden."

Reif testified that he believed that the absent witnesses would have been important to his case because they had been unable to identify McFadden at the lineup.

Reif also testified that he had been so "shocked and outraged" by what he considered to be prosecutor Cannon's broken promise that, on the following day, he failed to seek a mistrial or object to a series of remarks made by Cannon during closing arguments that Reif considered improper. He testified that he had no tactical reason, such as fear of emphasizing the remarks to the jury, for sitting quietly:

"I take complete responsibility for it. I just did a bad job, something in retrospect, and when I reviewed the record and saw what Cannon said and my failure to object, it's obvious that I did a bad job. That's the only explanation I can give for not doing it. I certainly didn't have—my reason for not objecting was certainly not to benefit Mr. McFadden in any way."

After Reif testified, Cannon took the stand and denied Reif's allegations.

Then, after the trial, in legal papers filed with Blake, the district attorney's office contended that "Reif's confession of ineffectiveness is not credible. . . . Mr. Reif, long possessed with the addresses of the witnesses, now urges this Court to believe that these same people would have provided valuable, exculpatory evidence and that it was only through his own sloth and Mr. Cannon's purported deception that these alleged witnesses were not presented. This testimony by Mr. Reif cannot be credited."

On Sept. 17, 1982, Blake refused to grant a new trial, saying the only reason to believe that the witnesses would have helped McFadden was the "unsupported surmise of former counsel Reif."

The judge wrote that the "record does not support Reif's testimony that he was misled" and that "we simply cannot rely solely on defense counsel Reif's description of these incidents as the defendant would have us do."

In June 1984, Reif testified in another case before Blake that he had erred in his representation of another man. The district attorney's office challenged Reif's credibility. In a written argument, the prosecutors said Reif's "over-eagerness to allege his own ineffectiveness is apparent" and contended that the admission was based upon "collusion" among Reif, defendant John McManus and McManus' new attorney, Pamela Higgins.

McManus, who was convicted in March 1980 of eight counts of receiving stolen property, contended that Reif had failed him twice—first by not presenting an adequate defense, then by never asking Judge Porter to reconsider the stiff prison term of 42 months to eight years imposed months after the conviction.

Reif, in sworn testimony, agreed: He said that he had erred by never telling McManus about a phone call he had received from another client, Willaim Ward, who reported that many of the seized goods belonged to him. Nor did Reif produce Ward as a witness at McManus' trial.

Additionally, Reif never filed a motion to reconsider McManus' sentence, saying he had misunderstood state criminal rules requiring that such motions be filed within 10 days.

It wasn't until McManus lost two appeals that he hired a new attorney, Higgins, who challenged the adequacy of Reif's counsel.

In that effort, Higgins filed an affidavit, signed by Reif, laying out Reif's admission of errors. The essential argument was that Reif had a conflict of interest in the case that proved harmful to McManus. Reif also represented Ward, whose testimony might have helped McManus but might have incriminated himself.

Reif testified during a hearing in June 1984 that sometime in the spring of 1979, Ward called him from a New Jersey prison and "said that he wanted to come in and try to help John McManus, that he felt bad because of the fact if it wasn't for him, McManus would not have been arrested in this case and that many of the items that were taken and that John was charged with were items that he had brought into the house, that John had no way of knowing were stolen."

Reif, who testified that by the time of the telephone call he was representing Ward in connection with a separate credit-card-fraud case, also testified that he had advised Ward against admitting in court that McManus was being charged with Ward's crimes:

"I did not think it would help with John McManus, and all it would do, in my opinion, if he came in and testified in that fashion would cause him, William Ward, to be arrested for the same thing."

Asked whether he may have had a conflict of interest in representing both Ward and McManus, Reif testified: "I did not, in my own mind and based on my experience as a criminal lawyer, see the possibility of a conflict. If I had, there's no way I would have handled it."

The state Code of Professional Responsibility prohibits attorneys from representing two clients if his judgment in behalf of one is likely to harm the other. The only exception is if both clients, knowing the potential problems, agree to the multiple representation.

Reif stated during the hearing on the request for a retrial that he had never advised either client about the potential conflict of interest.

According to testimony, Ward was murdered in 1982, so his side was not told at that 1984 hearing.

In addition to the conflict argument, Higgins contended that Reif had failed to perform competently by not requesting that Porter reconsider McManus' sentence.

Reif testified that McManus had wanted him both to file an appeal to the Superior Court, which must be done within 30 days of sentencing, and to ask the judge to reduce the sentence, which must be done within 10 days of sentencing.

Reif never filed a motion to reduce the sentence.

He did file the appeal on time, but Reif said during the hearing that despite his extensive experience, he had not realized he could ask for a lighter sentence while the appeal was pending. He said he believed that the 10 days to seek reconsideration of sentence began after the appeal was resolved.

In legal papers filed with Judge Blake after the hearing, Assistant District Attorney Clifford Goldstein wrote: "In this case [the court] must be very hesitant to accept the testimony of Reif" about his conversation with Ward.

He further wrote that "it is ridiculous to believe that an attorney with [Reif's] experience . . . who has tried thousands of cases, and served as an Assistant District Attorney, could have simply not known as basic a rule as the rule on reconsideration of sentencing." Citing the affidavit that Higgins had taken from McManus, Goldstein also contended: "This case presents a classic example of collusion between the petitioner McManus, petitioner's new counsel, and trial counsel."

In a reply, Higgins denied any collusion, writing: "It is difficult to counter with restraint the baseless and reckless allegations of 'collusion' between present and past counsel for petitioner."

In January 1985, Blake issued an eight-page decision denying McManus' petition. He found that no conflict of interest had existed, since Reif was representing McManus and Ward on different cases.

Blake concluded also that Ward's testimony would not have helped McManus, and that Reif's strategy of not calling Ward as a witness was "very reasonable." Blake did not address the question of Reif's credibility.

LAWYER SAYS HE JUST 'FORGOT'

In November 1979, Davico Cabeza was convicted of first-degree murder for his role in the shooting death of bartender Helen Cook in the Pony Tail Bar in South Philadelphia. It was, by all accounts, an odd result, because the person accused of the actual shooting was tried separately and convicted only of voluntary manslaughter.

According to trial testimony, Cabeza guarded the door as Paulette Cabeza, his mother, drew a pistol inside the bar and aimed at a woman with whom she had been fighting. As Paulette Cabeza pulled the trigger, the woman fainted and the gun misfired. Paulette Cabeza pulled the trigger again. The bullet flew over the head of the unconscious woman, striking bartender Cook between the eyes. Both Cabezas were charged, and the younger Cabeza came to trial first.

Cabeza was found guilty of first-degree murder after a trial in which his attorney, Timothy Crawford Jr., presented a defense consisting of four character witnesses.

In post-trial arguments, Crawford contended that he had erred at trial. The trial judge, Common Pleas Court Judge John A. Geisz, refused to allow Crawford to raise that issue while he continued to represent Cabeza, and a new attorney, Ronald Merriweather, took over the case.

At a June 1980 hearing, Crawford testified that he was remiss in his defense because he "forgot" to call his client to the witness stand.

Cabeza was prepared to testify, and it was in his interest to testify, contended Crawford, who added that he realized his mistake only after the verdict had been announced and he was talking to a juror. The juror asked why he had not called Cabeza. "And then, that's when it came to my attention that I hadn't called the defendant to the stand," Crawford testified. He said there was no strategic reason for not calling Cabeza.

Assistant District Attorney Ronald Kovlar took the stand during the same hearing and challenged Crawford's testimony. Kovlar contended that Crawford had told him during the trial that he faced an ethical dilemma in whether to call his client, whose testimony would have implicated Paulette Cabeza. Later, upon hearing what he regarded as Crawford's contradicting himself, testified Kovlar, "I was taken aback, to say the least."

Geisz wrote in an August 1981 opinion: "The Trial Judge has been put in the unenviable position of determining the relative credibility of trial counsel. . . . After serious deliberation, the Trial Judge cannot escape the conclusion that defense counsel's statement that he 'forgot' to call the defendant lacks crediblity."

Geisz added, "The Trial Judge cannot believe that he not only 'forgot' to call the defendant but that the fact that he did not failed to dawn on him until one of the jurors questioned him about it. . . . The Trial Judge is forced to conclude that trial counsel testified that he 'forgot' to call his client for the sole purpose of obtaining a new trial for him. The Court cannot condone such a course of conduct."

Crawford, in a recent interview, said of the case: "It was a jury trial, and I was in shock at the result. The only reason that I did that [testifying that he had forgotten to call his client] was that I felt so bad about the result, and I saw this as the only way out."

Though there were tactical reasons not to call Cabeza, he said, "I got on the stand and tried to take the weight on me. But even then, the judge still wouldn't overturn it."

After denying the new trial, Geisz sentenced Cabeza to life in prison. Another lawyer, Norris Gelman, took over the case on appeal and persuaded the state Supreme Court to order a new trial for Cabeza, after finding that Geisz had allowed the prosecutor to ask improper questions of character witnesses.

After four years in jail, Cabeza was released in June 1984. He had agreed to plead guilty to voluntary manslaughter in return for a sentence amounting to the time he had already served.

A CLIENT IS GIVEN ADVICE TO LIE

Joshua Lofton was convicted at a 1978 non-jury trial before Common Pleas Court Judge Charles Lord on drug and conspiracy charges and was sentenced to five to 10 years in prison. After Lofton had exhausted his appeals, he hired lawyer Barry Denker to represent him in challenging the representation he had received at trial from Vincent Ziccardi.

Lofton contended that Ziccardi had improperly decided for Lofton that the case should be tried without a jury.

"He wanted a jury trial and wanted to protect all his rights," Ziccardi testified during a November 1981 hearing before Judge Blake. "I said to him, 'You know, if you go through a jury trial and get convicted, you're going to get substantial time.' " But, Ziccardi testified, he "basically guaranteed" Lofton that he would be put on probation if convicted at a non-jury trial.

Denker questioned Ziccardi about a colloquy that had taken place at the start of the trial. In that exchange, Lofton had assured Judge Lord that he had not been threatened or been given any promises in giving up his right to a jury trial.

"Did you advise him beforehand to say no?" asked Denker.

"Absolutely," said Ziccardi.

At the end of the hearing, Blake said to Ziccardi: "You're telling me that you advised your client to lie when he answered the question with respect to promises—is that what you are telling me?"

"Yes," responded Ziccardi.

"He was under oath?" asked Blake.

"I guess so," said Ziccardi.

In September 1982, Blake denied Lofton a new trial, ruling that "we have absolutely no doubt" that he had "knowingly and voluntarily" waived his right to a jury trial. Blake added that Ziccardi had "competently and effectively represented this defendant."

Nowhere in his opinion did he address Ziccardi's statement that he had counseled his client to lie. The disciplinary rules prohibit attorneys from counseling and assisting clients in fraudulent or illegal conduct.

Ziccardi, in a recent interview, called the case "a very bad deal, very, very bad." No one will waive a jury trial, or plead guilty, without a guarantee that it will help them, he said. But no judge will grant the waiver without first putting on the record the client's sworn statement that there has been no such guarantee.

"It is all part of the play," he said of the ritual colloquy. "The case isn't the witness. It isn't the jury. If you had to, you could even rent a defendant. The case is the two lawyers and the judge."

POINTING OUT ONE'S OWN ERRORS

Generally, the question of a trial lawyer's effectiveness is raised by a new attorney retained for the purpose. In fact, state Supreme Court decisions make clear that a defendant should not be expected to attack the effectiveness of his attorney until a new lawyer has been retained. Trial lawyers cannot be expected to argue their own ineffectiveness, the court says.

In some cases, however, trial attorneys have done precisely that. In such instances, the trial attorney, instead of testifying about his incompetence, merely alleges his failings in unsworn written or oral arguments. As a result, the prosecutors lack the opportunity to cross-examine the attorney making the claim.

In such cases examined by The Inquirer, appellate courts have regularly refused to grant new trials as long as the trial attorney continues to represent the client.

However, the Superior Court did award a new trial last year to Christina Lobel in a fraud case, even though she had the same lawyer, Robert Gabriel, both at her trial and on appeal.

Gabriel, because he still represented Lobel, could not be cross-examined about the error he said he had made during the trial. The Philadelphia district attorney's office has asked the state Supreme Court to review the case, saying the decision was "particularly repugnant" because Gabriel could not be questioned about his trial tactics.

In a more typical case, lawyer Darryl Irwin raised questions in post-trial arguments about his own representation after his client, Daniel Roy, had been convicted of third-degree murder. The charges involved the shooting of William "Reds" Johnson inside a South Philadelphia bar in February 1979. Roy contended during the trial that he had shot Johnson in self defense.

After the conviction, Irwin, a former prosecutor and an attorney since 1974, contended that the trial judge had failed to instruct the jury on the law of voluntary manslaughter—a crime that includes situations in which a defendant unreasonably believes he is justified in killing someone.

Irwin had never asked the judge for such an instruction; but in post-trial arguments, he contended that he should have, and that the judge also erred in not giving such instructions on his own.

During an October 1980 hearing on Roy's request for a new trial, Irwin told the trial judge he had "no shame in saying that I had made a mistake" by not asking for the instruction. "I say the court failed its obligation. I failed my obligation. But Mr. Roy should not have to sit in jail three years, 10 years, to wait for the Supreme Court to tell us what we all know is going to be told to us. . . . I am asking you, Judge, to be a special man, to say, 'I know I made a mistake. I know Mr. Irwin made a mistake.' "

The trial judge, Common Pleas Court Judge Joseph T. Murphy, refused to grant a new trial, stating in an August 1981 opinion that because Irwin "continues his stewardship on appeal, the issue of his ineffectiveness cannot be raised at this time."

Arthur James replaced Irwin as attorney and appealed to the Superior Court in Roy's behalf, again challenging Irwin's performance.

The challenge left the district attorney's office in the ironic position of vigorously supporting Irwin's original trial strategy. Prosecutors contended that seeking an instruction on voluntary manslaughter could have been "devastating" to Roy at trial, since Roy's whole defense was that the act was justified.

In their legal argument, the prosecutors wrote: "The fact that a defendant is fortunate enough to have a trial counsel who is willing to 'confess' to his incompetence is of no legal significance." To allow the defendant to win a new trial on that basis, they contended, "would impermissibly encourage and condone 'sandbagging' by defense counsel. . . . Equally important, it would make ineffective assistance of counsel 'the most effective representation of all.' Such manipulation of the criminal justice system cannot be tolerated."

In November 1983, the Superior Court rejected the appeal, saying that if Irwin had sought an instruction on voluntary manslaughter it "would have seriously detracted from the possibility of convincing the jury to acquit the defendant."

Similarly, after a jury convicted Wallace Feaster of third-degree murder, his defense attorney, Nino V. Tinari, one of the city's busiest lawyers, contended in post-trial motions that the judge, Common Pleas Court Judge Matthew W. Bullock Jr., had erred in not instructing the jury in the law concerning temporary insanity.

Tinari had never asked for such an instruction, and he wrote in arguments: "Defense counsel is also willing to admit his own mistake and allege his own ineffective assistance. The failure of defense counsel is inexcusable. However, the appellant should not be made to suffer for this oversight."

Feaster, 69, had shot Roosevelt Davis, also 69, five times in the back on a South Philadelphia street after an argument over a numbers bet that Davis had won, according to trial testimony.

On Jan. 30, 1979, Bullock rejected a request for a new trial. He said that because Tinari was arguing his own ineffectiveness, "we have only trial counsel's 'second-guessing' his trial performance, as it were." The judge noted that Tinari had many years' experience trying criminal cases and wrote, "We have no reason to assume that through ignorance or inadvertence, he simply overlooked the possibility or desirability of pleading insanity as a defense. Defense counsel may well have concluded that it would hurt his client rather than help him" to have such an instruction given.

The case went to the state Supreme Court, which also denied the appeal.

CONCERN FROM STATE'S TOP COURT

Recent decisions by the state Supreme Court offer the first instances in which justices are expressing concern about the possibility of defense attorneys' helping their former clients by testifying to their own incompetence.

One such case involved the conviction of Gerard Paul McKenna, who was sentenced to death in 1974 for the rape and murder of a 16-year-old girl in Bradford County.

During a post-conviction hearing, McKenna's trial counsel, Thomas Walrath, testified that he believed during the trial that Bradford County President Judge Evan S. Williams had erred, and that a new trial would be granted on appeal. As a result, Walrath testified, he had not bothered to present witnesses who he contended could have helped McKenna's case.

"I just didn't want to waste any more time," he testified. "I felt that the trial was a complete waste of time."

After reviewing that testimony, state Supreme Court Justice John P. Flaherty wrote in January 1982, in behalf of a unanimous court, that McKenna was entitled to a new trial because "counsel provided ineffective representation by, in effect, taking it upon himself to terminate the trial" without calling witnesses.

Flaherty added that the court "is astonished at the method employed by counsel in this case, so much so, that we are submitting the record to the Disciplinary Board."

Within a month, McKenna filed a petition with the trial court, asking that Walrath—the lawyer who had just been found ineffective —be appointed to represent him in his retrial.

That petition was sent to the state Supreme Court by special prosecutor Arthur Shuman, who asked the court to reconsider its earlier opinion.

On June 30, 1982, in an extraordinary move, the court reversed itself by a 4-3 vote.

The new opinion was written by Justice James T. McDermott, who now described Walrath's testimony during the hearing for a new trial as "synthetic," "artificial" and "self-serving."

Although McDermott did not say what had made the court change its opinion, he wrote that the evidence contradicted Walrath's contention that he had failed to offer evidence helpful to McKenna. Citing Walrath's testimony, he added, "We shall refrain from comment, for the purposes here, upon such unprofessional conduct, as there is no merit" to McKenna's contentions.

There is no record of the Disciplinary Board's acting on the matter.

In April 1984, the Supreme Court was reviewing the death sentence of Richard Stoyko of Fayette County, who had been convicted of murdering Shelby Jean Storm and Joseph Glad in 1980. Under state law, the Supreme Court reviews all death penalties, and if any error is found to have occurred during sentencing, a defendant automatically is sentenced to life imprisonment.

The court, in deciding that case, noted that unless it carefully reviewed claims of ineffectiveness by the trial attorneys during such proceedings, "we could invite a Catch-22 situation. . . . A zealous, but misguided, defense counsel might be tempted, at this point, to 'throw the case,' " to ensure that a death sentence could be overturned.

"Accordingly, this court will scrutinize the record for bogus 'ineffectiveness' claims and should not hesitate, if the facts and inferences so warrant, to refer the matter to the Disciplinary Board."

HOW POLITICAL INTERESTS STAND IN THE WAY OF CHANGE

FRIDAY, JANUARY 31, 1986

BY H. G. BISSINGER
AND DANIEL R. BIDDLE

To keep politics from dominating the courts, 22 states have panels to screen judicial candidates for experience, skill and integrity, and try to select only the best.

Pennsylvania doesn't.

Thirteen other states pick judges in nonpartisan elections.

Pennsylvania doesn't.

Several big-city court systems have tough rules to curtail personal and political ties between judges and the lawyers who have cases in front of them.

Philadelphia doesn't.

Many city courts have sharp limits on nepotism and political patronage.

On Philadelphia's court payrolls, it sometimes seems as if nepotism and patronage *are* the rule.

With some exceptions, changes that work well in other court systems have not been tried here.

Why?

Generation after generation of judges, lawyers and public-interest groups have complained of slack ethical standards and the ever-present drag of political influence on Philadelphia's Common Pleas and Municipal Courts—indeed, on the state's entire court system. But the problems outlast the critics.

"Our experience," says Bennett G. Picker, Philadelphia Bar Association chancellor and an advocate of change, "has been very frustrating."

Judge William M. Marutani, a firm believer in tough ethical standards, says after 10 years on the Common Pleas Court bench: "I've pushed for a lot of things. Pretty soon, you stop pushing."

The system does have its supporters, who say that partisan election of judges is a good thing, and that it is unrealistic to expect a court system as big as Philadelphia's—120 judges and 2,441 employees handling tens of thousands of cases a year—to exist without some problems here and there.

Those supporters include some of the city's best-known politicians and labor leaders, and some judges.

Patrick B. Gillespie, business manager of the 14-union, 60,000-member Building Trades Council of Philadelphia, says, "Don't take the right to vote away from the people." The council puts its money where its mouth is: Along with the Teamsters, building-trades unions rank among the biggest donors to judges' campaigns here.

"There may every now and then be a bad apple that gets elected," says Gillespie. "But they should not throw the baby out with the bath water."

James J. Tayoun, Ward 1 Democratic leader and former city councilman, goes even further, saying, "The overwhelming majority of the judges have acquitted themselves extremely well. . . . I find them all to be totally conscientious and sensitive."

State Sen. Vincent J. Fumo (D., Phila.) says of the court system here: "It's running pretty good. . . . It has its problems, as does any other political entity."

Yet a broad range of individuals—from Chief Public Defender Benjamin Lerner to former District Attorney Edward G. Rendell, from veteran plaintiff lawyer Marshall Bernstein to judges such as Marutani —see it differently.

They say that the court system too often fails to project an image of integrity, impartiality and competence, and that the failures are deeply rooted in how the city chooses its judges. The basic problem, they say, is that Fumo is right: The courts here are a political entity.

For decades, they say, the parties have endorsed and elected judges more for their party loyalty than for their competence or integrity, enabling them to decide between plaintiff and defendant, incarceration and freedom, innocence and guilt.

Politicians—ward leaders, party chiefs, City Council members, state legislators—also hold considerable sway in hiring many of the courts' employees. And worst of all, say Marutani and many others, some politicians seek favors from judges in court cases.

"As long as you have the political process of picking judges, there's no way you're going to have people who are completely free of political pressures," says Marutani. "All of us are subject to the political barons. . . . This system does require a major overhaul."

Says Chief Public Defender Lerner: "The problems are so ingrained in the political process that speaking out . . . even if you're head of the bar association, speaking out if you're a powerful district attorney, speaking out if you're writing editorials . . . makes no difference whatsoever. . . .

"There's a relatively small handful of people in the commonwealth who presently wield the political power needed to make the kind of basic decisions necessary. And those people are not interested in making those changes, because it would dilute their own power.

"We're talking about the governor, leaders of the state legislature. We're talking about the leaders of both political parties in this city."

Lerner's view of the court system is shared by many of the city's prosecutors. One well-known prosecutor, former Deputy District Attorney Eric B. Henson, says, "In many ways, Philadelphia has the judiciary it wants."

If lawyers seem to do better in court after donating to judges' campaigns, Henson reasons, those lawyers' clients probably don't object. If a private conversation with the judge seems to help the case— or if a ward leader offers to call the judge for a favor—the client isn't likely to care about the impropriety of what lawyers call "ex parte" contact.

"The reason there isn't change is because enough people are satisfied that they can do as well in the system . . . through inappropriate behavior," Henson said. "Enough of them that there's not an outcry. Somebody or other benefits from the manner in which the courts' business is conducted."

Those familiar with problems of big-city courts here and elsewhere offer a number of fundamental proposals to improve the court system:

• Screen and appoint judges. Under this so-called merit selection system, used in varying degrees in 22 states, a politically balanced nominating panel that includes lawyers and lay people screens potential judges. A list of the best-qualified is sent to the governor, who chooses one. Judges later run in retention elections on a yes-no basis.

• Have a meaner watchdog. Some lawyers and judges say the state agency that monitors judges' conduct, the Judicial Inquiry and Review Board, needs to be more visible and less dominated by judges. As it is, most of the board's work is secret; the board may charge a judge with grave misconduct and not announce it for months. Five of the nine review-board seats automatically go to judges; on similar boards in most other states, non-judges are the majority.

• Ban or limit contributions by lawyers to judges' campaigns. If contributions are permitted, there should be rules to curb the appearance of impropriety, critics say. For example, if a case involved a lawyer who helped the judge's campaign, the judge would be required to disclose the campaign tie in court before hearing the case.

• Impose tougher restrictions on private communications between judges and lawyers for only one side in pending cases. Though such communication is illegal when it concerns the merits of a case, many judges and lawyers say that such ex parte contact occurs regularly. Pennsylvania's rule is less strict than the American Bar Association's model canon, which many states have adopted: "A judge should . . . neither initiate nor consider ex parte or other communications concerning a pending or impending proceeding."

• Adopt rules to discourage defense lawyers from pleading their own incompetence to get convictions reversed. Experts suggest the creation of a central registry to report each time a criminal lawyer makes such a plea. Experts also say the state's lawyer disciplinary mechanism doesn't deal with such cases, and that even if it did, it would be understaffed to deal with the volume.

• Require more disclosure of judges' finances. Though Pennsylvania judges do file disclosure forms, they aren't required to include much detail. The forms are filed in a place most citizens have never heard of: the Administrative Office of Pennsylvania Courts. Critics say the disclosures should be much more thorough and should be readily available in Common Pleas Court—as a guard against conflicts of interest in court cases.

• Hire only on merit. As it is, nepotism and patronage in court hiring are rampant; at least 30 of the 120 judges in Municipal and Common Pleas Courts have a relative on the court payroll. Some critics suggest a civil-service system for court employees. Others say Philadelphia could adopt the rule that exists in most other states: Avoid nepotism in hiring.

• Have a more independent president judge. Judges and lawyers say that the president judges of both Municipal and Common Pleas Courts are hamstrung as administrators because they must seek their colleagues' votes for re-election. Some critics suggest the job should be for one term only. Others say an independent authority, such as the chief justice of the state Supreme Court, should appoint the president judges.

• Increase judges' salaries. Many lawyers say that the best people in their profession don't consider becoming a judge in Philadelphia because the job doesn't pay enough. Common Pleas Court judges earn $65,000, Municipal Court judges $63,000. With those rates, says Bruce Franzel, chairman of the bar association's judicial selection committee, the image of Philadelphia judges is "not sufficiently glowing" to attract the best lawyers.

THE ELECTION OF JUDGES

There are differences of opinion regarding many of the proposals for change, but on one point people such as Lerner, Picker, Franzel and Rendell agree: Philadelphia needs a better way to choose its judges.

Bar chancellor Picker put it this way:

"We potentially compromise the integrity—and we absolutely compromise the appearance of independence—of our court system by having our judges go through the election process. And specifically, the problem arises with judges and judge candidates campaigning among lawyers who may appear before some of these judges at a later date."

Choosing his words with care, Picker said that elections also failed to produce the best judges. "The present system is not one which is designed to bring to the court judges who are of high quality—although many are—or who are independent," he said.

Says Public Defender Lerner: "We do have some good judges. . . . But under the system we have, it's more an accident than anything else."

Says Marshall Bernstein, a plaintiff lawyer who has tried cases here for 35 years: "I would say that because the political process is so deeply into the selection of judges, the quality of judges leaves something to be desired."

Says Rendell: "If a genie woke me up in the middle of the night and said, 'Mr. Rendell you have one wish to [use to] clean up the judicial system in Philadelphia,' I'd clearly spend the wish on merit selection of judges. Then I'd go back to bed. I think until merit selection is in place, we will never totally cure the problems of the Philadelphia judicial system."

Even Edward J. Bradley, president judge of Common Pleas Court since 1975, praises the status quo with a faint damn. "I believe we have a good corps of judges," Bradley says. "I think the system of selecting them could damn well be improved."

Although two previous campaigns to adopt a merit-type system of choosing the state's appellate judges have failed, Picker and others still are optimistic on that point. But they say merit selection for the city's judges faces a much tougher battle.

Short of changing the method of choosing judges in the state, Bernstein says one simple step would help improve the existing process:

"Prohibit lawyers from contributing to the campaigns of judges."

Judge Marutani agrees, saying that such a ban also would eliminate what he called the *terrorum* effect on lawyers who felt they had to donate, or else face the judge's wrath in court. *Terrorum* is Latin for terror.

Cleveland's bar association has confronted the problem by urging all judicial candidates to pledge not to seek or accept donations larger than $50 from individual lawyers. Members of law firms can give $50 each—but with a ceiling of $500 per judge for the firm.

There is a built-in incentive for candidates who make the pledge and then get approved by a bar screening panel: The bar endorses and advertises them as a slate. Tom Brady, the association's executive director, says roughly 90 percent of judicial candidates make the pledge.

The Philadelphia Bar Association experimented with a similar rule last year but applied it only to incumbent judges rated as qualified by the association's screening panel.

CONTROLLING PRIVATE CONTACTS

As Rendell points out, the ex parte problem—judges having private contact with lawyers or others interested in court cases—is perhaps the hardest to control. "There are so many judges and so many ways to have ex parte contact," he said. Some lawyers and judges say that Rendell's own prosecutors have not been faultless on this issue.

In Chicago, after the FBI's Greylord investigations produced federal corruption indictments of nine judges and 22 lawyers, a new rule was adopted last year. It gives lawyers 48 hours to report, in court or in letters to all parties, any private contact with the judge in a pending case. Failure to report can result in disciplinary charges.

Lawyer Jerold S. Solovy, chairman of the commission that wrote the rule, says he does not want to hear about how some private communications with the judge might be too petty to report. "Look," Solovy says, "ex parte communication is the first step in corruption. You cannot corrupt a judge if you can't talk to him."

Solovy acknowledges that enforcement of the new rule will depend largely on lawyers' honesty. He is mindful of the common wisdom: "You always hear the cry, in a big-city court system, that the system cannot go on without ex parte communication." He says that if lawyers think that way, they should imagine themselves in a case in which they learned the other side's lawyer had spoken privately with the judge. "You'd be apoplectic," he said. "And rightly so."

"When a judge does something he knows, or ought to know, is clearly illegal . . . nothing happens to that judge," says Public Defender Lerner, whose office represents the vast majority of defendants in criminal cases here. "The judicial inquiry and review system here is a joke."

Here, again, top prosecutors share Lerner's view. Rendell said his office got "almost uniformly unsatisfactory results" when it complained about judges to the review board.

Part of the problem is secrecy: It is almost impossible to find out whether the review board thoroughly investigates complaints against judges here. Under rules laid out in the state constitution, the review board carries out nearly all of its work behind closed doors.

Investigations, formal charges against judges and hearings on those charges are confidential. Cases against judges become public only if the board asks the state Supreme Court to censure, suspend or remove a miscreant judge. And that happens rarely.

Richard E. McDevitt, the review board's executive director since its inception in 1969, countered, "We have looked into every complaint." He added a complaint of his own: Rendell's office often contacted the review board about judges' conduct but failed to follow up with written complaints, as required by review-board rules.

While agreeing that more public information about review-board cases could work as a deterrent to judicial misconduct, McDevitt maintains that the secrecy rule has its value: When the board privately tells judges to stop misbehaving, those judges often comply, rather than risk having their cases go public in the state Supreme Court.

Another problem, in the eyes of critics, is the review board's composition: five judges, two lawyers and two non-lawyers. According to the nonprofit American Judicature Society's 1980 survey, Pennsylvania is one of only 13 states in which judges are a majority on the board that polices judges.

In the last decade, the board has called for the censure of two Philadelphia judges. One of them, Common Pleas Court Judge Bernard Snyder, was defeated by the voters last November before the state Supreme Court could rule on the review board's recommendation to remove Snyder because of his alleged contacts with the winning side's attorney in a lawsuit.

In 1981, Municipal Court Judge Mitchell S. Lipschutz was publicly censured for what the high court called "arrogant, rude, ill-tempered and demeaning conduct" in jailing a public defender and a prosecutor. Among other things, Lipschutz said he had been angered by the public defender's refusal to tell him what she had said to a client and the prosecutor's failure to produce a witness on time.

The Democratic Party slated Lipschutz last year for a Common Pleas Court judgeship, despite the 1981 censure—and despite a "not-qualified" rating from the Philadelphia Bar Association committee that screens and rates judicial candidates. Lipschutz won. He was sworn in Jan. 3.

AN AGREEMENT THAT WAS BROKEN

To those who criticize the judicial election system, the slating of Mitchell Lipschutz represented the most telling evidence of just how little the political parties care about the quality of the court.

Both parties had agreed in advance to slate only judicial candidates given a "qualified" rating by the bar association's selection commission.

"We look forward to continue our cooperative efforts in providing the citizens of Philadelphia with the best possible candidates for judicial office," bar commission chairman Bruce Franzel wrote to Democratic city chairman Joseph F. Smith last Feb. 1.

But even as the commission was concluding that Lipschutz was "not qualified," the Democratic city committee was endorsing him. That meant most, if not all, party ward leaders would feature Lipschutz on the sample ballots passed out to voters in the spring primary, virtually assuring his nomination to Common Pleas Court. Bar association executive director Kenneth Shear wrote to Smith on March 6 urging the party to "immediately rescind its endorsement of Judge Lipschutz."

Smith never responded.

Several attempts to interview Smith about the incident have been unsuccessful.

Ian Lennox, head of the Citizens Crime Commission and a member of Franzel's panel, said that the incident showed that the city's majority party leadership wasn't really serious about choosing good judges. The Lipschutz endorsement, Lennox said, "throws the lie at all they've been saying."

Why, then, did the Democratic leadership back Lipschutz?

Part of it was his reputation as "a compassionate guy, an understanding judge," said labor leader Gillespie, who serves on the party's policy committee. Then there was "his track record in the political field. He paid his dues in the vineyard prior to becoming a judge." Most of the 69 Democratic ward leaders backed Lipschutz, Gillespie said, because "he was a sensitive person towards the Democratic Party, and the committee people and the like."

Ward 27 Democratic leader Kevin Vaughan—who opposed slating Lipschutz—said that other ward leaders had pressed him to change his mind because the judge was "responsive to the needs of ward leaders."

Lipschutz, in the recent telephone interview, said that he had never done anything improper at the suggestion of a ward leader or other politician. He said he sometimes found party officials' calls about consitituents to be useful in making such routine decisions as setting bail. Lipschutz said such calls are "not the same as, 'Hey, pal, do me a favor.' "

SELECTING PRESIDENT JUDGES

Although they differ over how to change it, many of the judges and court observers interviewed criticized the method of picking president judges for Common Pleas and Municipal Court. Each court's active judges meet once every five years and vote for the so-called PJ.

That, critics say, puts the president judge in no position to make his colleagues more accountable. Some would empower the chief justice of the state Supreme Court to appoint president judges; others say the job should be elected—but for one term only.

Speaking privately, many judges feel that Common Pleas Court President Judge Bradley is looking for votes when he hires judges' relatives for court jobs, or passes out choice assignments.

Bradley concedes that "it might not be a bad idea" for president judges to serve just one term. But he denies using his appointment power to win votes. "If you're going to do that," he says, "you might as well chuck it in."

Likewise, Municipal Court President Judge Joseph R. Glancey sees no problem in having to seek his colleagues' votes. He argues that the main burden of disciplining judges should reside elsewhere: "They've got to have a good Judicial Inquiry and Review Board—with muscle."

MISSOURI PLAN: IS IT FAIR?

Many Democratic Party leaders say they don't believe that merit selection of judges would give fair treatment to minorities, women or labor, or to lawyers who don't come from big law firms with giant corporate clients. They say the very words "merit selection" are a euphemism for removing judicial selection from the voters and giving it to an elite few.

Adopted first by Missouri in 1934, the screening-and-appointment method became known as "the Missouri plan" and has long been suspected by its critics as the thinly-gloved hand of the upper classes and their WASP-dominated law firms seeking to wrest control of the courts away from less-powerful groups: white ethnics, nonwhites, organized labor and Democrats.

In 1948, a Missouri judge, James G. Wallace, wrote a song:

Oh, the Old Missouri Plan,
Oh, the Old Missouri Plan,
When Wall Street lawyers all judicial candidates will scan
If you're not from Fair Old Harvard
They will toss you in the can,
And they'll hand the buns
To their younger sons
On the Old Missouri Plan
Oh, the Old Missouri Plan,
Oh, the Old Missouri Plan,
It won't be served with sauerkraut nor sauce Italian
There'll be no corned beef and cabbage,
And spaghetti they will ban,
There'll be no such dish
As gefilte fish
On the Old Missouri Plan.

A study published earlier this month actually suggests that non-whites and women have been better served by the merit selection system. M. L. Henry, director of New York's nonprofit Fund for Modern Courts, says his two-year study covered virtually every judgeship in the country and found that about 17 percent of merit-selected judges have been women or minorities, while the comparable figure for elected judges is about 11 percent.

STEPPING IN FOR A CONSTITUENT

What advantages do some Philadelphia politicians get from a politically elected judiciary? The critics offer several: frequent hiring of patronage employees on the courts' $55 million payroll; lobbying the Board of Judges (which consists of all 81 Common Pleas Court judges) to support the parties' hand-picked choices for various city commissions such as the Board of Revision of Taxes that are filled by a vote of the judges; and above all, access to judges on constituents' court cases.

Few of the politicians interviewed for these articles acknowledged having contacted judges about court cases. City Controller Joseph C. Vignola, Democratic leader of Ward 2 in South Philadelphia since 1978, was an exception.

A ward's committee people, Vignola said, believe that when someone gets arrested, ward leaders "can go to the judge and say, 'There's a neighborhood connection here' "—in other words, a family or community tie that would make the defendant a better bail risk, or someone who deserves less jail time.

Vignola estimated that before he became city controller in 1983, he made an average of one call per month to judges about setting bail for criminal defendants. He said he has also written to judges asking for leniency at sentencings. He said he always asked judges to put his letters in the court record.

"The way I used to do it, I would call up the judge. . . . I would say, 'Judge, hi, this is Joe Vignola.' I would say that 'John Livingston is scheduled to be arraigned in front of you. I don't know what the charges are; I don't care. I just want you to know that his mother called me, and, you know, is concerned about his spending time in jail prior to trial, and that she lives in my community and she'd hope that you would consider that in setting bail."

"You have to remember," Vignola said in a telephone interview, "as long as you're not trying to influence the outcome of a case, there is nothing illegal about expressing an interest in a defendant."

While saying he had never tried to lobby a judge about a case's actual outcome, Vignola estimated that 10 percent to 12 percent of the city's ward leaders and local elected officials would seek favors on case outcomes.

Who seeks such favors? "I would say the older style of politician," said Vignola, "whether that person is an elected official or a political party official."

Politicians' favor-seeking, says Common Pleas Court Judge Leon Katz, taints even those judges who *never* take a politician's wishes into account on a case.

"What's nefarious about this is, if somebody calls you, let's say, about a resident that's arrested for a fight . . . and it turns out that the defendant is not guilty," then, even if the judge decides the case honestly, Katz says, "the committeeman is going to brag all over the place that he's 'got' the judge."

Clearly, many judges refuse to let such calls enter their thinking on cases. Those interviewed spoke again and again of judges who, early in their terms on the bench, hung up the phone, cut off the conversation or otherwise made it clear that they were unapproachable.

But even when a judge wants to keep such elements out of the court, it may be impossible.

Shortly after Carolyn Temin became a Common Pleas Court judge in January 1984, the calls started coming in to her office from politicians. The first two were handled by people in her office. But the third came late one night when everyone else in the office had left.

"It was someone I knew," she recounted in an interview. "What was said could have been construed as someone trying to fix a case." Temin said she stopped the conversation as quickly as she could. But the damage had been done. Outraged by the call and afraid she might take out her anger on the defendant, she recused herself from the case.

"You don't become a judge without becoming aware this might happen," she said.

When Common Pleas Court Judge Harry A. Takiff learned how some politicians seek favors from judges, it was by accident.

Once, Takiff recalled in a 1984 interview, he was sitting in for another judge—he declined to say which one—when a ward leader or ward committee chairman called about a criminal case due to be heard that day.

Mistaking Takiff for the judge normally in that courtroom, the caller said in matter-of-fact tones that he would like the judge to favor the defendant. The case involved a question of probation or parole for a man already convicted of a crime, Takiff recalled.

After the caller had spoken for a moment, the judge said: "This is Harry Takiff."

The caller hung up.

Takiff, who is now a senior judge and became court administrator under Bradley in 1984, reflected later: "Does it happen? Obviously it does. I was witness to it."

"How frequently? I can't begin to say. It could have been a totally isolated, never-to-be-repeated experience. It could have been commonplace.

"I was taken aback. I thought, 'Maybe this is the real world.' "

Sometimes a politician's private calls to a judge show up in the public record of a criminal case.

On June 2, 1983, Common Pleas Court Judge Lisa A. Richette was deciding whether to jail a woman named Millicent Curry for violating probation. She had previously given Curry 10 years' probation for her role as an accomplice in a holdup. Now, Curry had been caught using a stolen credit card to buy a diamond ring and had pleaded guilty to forgery.

It happened that Curry also did volunteer work in the office of then-City Councilman James J. Tayoun.

"Millicent thinks she has Councilman Tayoun on her side," Richette said in court. "I'm tired of the phone calls. I want you to know he can't influence me one bit. I resent it. . . . He's been calling me for days on this. I told him to come up to the courtroom and put it on the record." She said Tayoun later did place a letter in the court record.

In a telephone interview, Tayoun said that he could not remember exactly what had happened in Curry's case, but that if he had called Richette more than once, it was only to leave messages until he could speak with the judge directly.

Tayoun said he had made many similar calls to judges throughout the city's courts. "I might not call for six months; I might call twice in a week." In 99 percent of his calls, he said, he offered to testify as a character witness—although he said he actually testified in only about a third of the cases. He said he was selective. "I wouldn't go to bat for a murderer or a rapist or something like that," Tayoun said.

At Millicent Curry's hearing, Richette said Tayoun had complied with her wish by putting a letter in the court record.

Richette said Curry's temporary job with Tayoun, plus her expectation of getting a full-time housekeeping job, showed "a good attitude." That, she said, was why Curry deserved to stay on probation.

• • •

In one area, prosecutors and many defense attorneys say the current rules don't need changing—just better enforcement. These lawyers say the state board that polices lawyers should take action against defense attorneys who testify that because of errors they have committed that violate disciplinary rules, their former clients deserve new trials.

In many cases, as The Inquirer reported yesterday, prosecutors say the defense lawyers falsely testify to improperly representing clients in an effort to help those clients win new trials.

But state Disciplinary Board officials say they often are not told of such instances. Many prosecutors contend that it would appear vindictive for them to report the lawyers, and that such responsibility rests with judges. And some judges contend that their role is that of neutral arbiter, making it inappropriate to make such referrals.

Chief Public Defender Lerner, among others, contended that too many judges are willing to protect lawyers from discipline, in part because they rely upon attorneys for campaign support. And, he said, prosecutors are reluctant to report such instances because they "don't want to make judges angry."

Staff members of the President's Commission on Organized Crime have suggested as a remedy that each state establish a central register, where all such admissions would be recorded. The bar would be required to investigate and discipline lawyers who make such claims.

While defense attorneys contend such instances are rare, Second U.S. Circuit Court of Appeals Judge Irving R. Kaufman has said that whatever the number, the bar must respond.

As Judge Bradley, an accomplished distance runner, has often said, changing the judicial selection system is "not a race for the short-winded."

No one disagrees. Judicial elections are mandated by the state constitution, and the only way to amend it is the long way. Two consecutive sessions of the General Assembly (the sessions are two years apiece) must approve any proposed amendment. Then a statewide referendum gives Pennsylvania's voters a chance to ratify the amendment or kill it. In the best circumstances, says the bar's Picker, the soonest all this could happen would be 1988.

Likewise, any bid to change the judicial review board's judge-dominated, secrecy-bound style of policing the judiciary would move at the same sluggish pace. The review board's composition and rules are all written into the state constitution.

So it is not surprising that many of those who discuss changes in the court talk not of years, but of *decades*.

In his last month as district attorney, Rendell was asked to predict when the city and the state might abandon political elections of judges.

"It won't be an easy fight, but I think it's a winnable fight," Rendell answered, sounding full of hope and conviction. "It can happen before the century's over."

FOUR

BLOOM COUNTY

1987 WINNER IN THE EDITORIAL CARTOONING CATEGORY

"For a distinguished example of a cartoonist's work, the determining qualities being that a cartoon shall embody an idea made clearly apparent, shall show good drawing and striking pictorial effect, and shall be intended to be helpful to some commendable cause of public importance . . ."

The Washington Post
Berke Breathed

Berke Breathed's comic strip is required reading for power brokers as well as for those who are just plain broke. His characters pack a punch, albeit a gentle one and always with a dose of humor to make the message sink in.

Since Berke Breathed's comic strip "Bloom County" was first offered in syndication on December 8, 1980, it has combined humor and satire in novel ways. President Reagan's foreign policy is symbolized as a confused "basselope" stranded on a fence. The hypocrisy of the the corporate drug hysteria is illustrated by marching out the chief executive officer of Bloom County Enterprises for a lecture.

Such is the oblique and subtle manner by which Berke approaches editorial commentary on the comic pages.

The key to outstanding comic strips is in the writing. Berke makes every word count, and has an unusual understanding of the rhythm and pungency of language. "Bloom County" has become the major new comic strip of relevance in this decade.

Berke's work is both distinguished and accessible. It has brought readers of all ages and persuasions closer to the cutting edge of social and political issues, and all with good humor.

"Bloom County" lies somewhere between a comic strip and political cartoon. Opus, the opinionated and adorable penguin who delves into political issues, leads the list of unique characters. Others include Milo, who alternately runs the local newspaper, conducts political campaigns and otherwise stirs things up; Steve Dallas, a self-absorbed and rumpled lawyer; Binkley, the intellectual who is tormented by characters from the Binkley Closet of Anxieties; Bill the Cat, who has been a vice presidential candidate, a rock star and a hostage in a New York City cab; and Oliver Wendell Jones, a computer whiz kid.

"What I like to think," Berke says, "is that with the help of metaphor and allegory, my editorializing is slipped under the reader's door, so to speak, rather than thrown briskly upon his face."

—Washington Post Writers Group

The Washington Post

THE COMICS

BLOOM COUNTY / By Berke Breathed

The Washington Post

THE COMICS

BLOOM COUNTY / By Berke Breathed

GOOD MORNING,
LADIES AND
GENTLEMEN...
W.A. THORNHUMP III HERE...
CHAIRMAN OF THE BOARD,
"BLOOM COUNTY
FEATURES, INC..."

...NAMELY, MANDATORY DRUG
TESTING. YES, WE WANT TO
KNOW EXACTLY WHAT POISONS
OUR EMPLOYEES HAVE
PUT IN THEIR BODIES.
THE LATEST LAB
RESULTS ARE AS
FOLLOWS...

DRUGS, LADIES AND
GENTLEMEN...DRUGS. THEY'RE
DESTROYING THIS NATION.
BUT THEY WON'T INFECT
THIS COMPANY...
AND WE HERE IN
UPPER MANAGE-
MENT HAVE
TAKEN DIRECT
ACTION TO
INSURE JUST
THAT...

5-11

1986, Washington Post Writers Group

MILO BLOOM...actor:
(tests indicate re-
cent ingestion of...)
• One avocado bagel.
• 23 potato chips.
• 16 ounces "Squirt."

Verdict: DRUG FREE

OPUS...actor:
• One herring wiener.
• "V-8 tomato juice."
• Nine ounces squid
  pâté.
• 73 Hostess Ding
  Dongs

Verdict: DRUG FREE

Steve Dallas...actor:
• Four mustard
  Whoppers.
• Two Pepsis.
• 3 ounces cashews.
• Six "Magic hair
  growth" tablets.

Verdict: DRUG FREE

YES, WE'RE THE NATION'S
TOP CORPORATE EXECUTIVES:
THE VALIANT
FRONTLINE IN
THE BATTLE
FOR A PURER
AMERICA!

YOUR SIX-
MARTINI
LUNCH,
SIR.

BILL THE CAT...actor:
• "Tender Vittles".
• Two fish heads.
• 139 ounces Brazilian
  cocaine.

Verdict: DRUG
ADDICT. BUT NOT
EXPENDABLE. PROBA-
TION RECOMMENDED.

BERKELEY BREATHED
staff artist/writer:
• Two tacos.
• A small root beer.
• One marijuana
  brownie eaten six
  years ago.

Verdict: DRUG
ADDICT. RECOMMEND
EXECUTION.

AND IN THE INTEREST
OF BASIC FAIRNESS, WE
IN UPPER MANAGEMENT
WERE TESTED AS
WELL. AND AS
YOU CAN SEE,
WE HAD NOTHING
TO HIDE...

W.A. THORNHUMP III
Chief executive:
• One breakfast Bloody
  Mary.
• Two whiskey sours.
• One bottle Château '63
• After-dinner cognac.
• One brandy nightcap.

Verdict: DRUG FREE.

BERKE

The Washington Post

THE COMICS

BLOOM COUNTY / By Berke Breathed

The Washington Post

THE COMICS

BLOOM COUNTY / By Berke Breathed

The Washington Post

THE COMICS

BLOOM COUNTY / By Berke Breathed

The Washington Post

THE COMICS

BLOOM COUNTY / By Berke Breathed

ROSEBUD WAS HAVING ONE OF THOSE DAYS.. IN AN UNEXPLAINED FIT OF OPTIMISM, HE TRIED A LEAP OVER THE FENCE ON HOOPER'S RIDGE.. MILO FOUND HIM SOME HOURS LATER.

WHAT HAPPENED?

I'M HAVING ONE OF THOSE DAYS.

WORD SPREAD QUICKLY AND A CRISIS-MANAGEMENT TEAM WAS DISPATCHED...

WE NEED A CRANE.

LET'S BLAST 'IM OFFA THERE!!

LET'S NOT PANIC, GENTLEMEN.

CRISIS CONTROL

1986, Washington Post Writers Group

12-14

THINGS WERE TRIED...

PULL! OUCH!

PULLING!

AND OTHER THINGS WERE TRIED...

PUSH! OOF!

PUSHING!

ARGH...

BUT IN THE HARSH FACE OF FUTILITY, ALL THERE WAS LEFT TO DO WAS FIND THE LARGER MEANING IN THIS DEBACLE...

MEN.. I SEE THIS WHOLE THING AS A METAPHOR FOR THE LIMITS OF U.S. POWER.

GREAT. LET'S GO HOME AND HAVE A "POP TART"...

OF COURSE.!

AND SO.. AS THE LIVING SYMBOL OF AMERICA'S TROUBLED FOREIGN POLICY PRAYED FOR A LARGE SNOW DRIFT TO COME ALONG AND PROVIDE A DIGNIFIED ESCAPE, HE, TOO, REALIZED THAT BASSELOPES, LIKE NATIONS, SHOULD NEVER LET THEIR REACH EXCEED THEIR GRASP.

THE MORAL: I WANT A "POP TART"...

FIVE

THE CONTRA CONNECTION AND THE CHALLENGER EXPLOSION

1987 WINNERS IN THE NATIONAL REPORTING CATEGORY

"For a distinguished example of reporting on national affairs . . ."

The Miami Herald
Staff

The New York Times
Staff

THE CONTRA CONNECTION

During the spring and summer of 1987, the Iran-contra affair became a daily staple for the American public. *The Herald* had done much of the preliminary work in tracing the path of the arms and money trails that eventually uprooted a private network that was secretly carrying out American foreign policy.

Months before the Iran-contra scandal captured the nation's political consciousness, *The Miami Herald* was virtually alone on the contra story. One major story after another made the paper the primary source of information for Congress, for the Washington press corps and for the American people.

In Washington, 10 months before Attorney General Edwin Meese acknowledged that Lieutenant Colonel Oliver L. North diverted profits from Iran arms sales to the contras, *Herald* correspondent Alfonso Chardy disclosed that the obscure White House aide directed secret operations and arms transfers.

In Costa Rica, foreign correspondents Sam Dillon and Tim Golden discovered blatant misuse of American funds by the contras, information later confirmed by the General Accounting Office.

On the streets of Miami, reporters Sandra Dibble and Andres Oppenheimer revealed how the city—from its bilingual banks to its international airport—was the command center for the secret war against Nicaragua's Sandinistas.

After the Iran-contra scandal broke, investigative reporter Jim McGee disclosed that even while it was arranging the sale of arms to Iran, the White House had proof that Iran had ordered and financed the 1983 bombing of the Marine Corps barracks. Reporters Chardy and Dillon disclosed that Colonel North personally supervised an election advertising campaign for sympathetic members of Congress.

Alfonso Chardy explains how he pieced together fragments of information that provided a glimpse of a vast private supply network for the contras:

"After Congress moved to suspend official aid to the contras in mid-1984, we knew that private aid, gathered and channeled by private individuals who also were close friends of high-level government officials, would replace Central Intelligence Agency supplies to the rebels.

"Foreign editor Mark Seibel issued the first of what would be a seemingly endless string of assignments on private aid. His interest had been piqued by the death in August 1984 of two Americans when their helicopter was shot during a contra attack on a Nicaraguan military school.

"That led to a story in September 1984 on the private aid network that had sprung up. A few months later, we updated that with a story that examined the aid to the contras from Taiwan, South Korea and Saudi Arabia. In June 1985, I wrote the first story in a major American newspaper that linked Oliver North to the aid network—16 months before North's name became a household word after President Reagan fired him on November 25, 1986, for his role in the Iran-contra affair.

"Even after other papers lost interest in Oliver North, *The Miami Herald* continued to expose his involvement. *The Herald's* interest grew in December when a contra unit shot down a Sandinista Soviet-made helicopter with a Soviet bloc SAM-7 surface-to-air missile.

"Heath Meriwether, executive editor of *The Herald,* directed me to find out whether, despite denials, the Reagan Administration had played any role in supplying or helping the contras acquire the missile that brought down the Sandinista helicopter. In talking to various American and contra sources, it became obvious very quickly that Oliver North was once again playing a role.

"That was the first story of 1986 on North's involvement, and it was to be a prophetic one. Not only did it link North to the contras' acquisition of SAM-7s and other surface-to-air missiles, but it also revealed that Portugal was one of the trans-shipment points. Investigations in the aftermath of the Iran-contra scandal have borne out that North and Portugal did play significant roles in securing the missiles for the contras.

"In April, as charges surfaced of alleged corruption in the contra movement, a conservative activist from the Dallas-Fort Worth area,

Philip Mabry, went public with the first evidence of how North set up secret private agents as liaisons with the contras to circumvent the Boland amendment. Mabry had letters from Fawn Hall, North's secretary, and Meese, then a White House counselor. Mabry gave those letters to *The Herald.*

"By the summer of 1986, some contra aid critics in Congress made the first feeble attempt to investigate North's activities. I re-examined the issue and put together details on how high-level White House officials, perhaps even the President, had ordered the continuation of assistance to the contras despite Congress's ban. In October, I put together the most complete roundup story of my journalistic career: an examination of North's network that included most of the principals in the Iran-contra scandal."

Meanwhile, *Herald* reporters in Miami and in Latin America were pursuing other angles of the story.

Andres Oppenheimer tells how he uncovered evidence of misuse of Congress's humanitarian aid to the contras:

"Through congressional sources, we learned that the contras were using several Miami banks that had not been previously named. I called several of my sources in the Latin banking community, and, with the help of some disaffected contras, we soon identified four Miami banks that carried the bulk of the contra funds (Popular Bank, Citizens and Southern International Bank, Consolidated Bank and Republic National Bank.)

"An official in one of the banks allowed me to see records of two contra accounts. I took notes of the names to which the checks and wire transfers were made, and then called the other banks to confirm that those specific transactions had taken place. That, in turn, led to admissions of larger contra accounts in these and other banks.

"A few weeks later, I obtained from a congressional source a detailed list of suppliers of boots, uniforms and food to the contras in the United States, Honduras and Costa Rica. The list had been provided by the contras' United Nicaraguan Opposition to the State Department's Nicaraguan Humanitarian Assistance Office. The list allowed us to prove that—contrary to the contras' assertion that they were directing their activities from Costa Rica—their operation's center was in Miami.

"The list included the names of contra suppliers in Honduras and Costa Rica, such as the Hermano Pedro supermarket in Honduras and the Creaciones Fancy store in Costa Rica. I passed the information to Sam Dillon and Tim Golden."

Tim Golden, who was in Costa Rica, tells how he used that information:

"I began leafing through old telephone books, calling contras, their friends and their old suppliers. Within a couple of days, I knew I had something. I got to a man who had been a key supply officer. After talking a while, he agreed to explain the system in detail: who bought what, where, when, how, and how bogus receipts were central to the process. Nearly everywhere I followed the paper trail, his story turned out to be accurate.

"Store owner after store owner who knew the local contras recalled having sold to them, but said they would be in Las Vegas if they had sold as much as the State Department's balance sheets showed. (The Nicaraguan Humanitarian Assistance Office later said a secretary had transposed the figures on the balance sheet.)

"The one store I found last was Creaciones Fancy, a hole-in-the-wall discount store on a dirty, downtown San Jose street. Yet the storekeeper recalled the contras' purchase, and she produced documentation that eventually led to the contras' admission that they had submitted an estimate as a receipt and used more than $25,000 of humanitarian aid to purchase grenades and ammunition. The money was subsequently returned."

The Miami Herald published more than two dozen exclusive stories about covert operations, lawbreaking and questionable conduct that the United States Government wanted kept secret. The newspaper's labor—more than 171 staff-produced stories on the contras and the Iran arms sales—is a textbook illustration of international reporting.

—The prize-winning team
The Miami Herald

U.S. HELPED CONTRAS GET MISSILES

SANDINISTA COPTER DOWNED BY SAM

SATURDAY, JANUARY 18, 1986

BY ALFONSO CHARDY

WASHINGTON—Reagan administration officials played a role in helping U.S.-backed Nicaraguan insurgents to buy an anti-aircraft missile that downed a Nicaraguan helicopter in December, according to administration officials and congressional sources familiar with the case.

Senior officials, including Secretary of State George Shultz, have denied charges by the Sandinista government in Managua that the United States provided the rebels with the heat-seeking, surface-to-air SAM-7 missile that downed the Soviet-supplied Mi8 Sandinista helicopter on Dec. 2. Twelve Nicaraguan soldiers and two Cuban pilots were reported killed.

Knowledgeable sources, while confirming that the United States did not supply the Soviet-made SAM-7 missiles, said officials who monitor the rebels' activities passed information to the rebels through third parties on how to secure the weapons through foreign arms dealers.

In another instance of U.S. involvement, administration sources said that while the contras awaited delivery of the missiles, U.S. officials in Central America, acting on their own, described for the rebels the vulnerabilities of the Russian helicopters so they could use their new weapons effectively.

The rebels, or contras, reportedly purchased their first missiles from European arms dealers in February or March, took delivery in April at their Honduran camps and were trained in their use by private American arms experts.

"It wasn't a question of U.S. officials meeting secretly with guerrillas in the basement of the White House in the middle of the night and telling them 'Now boys, you gotta get surface-to-air missiles' and 'don't worry, we'll get them for you,' " said one official aware of contra activities.

'INDIRECT HINTS'

"But there were enough indirect hints from officials through third parties as to where they could go and get the weapons and training. The whole thing would have been impossible without some sort of U.S. participation."

The part American officials played was so discreet that it is unlikely that it could be conclusively established that they circumvented a congressional ban on assisting the contras, which was in place when the missiles were acquired in early 1985, the sources said.

"Those who helped covered their tracks so well that enough deniability was preserved," said a congressional source who was briefed by U.S. intelligence officials. He said there is no evidence the administration had a policy of supplying missiles to the rebels.

To understand the context in which U.S. officials became involved, it is necessary to review chronologically how the contras came to acquire the SAM-7s.

The process began election night, Nov. 6, 1984, when American intelligence sources reported that a Soviet merchant ship, the Bakuriani, was en route to Nicaragua reportedly carrying crated MIG-21 combat jets.

The report was wrong, but the crates did contain a new weapon for the Sandinistas: the first of several sophisticated Mi24 helicopter gunships that the Soviets have used against rebels in Afghanistan.

Within days U.S. officials warned the contras that the Sandinistas planned to employ the Mi24s against the Nicaraguan guerrillas and suggested that they needed anti-aircraft weapons.

At the time, contra leaders Adolfo Calero and Enrique Bermudez raised the possibility of obtaining U.S.-made Redeye surface-to-air missiles but the effort failed because of the congressional ban against supplying the contras with weapons, the sources said.

PRIVATE FUND-RAISERS

They added, however, that National Security Council staffers involved with the contras, particularly While House liaison Lt. Col.

Oliver North, suggested to private contra fund-raisers the possibility of steering the guerrillas toward an arms market source.

North did not talk to the rebels about the missiles but discussed the issue in conversations with individuals who raised private funds for the insurgents.

Chief among them, the sources said, was retired Army Maj. Gen. John K. Singlaub who, in 1985, became the contras' chief private fund-raiser and military adviser. Singlaub, 65, was removed as chief of staff of U.S. forces in South Korea in 1977 after publicly disagreeing with President Carter's decision to reduce the level of American troops there.

"I was instrumental in helping the freedom fighters get the missiles," Singlaub acknowledged in a telephone conversation last week from Hawaii, where he was attending a military conference.

Singlaub denied that North or any other U.S. official guided him or the contras to arms dealers. But he admitted "discussing" the subject with North.

"I was not told by any official that this is what I had to do," said Singlaub, "but I did advise them of the plans so as to keep them informed and so they wouldn't be surprised." North's officer offered no comment and refused a request for an interview.

Singlaub said he recommended the SAM-7s because they are the only portable ground-to-air missiles "freely" available through arms dealers who obtain them from East bloc countries or from warring factions in Lebanon.

Singlaub said that while he raised "a lot of money" for the contras in the United States in 1984 and 1985, all of the funds used to purchase the SAM-7s came from contributors outside U.S. territory or from foreign bank accounts where American donors deposited money. The reason, he said, was to avoid violating the 188-year-old Neutrality Act. The act prohibits arming expeditions from U.S. soil against a country with which the United States is not at war.

In January 1985, Calero said that a rich U.S. donor, whom he declined to identify, had deposited enough funds in a foreign bank account to purchase the first missiles.

Congressional sources said they were told by U.S. intelligence officials that in February or March of last year a contra representative traveled to Western Europe, either Portugal or Belgium, and met with an arms dealer for the missile transaction. Singlaub said the contras paid about $45,000 per missile, including about $5,000 per launcher.

Administration officials said the contras took delivery of the first four SAM-7s in April and began training on the weapons at their camps in Honduras. Singlaub said Americans taught the contras how to fire the missiles. He declined to identify the Americans and denied that U.S. government personnel were involved.

But a prominent contra fund-raiser, who requested anonymity, said some of the trainers were retired Pentagon and CIA officers who went to Central America perhaps with the discreet approval of their services.

WOULDN'T FIRE

CIA spokeswoman Patti Volz declined comment but her counterpart at the Pentagon, Maj. Fred Lash, said "the possibility does exist, and would not be remote, that former military personnel have been involved or are currently involved in training or assisting the Nicaraguan anti-government forces."

The contras, however, failed to make use of the first delivery of missiles because at least three of them would not fire, a U.S. official said. He said moisture had damaged the missile launchers' delicate trigger system that responds to electronic commands.

Additional missiles and launchers were bought during the summer, and by August the contras had an arsenal of 13, said a congressional source who visited the area at the time.

A U.S. official said last week that the contras may now have "more than 30" missiles. Contra leader Calero declined to provide a precise number, saying that he did not want to "give away" sensitive data to the Sandinistas.

Calero said in a recent interview with The Herald that the contras plan to buy additional missiles and disclosed that a "rich lady" outside the United States had provided the movement with $1 million for more such weapons. He refused to identify the woman by name or nationality.

CONTRAS BILK U.S. ON SUPPLIES, COSTA RICAN MERCHANTS SAY

SUNDAY, JUNE 1, 1986

BY TIM GOLDEN

SAN JOSE, Costa Rica—Anti-Sandinista rebels in Costa Rica have billed the United States for thousands of dollars in food, clothing and other supplies that merchants say they never sold or delivered to the insurgents.

The Costa Rica-based rebels also apparently charged the United States for enough supplies to outfit 2,000 or 3,000 guerrilla fighters, even though their numbers never have totaled more than 385 and actually were declining during several months when expenditures were at a peak.

The Costa Rican allegations involve the Nicaraguan Revolutionary Armed Forces (FARN), a tiny guerrilla group led by Fernando "El Negro" Chamorro, and the Costa Rica-based branch of Kisan, another small, anti-Sandinista group made up of blacks and Indians from Nicaragua's Atlantic coast. Both groups are affiliated with United Nicaraguan Opposition (UNO), the U.S.-backed anti-Sandinista contra umbrella organization whose leaders just concluded a 2½-week summit meeting in Miami.

Knowledgeable rebel sources say that soon after Congress approved $27 million in nonlethal "humanitarian" aid for the rebels last summer, FARN leaders began planning ways to win as much of that aid as possible.

"We began to get blank receipts from all over the place," said one rebel source with access to guerrilla financial records. Like many others interviewed for this article, he requested anonymity out of concern for his security.

The allegations that rebel forces misused or misappropriated U.S. aid in Costa Rica come amid growing concern in Congress that rebel leaders have profited personally from the U.S. aid program or diverted it for weapons purchases. One congressional subcommittee and the

General Accounting Office are investigating alleged irregularities in the handling of the money, and the GAO, Congress' auditing agency, has issued a report saying that it cannot verify how a large percentage of the money was spent. Three other congressional committees are investigating other rebel activities.

Most of the congressional questions surrounding the use of U.S. aid money have centered on rebel activities in Honduras, base of the largest rebel fighting force, the Nicaraguan Democratic Force (FDN). The FDN, which also is affiliated with UNO, does not operate from Costa Rica.

Interviews in Costa Rica and examination of classified U.S. records of rebel expenditures show that although only about $2 million of the $27 million has been spent in Costa Rica, the support has left a long trail of financial irregularities, questionable business practices and missing funds.

Chamorro, a seasoned guerrilla opponent of the Sandinistas who also fought President Anastasio Somoza and once was a Chevrolet salesman in Managua, declined through aides to be interviewed on FARN's use of the aid.

However, other FARN leaders denied any misuse of American aid, praising Chamorro's management style as honest and "tight-fisted."

Ivan Fonseca, in whose Miami bank account the U.S. money was deposited, could not be reached for comment. Some relatives said he is out of the country. His brother, Ulises Fonseca, said that Ivan had no desire to comment on the report about his involvement in use of the rebel aid.

'ACCOUNTING IS OURS'

Ulises Fonseca is FARN's principal administrator for the U.S. aid. He said Saturday that he had signed receipts from all foreign suppliers, which matched the figures on U.S. records. However, he said, "Our accounting is ours and not for any journalist."

Fonseca suggested that discrepancies between the amounts that merchants said they had been paid, and what U.S. records show, had arisen because suppliers had understated the business they had done to avoid paying Costa Rican taxes.

A State Department official, told about the questions surrounding the Costa Rica purchases, said Saturday that "We are unaware of these new allegations."

"Certainly it has been very difficult for the Department of State to conduct a foolproof program of this nature given the restraints placed on the program by the host countries in the Central American region," the State Department official, who asked not to be named, said. "This specifically includes the ability to conduct an open and effective verification program.

"Should concrete evidence be established lending credence to these allegations it will be incumbent on the U.S. government to follow up the charges."

According to Ulises Fonseca, money destined for FARN purchases has flowed exclusively through his brother Ivan's account at Citizens and Southern International Bank at 1101 Brickell Ave. in Miami.

The account also received part of the funds going to Kisan-South and UNO's political representatives in Costa Rica.

The money is deposited in that account by the State Department's Nicaraguan Humanitarian Assistance Office (NHAO), which was established last year to oversee the $27 million aid package. A knowledgeable U.S. official said FARN had received about $1.89 million of the $27 million.

SPOT CHECKS

The NHAO, however, makes no on-site inspections in Central America to determine how money is spent, and relies on spot checks by U.S. intelligence agencies. The lack of on-site inspections was one of the GAO's main criticisms of the aid program.

Interviews raise questions about most of the expenditures shown in classified U.S. records of rebel purchases in Costa Rica. The records cover purchases through mid-February.

For example, U.S. records show that on Nov. 6 the NHAO paid $16,764—$15,907 for "foodstuffs and sundries" and $857 for pharmaceuticals—to the Farmacia Upala, a small drugstore in a town near the Nicaraguan border.

But the owner of the cramped, one-room outlet, Judith Sanchez Alfaro, 31, was mystified at the idea.

"If I had written receipts for millions of colons," she said, referring to the Costa Rican currency, "I wouldn't be here." A dollar is currently worth about 55.10 colons.

Sanchez said rebels bought cold medicines, Alka-Seltzer and prescription medications at her store on four or five occasions, paying cash. The neighborhood pharmacy stocks nothing that could be considered food.

"The purchases were very sporadic and very small," Sanchez said. "I suppose they went to another pharmacy to buy what they needed."

On the other side of Upala, four muddy blocks away at the Abastecedor El Puente, a store owner Coralia Valverde, 38, was similarly unaware that, as U.S. records indicate, she had sold $26,766 in food to the rebels on Nov. 6. Valverde said she had sold about $370 worth of jeans, dress shirts and underwear to FARN members in January, but little if anything since then.

Ulises Fonseca said that El Puente may have been billed for a purchase of food at the Almacen Upala, but he had no record available of such an indirect charge.

Valverde, like many Upala residents a strong rebel supporter, proudly described her establishment as the town's fashion mecca. It stocks no food.

Skepticism about the accuracy of rebel accounting was also raised by Alejandro Gonzalez, 38, one of three brothers who manage the Almacen Upala, which U.S. records show was reimbursed on Nov. 26 and Dec. 18 for a total of $50,211 spent on food and clothing.

Gonzalez acknowledged that FARN officials, who had been spending as little as $500 a month at his store, began to buy "mountains of stuff" after Congress approved aid to the rebels.

But he said that since October, the most FARN had spent in one month at the store was about $22,000. He said they spent that sum in both December and January.

Gonzalez said the store billed the rebels more or less monthly. They asked for blank receipts "very few times," he said.

An interview with the rebels' Costa Rican physician, Dr. Luis Blanco Rojas, also raised questions. U.S. State Department records show that Blanco was paid $14,266 on Dec. 17.

But Blanco, interviewed Saturday at his home in Zarcero, said he believes he has received no more than $3,000 from FARN during the past 18 months. He said he signed a receipt in late 1985 for about $2,200 as an honorarium for his year's work for the rebels, but that he had not yet received the money.

He said he received some $2,700 from the rebels for participating in an arterial bypass operation in December, but that he had used most of that money to pay other doctors involved in the procedure and other costs.

He also said he believed that about $4,700 in supplies had been purchased in 1986 in his name for a rebel clinic.

"They give me a little money to get from place to place," he said. "I have mostly treated them for free."

Blanco later phoned The Herald to say that a bill for some $15,000 had been written under his name at the end of the year to cover debts to the Costa Rican social security system for the hospitalization of 17 rebel patients at a government facility in Upala between July and October 1985.

Questions also arise over the selection of businesses that were to benefit from the U.S. aid.

One of the largest recipients of rebel business in Costa Rica, according to U.S. records, is the Farmacia San Luis, a downtown San Jose drugstore that rebel banker Ivan Fonseca and another brother, Marco Antonio, manage for their mother. U.S.-funded FARN purchases at the pharmacy from Nov. 6 to Feb. 4 totaled $47,853, documents show.

STOCKING A CLINIC

Ulises Fonseca justified the large expenditures by saying that in addition to immediate needs, the rebels were buying supplies to stock at a clinic and supply warehouse. Other knowledgeable rebel sources critical of the handling of the U.S. funds said, however, that they believe actual purchases totaled only one fourth to one half what U.S. documents show was spent at the pharmacy.

Another accounting black hole appears with Creaciones Fancy, a closet-sized discount clothing store on a bustling San Jose street. On Nov. 26, U.S. officials budgeted $14,300 for 1,000 pairs of pants, $5,720 for 1,000 shirts and $6,200 for 1,000 pairs of rubber boots for the Indian group Kisan. The U.S. government paid $25,870 on Jan. 24, the documents show, $350 less than originally estimated.

But two managers for Creaciones Fancy denied selling anything to Kisan and said they never received any U.S. funds.

The managers, who asked not to be named, dug into store files and pulled out two estimates that they said they had given to a youngish, Nicaraguan-sounding man who said he wanted to buy the clothing— green Lee brand jeans, green T-shirts and boots—for his cattle farmers' cooperative in the northern Costa Rican province of Guanacaste.

Both a green duplicate copy dated Nov. 18 and a white original dated Jan. 8, listed the pants, shirts and boots and set their prices in colons. At the time, a dollar was worth about 52.45 colons.

One of the store managers said that the man, who identified himself as Victoriano Morales, specifically asked her not to write "estimate" on the November receipt and requested and received the original rather than the copy she would normally have given a customer.

LOST INVOICE

The man returned in January, with two fair-skinned "gringos," she said, including one who was well-dressed and spoke no Spanish. She said the Nicaraguan told her he had lost the invoice and requested another, insisting he would return to arrange for payment and delivery of the order. He never did.

"We didn't sell him anything," she said.

Jenelee Hodgson, a Kisan official who handled some of the nonlethal aid purchases, said she knew nothing of Morales or Creaciones Fancy.

Hodgson said the southern Indian front had used the aid to buy food and medicines—some at Farmacia San Luis. Kisan, which was formed last September, is not known to have sent combatants into Nicaragua.

Questions also surround the reported purchase of 2,000 uniforms by FARN from Duque-Estrada y Ortiz, S.A. The United States paid Duque-Estrada $56,745 for the uniforms on Jan. 31, U.S. documents show.

The concern, owned by Carlos Jose Duque-Estrada, who describes himself as a "very good friend of El Negro" Chamorro, is registered with Costa Rican authorities as a technical and financial consulting corporation.

But Duque-Estrada says that the company manufactures clothing, made the 2,000 uniforms and sold them to FARN at close to cost.

Two rebel sources insisted there were no uniforms. Two others, however, said 400 or 500 had been delivered.

Duque-Estrada said the uniforms had been manufactured at a rented house by unemployed Nicaraguan refugee seamstresses who brought their own sewing machines. But he declined to take a reporter to the house, saying the locale had been rented by new tenants, he did not know where it was located and did not know where to find the young Nicaraguan who managed the operation for him.

SECURITY CONCERNS

"There are some things here that just can't be clear," because of the security concerns of a guerrilla insurgency, Duque-Estrada said.

Rebel sources also said FARN gathered blank receipts from Industrias Quimicas Don Sam, a one-room laboratory run by another Nicaraguan rebel supporter.

The lab's owner, Samuel Reñazgo, said his sales of homemade talc, foot powder, insect repellant and rifle lubricant had jumped considerably since the United States began providing aid to the rebels. He said that since the funds began to arrive, the rebels had been spending a monthly average of $1,550 on his products and had made purchases of about $3,050 during October and November. NHAO records show that Reñazgo was paid $4,770 on Nov. 26 and $9,100 on Feb. 13 for pharmaceutical supplies.

Separate from the government accounting, Fonseca said FARN also had purchased a Toyota jeep and pickup truck from Comercial Tulin, a corporation run by three close political associates of UNO director Alfonso Robelo. Fonseca said two more jeeps were being purchased from the company.

DESPITE BAN, U.S. HELPING CONTRAS

SUNDAY, JUNE 8, 1986

BY ALFONSO CHARDY

WASHINGTON—Despite congressional restrictions, the Reagan administration has continued secretly to assist anti-Sandinista rebels in finding weapons and plotting military strategy through a network of private operatives overseen by the National Security Council (NSC) and the CIA, administration and rebel officials say.

The system has been overseen by Marine Lt. Col. Oliver North, a senior staff member at the NSC, who has operated with advice from CIA officers attached to the Central American division of the agency's clandestine branch, the officials said.

The NSC and CIA involvement in contra activities comes in spite of an Oct. 10, 1984, law that forbids U.S. officials from direct involvement in planning or executing military operations inside Nicaragua. The prohibition was relaxed—but not lifted—last summer when Congress authorized $27 million in so-called humanitarian aid to the rebels.

The officials said the system's main private agents include retired Maj. Gen. John Singlaub, the former commander of U.S. forces in South Korea, and Robert Owen, a 32-year-old Stanford graduate who until May 28 worked as a paid consultant for the State Department's Nicaraguan Humanitarian Assistance Office (NHAO).

PRIVATE CHANNELS USED

While any official military assistance to the contras would violate the law, the sources—two administration officials and a knowledgeable rebel leader—said the administration feels it has honored the restrictions by channeling its involvement through private citizens.

But the arrangement still is expected to be a central focus of congressional investigators looking into the contra movement. The investigation is expected to begin after the vote later this month on President Reagan's request for an additional $100 million in aid to the rebels.

North declined comment, but an administration official said North "has not been involved in illegal activities." CIA spokeswoman Kathy Pherson said the agency has "adhered" to congressional requirements.

The contra rebels were organized by the CIA and Argentine military officers in 1981 and began fighting the Sandinista government in Nicaragua in 1982 with CIA guidance and supplies.

In 1984, Congress banned CIA assistance for military actions inside Nicaragua after the CIA directed the mining of Nicaraguan harbors.

Under the ban, the CIA was allowed to receive intelligence from the contras but was barred from advising them.

CAN SHARE INTELLIGENCE

After Congress approved $27 million in U.S. aid to the contras last year, the CIA was allowed to share intelligence on Sandinista troop movements, but U.S. government officials were still prohibited from helping the contras plan strategy or procure weapons.

According to administration officials, North was first told to organize a network of private supporters for the contras in 1984, when it became apparent Congress was about to end CIA involvement in the rebel movement. It's not clear who in the administration told North to form the network.

Conservative activists were contacted and raised almost $30 million.

After Congress' ban prohibited North from dealing directly with the contras, private individuals were used as bridges between the administration and the rebels, officials said.

Singlaub, officials said, became the de facto military adviser to the contras while Owen served as a secret conduit for messages, advice and funds.

Both reported to and consulted with North frequently by phone and at North's office in the Old Executive Office Building next to the White House, the officials said.

"That's how the system worked," said one official who monitors contra activities. "Owen was the messenger boy and Gen. Singlaub the military commander, chief fund-raiser and arms adviser and broker."

Owen refused to be interviewed.

Singlaub, in an interview earlier this year, acknowledged being in contact with North but denied receiving instructions from him. Singlaub also acknowledged having raised funds for the contras to buy weapons, but said transactions were made outside the United States to avoid violating the 188-year-old Neutrality Act.

Singlaub said he also advised the contras on types of weapons they needed.

A knowledgeable contra official said Owen was North's "gofer" and kept in touch with rebel leaders in Honduras and Costa Rica.

An administration official intimately familiar with contra affairs said he had been instructed by the NSC to refer to Owen anyone offering supplies or funds to the contras during the time of the prohibition.

'BAD ORGANIZATION'

The contra official said Owen also had been assigned the role of organizing a southern front that would be supplied from Costa Rica. But the contra said the project never prospered because of "bad organization."

Rebel officials said that since last summer the CIA has gradually widened its involvement by paying for the travel and living expenses of contra leaders and financing their propaganda projects. The increased CIA role, the rebels said, has displaced the NSC, diluting the council's influence.

Administration officials said that since last year, the CIA has secretly funneled between $1.5 million and $3 million to the contras' umbrella group, United Nicaraguan Opposition (UNO), to pay rebel officials and supporters, and to open offices in Western Europe and Latin America.

A rebel official said CIA officers also have intervened in internal contra political disputes in a bid to bring about unity in the fractious anti-Sandinista movement.

The rebel said the CIA played a key role in persuading Eden Pastora's six senior commanders to desert their leader in May after he refused to ally himself with UNO. Pastora later gave up his fight and sought political asylum in Costa Rica.

Rebel officials said the CIA's main goal now is to consolidate a totally unified contra alliance and prepare it for a major offensive against the Sandinista government if and when Congress approves Reagan's $100 million proposal for military and logistical aid.

If Congress approves the package as the administration has proposed, all restrictions on CIA involvement will end and the agency again will be able to plot the contras' military moves.

HOW U.S. OFFICIALS CREATED A NETWORK FOR CONTRA FUNDING

TUESDAY, OCTOBER 28, 1986

BY ALFONSO CHARDY

WASHINGTON—A private supply network for anti-Sandinista rebels was the idea of CIA director William Casey, and President Reagan and Vice President George Bush attended meetings in late 1983 and early 1984 where it was discussed, administration and rebel officials say.

U.N. Ambassador Vernon Walters, then-White House counselor Edwin Meese and then-Interior Secretary William Clark played key roles in helping organize the network, but day-to-day operations were left to retired American intelligence and military officers, the sources said.

In all, the sources said, the network provided the contras with about $50 million in weapons, ammunition, training, uniforms, boots, food, medicine and cash from 1984 to 1986.

The existence of the aid network has been known since the first stories about the program were published in The Miami Herald in September 1984. But its outlines have remained sketchy because those involved were reluctant to discuss it.

Now, however, with a new $100 million contra aid program approved and the surrogate network no longer necessary, rebel and administration sources with knowledge of the program have for the first time provided details of how the network was organized

Their accounts do not provide specifics on many aspects of the contra aid network, particularly how it functioned on the ground in Central America.

But it clarifies several disputed aspects and reveals several previously unknown details, including:

• That the program was discussed and approved at the highest levels of the U.S. government. The sources say Casey first broached the idea to the President and that many of the President's closest advisers were actively involved at least in the initial stages of the program. Previously, Reagan administration officials have denied any organizational involvement. "We have not violated the law, nor have we directed, coordinated or overseen any private operation," White House spokesman Don Mathes said Monday.

• That the CIA initially asked for help from Saudi Arabia in 1984, but that the request was turned down. It was not until this year that the Saudis agreed to help, and then only through private Saudi subjects, not the government.

• That citizens of Taiwan and South Korea provided cash for weapons, while conservative political activists in Colombia and Venezuela picked up the tab for anti-Sandinista political activities, including the living expenses of contra leaders.

• That many of the weapons given the contras came from stockpiles captured by the Israelis in Lebanon or left by the Soviets in Egypt.

'FOUND THE LEGAL EDGE'

The sources said they do not believe that any U.S. official violated the letter of congressional restrictions on aiding the contras or U.S. neutrality laws. As one administration official put it in describing what his colleagues did, "they found the legal edge of the restrictions and danced consciously around it."

Some of the top U.S. officials aware of or involved in the system, the sources said, included Reagan, Bush, Bush's national security affairs assistant Donald Gregg, Casey, Walters, Meese and National Security Council aide Lt. Col. Oliver North.

Casey, North and Gregg oversaw the system from Washington at different times, the sources said.

Two retired U.S. generals, John Singlaub and Richard Secord, acted as the primary advisers to the system and procured funds and weapons abroad for the contras, the sources said.

They said Singlaub worked the Far East in 1984 and 1985 and Secord the Middle East in 1986. Singlaub's funding came mostly from Taiwan and South Korea, including the Unification Church of the Rev. Sun Myung Moon, the sources said.

Secord secured money from Saudi Arabian sources to acquire Soviet-made weapons from Egypt, Israel and international arms dealers, the sources said. They said funds Secord raised also paid the salaries of U.S. specialists helping the contras and bought planes to transport the weapons to them. Secord could not be reached for comment.

Honduras, Guatemala and El Salvador provided facilities for contra supply flights, the sources said. The Honduran military also provided some weapons, and the Salvadoran military allowed use of its Ilopango Air Base near San Salvador as the control and command center to run the network's delivery system. At one point, the sources said, groups in Brazil provided some grenades.

Conservative political groups in several Latin American countries, among them Venezuela and Colombia, also provided funds, mostly to finance travel and other expenses of contra leaders, the sources added.

Wealthy U.S. businessmen such as Nelson Bunker Hunt, Joseph Coors and Peter Grace donated money for nonlethal relief supplies. Their example led to the formation of pro-contra "humanitarian" aid groups in the United States.

PLANE SHOT DOWN

It was this intricate network that was responsible for a camouflaged C123 cargo plane shot down over Nicaragua Oct. 5 as it ferried weapons and ammunition for the contras.

The American pilot and co-pilot and a Nicaraguan rebel aboard the plane were killed and a third American, retired CIA cargo handler Eugene Hasenfus, 45, of Marinette, Wis., was captured. He is now being tried in Managua.

The downing of the C123 renewed debate on whether the existence of the network and U.S. involvement in it violated previous congressional restrictions on assisting the rebels.

Congress prohibited further military assistance to the rebels in October 1984 after two years of CIA covert support.

This summer, Congress reversed itself and approved a new $100-million contra aid program. Reagan activated the program last week, enabling the CIA to resume day-to-day management of the rebels.

While those involved are convinced they did not break the law during the Congressional bans, several sources acknowledged that U.S. officials circumvented the restrictions to avoid the collapse of a high-stakes policy in Central America.

"The objective of those in Congress who designed the law prohibiting aid was to force President Reagan to walk away from Central America, leaving it to the Communists," one official said. "Had we adhered strictly to their dictates, we would have abandoned the freedom fighters."

According to this official, the fear within the CIA and the White House was that if the United States abandoned the contras, the action would have led to a rebel defeat.

"That would have been a second Bay of Pigs fiasco," the official said. "It would have had wider implications than just the loss of the contra program. It would have damaged the prestige of the United States and would have amounted to a strategic triumph for the Soviet Union."

BEGAN IN 1983

According to the sources, all of whom spoke only if promised anonymity, the network began to take shape in October 1983, a month after Congress imposed the first restrictions on contra funding, limiting CIA spending to $24 million during 1984 and barring the agency from dipping into its contingency fund to cover additional costs.

The law did not prohibit U.S. officials from seeking alternate sources of contra funding.

Casey, told by officers in charge of the contra program that the $24 million was not enough, alerted Reagan.

In a series of meetings in December 1983 and January 1984, Reagan approved Casey's proposals that an alternate means of support be found to supplement the $24-million program.

A former administration official familiar with those meetings said that Lt. Col. North, deputy director of the NSC's political development and political-military affairs branch, devised the plan for the system in a series of memorandums discussing private aid.

At the same time, Meese and Clark, a trusted friend who had been Reagan's national security advisor until October 1983 when he was named interior secretary, joined with the president's so-called kitchen cabinet of close conservative friends in contacting wealthy Republicans and U.S. conservatives to solicit aid. Clark was interior secretary until January 1985.

Casey and Walters, then Reagan's personal diplomatic trouble-shooter, traveled abroad to persuade friendly foreign governments and intelligence services to cooperate in assisting the contras.

"There were trade-offs," said a former intelligence officer who worked closely with North on contra-related projects in 1985.

A knowledgeable intelligence source said Casey initially asked the Saudis in June 1984 to contribute $20 million to the aid efforts. But the Saudis rejected the request, saying they disagreed with Reagan's Central America policy and feared that their role would be exposed by U.S. news organizations.

The source said that earlier this year the Saudi government, while remaining aloof from the program itself, did permit private Saudi subjects to provide funds after an appeal by Secord. The source said the Saudi contribution was about $15 million and was used to buy aircraft, including the downed C123, that transported weapons to the contras from El Salvador.

The Saudis provided assistance after it was pointed out that the United States had defied the pro-Israeli congressmen in selling AWACS early warning aircraft to Riyadh in 1981, a deal worked out by Secord and North, the source said. He said Egypt and Israel also cooperated when reminded of the substantial aid they received from the United States.

When the last CIA covert money was spent March 8, 1984, North was informally made chief coordinator of the emerging surrogate system.

In October 1984, when Congress barred all funding for contra military operations, the CIA withdrew from the program and North delegated responsibility for direct contact with the rebels to at least two private agents: Singlaub and a conservative political activist and public relations specialist, Robert Owen.

Singlaub's role was solicited by Casey. They had known each other during World War II as members of the Office of Strategic Services, the U.S. intelligence agency that preceded the CIA.

After President Carter removed Singlaub as commander of U.S. forces in South Korea in 1977 in a dispute over reduction of U.S. forces there, Singlaub became a hero to conservatives in the United States and the Far East. He was rewarded with the chairmanships of the U.S. Council for World Freedom and the Taiwan-based World Anti-Communist League.

As a leader of the contra surrogate supply system, Singlaub's mission was to return to South Korea and Taiwan to secure funds with which to acquire guns and ammunition in lieu of CIA cash.

Singlaub's spokeswoman Joyce Downey in a telephone conversation last week confirmed that Singlaub secured funding from "groups" in South Korea and Taiwan.

SECRET BANK ACCOUNT

In a telephone interview last year, Singlaub acknowledged that some of the funds he obtained were deposited in a secret foreign bank account to finance arms purchases. One of the items he helped acquire was Soviet-made SAM-7 portable surface-to-air missiles with which a rebel unit shot down a Soviet-supplied Mi8 Sandinista transport helicopter piloted by Cuban officers in December of last year.

Singlaub also acknowledged that he advised North of his actions to keep him and the U.S. government informed of what the contras were up to. But he denied that he received instructions from North or any other administration officials.

In an interview with CBS News' 60 *Minutes* program shown Oct. 5, the day the C123 was shot down, Singlaub also revealed that he discussed the contras with Casey, his old OSS case officer.

"Well," Singlaub told interviewer Mike Wallace, "[Casey] has indicated approval, and he has been encouraging. He introduces me to the people that need to have the detailed information. So he's been cooperative, and sees me when I come into town on short notice."

Owen, a 32-year-old Stanford graduate who once worked for Sen. Dan Quayle, R-Ind., and for the high-powered Washington public relations company Gray and Co., owned by one of Reagan's friends, William Gray, primarily ferried messages to the contras in Central America and reported back on their activities.

Contra sources said that in 1985 Owen was assigned to help Costa Rica-based rebel factions open a southern front against Nicaragua, a mission that failed.

CUBANS RECRUITED

As part of the mission, the sources said, private American volunteers overseen by Owen recruited Cuban Mariel boatlift refugees in Miami to fight with a contra faction based in Costa Rica with promises of American citizenship in the future.

Former contra supporters in Miami have also linked Owen to an alleged illegal shipment of weapons in early 1985 aboard a cargo aircraft that left from Fort Lauderdale-Hollywood International Airport bound for Ilopango air base in San Salvador.

From late 1985 to last spring, Owen worked as a consultant for the Nicaraguan Humanitarian Assistance Office, the State Department agency that administered a now-defunct $27 million program of "humanitarian" aid for the contras.

As the contras received foreign funding for weapons and supply aircraft in 1984 and 1985, private groups emerged in the United States to provide nonlethal assistance such as clothing, food and medicine.

More than 20 such groups, most created or led by conservatives, emerged to aid the contras. These included the Air Commando Association of Forth Walton Beach, Fla.; Friends of the Americas of Louisiana; Civilian Military Assistance—later renamed Civilian Materiel Assistance—of Alabama; the Knights of Malta and the Rev. Pat Robertson's Christian Broadcasting Network.

The critical assistance—weapons and funds for the supply aircraft —came from abroad, a rebel source said last week. In 1984 and 1985 they came from Asia, arranged by Singlaub, and in 1986 from Saudi Arabia through Secord, he said.

Secord, a West Point graduate and former deputy assistant secretary of defense, was described by some administration officials as key to the supply network, perhaps more effective than Singlaub.

Officials said Secord, who lives and maintains an office in Virginia, essentially took over the supply network in 1986 after the funding that Singlaub had arranged began to dry up. The sources attributed the decline to passage by Congress in 1985 of the $27-million "humanitarian" aid program.

"Many of the foreign and private contributors thought that the humanitarian aid would be enough and stopped giving," a rebel source said.

At the same time, other sources said, the North-Singlaub-Owen connection had become a liability amid allegations that the contras and their private supporters had engaged in gun-running, drug-trafficking and murder and terrorist plots.

Congressional investigators demanded an accounting and Rep. Ronald Coleman, D-Tex., introduced a resolution in Congress asking Reagan to provide information on North's contra dealings.

Gradually, the sources said, North, Singlaub and Owen were eased out and Gregg and Secord took over.

The Gregg-Secord involvement remained largely unnoticed until the C123 was downed. After Hasenfus was captured, he told his Sandinista interrogators that a man named Max Gomez directed the supply operation at Ilopango. Gomez's real name is Felix Rodriguez. He's a Bay of Pigs veteran, member of a CIA team that helped track down Che Guevara in Bolivia and was a combat helicopter pilot in Vietnam.

Administration sources said Rodriguez was introduced to Bush and the contra supply network by Miami's Cuban American leaders.

Gregg, Bush's national security affairs assistant, apparently had no trouble in recommending Rodriguez for a post in El Salvador since he knew the Cuban from their days together in Vietnam working for the CIA.

Administration officials said Gregg introduced Rodriguez to North during a Jan. 24, 1985, meeting in Bush's office during a discussion on how to assist El Salvador in its fight against leftist guerrillas.

Critics contend that the entire network raises serious questions about whether U.S. neutrality laws and Congressional restrictions were violated but that the Justice Department, now headed by Meese, is not likely to prosecute any officials or private citizens who aided the contras.

Supporters and critics of contra aid acknowledge it will be difficult to prove that the administration has violated any laws because of the Justice Department's narrow interpretation of these laws.

On Oct. 17, a majority of the Democrats on the House Judiciary Committee asked Attorney General Meese for the appointment of a special prosecutor to investigate whether administration officials have been illegally authorizing military aid to the contras.

Critics say, however, that the only way a wide-ranging congressional investigation will take place is if Democrats wrest control of the Senate from Republicans in the November elections.

But administration officials contend that the question is moot since it is again legal for the Unitied States to provide the contras with military aid.

U.S. KNEW IRAN ORDERED, FUNDED BEIRUT BOMBINGS, INTERCEPTS SHOW

SUNDAY, DECEMBER 7, 1986

BY JIM McGEE

Two years before Marine Lt. Col. Oliver North arranged shipments of arms to Iran, the White House had precise evidence that Iran paid for the terrorist bombing in Beirut that killed 258 U.S. servicemen and diplomats.

The secret eavesdropping network of the National Security Agency intercepted diplomatic messages in 1983 showing that the government of Iran ordered and financed the Beirut bombings, according to information obtained by The Miami Herald and confirmed Friday by a White House official.

The intercepted diplomatic messages enabled U.S. officials to trace the movement of more than $1 million from the government of Iran to the Iranian Embassy in Lebanon, where it was disbursed for the bombings of the U.S. Embassy and the Marine barracks.

The money was earmarked for the 1983 campaign of terrorist actions against U.S. targets in Lebanon, according to U.S. intelligence reports prepared after the attacks.

"Looking at it [the intercepted messages] after the fact, it was a clear indication the money was going for the attack," said an official familiar with reports based on the intercepts. "There was no doubt in our minds."

On Friday, a White House official involved in national security matters described The Herald's account of the material intercepted by the NSA as "damn good."

"Obviously, the NSA knew about this, and I would have to surmise the president knew about it, too," the White House official said. "After the bombing, [President Reagan] took a keen interest in who did it."

The new information on Iran's involvement in the bombings underscores the dramatic change in U.S. policy toward Iran that took place in June 1985—after the Reagan administration realized that Iran had used its influence with Lebanese Shiite Moslems to free the Americans seized in the Trans World Airlines hijacking.

The NSA intercepts in 1983 were consistent with other information obtained by CIA officers investigating the embassy bombing, a source familiar with the U.S. investigation told The Herald.

Under interrogation by U.S. and Lebanese authorities, a suspect in the embassy bombing confessed to being the paymaster for the attack and told interrogators that the money he used originally came from Iran.

A third corroborating link to Iran was disclosed in 1984 with published reports that a Lebanese "fixer" involved in staging the barracks attack cashed a $50,000 voucher at the Iranian Embassy three days after the bombing.

It is not clear how long before the attacks the communications were intercepted or why the NSA intercepts were not used to warn American personnel. One official familiar with the situation said there often are long delays in analyzing the intercept communications.

"There is so much stuff coming in all the time that it is not translated and analyzed on a real-time basis," said the official. "There is stuff on the tapes that isn't analyzed until months later."

The U.S. government has never publicly disclosed what it determined about the two bombing attacks, which led to the largest loss of American military personnel since the Vietnam War.

A month after the Marine bombing, Secretary of Defense Caspar Weinberger told reporters that the perpetrators were "basically Iranian with sponsorship, knowledge and authority" of Syria.

In November, The Washington Post reported that Israeli and American intelligence agencies had developed information that the Iranian government was a "chief supporter" of the terrorist groups responsible for the attacks.

Recent interviews in Washington and elsewhere, however, indicate that the information available to the Reagan administration in early

1984 showing direct involvement by the Iranian government was more precise than has previously been reported.

"It was Iranian money and Syrian expertise and direction," said one source familiar with the subsequent investigation. "The Syrians don't have the money to burn. The Iranians do."

The Herald reported in August that the CIA had obtained confessions from five Syrian-backed participants in the bombing of the U.S. Embassy and established that Syrian intelligence officials supervised the attack. The confessions were subsequently confirmed by a CIA-administered polygraph test.

That account, which described the confession of the paymaster, was subsequently confirmed by the Reagan administration.

Seventeen Americans were killed in the bombing of the U.S. Embassy in Beirut April 8, 1983.

The attack on the Marine compound at Beirut International Airport came six months later.

Early on Oct. 23, 1983, a truck carrying about 2,000 pounds of explosives wired to tanks of propane gas erupted in a blast that demolished the four-story main building and left a crater 40 feet deep and 30 feet wide.

Dozens of young Marines were killed instantly in their bunks. Many more were buried under the rubble.

It has been publicly reported that North, a career Marine reputed to have expertise in counterterrorism, was assigned to investigate the barracks bombing for the National Security Council.

One official source said it is inconceivable that North was not made aware of the NSA intercepts and other evidence implicating Iran. North has repeatedly declined to be interviewed.

After Iran cooperated in the TWA jetliner crisis, North's former boss, ex-national security adviser Robert McFarlane, argued that better relations with Iran were desirable because of its pivotal role in the Mideast.

In September 1985, North arranged to ship the first planeload of U.S. arms to Iran, according to administration officials.

There was considerable debate within the intelligence community about avenging the Beirut bombings, an official told The Herald.

William Buckley, the former head of the CIA station in Beirut until he was kidnapped, had advocated in at least one meeting that the United States retaliate against Syria.

"It was one of his great frustrations with this," said an official. "The Syrian connection, what they did and the fact that the U.S. government didn't pay attention."

THE CHALLENGER EXPLOSION

The nation, united in mourning for the seven astronauts who died in the explosion of the space shuttle, wanted to know why it happened. Reporters for *The Times* pored over documents, interviewed officials, challenged accepted explanations and helped bring about important changes in the space program.

The story of the disaster of the shuttle Challenger was not so much what happened. America knew only too well. It had seen the tragedy unfold in 73 seconds on television screens across the nation.

The story to be told now, against a long backdrop of seeming excellence in space, was why.

What had gone wrong with the program that had landed man on the moon, launched the first shuttle between Earth and space and led the world in all manner of space exploration?

Within hours of the Challenger explosion, Richard Flaste and Holcomb B. Noble, directors of science news of *The New York Times*, and the special team they headed—Philip M. Boffey, William J. Broad, Stuart Diamond, David E. Sanger, William E. Schmidt, John Noble Wilford and Richard Witkin—were at work on the answers. With disclosure after disclosure, they not only told that story, but in the process they also played a key role in bringing about important changes in the American space program.

Mr. Witkin, a veteran reporter who had covered aviation for many years and who could turn to valuable old sources, struck first. Just three days after the accident, he learned that NASA was already zeroing in on what, indeed, proved to be the cause: a faulty solid-fuel booster rocket.

There were reasons why the space agency's technicians, weeks before telltale wreckage could be salvaged from the ocean floor, could move so fast. Mr. Sanger discovered that the booster rocket was known not to have been designed for use below 40 degrees Fahrenheit; the temperature at launching was about 33. Mr. Boffey discovered that NASA had been specifically warned six months before the accident that defective seals on the booster rockets could cause a catastrophe, and his report immediately changed the course of a presidential commission's inquiry. William P. Rogers, the commission chairman, cited the Boffey account and ordered NASA to produce all records relating to previous booster-rocket problems.

There were other devastating disclosures. Mr. Broad reported that accidents and personnel problems had plagued Cape Canaveral for months. Mr. Diamond wrote that NASA had received a report two years before that criticized safety planning and estimated the chance of catastrophe involving the booster rocket at 1 in 35. Mr. Boffey found that NASA had waived its requirement for backup safety seals. And Mr. Sanger reported that a chief engineer for the company that built the rocket, the senior engineer present at the launching, said he argued for hours with NASA officials, urging them not to launch because of the cold weather. That was something that the commission had been told but that the American people, who had paid for the program and who were deeply disturbed by what had happened, had not.

Mr. Boffey and Mr. Sanger covered the Rogers commission hearings with clarity, technical authority and thoroughness. But perhaps more importantly, they and the other team members probed deeper than had the commission investigators themselves, hitting areas the commissioners had not reached. The reporters' work influenced, and sometimes redirected, the course of the hearings.

In fact, though the reporting fully reflected tough criticisms made of the commission, Mr. Rogers called *The Times*'s publisher, Arthur Ochs Sulzberger, to congratulate him for the newspaper's "remarkable coverage" of the hearings. The former secretary of state said that he had "never seen better coverage anywhere" and that he wanted the newspaper to know how appreciative he and the rest of the commission were.

The Times dug deeper.

Mr. Boffey went to the Marshall Space Flight Center in Huntsville, Alabama, where manufacture of the rocket was supervised, and found a climate of fear on the part of employees and a reluctance to talk openly about what might have gone wrong.

Mr. Diamond spent weeks poring over 15 years' worth of government documents and then brilliantly pieced together the startling story of billions of dollars in government waste on the shuttle and on other space programs. He found, with the help of the Freedom of Information Act, that these documentable losses—in an amount exceeding $3.5 billion—occurred despite explicit warning by the Defense Department, the General Accounting Office and NASA's own Inspector General's office on cost abuses and mismanagement.

Most important in terms of the Challenger's destruction and the loss of the lives of its seven astronauts, Mr. Diamond found that this enormous quantity of money was being wasted at a time when NASA was cutting back or delaying a half billion dollars in safety and development programs on the grounds of lack of funds.

Finally, drawing on what Mr. Witkin, Mr. Broad, Mr. Boffey, Mr. Sanger, the Rogers commission and all he had learned himself, Mr. Diamond set forth for the first time a full picture of the fundamental, built-in causes of a major disaster: the overselling of the program from the outset, the unrealistic promise to make it not only pay for itself but also show a profit, the consequent unrelenting pressure to launch at a dangerously rapid pace and the sacrifices made along the way.

Key solutions that Mr. Diamond aired in the two-part series in April were, in fact, ordered later by the president: Clarify NASA's lines of management authority, monitor safety far more carefully and separate the commercial aspects of the American space program from the noncommercial ones to eliminate the dangerous scheduling pressures.

The Times did not stop there. Would NASA really change its ways or would it rush to a quick fix? The day before the Rogers commission was to deliver its report, Mr. Sanger wrote that there might be cause for pessimism: Some members believed the Rogers findings and recommendations to be so watered down as to encourage the more superficial approach.

Indeed, Mr. Broad learned in September that no basic redesign of the defective booster rocket was planned—that, in fact, the principal element proposed to correct the flaw was actually devised nearly five years earlier, indicating that the problem itself was much older than the public had been led to believe. And Mr. Sanger followed with the report that, by taking this approach, NASA may be discarding more reliable systems for the same underlying reason that caused the problem in the first place: an effort to save time and money.

America's space future, Mr. Wilford wrote in a review of the effects of the disaster, seemed badly clouded.

Did the story go deeper still? Yes. On December 7, on the basis of newly disclosed documents and dozens of interviews, Mr. Broad reported that Dr. James C. Fletcher, the NASA administrator, could have had the appearance of bias in awarding the original contract for the shuttle's booster rockets. As a result, Dr. Fletcher said he would seriously consider removing himself from all future determinations on shuttle contracts.

The documents uncovered by Mr. Broad and the information provided him in the interviews showed evidence, critics charged, tying Dr. Fletcher to Utah and the contractor, Morton Thiokol. Mr. Broad reported that Dr. Fletcher had served on a Utah industrial development board at the time of his Senate confirmation, that he was aware that two former Thiokol employees served in top positions on the NASA board that evaluated the contract and that Dr. Fletcher ignored a previous, 10-year research program for a booster rocket of alternate design. Thiokol's contract to participate in that program had been canceled after its rocket candidate blew up.

The issue had renewed relevance because NASA again was faced with deciding who would fix the flawed booster rocket, and how.

Indeed, following Mr. Broad's disclosures, Senator Albert Gore called for an inquiry by Congress's main investigative arm, the General Accounting Office, into the original contract award. Senator William Proxmire said Dr. Fletcher should remove himself from future booster-rocket decisions.

As the year of the American tragedy came to a close, Mr. Boffey, Mr. Diamond, Mr. Sanger and Mr. Wilford reported that NASA had, indeed, instituted some important reforms. But substantially more needed to be done in overall, long-term redirection of the American space program. Mr. Wilford wrote with sensitivity, perspective and a kind of somber poetry that the leadership and vision needed to recapture a dream and redirect a national mission were still missing.

—The editors
The New York Times

NASA HAD WARNING OF A DISASTER RISK POSED BY BOOSTER

ENGINEERS FEARED LEAKS; INTERNAL REPORTS CITED EROSION OF ROCKET SEALS—AGENCY DECLINES TO COMMENT

SUNDAY, FEBRUARY 9, 1986

BY PHILIP M. BOFFEY

WASHINGTON, Feb. 8—The space agency was warned last year that seals on the space shuttle's solid-fuel booster rockets might break and cause a catastrophic accident, according to documents from the agency's files.

The documents show that engineers at the headquarters of the National Aeronautics and Space Administration and its Marshall Space Flight Center in Huntsville, Ala., were concerned that leaks might occur where segments of the booster rockets are mated.

Such leaks would allow hot gases and flames to escape through the side of the rocket instead of through the nozzle that channels the gases out the rear, possibly causing severe damage to the shuttle or an explosion, according to space experts.

A STARK WARNING

One NASA analyst warned in an internal memorandum last July that flight safety was "being compromised by potential failure of the seals." He added: "Failure during launch would certainly be catastrophic."

A 1982 "critical items list" for the booster also warned that if the seals should fail the result could be "loss of vehicle, mission, and crew due to metal erosion, burnthrough, and probable case burst resulting in fire and deflagration," or rapid, intense burning.

It is not clear what action if any NASA might have taken in response to the warnings in the documents, but the issue was listed as a matter of concern in agency documents as recently as December.

Space agency officials declined today to respond to questions about the concerns raised in the internal documents.

David W. Garrett, chief of the agency's news and information branch, was informed of the substance of those documents and said he had informed both L. Michael Weeks, deputy associate administrator of the office of space flight, and David L. Winterhalter, acting director of the agency's shuttle propulsion division. He said they had declined to comment.

Jesse W. Moore, associate administrator for space flight, the agency's top shuttle official, did not return a telephone call to his home, although a family member said he was there.

The internal documents describing problems with the seals were made available to The New York Times by a solid-fuel rocket analyst who has worked closely with propulsion engineers from the Kennedy Space Center in Florida, which assembles the booster rockets; the Marshall center in Alabama, which is responsible for their design, and NASA headquarters in Washington.

THE LEADING THEORY

Although no one knows exactly what caused the explosion that destroyed the Challenger Jan. 28, space agency officials have said that the leading theory, based on films of the flight, is that a plume of flame emerged from one side of a booster and set off an explosion of the shuttle's giant external fuel tank.

Space officials have said they cannot identify precisely where the plume emerged and thus do not know whether it burned through a seam or through the metal side of the rocket. "It did appear to happen at least near a seam," Dr. William R. Graham, Acting Administrator of the space agency, said last Sunday. He said the plume appeared to start "near one of the field joints" but that measurements had not yet established whether the plume occurred "at the seam or just near the seam."

The safety of the seals also became an important issue Thursday at the first meeting of a Presidential commission that is investigating the causes of the accident. The space agency acknowledged that it had consulted with the rocket's manufacturer, Morton Thiokol Inc., about concerns that cold weather at the launching site might have weakened the seals. But an agency official told the commission the manufacturer had concurred that the launching should proceed.

The official, Judson A. Lovingood, deputy manager of shuttle projects at Marshall, also acknowledged that there had been concern after previous shuttle flights about erosion damage to some of the seals, but he indicated that this problem had been thoroughly investigated.

The seals are needed because the booster is not a single long structure but rather four large cylindrical segments that are bolted together, along with other components, at the Kennedy Space Center when the rocket is being prepared for launching. Although the side of the rocket may look leakproof to the naked eye, there is room for gases to escape at the seams. Thus rocket engineers have devised a series of seals and other barriers to keep the gases in.

The two most important seals are O rings, essentially large doughnut-shaped pieces of synthetic rubber that fill the tiny gap between two cylindrical segments that are bolted together. The O rings are themselves protected from heat and flame damage by an initial barrier of putty.

TIGHTER UNDER PRESSURE

If flames and hot gases are to escape through the joint between segments of the rocket, they generally must first pass through the putty, then through the primary O ring, and finally through the back-up ring. The rubbery O rings are designed to seal especially tight when they are hit by the high-pressure gases, much as a rubber washer on a faucet seals tight to prevent water from leaking.

At the Presidential commission's meeting Thursday, Mr. Lovingood, from the Marshall space center, was asked if experts had looked at the joints in the re-usable boosters after previous shuttle flights to see if there was any evidence of leakage. "We have seen some evidence of erosion of those seals, the primary seal," he said. "We've never seen any erosion of a secondary seal. But we have seen evidence of soot in between the two seals."

When asked if this was a cause for concern, he replied: "Oh, yes, I mean that's an anomaly and that was thoroughly worked, and that's completely documented on all the investigative work we did on that."

The possibility that cold weather might weaken the seals, by causing shrinkage or stiffening or through some other effect, is not explicitly addressed in the internal documents. Instead, those memorandums focus on erosion and heat effects observed on the seals after previous flights. One memorandum does suggest, however, that "environmental effects such as moisture" could be an indirect factor in causing erosion.

A memorandum prepared within the comptroller's office at NASA headquarters last summer used dire terms to describe the potential problems of charring and erosion that might damage the effectiveness of the seals. The memorandum, dated July 23, 1985, was addressed to Michael B. Mann, head of the resources analysis branch for the shuttle program, from Richard C. Cook, a subordinate.

RING WAS 'DESTROYED'

Mr. Cook warned that "the charring of seals," which had been observed on recent shuttle flights, posed "a potentially major problem affecting both flight safety and program costs." In the joint between the nozzle section of the rocket and the adjoining segment, the memorandum said, "not only has the first O ring been destroyed, but the second has been partially eaten away." The memorandum did not say how often this had occurred.

The joint referred to in the memorandum is the one nearest the spot where the plume of flame was seen to emerge from the side of the rocket just before the explosion that destroyed the Challenger.

The memorandum said the cause of the erosion problem had not been determined. "There is little question, however, that flight safety has been and is still being compromised by potential failure of the seals," it said, "and it is acknowledged that failure during launch would certainly be catastrophic."

The memorandum said the leadership of the space flight program "is viewing the situation with the utmost seriousness."

Another memorandum prepared at roughly the same time by Irving Davids, an engineer in the shuttle rocket booster program at NASA headquarters, described a visit he made to the Marshall Space Flight

Center on July 11, 1985, to discuss "seal erosion problems" that had affected the O rings on several shuttle flights.

A DOZEN INSTANCES

This memorandum said there had been "12 instances during flight" where there had been some erosion of the primary O ring at the seam where the nozzle segment of the rocket is bolted to the adjacent segment.

The memorandum said that in two cases soot actually blew by the primary seal, and in one case the backup seal showed erosion as well. Both this observation and Mr. Cook's memorandum appear to contradict Mr. Lovingood's assertion that no erosion of a secondary seal had been observed.

The document added that the prime suspect in causing the erosion was the type of putty used. It said Morton Thiokol, the manufacturer of the booster rocket, believed that the putty, made by another, unidentified manufacturer, could develop holes under certain conditions and that these holes would have a "jetting effect," an indication, apparently, that the holes could focus hot gases on the seal. "There doesn't appear to be a validated resolution as to the effect of the putty," Mr. Davids wrote.

The memorandum also described erosion of the O rings at the joints between other major segments of the rocket. It said there had been five occurrences during flight where the primary ring showed erosion and one case where the back-up ring was affected by heat although not actually eroded.

PROBLEM WITH BACK-UP RING

One critical problem, it added, was that rotational forces generated as pressure builds up within the rocket caused a "lifting off" or "unseating" of the secondary ring, a problem which "has been known for quite some time." One proposal for eliminating this problem, the memorandum said, was a "capture feature," not otherwise described, which would prevent the seal from lifting off.

The memorandum from Mr. Davids was addressed to Mr. Moore, the associate administrator for space flight.

Through the rest of the year, the O rings continued to be a concern to some engineers and budget analysts.

On Aug. 21, 1985, a budget briefing prepared for top-level NASA officials listed charring of the rings as one of the top "budget threats" to the solid-fuel booster program, apparently a reference to the fact that fixing the problem could become costly.

OTHER RECENT REPORTS

On Sept. 10, 1985, a status report and briefing prepared by NASA's propulsion division said that the most recently completed shuttle mission showed "one minor erosion" on the primary ring at the joint between the nozzle and the adjacent segment but no such damage at the other joints. It also listed charring of the rings at the top of the list of "solid rocket booster issues."

In December 1985, a monthly status report again listed ring charring as one of seven issues regarding the booster.

Concerns about the seals had been expressed in agency documents at least as far back as 1982. A "critical items list" for the solid-fuel booster rocket, dated Dec. 17, 1982, described the joints as in the most important category.

The document also said that "joint rotation" as the pressure rose in the rocket might knock out the back-up ring. This was the same problem that, according to Mr. Davids's memorandum, had still not been solved in July 1985, although it had been "known for quite some time."

ROCKET ENGINEER DESCRIBES ARGUING AGAINST LAUNCHING

SAYS HE WAS OVERRULED: TOP EXPERT FOR THIOKOL AT CAPE REPORTS 11TH-HOUR ADVICE ON DANGER FROM COLD

WEDNESDAY, FEBRUARY 19, 1986

BY DAVID E. SANGER

WASHINGTON, Feb. 18—The top Morton Thiokol engineer present at the Kennedy Space Center before the Jan. 28 liftoff of the space shuttle Challenger said tonight that he had argued for hours with space agency officials not to launch the craft because of low temperatures.

He said that he persisted even after his own superiors had overruled him and given the agency a go-ahead.

The engineer, Allan J. McDonald, a 26-year veteran of Morton Thiokol Inc., which made the solid-fuel booster rockets for the shuttle, said that at a closed session last Friday before the Presidential panel investigating the explosion he recounted his "somewhat heated" exchanges with officials of the space agency.

NOTES TO COMMISSION

He said in a telephone interview tonight that those exchanges centered on the rocket seals that have become a major suspect in the explosion that killed the shuttle's seven crew members.

Mr. McDonald, who is the director of Thiokol's solid-fuel rocket motor project, also said he turned over to the commission detailed notes made in the course of his dispute with the officials of the National Aeronautics and Space Administration.

He said he first warned NASA officials about potential dangers after calculations performed by Morton Thiokol engineers in Utah showed that the temperature of the O rings, which seal joints in the booster rockets, was about 30 degrees Fahrenheit. That is about 23 degrees lower, he said, than the temperature of the rings in a January 1985 shuttle launching that resulted in the largest amount of ring erosion ever seen by NASA officials.

SEALS SUSPECTED IN DISASTER

The O rings are the leading suspect in the apparent failure of the right-hand solid-fuel booster rocket. It is now believed that they may have set off events that led to the fireball that consumed the Challenger.

In testimony before a Senate subcommittee today, Jesse W. Moore, the space agency's top shuttle official, said he was not told about low temperature readings on one of the rockets the morning of the launching and would have asked more probing questions had the issue been brought to his attention.

Mark Weinberg, a spokesman for the Presidential commission, said, "It would not be appropriate" to say whether Mr. McDonald had appeared before the commission in its closed session at the Kennedy Space Center last week. Mr. McDonald said it was likely he would be called to appear at an open hearing of the commission next week. The commission has confirmed that it took testimony from several Morton Thiokol officials on Friday.

NASA officials said today that technical crews on the launching pad, using infrared sensors, had measured temperatures as low as 7 to 9 degrees Fahrenheit on the surface of the right-hand booster rocket, near the O ring seals that are suspected of failing.

A breach of the O rings would allow superhot gases to escape through the side casing of the 149-foot-long rocket, an event that NASA officials had previously considered unlikely, although some NASA engineers had warned more than a year ago that such a breach could be catastrophic.

Mr. McDonald said today that on the night of Jan. 27 he was arguing primarily with Lawrence B. Mulloy, who heads NASA's solid-fuel booster rocket project at the Marshall Space Flight Center in Huntsville, Ala.

"It was a very prolonged discussion, Mr. McDonald added. "The engineers in Utah were largely in agreement with me."

Nonetheless, he said, his superior, Joseph Kilminster, overruled his objections around 11:30 P.M. and transmitted to NASA a copy of a letter approving the launch. But Mr. McDonald said he believed the situation was so serious that he continued arguing his point even after the letter had arrived at Cape Canaveral.

"I argued before and I argued after," he said by telephone from his home in Ogden, Utah. "The low temperatures make the O ring seals much harder, stiffer, and it caused them to shrink. It is hard to quantify, but qualitatively that is what happened."

Mr. Mulloy did not return a message last night left on an answering machine at his home in Huntsville. There was no answer at Mr. Kilminster's home in Utah.

Mr. Mulloy has testified before the commission on the effects of the cold on the O rings. Mr. Kilminster has not, but his name has been mentioned before the commission in discussions about Morton Thiokol's agreement to go ahead with the launching.

TESTIMONY BEFORE PANEL

In testimony before an open session of the Presidential commission last week, Mr. Mulloy, confronted with an impromptu test of the resiliency of the O rings by a panel member, Richard P. Feynman, said tests indicated that the rings lost resiliency as the temperature dropped toward 50 degrees Fahrenheit. But he added that specifications indicated they could operate safely down to 30 degrees below zero.

In his testimony Feb. 11, Mr. Mulloy said that data presented on the night before the launching by Morton Thiokol indicated that the resilience of the seal drops even further at temperatures of 20 or 25 degrees Fahrenheit. However, Mr. Mulloy said that "under the conditions that we would see on launch day, given the configuration that we ran, that the seal would function at that temperature. That was the final judgment."

He added, "Ah, there were data presented as we have discussed, by some, by Thiokol engineering, that there was a suggestion that possibly the seal shouldn't be operated below any temperature that it had been operated on previous flights."

Mr. Mulloy also said last week that Morton Thiokol had originally recommended against launching but reversed that position later on the evening of Jan. 27.

At NASA headquarters tonight, Charles Redmond 3d, a spokesman, said, "Clearly, the Morton Thiokol engineer has a point of view he is allowed to make, but beyond that I don't think we have any comment."

At least some of Mr. McDonald's comments today appeared to contradict Mr. Mulloy's statements last week concerning the relationship between the cold and erosion of the O rings in previous launchings.

Last Wednesday, at a news conference, Mr. Mulloy was asked about the decision to launch despite the cold. "What we went on," he said, "was the basis of the data that we had that indicated that there was no direct correlation between the erosion and blowby on the primary ring and temperature, based on the previous flight data."

"Blowby" refers to a rush of gases past a seal.

But Mr. McDonald said today, "That is not quite correct."

"There is not a strong correlation," he said. "But there is evidence that things got worse with low temperature." Before the Challenger launching, he said, the O ring was particularly cold because it had sat, uninsulated, in below-freezing temperatures the night before the launching.

Mr. McDonald, who is 48 years old and holds a bachelor's degree in chemical engineering from Montana State University and a master's degree in engineering administration from the University of Utah, said tonight that he was uncertain why his recommendation against the launching had been overruled.

"They felt, I am sure, that the basis for the concern was not fully conclusive," Mr. McDonald said.

NASA CUT OR DELAYED SAFETY SPENDING

THURSDAY, APRIL 24, 1986

BY STUART DIAMOND

The space agency cut or delayed half a billion dollars in spending on safety testing, design and development from the time the shuttle program began to when the Challenger exploded in January, Federal audits show.

The range of work included testing the shuttle and its main engines for vibration, developing the booster rocket that probably caused the explosion and conducting communications and thermal tests.

For years Government auditors and aerospace experts implored the National Aeronautics and Space Administration not to cut testing and other development work. They said eliminating the spending or significantly delaying it—some of the money has still not been spent—would mean equipment would be assembled before components were fully tested. It would then be very difficult and costly to make changes. Ultimately, this would compromise reliability and make the machine less cost effective and less safe, they said.

But the agency, faced with ever-tightening budget restrictions, refused, saying the eliminated procedures were "not cost effective," said the General Accounting Office, a Congressional investigative agency.

The cutbacks came in the same general period in which Government inspectors repeatedly warned NASA that it was wasting large sums of money through faulty management. This money, more than $3.5 billion in all, in turn helped create the budget problems.

REVIEW OF 500 AUDITS

The reductions in safety testing, design and development and the patterns of excessive spending and mismanagement at NASA emerged in a review by The New York Times of more than 500 audits of the space agency by its own Office of Inspector General, the General

Accounting Office and the Pentagon's Defense Contract Audit Agency. Interviews with space experts inside and outside the Government generally confirm the audits, most of which have not been made public. Many were obtained through the Freedom of Information Act.

The agency issued a statement yesterday saying some of the problems cited in the audits "are related to activities several years ago and have been corrected or are being corrected."

"Furthermore," the statement said, "during the existence of NASA it has used its own internal audits to uncover and correct deficiencies and to strengthen internal controls."

NASA officials said in interviews that the audits had been fair and generally accurate. They also contended that the mismanagement was administrative, not technical, and insisted that it did not result in safety compromises.

Among the chief findings of the audits were the following:

• On the Challenger, faulty welds concealed through falsified X-rays by a subcontractor to avoid the cost of repair. They went undetected and uncorrected until NASA auditors received tips from former employees of the subcontractor.

• After a reduction in its inspectors' ranks, the Johnson Space Center, in direct charge of the shuttle flights that were to begin a year later, failed to detect equipment flaws so critical that they could cause loss of life or destruction of the spaceship.

• NASA misled Congress about costs and schedules for the shuttle and other programs, withheld critical documents and violated Federal codes in thousands of instances.

• NASA violated Federal policy by spending billions of dollars on shuttle equipment that had not been thoroughly tested.

• By 1976 the shuttle had become "a higher risk program" in terms of economics and performance than conceived, the General Accounting Office said.

THE TRANSITION FROM THE APOLLO ERA

Experts familiar with this history of NASA say problems at its headquarters in Washington and 16 other space centers began shortly after the agency reached its founding goal of landing men on the moon in 1969 and after the Administrator who led NASA there, James E. Webb, resigned after eight years in office.

"There was a distinct change after Mr. Webb left," said Elmer B. Staats, who from 1966 to 1981 was the United States Comptroller General, the top position at the General Accounting Office. "Mr. Webb was a good manager. He put together a good team. But afterwards, there was less openness, less willingness to listen to the kind of challenges we were making. It was an institutional thing; it was the whole system."

One of the major changes was the way the agency viewed the design, testing and development of new space systems.

On the Apollo moon program and others of that era, each component was designed, built as a prototype and then tested, space experts say. Thus when the final system was assembled for a test, scientists had a high degree of confidence that it would work.

But NASA decided that to save money it would cut back on the kind of testing done in earlier programs and instead build major components and systems before they were fully tested, according to auditors, space experts and NASA officials themselves, including C. Thomas Newman, the NASA comptroller, who has been with the agency since 1963.

"The shuttle set out with some different objectives," Mr. Newman said. "To produce a system of moderate costs, the program was not as thoroughly endowed with test hardware."

CUTTING OF COSTS BEGINS IN EARNEST

Most of NASA's money problems—overspending for equipment and personnel and shortages of funds for testing—coalesced on the shuttle program, the auditors conclude. The program started as a relatively modest project and eventually took up 60 percent of the agency's budget.

The shuttle was NASA's choice to succeed the Apollo program as the agency's major endeavor after NASA was rejected in its attempt to undertake a manned flight to Mars and build a space station. The Nixon Administration backed the shuttle to aid scientific and military goals and help shore up the aerospace industry, according to experts familiar with decisions then.

But space experts said the program was sold to Congress, essentially by Dr. James C. Fletcher, NASA's Administrator at the time, based on the idea that it would pay for itself through commercial business, deploying and repairing private satellites and selling other space services. Dr. Fletcher has been nominated by President Reagan to head the agency again, and his confirmation hearings got under way in Congress yesterday.

The shuttle's economics, however, depended on relatively low operating costs to offset the high development costs.

To meet budget restrictions, NASA proposed a shuttle that would be reusable only in part. That kept down the development cost but made operating costs much higher, as the huge external fuel tank and other components had to be replaced each time.

To further cut costs, NASA projected 60 flights a year. "They were assuming a ridiculous number of flights," said John E. Pike, space policy expert at the Federation of American Scientists. Since the Challenger explosion, some astronauts have said that any more than nine flights a year can put dangerous pressure on those preparing each flight.

C. Robert Nysmith, the agency's Associate Administrator for Management, said NASA officials consistently believed that, despite the cuts, enough protections remained to keep the space programs safe even if some testing was delayed.

The risk of the reduced or delayed testing, however, was that if major problems developed, costs would rise greatly as they were fixed and, in reality, safety might well be compromised, said auditors and such space experts as Dr. Albert J. Kelley, a vice president of Arthur D. Little Inc., the management consulting concern, who was once a NASA project manager.

"It's not the optimum way," Dr. Kelley said, "and you take a risk. When you have pressures, you look for ways to cut corners, and you manage differently. What usually goes is design planning and hardware testing."

THE ISSUE OF SAFETY

Despite NASA's views to the contrary, the Government auditors argued that there was no clear distinction between technical and administrative management, particularly because it often involved the same people.

And if there is no real distinction, they argued, safety issues cannot be considered separately from administrative problems.

Dr. Kelley, who holds a Ph.D. in aeronautics and astronautics from the Massachusetts Institute of Technology, said: "Outside the laboratory, there are very few decisions that are only technical. The whole technical, management, procurement, schedule and cost issues are interrelated."

The cuts and delays in early shuttle spending included $147 million of testing for the main engines, the most advanced ever developed for use in space, audits by the General Accounting Office said. About $118 million for testing and developing the orbiter was cut, $10 million for developing the external tank for liquid fuel, $68 million for developing the solid-fuel booster rocket and $70 million for launching and landing development.

Vibration tests for the orbiter and for the shuttle assemblage were deleted. Tests of tires and landing gear were cut back. Testing and development were eliminated or postponed for years on a wide variety of radar, communications links and other equipment, including that needed to operate shuttles in orbit.

The audits give numbers for a total of about $500 million of cuts, but not all of the deletions have price tags attached.

Some of the development work was moved to the production phase of the program and some to the operations phase, but a substantial portion was deleted: at least $110 million by 1976.

The cuts worried experts both inside and outside NASA. They warned that because the performance of much equipment could not be verified early in the program, the agency might wind up with unreliable and unsafe equipment. It also would not find out about major problems until an advanced stage of production, meaning that any changes could be very costly.

Some of those concerns were raised in 1974 in a study by 35 aeronautical and space experts led by Willis Hawkins of the Lockheed Aircraft Corporation. The team said it was worried that testing was being "highly compressed." Orbiter testing, for example, was cut from 16 months to three. Main engine testing was slashed, the report said. It said there was little backup equipment for use in tests, so failures would delay the schedule.

The experts said that the likelihood of unforeseen technical problems was high because of the "difficult technical goals" but that there was little margin for error. Those concerns were echoed by three studies at NASA's Goddard Space Flight Center. And they were repeated by Congressional auditors in 1975 and 1976.

In 1977 the auditors said deletion of tests of tires, brakes and landing gear "may result in loss of vehicle and crew." These systems have consistently caused problems on shuttle landings.

But NASA consistently disagreed with the auditors and experts. The agency rejected a plea by the Hawkins team to stop compressing the test schedule "as not being cost effective."

MAJOR TROUBLES BEGIN TO DEVELOP

NASA officials said they did not need all the tests because of experience gained from the Apollo program, though many experts argued that the shuttle was a new venture with its own potential problems. The General Accounting Office noted that some of the deleted tests had turned up many problems that required changes in design and other areas. Yet they were deleted, the auditors said, because NASA thought them "too costly."

On Feb. 27, 1975, Dr. Fletcher wrote to the General Accounting Office that NASA had a "sound management process" for the shuttle, adding, "I have no reason to anticipate cost overruns" beyond the original commitments. Two years later Dr. Fletcher said, "The shuttle has encountered normal technical problems of a complex program."

But major problems were beginning to develop by the late 1970's with the shuttle's thermal protection system, about 30,000 lightweight tiles that cover 65 percent of the vehicle and protect it from the heat of re-entry. Tiles kept falling off.

Moreover, the main engine, when built, kept blowing up in full tests. Pumps, valves and other equipment failed when completed. Hundreds of millions of dollars more were expended for corrections.

Ever since the shuttle started flying in 1981, flights have been delayed and problems have developed in flight as some of the equipment not fully tested failed. At least 7 of the 25 flights have been delayed a total of nearly seven months because of problems with engines, onboard power units or the solid-fuel booster rockets.

In May 1982 NASA's inspector general said, "Technical difficulties and problems have occurred across the entire spectrum of the Space Transportation System development activity."

As recently as March 27, NASA's own Office of Inspector General reported that administrative practices at the Marshall Space Flight Center in Huntsville, Ala., were so lax before the Challenger explosion that the center could not properly determine whether defective equipment had been fixed. Marshall officials, who had responsibility for the booster rockets, have declined to comment on the findings.

DEFECTIVE WELDS FOUND ON CHALLENGER

The link between NASA's administrative and safety problems was apparent in various aspects of the shuttle program, the audits show.

In reports by NASA's Inspector General in 1979 and 1980, the Rockwell International Corporation, prime contractor for the shuttle orbiter, was found to have failed to detect promptly and report defects in items whose malfunction could be threatening to a spaceship or its crew. And the NASA managers at the Johnson Space Center who supervised Rockwell did not correct the problems for at least 14 months, the inspectors said.

Three years later, the auditors reported that a Rockwell subcontractor had routinely submitted falsified X-rays to conceal safety defects in welds on the Challenger "to avoid the cost of rewelding." The auditors said the subcontractor, Jet Air Inc., of El Cajon, Calif., had given its welding work to unapproved machine shops and then falsely certified that it had done the work.

The problem was caught only after former workers of Jet Air informed NASA auditors.

Rockwell, at the auditors' request, reviewed more than 1,800 parts on the Challenger and found a number it could not certify as proper. But the company suggested that the Challenger "fly as is" because of the "high design margin" and "noncritical" function of the parts. It suggested repeated inspections and limits on use of the parts because of possible "crack growth." One part carried the warning, "May yield under load, but no catastrophic failure."

The documents of the three inspection agencies contain no specific references to administrative procedures or safety cutbacks related to the rocket joints suspected as the cause of the Challenger's explosion, in which the seven crew members died.

But the head of NASA's shuttle program, Arnold Aldrich, told the

Presidential commission investigating the Challenger explosion that a serious management flaw had preceded the tragedy. He was never told, he said, that engineers had complained about troubles with the rocket seals. The complaints, made for several months in 1985, had reached lower-level officials, NASA said.

The Federal auditors warned that reducing tests of safety and design would lead to miscalculations about equipment performance. Indeed, one miscalculation occurred on a system that was designed to blow up the shuttle if it went out of control within range of populated areas.

Air Force personnel, who monitor shuttle launchings, used the range-safety system to blow up the booster rockets that were flying wildly after the Challenger broke apart. Yet in 1974 NASA told the Air Force that such a system would not be needed after the first few flights. "Adequate safety would be attained through system design reliability" of the shuttle, NASA argued.

NASA did adopt a system by which the crew could terminate a malfunctioning flight, the Congressional auditors said, but its choice still did not meet Air Force's requirement for a remote control. The Air Force imposed this requirement to protect people on the ground in case disabled astronauts were unable to control the flights.

NASA is said to have continued developing its crew-operated system for more than a year over Air Force objections, while deleting $10 million for testing a remote-controlled system.

Late in 1975 NASA decided to install an Air Force-approved system. It cost millions of dollars more than the agency anticipated.

Among the other development work that suffered was designing equipment for ease of maintenance. In 1975 NASA canceled a contract with American Airlines for a study of maintenance considerations. The agency's inspector general said years later that the lack of such considerations was a major reason for the greatly increased time it was taking for preparations between launchings, 1,240 hours instead of 160. This meant increased pressures on personnel, and an added threat to safety, auditors and space experts alike have said since the Challenger exploded.

CONGRESS WAS MISLED, AUDITS ASSERT

Audits of the space agency since 1971 allege that NASA consistently misled Congress on projects, whether on costs or feasibility, in violation of various Federal laws.

At one point NASA told Congress that the agency had $2.7 billion to work with when it actually had $4.3 billion, counting surpluses and other funds, the auditors said. The General Accounting Office said that "NASA's data is inaccurate and incomplete" and that Congress should not rely on the data. The auditors said NASA's actions violated its own guidelines for providing Congress details about projects. But the dispute continued all through the 1970's, as the General Accounting office repeatedly said NASA was misleading Congress.

The auditors said the agency's reports to Congress contained some direct misstatements, usually underestimating costs, but auditors and space experts say the reports were also misleading in what they failed to report: that budget cutbacks could not be separated from possible safety problems.

As auditors' criticisms intensified over the last decade, there were some expressions of concern in hearings by the five Congressional subcommittees with jurisdiction over NASA. But Congress kept approving budgets for the shuttle project and usually accepted NASA's explanations or pledges to change.

The committees were too soft on NASA, according to the auditors, various Government experts and even some legislators. One of the auditors, Donald E. Day, senior associate director of the G.A.O.'s Division for National Security and International Affairs, observed, "The committees have been very supportive of the agency. They have gotten too close to the agency and have been less objective than they should have been."

Mr. Day singled out Representatives Don Fuqua and Bill Nelson of the House Science and Technology Committee, both Florida Democrats. And he pointed to Senator Jake Garn, whose Utah constituency includes Morton Thiokol Inc., maker of the suspect rocket boosters.

Those and others on their committees, Mr. Day said, "are NASA's biggest fans when you get right down to it." He said that was why auditors' warnings on cost and safety mismanagement had been so consistently ignored. "Even though we bring things to the Congress, there is this shield," he said. "They say, 'Thank you, G.A.O., for your work,' " and then ignore it.

Each lawmaker denied vigorously any support of NASA by virtue of their constituencies. They acknowledged certain shortcomings in the process and affirmed their support of NASA.

Auditors said other reasons for ignoring warnings included NASA's remarkable success with the moon landing as well as a public belief in the space program in general.

"The shuttle had a kind of special appeal in this country," said Mr. Staats, the former Comptroller General. "We had many meetings with NASA, but we couldn't convince them to make the changes. And there wasn't enough support for our position in the top levels of Congress or in the Administration."

Bill Green, Republican of Manhattan and ranking minority member of the House Appropriations Subcommittee on H.U.D. and Independent Agencies, said "there was an assumption of managerial efficiency" with NASA.

"Certainly the success of the programs helped the Congress give NASA" what it wanted, Mr. Green said. "But the shuttle program has very much eroded that. The oversight will be a lot tighter."

Walter F. Mondale, who was a vocal opponent of the shuttle when he was a Senator, agreed. "The information, the statistics, the facts simply didn't matter to NASA's sponsors in Congress," the former Democratic Presidential candidate said in an interview. "There was this whole empire of people left over from the Apollo program with nothing to do. And to sustain their efforts, they needed show business. And manned flight was the drama."

Mr. Fuqua, a Democrat who has headed the House Committee on Science and Technology since 1979, said he and others did raise questions about cost and testing, but generally let the agency have its way. "We raised questions. But we said, 'If it works, you look good. If it doesn't, we all are going to have egg on our face.'

"We are strong proponents of the space program," he said. "I think we wanted NASA to do well. We had to trust their judgment. They have some very competent people."

Now, he said, the agency must make its management more centralized. "I don't think we have to legislate it," he said, "but there will be a lot closer scrutiny."

Mr. Garn, who heads the Senate's counterpart to Mr. Green's sub-committee, has been on Senate science committees since 1974 and flew aboard the shuttle Discovery in April 1985.

"Of course NASA has troubles in management," he said. "Of course there are things that could have been done better over the years. There were inefficiencies in the way money was spent. NASA has been wrong in its estimates."

But he argued that many Government agencies wasted money and that NASA had done a "remarkable" job, given the complexities of its projects. "Someone has to stand up for this agency when everyone else looks for the negative," Mr. Garn said. But he, too, added that there would have to be management changes.

AUDITORS AND EXPERTS OFFER CONCLUSIONS

The space shuttle, it is clear from the audits, is far less re-usable than planned. The main engines, which were supposed to last 55 flights without major overhaul, for one example, barely last five flights before major components have to be replaced. Vibration is causing premature wear of a main pump, including blades and bearings. The engines are operating at 5 percent less power than their design goal.

And some of the rocket boosters have lasted less than their predicted 20 uses due to various problems such as damage from impact with the ocean.

The result is far greater cost for replacements, lower safety margins and a nearly eightfold increase in turnaround time. Major multimillion-dollar development work for the program is still continuing even as the orbiters are considered "operational."

The shuttle will cost at least $2.4 billion a year to operate and another $1.9 billion a year to amortize the investment, the Congressional Budget Office says. Those costs mean the shuttle is significantly more costly than the expendable rockets it was to replace, according to shuttle economic experts, and is not even close to paying for itself.

Thus nearly everyone interviewed, both inside and outside NASA, agreed that the original goal of commercial competitiveness for the shuttle should be abandoned. Mr. Newman, the NASA comptroller, said, "I doubt the shuttle itself is a commercial venture."

But most agreed, too, that the shuttle was an extremely valuable scientific and military asset. And they contended that if the commercial pressures for the frequent launchings were eliminated and the shuttle was used more selectively when needed, it would become a safer and more valuable national enterprise.

NASA HAD SOLUTION TO KEY FLAW IN ROCKET WHEN SHUTTLE EXPLODED

MONDAY, SEPTEMBER 22, 1986

BY WILLIAM J. BROAD

The key solution proposed by the space agency to the problem that caused the Challenger explosion was devised years before the disaster and was being systematically applied to the entire space shuttle fleet, interviews, documents and testimony show.

The record shows longstanding worry about seals on the shuttle and application of an innovative remedy to generations of booster rockets. It also shows why the solution was unavailable for the Challenger flight of Jan. 28, in which a leaky booster seal touched off an explosion that destroyed the craft and killed its seven astronauts.

To critics, this new history suggests duplicity on the part of the National Aeronautics and Space Administration: While publicly declaring the shuttle safe to fly, these critics say, NASA officials knew the flaw was grave and had quietly embarked on a major program to fix it.

DENIAL FROM NASA

NASA officials vigorously deny this charge, insisting they were unaware of the seriousness of the flaw and were simply trying to increase the booster's margin of safety.

No matter what prompted past action, the fact that NASA had almost five years of experience with the remedy explains how the agency was able to propose a $300 million seal redesign, unveiled Aug. 12, as fast as it did. Both critics and NASA officials agree that the space agency is now following the basic course it set for itself long before the Challenger disaster.

The key element of the redesign was invented in 1981 to lock seals tightly in place by latching down an element of the joint. This capture feature was applied to the design of booster rockets in 1982 and again in 1985.

In July 1985, amid growing fears of seal failure, NASA officials ordered 72 new steel cases so they could install capture features in boosters already in use. These new cases were in production at the time of the Challenger disaster and today they are the basis for the creation of improved boosters.

This history, gleaned from dozens of interviews, hundreds of newly released documents and thousands of pages of testimony, much of it originally kept secret, is sharply at odds with information previously made public. It had been thought that NASA officials were concerned about the booster seals before the Challenger disaster and were searching for a way to fix them. In fact, "the solution," as NASA engineers called the capture feature, was already being systematically if slowly applied.

The Presidential commission that investigated the Challenger disaster steered away from this history and the issues it raises. Among them are: Who knew replacement casings had been ordered? Did officials who knew about these casings press to continue flights? Why was the new design being applied slowly?

The commission's chairman, former Secretary of State William P. Rogers, said the panel should deal only with events leading directly to the disaster. But others are investigating deeply in other directions.

Representative James H. Scheuer, for instance, sits on a Congressional committee that recently reviewed the Rogers commission's findings and held hearings on the disaster. "It's remarkable how much NASA knew and how little they did about it," said Mr. Scheuer, a Queens Democrat. "There was no sense of urgency. There was no order or direction that went out. There was no mobilization of forces."

Richard C. Cook, a former NASA budget analyst who warned in 1985 that problems with the shuttle's booster joints might lead to a catastrophe, said: "The capture feature was to be the solution. It was clearly a big step. But it was happening very slowly." "The engineers knew about the big fix," he said, but until it was carried out, "they held their breath every time the shuttle took off."

John E. Pike, director of space policy at the Federation of American Scientists, called the situation at NASA "shocking."

"They were clearly covering up the magnitude of the problem," Mr. Pike said. "It raises the question of who knew what when. It's one thing to say this was a dinky little problem that a few engineers worried about, and another to embark on a major redesign of the system."

The fact that the space agency applied the "solution" as early as 1982 and again in 1985 could affect litigation over the Challenger disaster, according to a lawyer representing Cheryl NcNair, widow of Dr. Ronald E. McNair, one of the Challenger astronauts.

"Why fix the booster if it wasn't broken?" asked Ronald D. Krist, a Houston lawyer who has filed a suit in Texas in behalf of Mrs. NcNair.

"It makes the fact that they forced this launch all the more reprehensible," Mr. Krist said. "It shows a conscious indifference to the welfare and safety of the astronauts. Rather than postpone a launch, they pressed ahead."

Mrs. NcNair has sued the booster maker. In addition, Jane Smith, widow of the Challenger's pilot, Comdr. Michael J. Smith of the Navy, has filed an administrative claim against the Government.

In defending past actions, NASA officials insist the depth of the booster problem was unknown before the Challenger disaster. Casing design improvements, they assert, were part of a wide-ranging effort to make all flight equipment as safe as possible.

"Enhancement of that joint was just one of several things we were working on," said James E. Kingsbury, director of science and engineering at the Marshall Space Flight Center in Huntsville, Ala., which has responsibility for design of the booster rocket. "No one recognized the weakness it contained."

Thomas L. Moser, deputy associate administrator (management) for space flight at NASA headquarters in Washington, agreed. "In fairness I don't think you can say NASA was flying with a system it regarded as inadequate," he said. "The design was seen as marginal but adequate. It's just that there was an opportunity to increase the margin of safety."

HISTORY OF JOINT IS A COMPLEX ONE

The history of the capture feature begins in 1974 when the Thiokol Corporation, now part of Morton Thiokol Inc., won the contract to design and build the shuttle's solid-fuel booster rockets. They were to be 12 feet in diameter and 149 feet long. For ease of assembly, the boosters were built in parts, including four steel-walled, 27-foot-long fuel segments. These were cast in Utah and shipped to Florida, where they were bolted to one another with 177 steel pins at each seam. For strength at each joint, a three-inch tongue from one steel case fit snugly into a corresponding groove on the next, locking the segments tightly together. Or that was the plan.

In testing in 1977, the joint was found to be seriously flawed. As the rocket ignited, explosive pressures puffed out its half-inch steel walls. At the same time, the joint, where metal was thicker, resisted this motion. The result was a slight shift or rotation of tongue and groove in relation to each other, creating a gap between them. The design called for this gap to be filled by two rubbery O rings meant to prevent gases burning at 5,900 degrees Fahrenheit from leaking out of the rocket. The wider the gap, the greater the danger that the joint would not seal.

The discovery of the rotation prompted a series of memorandums at Thiokol in Utah and Marshall in Alabama. The existing tongue-and-groove joint was nonetheless deemed safe enough to fly. Tests showed that at least one of the O rings would hold in each joint. And they did, with few problems, in the first few shuttle flights.

Soon, however, two design changes to improve booster casings made joint rotation worse.

In April 1981, as the first shuttle flew into orbit, NASA engineers were planning two new generations of booster rockets. The first was to have lightweight steel cases so shuttles could carry heavier payloads into space, making the winged spaceships more cost-competitive. Shaving a few hundredths of an inch of steel from casings would lighten them by 4,000 pounds, or about 4 percent.

The second generation of casings was to replace steel altogether with lightweight carbon filaments and epoxy resins. These filament casings were viewed as critical for impending flights from Vandenberg Air Force Base, Calif., where shuttles would be sent southward into a polar orbit more difficult to achieve than the more equatorial orbit flown by shuttles launched from Kennedy. Vandenberg shuttles had to be as light as possible; filament casings made each booster 33,000 pounds lighter.

But both new casings were more elastic than the old ones, and their walls ballooned even more on rocket ignition, increasing joint rotation.

"We worried about the lightweight steel case," said Kenneth W. Jones, a Marshall booster engineer. "It aggravated the rotation. And the filament would aggravate it even more. So we were looking for a way to reduce it." Alternatives for the lightweight steel casings were limited because it was simply a pared-down version of the old one. No fundamental change could easily be made in its joint. So attention focused instead on the filament casing and its joint, which were altogether new.

ANOTHER COMPANY ENTERS THE PICTURE

In 1981, engineers from Marshall discussed the rotation problem with representatives of the aerospace division of Hercules Inc., in Murray, Utah, and Thiokol, and two companies seeking the contract for the filament casing. Later, in preliminary design studies, both companies sketched joints nearly identical to the steel-case joints. But on Dec. 4, 1981, a Hercules engineer hit on an altogether new idea.

"I'd been mulling over the problem for months," Frederick Policelli, the inventor, recalled in a recent interview. "Finally it just popped into my head. I was on my way out the door, so I sat down and sketched it out." At the time, Mr. Policelli was technical manager of the filament booster program at Hercules. His idea, which he called a "capture lip," came to him as he was leaving a meeting with Marshall officials in Alabama.

The capture feature was envisioned as a one-inch appendage on the tongue that inhibited movement of the opposing groove, which held the pair of critical O rings. The whole joint was to be machined from one solid piece of steel to be tightly bonded to the filament case. The capture feature would give the wobbly joint stability not unlike that of a firm handshake.

In early 1982, Thiokol and Hercules submitted rival bids and designs for the filament-cased boosters. Thiokol proposed the same joint as on the steel case. Hercules proposed the capture feature.

"I jumped on it and championed it," said William L. Ray, an engineer at Marshall who had long criticized the booster joint as unacceptable. "There was a lot of opposition."

"People didn't understand" the joint or its problems, Mr. Ray said.

Influenced by the strong advocacy of Mr. Ray and other Marshall engineers, the space agency in May 1982 awarded Hercules the contract to develop filament casings. "The capture feature wasn't the only reason they won it," Mr. Ray said, "but it clearly was a plus."

BITTER FIGHTING BETWEEN COMPETITORS

The capture feature received no patents for orginality or awards for elegance. But it did turn a flawed joint into one that was much less susceptible to rotation.

It also injected an element of corporate rivalry into the manufacture of shuttle boosters, one that flared into bitter fights between Thiokol and Hercules. The new joint, after all, could be viewed as an indictment of the old one. Tension ran especially high because Thiokol was still to be in charge of filling the filament casings with fuel and readying them for flight. At one point in late 1982, Thiokol, exerting its influence, stopped Hercules from releasing plans for the filament joint to a forger, the Ladish Company in Cudahy, Wis.

"It came to a showdown," Mr. Policelli of Hercules recalled. "We went to NASA and they supported our side."

A spokesman at Thiokol's facility in Brigham City, Utah, defended the company's unwillingness to add a capture feature, saying that even today there are questions about its effectiveness. "It takes time to learn what changes are necessary," said Rocky Raab, the Thiokol spokesman.

At the time, the future of the filament casings was additionally unclear because NASA officials were unsure whether the new design might become the mainstay of the shuttle fleet, replacing steel casings altogether. Use of the lightweight filament casings would greatly increase the weight of the payload each shuttle could carry into space.

In 1982, the space agency's master plan was to begin using filament casings in Vandenberg launchings by October 1985. At first, these filament casings were to be used once and discarded, unlike steel casings used at Kennedy that were meant to be cleaned, refilled and reflown up to 20 times. But over time, with more research and development, filament casings, too, were to become re-usable, which would make them practical for use throughout the shuttle program.

Re-usability "was a goal, not a firm requirement," said a Hercules official in Utah, who spoke on the condition of anonymity. "We were to see if it would work for the program as a whole. And one of the beauties was that it had the capture feature."

PUTTING THE DESIGN INTO PRACTICE

In 1982 and 1983, however, space agency engineers were loath to gamble the program's future on the successful development of re-usable filament boosters. Hedging their bets, they discussed the possibility of creating steel casings with a capture feature, according to Mr. Ray. All it would take was casting new steel casings with an additional three inches of steel around the inside of one end, into which a capture lip could be machined.

Each two-part, 27-foot fuel segment would then comprise one new casing with the capture feature and one old casing, the pair sturdily joined at the factory in Utah. These segments, each with a capture feature at one end, could then be pinned together at the Kennedy Space Center. Alternating new and old casings would mean that, as the shuttle fleet expanded, all of the old metal casings could be used.

But there would be drawbacks as well. Capture features would add about 200 pounds each, or a total of 600 pounds per booster rocket—a small but significant amount. Assembly of segments with a capture feature would also be more complex. Moreover, engineers estimated it would take 27 months for new steel casings to be forged, machined, filled with fuel and readied for flight. Finally, in 1982 and 1983, no one was sure the capture feature was the best solution.

"There was great interest in incorporating the capture feature in the steel case," Mr. Ray of Marshall recalled, "The reason it wasn't done quicker is that we wanted to be sure it worked. That joint looks simple, but it's very complex. You don't want to accidentally make it worse." Marshall decided to wait for results from the testing of the filament case, and then make a decision about using it in new steel casings.

Meanwhile, steel booster performance problems increased, in part apparently because of adoption of the lightweight steel casings. These were first used to boost the shuttle aloft in April 1983 and thereafter became a standard feature of all flights. In 1984, O rings in light-weight steel boosters were found to have been damaged by hot gases on successive shuttle flights in February, April and August.

Fortunately, a rich harvest of data had been gathered starting in late

1984 on the effectiveness of the capture feature. The first full-scale filament test firing took place in Utah in October 1984, and others quickly followed. Moreover, laboratory tests were begun to investigate the dynamics of the capture feature. This testing program ended in the spring of 1985. "We were convinced the capture feature was a good thing," Mr. Kingsbury of Marshall recalled.

PROBLEM IS SEEN WITH THE O RINGS

Then, in June 1985, engineers discovered for the first time that hot gases had gone past a primary O ring on a shuttle flight and had started to erode a secondary ring.

A month later, Marshall officials responded by putting a "launch constraint" on all shuttle flights; from then on, the latest available information on joint problems would have to be discussed in readiness reviews before each flight.

The steel booster program had reached a turning point. In July 1985, more than three years after NASA decided to put the capture feature in the filament casing, Marshall and Thiokol officials acknowledged that the steel boosters needed them, too. They ordered the Ladish Company to begin forging 72 new steel casings for the booster rockets, according to secret testimony recently made public by the Rogers commission and in Congressional hearings.

On Aug. 19, 1985, Thiokol and Marshall officials briefed officials at NASA headquarters in Washington on the erosion of the O rings. Documents prepared for the briefing made reference to the "potential long-term solution," the capture feature. The documents said it could have its "earliest possible implementation" with a shuttle mission then scheduled for August 1988.

The Rogers commission later concluded that O ring erosion information presented at this August meeting had been "sufficiently detailed to require corrective action prior to the next flight." But nothing was altered in the following shuttle missions.

On Jan. 16 and 17 of this year, less than two weeks before the Challenger disaster, NASA engineers and those from Thiokol met at Marshall to review the history of O ring problems and possible solutions. The first item on the agenda was the capture feature, its status in the filament casings, and its future in the steel ones. A briefing paper prepared for the meeting noted that steel casings with a capture feature were due for delivery by February 1987.

On Jan. 28, the Challenger exploded, killing all seven crew members. According to the Rogers commission, the disaster was triggered when hot gases leaked past O rings through the lower field joint of the right booster rocket.

WORK IS ACCELERATED AFTER EXPLOSION

On Feb. 4, Marshall officials met with shuttle contractors to discuss "acceleration" of work on new steel casings, according to documents released by the Rogers commission. The February 1987 arrival date was abandoned for more urgent application of the new design.

Lawrence B. Mulloy, who then headed the booster program at Marshall, told the Rogers panel six days later, "We now will have the first of those parts delivered in 1986, in August of 1986."

Mr. Mulloy's testimony, at the commission's first closed session, contained his first reference to the new booster casings. His remarks troubled the commissioners.

Neil A. Armstrong, former astronaut and panel vice chairman, said he thought the public would not understand why the proposed solution to the booster joint problem had not already been applied.

Mr. Armstrong said: "I am concerned, Mr. Chairman, in looking ahead at the perspective of the audience and the people listening, that we will have demonstrated that there was a concern in this particular technical area, but it wasn't deemed dangerous to fly, it was deemed safe to fly, but it was also deemed that it ought to be fixed and be better, and work was going on, which makes an understandable story to me, but I am not sure that it will be understandable to everybody else."

" 'Why was it safe?' " he said people would wonder. " 'And if it was, why were you fixing it?' And that concerns me a little bit."

"It concerns us as well," said Jesse Moore, then director of the shuttle program.

Dr. Richard F. Feynman, a Nobel Prize winner in physics and one of the panel's most outspoken members, agreed. "It does look terrible," he said.

Mr. Rogers, the chairman, turned his colleagues away from this line of questioning, saying their investigations should focus on events leading up to shuttle mission 51-L, Challenger's last, rather than on planning that was under way at NASA. Mr. Rogers said: "If you went through all of the things that Larry has gone through and then the last question is, does any of this relate to 51-L, and the answer is no, everybody is going to say, well, why did you spend all of that time on it?"

Although the commission's final report did not deal with the capture feature's history, much of it is detailed in more than 122,000 pages of documents and 12,600 pages of testimony the panel made public.

In May the first of the new steel cases was delivered to a subcontractor in California for machining, including cutting the capture feature.

On June 6 the Presidential commission issued its final report. The text of the 256-page document made no mention of the capture feature or the 72 new steel casings.

On June 12, L. Michael Weeks, NASA's deputy associate administrator (technical) for space flight, told a Congressional hearing, "The 72 casings were ordered because we knew the rotation problem was serious." The fact that the work got under way in July 1985 "is now saving us six to nine months in the implementation program," he said.

Asked if shuttle flights should have continued in 1985 despite the program to fix the boosters, Mr. Weeks responded that NASA officials believed continued flights were reasonable given their knowledge at the time.

On Aug. 12 at a news conference in Alabama, Marshall unveiled its redesign of the booster joint. The main element was the capture feature.

THREAT TO NATION'S LEAD IN SPACE IS SEEN IN LACK OF GUIDING POLICY

TUESDAY, DECEMBER 30, 1986

BY JOHN NOBLE WILFORD

As workers at Cape Canaveral prepare for the somber task of burying the debris of the space shuttle Challenger in an abandoned missile silo, the greater wreckage of the American space program still lies everywhere, picked over but by no means reassembled into a vibrant whole.

Thus, 11 months after the worst disaster in spacefaring history, the United States finds itself well into the space age without a bold vision of where it is going and what it wants to achieve in space and without a coherent, comprehensive national policy guiding its diverse endeavors, according to aerospace experts, members of Congress and space officials.

As a consequence, they say, the nation is in danger of forfeiting its position as the leader in space, a loss that could have economic and strategic implications well into the 21st century. The non-military space program, its many triumphs in receding memory, is especially seen as in grave danger.

Once there were manned voyages to the Moon, regular, unmanned departures for the distant planets and a fair wind of shared national commitment that seemed sure to carry those who ventured far beyond the Earth. Once there were dreams of bases on the Moon, humans tramping on the red plains of Mars. The dreams, it once seemed, were so manifestly achievable as to be less like visions than expressions of tomorrow's reality.

Now the dreams seem empty of reality. Historians of the space program note that diminished political commitment, debates over manned vs. unmanned space flight, underfinancing, lack of leadership and the priority of military space interests have weakened the once-proud National Aeronautics and Space Administration. These conditions were exposed in the glaring light of investigation after the Challenger exploded Jan. 28, killing its crew of seven.

The shuttles will fly again, to be sure. A top priority at NASA is the redesign and testing of the flawed booster rockets. The agency also has reorganized and brought in new leaders in an effort to correct the deficiencies identified as contributing to the accident.

But if there was any agreement among political and space leaders in the aftermath of the tragedy, it was the recognition that the nation's space enterprise had lost its way, while the Soviet Union gained momentum and Western Europe, Japan and China accelerated their efforts.

Too much emphasis, it was said of the American program, had been placed on such short-term accomplishments as developing the shuttles and flying specific satellite missions. Little thought, it appeared, had been given to long-term goals for the civilian space program, and to a sustained commitment to the programs and technologies required to achieve them.

Many were the calls for a thorough reassessment of space policy leading to a clear, strong statement of direction and goals. Nearly everyone agreed that only firm Presidential leadership could provide the necessary vision and direction for the growing number of participants in the space program—the Defense Department, NASA, the Departments of Commerce and Transportation, thousands of research scientists and the companies seeking to operate private space launching services.

'WHAT POLICY?'

"We haven't done any of that," said Dr. Alex Roland, a historian of technology at Duke University who is a close observer of the space program. "It's difficult to make sense out of what we've done in response to the accident and all the problems it exposed."

Senator Donald W. Riegle Jr., a Michigan Democrat who will head a key space subcommittee in the new Congress, said flatly, "There is no clear space policy."

Dr. James C. Fletcher, the NASA Administrator, concedes that President Reagan gave him no specific policy guidelines when he assumed the helm of the agency last spring. "The White House expects me to recommend what our policy ought to be," he said.

White House officials insist that a cohesive space policy already exists in the sum of Administration directives. Several of these have been revised since the Challenger accident, though a definitive document explaining all aspects of the policy, now in draft form, will probably not be issued until summer, at the earliest.

Still many observers in and out of Government, when asked to comment on current space-policy developments, responded with the cynical question, "What policy?"

A senior NASA manager, when asked if he knew who was charged with formulating a Government-wide policy for the various space programs replied, "I'll be damned if I know where that bigger policy activity is going on."

THE MILITARY STEPS IN

Meanwhile, the Defense Department, now the dominant force in space activities, is aggressively pursuing its own agenda. It has won approval to do what it has wanted to do—have a large arsenal of its own launching rockets so it would not be dependent on the shuttles.

A new "Defense Space Policy" document, to be issued soon, will outline plans for the Pentagon to assert an even greater influence over the space program.

NASA, however, so preoccupied with cleaning its own house, has only recently begun weighing its prospects and goals. So far, all discussions of future policy and goals at NASA, and at the White House, have been predicated on the largely unexamined assumption that is increasingly seen as invalid: It is assumed that the centerpiece in future activities will be the orbiting manned space station, variously estimated to cost between $8 billion and $13 billion.

AN UNCERTAIN FUTURE

Although President Reagan has repeatedly endorsed the project, the space station has aroused little enthusiasm outside NASA. Most scientists argue that nearly all of the research and observations planned for the station could be done better and at less cost on unmanned vehicles and platforms. Private industry remains skeptical of claims that the station would usher in a lucrative space manufacturing business.

"It's a mess," said Dr. John M. Logsdon, director of the graduate program in science, technology and public policy at George Washington University. "The impression is one of drift and diffuseness and a lack of decisiveness. We still have not figured out how we want to recover and reconstitute our space program."

NEW PLAYERS IN SPACE

Never before has the nation experienced such confusion over what it wants to do in space, according to space officials and outside observers.

After the Soviet Union launched the first satellite in 1957, President Dwight D. Eisenhower accelerated existing rocket projects and moved to create NASA as the sole agency for non-military space exploration. In 1961, after the Soviet Union launched the first man in orbit, President John F. Kennedy responded swiftly with the Apollo Project to land astronauts on the Moon by the end of the decade. That gave NASA a major goal and the spending authority to achieve it.

Now, Dr. Fletcher of NASA said, the policy-making process is not so straightforward because there are "so many more players." NASA may still be the primary civilian space agency, but its influence has been diminished by straitened budgets and the ascendence of the Defense Department space program. The Pentagon's space budget this fiscal year is double that of NASA's $8-billion budget.

'NO UNIFIED MOTIVATION'

Increasingly active is the Department of Transportation, which established an office of commercial space transportation in 1984 to put into effect the Administration's directive to create private-industry launching services. And the Commerce Department has taken over operation of weather satellites and remote-sensing satellites from NASA.

With these and other "players" representing often conflicting viewpoints, the American Institute of Aeronautics and Astronautics concluded in a major assessment of the space program, to be issued soon, "There is no unified motivation to create policies which benefit the nation as a whole."

IMPONDERABLES: A CATALOGUE

"There's more to do, more we can do, but it's all more expensive," said Dr. Noel Hinners, director of NASA's Goddard Space Flight

Center, who is chairman of the agency's executive committee for strategic planning. But even in a more favorable economic climate, policy-makers would probably still have trouble setting new goals and choosing between proposals for new projects.

Other, more fundamental imponderables complicate the lives of those who must weigh space-policy choices.

The first is the manned shuttle. No one knows with any certainty how often the shuttles will be able to fly, once they resume operation. Until an answer can be determined from experience, space analysts noted, it is difficult to estimate how many conventional rockets—and what kind— will be needed to supplement them.

'STAR WARS' A CONSIDERATION

Another imponderable is the space station. It may be premature to base long-term planning on a station thought by many experts to be ill-defined in concept and design and which may not be in orbit in 1994, as scheduled. Moreover, if the station is given a major military role in return for Pentagon support, will that drive away the Europeans, Japanese and Canadians who have promised to finance parts of it?

A third imponderable is the "Star Wars" space-based missile defense program. "The whole Star Wars mentality has the potential of swamping NASA," said Senator Riegle, expecially when the value and place of a civilian space program deployment would require a massive build-up of launching capacity from both shuttle and conventional rockets.

Dr. Logsdon said there have been "no clear answers as to these questions" because, in part, no one has addressed the basic question of just how important the space program—and space leadership—is.

"This is a Presidential crisis," Dr. Logsdon said. "The President defines the national interest."

WASHINGTON TO THE DEFENSE

White House officials insist there has been policy leadership. Col. Gerald May, director of space programs for the National Security Council, said: "We have guidance, vision and goals. The President is very much in charge of the national space program and he's very much involved in several initiatives."

As examples, Colonel May cited the President's statements immediately after the accident affirming support for the space shuttle while directing NASA and the Defense Department to use both expendable rockets and the shuttle for their launching needs. This replaced the 1982 policy directives endorsing the shuttle as the primary launching system.

'PUSHING BACK THE FRONTIERS'

The White House also points to the decision to build a replacement for the Challenger as an important policy step. The statement announcing the decision on Aug. 15 also contained what is seen as the clearest declaration thus far of NASA's role in future plans.

In a paragraph concerning "the fundamental direction of the space program," President Reagan said: "NASA and our shuttles will continue to lead the way, breaking new ground, pioneering new technology, and pushing back the frontiers. It has been determined, however, that NASA will no longer be in the business of launching private satellites."

Critics say that, on closer examination, the Aug. 15 announcement betrayed the deficiencies in the Administration's space policy.

For one thing, several space-policy experts noted, the White House took eight months, marked by considerable internal debate, to decide to build the replacement shuttle. Donald T. Regan, the White House chief of staff, questioned the need for a four-shuttle fleet in view of plans to depend more on expendable rockets and a feeling that the shuttles represented outdated technology. President Reagan finally broke the impasse, presumably because at least four shuttles would be required to assemble and supply the space station and also handle Star Wars testing.

More disturbing to Congress and NASA was the fact that in the end the White House skirted the most difficult issue: how to pay for the 2.8-billion replacement shuttle. Critics saw in this a troubling tendency to revert to policy practices that had crippled the shuttle program from the start; that is, approving an expensive program without providing assurances of financing.

John E. Pike, a space specialist for the Federation of American Scientists, a Washington-based organization concerned with science and political issues, said the White House also "waffled" on encouraging private industry to enter the space-launching business with its own rockets.

After saying that NASA "will no longer be in the business of launching private satellites," the White House then agreed to let the space agency honor 14 of its 31 commitments to fly commercial communications satellites on the shuttles. Companies are concerned that continuing shuttle competition will leave them with too few customers to justify the risk of private ventures.

Above all, those concerned with the policy disarray contend that it will take stronger White House involvement to restore a sense of long-term purpose and clear direction to the nation's entire space program.

ALTERNATIVES TO THE SHUTTLE

The advantages of firm Presidential support and more generous budgets are seen in the Defense Department's rapid, vigorous response to the changed circumstances after the Challenger accident. The Pentagon had only reluctantly agreed in the 1970's to the policy of phasing out conventional launching rockets and relying almost exclusively on the shuttles. And even before the accident, with growing concerns over the shuttles' reliability and availability, the Air Force had moved to keep a fleet of its own expendable rockets ready to launch critical communications, navigation and reconnaissance satellites.

In 1985 the Air Force won approval to begin building 10 of the new, more powerful Titan 4 rockets, each capable of launching the equivalent of the payload carried by a shuttle. Then, after the accident, Congress appropriated funds to increase Titan 4 production by 13 vehicles, providing for the capability of launching four to six Titan 4's each year, beginning in 1989.

In addition, the Air Force expects to have medium-size launching vehicles available to handle at least four missions a year, also beginning in 1989. Contracts to build these rockets are to be announced next month.

The winner of this competition could be in a favorable position to mount a private space launching business. It could keep production lines open and make extra money on the side by turning out additional rockets for commercial launchings.

But a recent study by the Congressional Budget Office, "Setting

Space Transportation Policy for the 1990's," cautioned of the many uncertainties about future supply and demand for private-enterprise launchers. In the next few years, with backlog caused by the shuttle groundings, the prospects might be good. But if shuttles eventually fly 16 times a year, as sometimes predicted, the market for expendable rockets could diminish, especially if, as appears likely, more foreign launching services will become available.

Besides the Arianes, operated by a French-led European consortium the competition is expected to come from China and the Soviet Union. Commercialization may be "short-sighted" for American industry, the Congressional report concluded.

UNMANNED HEAVY-LIFT ROCKET

Also under study by the Defense Department are ideas for an unmanned, heavy-lift rocket to haul into orbit payloads that exceed the weight and volume that can be delivered by the shuttles. "The Air Force is running as fast as it can to get off the shuttle," said Dr. Logsdon. The Pentagon asked for money yesterday to speed up the research.

But for the next three or four years, the Defense Department will be depending heavily on the shuttles, often bumping other users by exercising its right to have first call for space aboard. Edward C. Aldridge Jr., the Secretary of the Air Force, said the military will have 21 payloads "sitting on the ground waiting to fly" in early 1988, when the shuttles are supposed to resume operations. The military demand will probably be so great that NASA will be hard-pressed to fly many of its own missions or meet its commitments to other Government agencies as well as foreign and commercial customers.

"The military are everywhere in NASA these days," Dr. Roland of Duke University said. "But they don't want to do away with NASA. They just want to bend it to their purposes."

Espousing an idea popular among many scientists, Dr. Bruce C. Murray, professor of planetary science at the California Institute of Technology and former director of the NASA's Jet Propulsion Laboratory, has written: "Our goals should be to use space to help the world manage the global environment and to begin a new era in U.S.-Soviet relations by collaborating with the Soviet Union in the human exploration of Mars after the turn of the century. Without clear Presidential goals such as these, the annual Congressional budget process and associated brokering among special interests will lead to a diffused, diminished and mediocre outcome."

Proposals of human exploration of Mars are likely to revive a bitter debate that has long riven the space program: the conflict between "manned" and "unmanned" approaches to space flight. NASA's leadership, conditioned by the Apollo experience, has generally favored big manned projects over the opposition of many scientists.

Writing in Issues in Science and Technology, a quarterly publication of the National Academy of Sciences, Dr. Murray argued that unmanned flights are a more cost-effective way to advance science and carry out practical civilian and military space activities.

The primary justification for manned flight, he argued, was political.

In developing a new "mixed space fleet" to supplement the shuttles, NASA has yet to resolve how much of an unmanned expendable rocket program to include.

Critics of manned flight point out that the journeys to Mars by the unmanned Viking 1 and Viking 2, for example, were able to gather valuable scientific data at far less cost than would have been required to make the trips safe for humans.

The counterargument, made now in favor of manned trips in the 90's, is that a wide variety of sophisticated experiments could never be done without man's presence.

THE PROBLEMS THAT REMAIN

Dr. Fletcher, head of the embattled NASA, said he would like to have President Reagan make a strong affirmation of the importance of a sustained national commitment of "will and resources" to space.

"We can't take America's leadership in space for granted," Dr. Fletcher said. "We've got to make up our mind that activities in space are an important national enterprise in the long run. These goals of ours at NASA ought to be accepted as goals for the nation."

By sustained commitment, Dr. Fletcher said he meant the kind of resolve displayed in the Apollo era and, on a practical level, the kind of multiyear guarantees of money for major undertakings that are given for some large weapons systems. As for the goals he spoke of, he conceded that the agency is only now trying to decide what they should be.

Among the issues under study are the agency's relationship with the military; how to strike a balance between big engineering projects like the station and a more vigorous space-science program; support for more advanced technologies, and the future of international cooperative ventures in space.

Even though the space station is considered a "given" in all planning, said Dr. Sally K. Ride, an astronaut who is Dr. Fletcher's special assistant for strategic planning, "One of the important things we have to do is make sure that the station fits into the context of the whole program."

NASA's own advisory council last month issued a report, "The Crisis in Space and Earth Science," expressing the "unease and frustration" among scientists who seek more support for the space-science undertakings but fear that rising costs of building the station will eat away at support for the very science projects it is supposed to be used for.

Dr. Hinners, the Goddard director and another architect of NASA's long-range planning, said: "We don't have the answers yet to some basic questions. Is the station only an earth-orbiting research facility? Is it a step to the Moon or to Mars?"

These unanswered questions reflect the quandary of NASA leaders. To sell the space station on the basis of its immediate uses—earth observations, scientific research and possible military experiments— seems to inspire little enthusiasm in Washington or even in the aerospace community. But to try to sell the station as the first step for ambitious planetary expeditions and space colonies might fire imaginations, but it might also scare off support.

All discussions of the space agency's future eventually lead to the matter of money. Since the end of the Apollo Project in the early 1970's, NASA has been given enough money to keep from starving, but not enough to aspire to the greater goals that are presumably within technology's grasp.

In its new assessment of the civilian space program, the American Institute of Aeronautics and Astronautics estimated that current

NASA budgets were less than half (in constant dollars) of what they were in the Apollo era. "This budget policy created a steady trend toward making the U.S. a second-class space nation," it said. It recommended that the budget be increased "as rapidly as practical" to about 40 percent greater than the 1987 fiscal year level and then maintained at a level adjusted to the growth rate of the gross national product.

The 1987 NASA budget of $10.4 billion represents a regular appropriation of $8 billion plus a one-time supplement to cover extraordinary costs associated with the Challenger accident. Efforts by Dr. Fletcher to persuade the Office of Management and Budget to make the $10.4-billion level the benchmark for all future budgets have so far met with little success. Anything much less, Dr. Fletcher cautioned, could delay completion of the replacement shuttle beyond 1991 and of the space station beyond 1994 as well as leave other NASA programs undernourished and in no position to pursue ambitious goals.

SIX

CENSORED IN SOUTH AFRICA

1987 WINNER IN THE INTERNATIONAL REPORTING CATEGORY

"For a distinguished example of reporting on international affairs, including United Nations correspondence . . . "

Los Angeles Times
Michael Parks

Although Pretoria proclaimed a state of emergency and tightened restrictions on the press, disorder further enveloped South Africa. Despite a threat of expulsion, Michael Parks continued to write about the consequences of apartheid.

As South Africa drifted deeper into disorder in 1986 and the authorities in Pretoria responded by throwing up a succession of barriers to covering the news, reporting on an already complex story became even more difficult, even more dangerous.

Despite the obstacles, including what finally amounted to formal censorship, no one rose to the challenge with more courage, more determination and more skill than Michael Parks, the *Los Angeles Times* correspondent in South Africa.

Parks showed the reader a South Africa seen by very few people, including South Africans.

Without taking sides, he described in moving detail the struggle of the blacks, still denied a voice at any level of government. He captured the indomitable spirit of Albertina Sisulu, whose husband has been in prison for 22 years and whose children had been detained or exiled. She fights the anti-apartheid battle with optimism and bags packed against the possibility of her own detention. Parks measured the growing support among blacks for the African National Congress and examined every facet of this key movement in the black struggle for political rights.

The terrible consequences of apartheid—a steady level of violence by blacks against whites, whites against blacks and blacks against blacks—were brought uncomfortably close in stories about the brutal warfare between black factions at the pathetic squatter settlement of Crossroads; the growth of vigilantism among whites convinced that the only way to survive is "to make sure we each kill 10 blacks"; and the mysterious disappearances of a schoolboy sent out to buy bread, a teenager serving Mass and a student who set out to spend the night with a girlfriend—all thought to be victims of government detention following imposition of a state of emergency.

Always on top of the breaking news as well, Parks had prepared *Times* readers for the imposition of the state of emergency. When it came on June 12, 1986, he laid out its terms as comprehensively as the government's deliberately vague regulations allowed.

In a year in which many American companies announced that they were pulling out of South Africa, Parks anticipated the decision of one industrial giant, General Motors. He talked to GM executives and workers in August about the factors that were then being considered for a pull-out decision that came in October.

One result of these decisions, and of the economic sanctions imposed by the U.S. Congress over a presidential veto, was a bitter backlash against the United States. Parks impartially recorded those feelings of deep anger, from the South African president's assertion that the United States "has yet again taken up the sword against us on behalf of the Soviet Union . . ." to the street-corner posters advising "Go Home Yanks."

The continuing crisis has had its toll on whites, too, and an economic recession springing in large part from the political troubles has put thousands of whites out of work. Parks described how soup kitchens and the sight of white children begging in the streets of white, working-class suburbs has brought home to the white community the consequences of their failure to share political power.

In perhaps his most vivid portrait of the sharp differences between the worlds of whites and blacks in South Africa, he told the story of one white's effort against segregation: the Rev. Nico Smith, who moved from a white middle-class suburb to a black ghetto and found, for instance, a world where no birds sing but where cocks put up a formidable dawn chorus, because a black ghetto has few trees for birds to nest in but poultry are an economic necessity.

Parks's uncompromising reporting did not go unnoticed by the authorities. At year's end, he was singled out by the Pretoria government and stood under threat of expulsion from the country. However, those who told him that his work permit would not be renewed could cite no story out of the 265 he filed in 1986 as inaccurate or unfair.

—The editors
Los Angeles Times

OUTLAWED BLACK S. AFRICA GROUP GAINS IMPETUS

J U N E   1 ,   1 9 8 6

B Y   M I C H A E L   P A R K S

JOHANNESBURG, South Africa—Sipho calls himself a "human radio." Each morning, he gets on the train near his home deep in Soweto, the sprawling black satellite city outside Johannesburg, and begins to repeat the news from the Radio Freedom broadcasts of the African National Congress.

As the crowded train rattles on toward downtown Johannesburg, Sipho, a brokerage clerk in his mid-30s, gives a detailed rundown on the growing unrest around the country; recounts the latest exploits of "our fighters" in the Spear of the Nation, the congress's military wing, and reports on the activities of the group's exiled leadership. Then he starts a discussion based on Radio Freedom's latest commentaries.

"Man, do I have an audience today!" he said. "Two years ago, people weren't interested, not at all, and I might have been talking to myself most mornings. Today, they want me to shout out the news, and they leave the train not just talking about the ANC but ready to work for it, to fight for it. . . . They know the ANC is going to lead us to freedom."

The fortunes of the African National Congress, outlawed here in 1960, have indeed soared in the last two years. Today, the group can probably claim the allegiance of more of South Africa's 25 million blacks than any other organization, and this makes it a major political force here.

The congress's black, green and gold flag is now seen at virtually every funeral for those killed in the country's civil strife. Its leaders, though just names to most blacks after years in exile or prison, are hailed at protest meetings with reverberating shouts of "Viva!" and "Long live!" Songs are sung praising the Spear of the Nation—Umkhonto we Sizwe, in Bantu—and its guerrillas and calling on the congress to give the people guns to fight the government. And

333

hundreds of black youths, joined by a few whites, have left the country to enroll in the organization's military wing in recent months.

For an organization long criticized as an exile group out of touch with events inside the country, this recognition is a major achievement —and an index of its strength within South Africa.

'PEOPLE LIFTED BAN'

"The people have lifted the ban on the ANC themselves," said Oliver Tambo, the president of the African National Congress since the imprisonment of Nelson Mandela in 1962. "They recognize us as their organization, as the vanguard of their struggle for liberation. According to the government, we are supposed to be illegal and nonexistent, but our support among the people grows daily."

The congress's guerrillas have doubled their attacks in the last 18 months so there are now two or three a week, according to both ANC and police sources, and with their AK-47 rifles and hand grenades, they have begun joining some of the fighting in the country's black townships.

They are also training more local recruits in the use of grenades, mines and various other weapons, these sources say. The huge arms caches found by police in recent months show greatly increased military capability despite the closure over the last three years of the easiest infiltration routes from neighboring countries.

Political cadres, most of whom work separately from the congress's military wing, are building up the group's underground organization in black communities and making some inroads among whites as well, according to senior officials at the organization's headquarters in Lusaka, Zambia.

Veteran leaders, who remained inside the country after the African National Congress was banned, often serving 12- and 15-year prison sentences in the notorious Robben Island penal colony, have helped organize the United Democratic Front, the Congress of South African Trade Unions and other new groups opposed to apartheid, the country's system of racial separation and minority white rule.

Younger congress members, many of them graduates of the 1970s' black consciousness movement and trained by Mandela while they were imprisoned on Robben Island, are at top levels of labor unions and working throughout a broad range of anti-apartheid groups.

Underground cells of the congress are now helping to organize the fast-growing networks of street committees taking over the leadership in many black townships.

Propaganda efforts, once confined to radio-listening groups such as Sipho's and clandestine distribution of smuggled leaflets, are expanding with videotapes on the life of Mandela, the history of the African National Congress and its guerrilla campaign.

"We are there, though the government pretends we are not," Tambo said in a recent interview on the organization, its current strategy and policies. "Our organizing work has been stepped up with good, loyal cadres, many more units and a network that is very alive now. . . . I can't tell you how much longer it will take, but we think that, at last, long last, victory is within sight."

Recognition of the African National Congress as a key player in shaping South Africa's future has come in recent months from a wide cross-section of the country's business, labor, student, church and political groups. Despite strenuous objections from the government of President Pieter W. Botha that the ANC is a terrorist group that should be shunned, many South African organizations have sent delegations to Lusaka and elsewhere for in-depth discussions with congress leaders.

"The ANC is undoubtedly the most popular organization among the oppressed masses of this country," Jan van Eck, a member of the Cape province council from the liberal white opposition Progressive Federal Party, told fellow legislators in Cape Town last month as he called for legalization of the congress. "It is the height of stupidity to ban an organization that commands the sort of mass support the ANC enjoys."

The African National Congress, once lumped by many Western diplomats with other exile groups still fighting for lost causes, has won increasing international acceptance as well.

As the South African government's international isolation grows, the group's leaders are warmly received on visits around the world. Tambo testified before a British parliamentary committee in London, held discussions with the West German foreign minister and is now planning a trip to the United States, his second in two years.

A special Commonwealth commission made up of "eminent persons" from Britain and six other countries last month urged negotiations between the Pretoria government and the congress, effectively recognizing the organization as the spokesman for South Africa's black majority.

And in Washington, the State Department, rejecting South African assertions that the African National Congress is primarily a terrorist organization, said last month that the United States believes the group must participate in determining the country's future.

To Tambo, all this affirms "the centrality of the ANC's role in resolving South Africa's problems, a centrality that we believe has always been there but which has been considerably enhanced and is now being recognized."

"There is a growing realization, a conviction even, that the ANC has everything to do with the solution of South Africa's problems, and without the ANC there can be no solution," Tambo, 69, a former Johannesburg lawyer, said while on his visit to Bonn. "This is what our people are saying, and the world and many white South Africans now see the truth of it, though not yet the Botha government."

Much of this recognition has come, Tambo and other congress leaders readily acknowledge, from the spreading anti-apartheid protests of the last two years here—protests whose origins were largely spontaneous and that still do not appear orchestrated by the group's underground network of guerrillas and political cadres here.

We don't claim responsibility for every protest, every development, but the felt presence of the ANC in South Africa is a powerful force that propels people into action," Tambo said.

"We gave the people a strategic objective in 1984—simply to make the apartheid system unworkable, to make the whole country incapable of government—and that is what they are doing. We have now set another strategic task—preparing and launching a people's war—and that is what we are moving toward."

The group's critics, such as Chief Mangosuthu Gatsha Buthelezi, the Zulu leader, contend that it is trying to profit from a situation it did not create and cannot control.

Its own efforts at armed struggle over the last 25 years have failed, the critics say, and the congress, as a result, had become almost irrelevant before the anti-apartheid violence began nearly two years ago.

"What is happening on the streets, it's true, is largely due to the people's anger over the (ruling) National Party's refusal to meet their demands," said Steve Tshwete, a graduate of Mandela's so-called "Robben Island University" and a regional president of the United Democratic Front.

"People do not need the ANC to tell them they are hungry, that they are homeless, that they are unemployed, that they are oppressed," he added.

"What the ANC does tell them is what they can do about it," he said. "Without a vanguard on the ground, it is not likely that our people would have risen to their present level of militancy. People needed to develop their political consciousness; they needed to know how to organize, how to draw up action programs. They also needed to know there was a big brother (the congress's military wing) to protect them.

"For years, the ANC has been the only organization on the ground, as a result, we suffered huge losses in casualties, but these did show people the ANC's commitment. If we have the people's allegiance today, we earned it."

Sipho—who uses that *nom de guerre* to protect himself from the security police and their informers—explained from his work as a "human radio" doing propaganda that blacks here see two qualities that they admire in the organization, now into its 75th year.

"The ANC has never sold us out like many black leaders have, compromised on its principles or given up the fight when it was toughest," he said. "If we are to have talks with the government, we want the ANC to represent us, not some sellout picked by the government.

"ANC policies are realistic and pragmatic and reflect the people's true aspirations for the country," he said. "The ANC is not dogmatic or ideological; it has Christians and Communists as members and there is even room for whites in it."

A third and increasingly important factor in its popular support, however, is the organization's armed struggle against the Pretoria government.

Once limited to bombings of government buildings and economic targets such as power substations, the group's offensive has been broadened in the last three years to include rocket attacks on oil-from-coal plants, land mines planted on farm roads, assassinations of black policemen and politicians seen as collaborating with the government and wider use of bombs and limpet mines in urban areas.

Despite government charges that these attacks, particularly those that have killed nearly 20 white civilians in recent months, have "confirmed the terrorist character" of the congress, its leaders argue that their use of violence remains selective, quite limited and "a response to the violence of apartheid."

"The armed struggle is very popular among the oppressed, who see it as a reply to the violence they suffer under apartheid and as a way to hasten their liberation," Tambo said. "And we, in fact, are expected to do more."

At a policy conference last June in the Zambian mining town of Kabwe, the African National Congress decided to expand and intensify its guerrilla efforts as a prelude to what it calls "people's war" and the eventual toppling of the white-minority government.

Ronnie Kasrils, one of the first members of the Spear of the Nation, explained in an interview in Lusaka that "the seizure of state power is our goal, and we must not stop short of that; otherwise, we won't be able to bring about fundamental changes in South Africa.

"With the transformation of the situation at home, our base is once more inside our country, among our people," Kasrils, who is also a South African Communist Party theoretician, said in the current issue of the congress's magazine Sechaba. "What has been a low-intensity war over 25 years is now taking off into fully fledged armed struggle and people's war involving our people in their hundreds of thousands."

Kasrils explained that guerrillas can now operate more freely than ever in the many black townships that have become virtual no-go areas for the police. In addition, he said, the government's informer network has been reduced considerably by the murders of many of those suspected of cooperating with authorities.

The "central task" of the Spear of the Nation now, Kasrils said, is to begin arming the congress's supporters in large numbers. "That army of stone-throwers (in the townships) has to be transformed into an army with weapons," he said. "Our people have the mood and spirit: Every stone-thrower wants a gun. We have to put guns in their hands."

The need for the full "armed insurrection" that Kasrils envisions is still debated within the African National Congress. But even those who hope for a negotiated "transfer of power" by the present government to minimize the loss of life argue for increased guerrilla efforts as essential pressure to break the white resistance to majority rule.

But the congress's current military capability is sharply disputed.

Police here say that ANC guerrillas, lacking bases inside South Africa, are stretched almost to the limit of their operational capacity. The congress resorts to terrorist attacks, such as the bomb that killed five Christmas shoppers south of Durban last year, out of its inability to attack the security forces.

"When their men come back into South Africa for a mission, we know very quickly, often before they start to operate, sometimes even with 15 minutes," a senior police officer said recently. "We have a sophisticated intelligence system that alerts us to any movement of their men and that ensures we find at least three-quarters of their weapons, explosives and other materials before they are used.

"The African National Congress is a terrorist threat, a very dangerous one, but not a true guerrilla or military threat to the state," added the police official, who asked not to be identified. "They are competent at hit-and-run tactics, but pose no credible threat to our security forces."

Over the last decade, about 500 guerrillas have been arrested or killed, he added. To limit its losses, the congress rarely has more than 10 to 20 trained military operatives inside the country at a time, he said. Even the increased level of two or three incidents a week represents no real threat to the state, government officials have said.

At its military camps in Angola and Tanzania, the African National Congress has trained between 2,500 and 3,000 guerrillas since 1976, according to Col. Jan Buchner, a police intelligence specialist on the organization, but about half of these are now in other jobs.

When politics cadres, administrative personnel, students and other exiles are included, Buchner said, the congress has a total strength of about 10,000 outside the country.

The group's internal strength is largely a matter of speculation.

"We know that 80% to 90% of their effort goes into political work, but we don't really know how successful it is," Buchner said."We see the flags at funerals, we know their use of front organizations, we are aware of the expansion of their cell network in the townships, but whether this would translate into real support in, say, an armed insurrection if we ever got to that is quite a different matter."

In pressing its military campaign, the congress, other analysts say, may also be underestimating the white-led government's determination to retain power, whether through gradual and limited political reforms, sheer military might or the present combination of the two.

Tom Lodge, a political scientist at Johannesburg's University of the Witwatersrand, who has studied the African National Congress closely for many years, predicts that a full-scale ANC offensive would bring an all-out government effort to destroy the organization, both within the country and abroad.

"We are not in a revolutionary situation here yet, and in terms of revolutionary theory itself, that makes any armed insurrection premature," Lodge said. "The ANC could also lose the support it is now cultivating among whites if it increased the level of violence considerably or launched attacks indiscriminately."

But the congress's leadership is under strong pressure from younger militants in the organization and from its supporters inside the country to "hit the government a lot harder and accept that many more white casualties will be necessary if we are to win," as one senior ANC official in Lusaka put it recently.

"We say we are at war against apartheid, and the younger generation says, 'Well, then, let's hit them with all we've got, because until they are hurt, badly hurt, they will never consider yielding to majority rule,' " he added, asking not to be quoted by name.

A younger ANC cadreman, Pappie Kubu, who left South Africa after the Soweto uprising 10 years ago, explained: "Youth, especially in the townships but also in our (military training) camps, want to do more. They want to rush in and destroy the whole apartheid system.

"The leadership has to hold them back and say, 'Not so fast, because destroying the system that way may destroy . . . the economy, many people's homes, the whole country even,' " Kubu said.

Another ANC cadre member who joined after Soweto, Susan Mnumzana, recalled that "we in the Soweto generation thought we were the revolution and would just push ahead and return home as great liberators in a couple of years.

"We were more angry than politically conscious, and . . . the

ANC's contacts with the country were not very dynamic," Mnumzana said, "Today, the young people who come to join us understand what the struggle is, and they identify with the ANC because they know what it stands for. . . . But that does not reduce the impatience of youth or the anger and bitterness of those who experience apartheid every day."

Under these pressures, the organization's conference at Kabwe last June decided to step up its military attacks, expanding the range of targets to those that might also mean civilian as well as military casualties.

"How hard to hit is one of the major policy issues within the ANC," Lodge said, "and there is a continuing debate over the merits of ruthlessness versus restraint. . . . It does not divide them, but it does preoccupy them."

Despite the Kabwe decision and the popularity of military actions among many blacks, the African National Congress remains notably cautious, more concerned at present with strengthening its underground organization than launching major offensives.

"We have always needed a compound strategy, not a simple, one-dimensional one," Pallo Jordan, the group's director of research and a member of its executive committee, said in an interview in Lusaka. "The major elements for us are mass mobilization, given cohesion by a strong underground, a growing military presence inside the country to reinforce this and to prepare for the seizure of power and, thirdly, international solidarity."

Jordan, an American- and British-trained historian, sees three likely scenarios for an ANC victory: a "protracted war" that shifts increasingly to the offensive until the government is defeated; "partial insurrections" combined with general strikes in key areas of the country, and a negotiated "transfer of power" by a weakened, isolated government "when it realizes that it has exhausted all possibilities except this—and fighting to the death."

"We are more interested than anyone else in a peaceful transfer of power, in reducing the violence," Jordan continued. "We know that our people will suffer the most casualties. We do not want to destroy the country—it is our country, too. And we do not want the bitter aftermath of a war.

"Yet even a negotiated outcome will be the result of a successful compound strategy. The element of armed struggle, of people's war, might not be of such a high profile, but it is essential, even decisive. The Botha government is not, quite obviously, going to give up power willingly and accept majority rule. It has to be forced to do so."

Despite the congress's hope for what Jordan called "a negotiated transfer of power" and its extensive talks over the last nine months with a wide range of South African groups and individuals to promote this, among blacks as well as the nation's 5 million whites, the organization does not feel the time has yet come for such negotiations.

"If the regime seriously, genuinely wanted to resolve the South African situation by negotiations, talks could begin very quickly, tomorrow, even while hostilities are in progress," Tambo said. "But the truth is that there is no readiness, no seriousness about ending apartheid. That is why we feel we must intensify our struggle, even if it means stepping up our armed attacks with the tragic loss of life that this may involve, tragic because it is unnecessary."

The main barrier to such negotiations, Tambo said, is Pretoria's insistence that the congress renounce violence as a precondition for negotiations.

"This is really laughable, for it is the violence of apartheid that gave rise to our violence, our very limited violence," he continued. "But we are prepared to renounce violence if this were a reciprocal action. . . . But they really can't as violence is inherent in the apartheid system. They would have to end apartheid, abandon it entirely, dismantle it. Then there would be no further violence against our people, and we would have no cause to continue our armed struggle."

A second obstacle to negotiations, ANC officials acknowledge, is their insistence that they concern the "transfer of power," not further reforms of the present system or the government's offer of power sharing.

"Political power, not simply ending racial discrimination, is the central issue, and anything short of that will be greeted with suspicion and probably rejection," Mac Maharaj, another member of the executive committee, commented during an interview in Lusaka.

"The government, we believe, is now in a crisis of such dimensions that there is no way out for it. However, like a cornered beast, it will use all its cunning to try and escape and, if it can't, to strike out madly. These are times to be cautious. . . .

"Many of the reforms Pretoria has undertaken are just shifts to maintain the system of minority rule, and we are talking about fundamental changes that can only come with a transfer of power," Maharaj said.

Although many whites interpret this as "discussing terms for our surrender and nothing less," as one National Party politician put it, the African National Congress has explained to the many South African delegations that have visited its Lusaka headquarters that transfer of power need not mean simply white capitulation but, rather, the establishment through negotiation of a new constitutional system for the country.

Majority rule, they similarly explain, should not be equated with black rule, but with a democratic political system in which all would have a voice.

"We are committed, and have been for decades, to a multiparty democracy with a constitution ensuring human rights and civil liberties for everyone," Jordan said. "The only thing we intend to declare illegal is the advocacy of racism and other forms of discrimination. There are many other aspects to our program in terms of the country's development, a new educational system, health care and the present monopolistic concentration of economic power, but these are all matters for discussion and democratic decisions."

For many whites and some blacks as well, the prominence of so many South African Communist Party members in the top ANC leadership—and their apparently much tougher line on military action, on negotiations, on the country's future—diminishes the value of such pledges.

Tambo, regarded as an African nationalist by even the Pretoria government, for many years fought what he himself saw as a Communist takeover of the African National Congress but eventually changed his mind.

"I have been in the ANC leadership since 1949, and I have found that the members of the South African Communist Party behave exactly as any other ANC person would behave," he said. "I know that Communist parties are normally credited with being able to influence everything and anything they come in contact with, but with us the experience has been that the Communists are very loyal, very committed members of the ANC. We are happy to have them on that basis."

Tony Bloom, a leading South African businessman, who was in one of the first groups to go from here to meet the ANC leadership, said later, "It is difficult to view the group as hard-line Marxists or blood-thirsty terrorists who are interested in reducing South Africa to anarchy. . . .

"They are people with whom serious negotiations can be undertaken," Bloom said, "and with whom a certain amount of common ground can be found."

In fact, the congress, founded in 1912, has become an omnibus liberation movement that seems to have room for a broad range of political persuasions, ranging from Christian activists to Communist Party members who still praise the leadership qualities of Soviet dictator Josef Stalin. "We do not want a one-party, everyone-think-alike state, and so it seemed wrong to turn this organization into that sort of thing," Jordan said. "So people will have to accept that we do have Communists as members of our ranks and our leadership along with devout Christians who say grace before meals."

The previous height of ANC influence in South Africa came during the 1950s, when it led protests against the Nationalist government's new apartheid laws, which instituted the system of strict racial separation.

But the organization was decimated by a police crackdown on its activities and members after it was outlawed in 1960 along with the Pan Africanist Congress of Azania, an ANC offshoot opposed to white involvement in the liberation movement and any subsequent government.

"We went through very, very rough years," Tambo recalled, "with the government tracking down hundreds and hundreds of our people, killing them, putting them into prison, driving them into exile. We struggled just to stay alive. If we are strong now, we developed much of that strength through those hard years."

S. AFRICA— FRATRICIDE AT CROSSROADS

JUNE 11, 1986

BY MICHAEL PARKS

CAPE TOWN, South Africa—Huddled together against the cold rains of the Southern Hemisphere's fast-approaching winter, the Temba family—mother, father, four children—had the forlorn look of refugees anywhere.

Their home, a three-room shack of wood, tin and plastic but with the luxury of real glass windows, was among those destroyed in the first round of fighting at the Crossroads squatter settlement outside Cape Town last month.

Sam Temba's head was still wrapped in dirty gauze bandages after a rifle bullet grazed him as he tried to salvage some of the family's meager possessions from their shanty. He complained of recurrent blackouts and dizziness. His wife, Elizabeth, was burned on the legs as she fled the settlement with their children.

WOUNDED BY MACHETE

Their oldest son, Andries, 19, was wounded when the machete of a black vigilante slashed his right arm almost to the bone as he and other youths tried to defend their homes against the vigilantes' repeated attacks.

The younger Temba children, all with sad, watery eyes, runny noses and dirty, ragged clothes, were wrapped in old woolen blankets in the corner of a leaky Red Cross tent.

"We're suffering, really suffering," Elizabeth Temba said, tending the crying child of a friend who had gone in search of her husband, missing since the worst of the fighting. "What are we to do now? Where are we to live? How will we survive?"

The Tembas, along with 50,000 others whose homes were destroyed in the Crossroads fighting, are not the first refugees in 21 months of South Africa's racial strife, but in their unprecedented

345

numbers they are testimony to how large and complex the conflict has become.

COMRADES UNDER ATTACK

The fighting at Crossroads last month and this, some of the worst yet in South Africa, pitted the Witdoeke, a conservative black vigilante group known by the white strips of cloth (*witdoeke* in Afrikaans) that they wear to identify themselves, against militant black youths called Comrades, who belong to affiliates of the United Democratic Front, a national coalition of anti-apartheid groups.

The Witdoeke support the long-time but now controversial leader of the Crossroads settlement, Johnson Ngxobongwana, and were commanded by his chief lieutenant, Sam Ndima. In some of the fighting, the Witdoeke, estimated to number more than 1,000 men, are alleged to have had police backing and to have been given guns.

The Witdoeke motive in launching their attacks on three sections of the Crossroads complex was clearly stated in angry meetings over the previous three months: The Comrades, some of whom had been recruited into new urban guerrilla units of the African National Congress, were endangering all the settlement's 120,000 residents by bringing increased police and army patrols into the area and, because they had refused to leave, had to be driven away.

"We did not mean to go to war, but we had to respond to the activities of these youths," said Edward Qhangana, a member of the Crossroads residents' executive committee under Ngxobongwana. "They may have militancy but they lack political maturity, and this makes them a danger to the whole Crossroads community. They had to go.

"When they attacked the security forces with their stones and petrol (gasoline) bombs and hand grenades even, we all suffered from the police retribution. Many of these youths were not even from Crossroads families but had fled here from nearby townships to escape the police. Finally, when they started attacking the Crossroads community leaders, we had to protect ourselves, and counterattack to drive them out. The Comrades bear the responsibility for all these deaths and all these people's misery."

The Comrades tell a different story. They see themselves as being in the vanguard of the black struggle against apartheid, South Africa's system of racial separation and minority white rule. And they see Ngxobongwana and members of his executive committee as "sell-outs" collaborating with the government, helping to maintain that system, for personal advantage.

"We are against exploitation, and Ngxobongwana's committee is exploiting the people of Crossroads," Mxolisis Tolbat, chairman of the Crossroads branch of the Cape Youth Congress, said, emerging briefly from a hiding place outside Crossroads.

"The committee is not democratic, and lately it has become a tool of the system. There is also a vast amount of corruption, with the committee taxing the people far too much and then helping themselves to the money to buy cars and cattle and maybe even farms. . . ."

The Comrades refused to leave Crossroads, according to Alfred Siphika, the leader of one of the three Crossroads sections that was razed in the fighting, because "the youths are part of the community, not some foreign force, and the ANC men, were they perhaps present in our area, certainly are our people, too."

The Crossroads committee, which was chosen in an election that it had managed itself and that drew no more than 5,000 of an estimated 87,000 adult residents, may have felt threatened by the growth of the United Democratic Front affiliates in the settlement, particularly in the newer sections of Crossroads where Ngxobongwana's leadership has been questioned recently.

Andries Temba, one of the Comrades, remarked to the nods of older Crossroads residents standing around him, "If we were not certain before about where Ngxobongwana and the other committee members stood ideologically, we knew when the Witdoeke attacked us. They were doing the work of the police, of the system. They were splitting the people in our struggle against apartheid and they had joined the enemy."

But the issue of land, perhaps even more than politics, appears to be at the center of the Crossroads fighting—and to have led directly to the razing of about 5,000 shanties in three sections of Crossroads last month. This week, fighting spread to a fourth section of the Crossroads complex where many had taken refuge, and thousands more shacks were burned.

After attempting for years to remove Crossroads' residents from the squatter settlement, either by returning them to the Xhosa tribal homeland of Transkei, where most had come from in search of work, or by housing them in a new black township farther from Cape Town, the government agreed last year to let about 40,000 stay and to develop the shantytown as a model urban community if the remainder moved.

Ngxobongwana, a former longshoreman, had led the decade-long fight to remain at Crossroads, becoming one of the most prominent community activists in the country. He felt the government's offer was fair because not only would Crossroads be redeveloped but most residents would get permission to remain in the Cape Town area and no longer be subject to deportation to the rural homelands.

But disputes arose immediately over who would remain in the upgraded Crossroads, about 12 miles southeast of Cape Town, and who would move, and under what terms, to the new town of Khayelitsha, about six miles away.

COVETED NEWER AREAS

And the deal led the 47,000 residents of the Old Crossroads, the oldest section of the settlement, to covet three newer adjacent areas, a total of 62 acres, whose 38,000 residents had come more recently and were refusing to move to Khayelitsha without explicit government guarantees that they would be allowed to remain in the Cape Town area permanently.

"We were here before them and have a right to stay here," Prince Gobingca, a member of the residents committee, said, referring to Old Crossroads, where most of the Witdoeke live. "We fought a long time, many years before they even came, for the right to stay here, and they were jeopardizing everything we had won. We do not want to continue living like this—look at these mud pools, we live like pigs—but to get better houses, to get Crossroads upgraded. We need to spread out."

To Sama Temba, this is simply an attempt to justify theft.

"They are saying, 'You have what we need, what we want, and we are going to take it from you,' and in the Bible that is called stealing," he said. "The truth is that I have been here since 1978, about as long as those in Old Crossroads, and in fact I used to live there until I brought my family from Transkei."

Although rival groups had fought at Crossroads several times over the years, the battle lines for the latest clash were drawn late last year when the Witdoeke, then known as the "Fathers," tried to drive the Comrades out of the settlement. They failed then, largely because the Comrades' numbers had increased with the inflow of hundreds of young militants from nearby black townships.

The Witdoeke attacked again in March, hitting at critics of Ngxobongwana and his committee, but were repulsed, suffering serious losses at the hands of the Comrades and armed African National Congress guerrilla cells.

Ngxobongwana's committee then struck another deal with the government, according to his critics. They agreed to demolish those squatter camps whose residents were still refusing to move to Khayelitsha. In return, he and his people would get the land adjacent to his Old Crossroads section, as well as guns and police and army protection for the Witdoeke, the critics say.

At the end of April, Sam Ndima, the Witdoeke commander, gave an ultimatum to Siphika and the leaders of the other two sections adjacent to Old Crossroads.

"Mr. Ndima said he wanted to flatten our camps, and that if we did not move out of the area he would destroy our camps by force," Siphika told the Cape provincial Supreme Court in an affidavit seeking protection for the remaining camps. "He said he had been given 200 guns by the police for this purpose."

Ngxobongwana, a charismatic leader and powerful speaker, was also reportedly promised a seat on the government's proposed national council that is to give blacks a share of political power.

If true—Ngxobongwana refused to be interviewed—this would be a political coup for the government, for Ngxobongwana is still chairman of the Western Cape Civic Assn. and until recently played a major role in the Cape Town branch of the United Democratic Front. But it would probably brand him a "sellout" in the eyes of many blacks for collaborating with the white-led government and abandoning the fight against apartheid.

Ngxobongwana, known as "Nobs" around Crossroads, had spent

much of 1985 in jail on murder charges. He was eventually acquitted, and on his release appeared to many who had worked with him over the past decade to be a broken man.

"Nobs was a different man when he came out," said a white clergyman who has worked in Crossroads for many years but asked not to be quoted by name. "Nobs was physically unwell, his mind was no longer as sharp as before and his personality had changed a great deal. How the police broke him, I can only speculate, but he came out of jail a compromised man."

Whatever deals may have been made, a ferocious Witdoeke attack began on Saturday evening, May 17, according to residents of the three sections adjacent to Old Crossroads. It continued for a week with little respite until the Comrades had been soundly defeated and all 5,000 shacks in the other areas were destroyed.

"First, they came in gangs of 50 and 60 looking for all the Comrades," Sam Temba recalled. "They were armed to the teeth with spears and clubs and *pangas* (machetes), and quite a few had rifles and pistols. All the youth had to flee because the Witdoeke clearly intended to kill anyone and everyone they thought might be a Comrade.

"Some of our young men did get together, and fought back with stones and petrol bombs and whatever weapons they could get. But the Witdoeke had more men and more guns, and whenever the battle turned against them, the police intervened with their tear gas and shotguns against the youth.

"They began burning our houses late on Sunday, and when they got the upper hand they set fire to everything. Many people saw some policemen even helping the Witdoeke to burn us all out. Of course, we all had to flee for our lives. And then the police and the army put up a barbed-wire fence to prevent us from returning. So there is no doubt in our minds that the Witdoeke were working for the system."

Tiaan van der Merwe, a member of Parliament from the opposition Progressive Federal Party, an organization of liberal whites, said after several visits to Crossroads during the battle that the police and army had "either been active in supporting the Witdoeke or, at the very least, were prepared to let them get away with what they were doing. They only interfered when the other side, the Comrades, were getting the upper hand."

The police strongly deny any involvement in the fighting, saying that they had difficulty separating the two sides. But a Supreme Court justice, hearing residents' accounts of the fighting, quickly granted a restraining order barring the security forces as well as the vigilantes from attacking another Crossroads camp.

The Witdoeke, however, ignored the court order and launched a new attack Monday on another section of Crossroads known as the KTC Camp after a nearby store. In two days of fierce fighting, the Witdoeke drove the Comrades away and burned the shacks that had been home to 50,000 people. Unofficially, the death toll is now at least 85, including 17 reported killed Monday and Tuesday.

The government has rejected "with the contempt they deserve" all suggestions that it conspired with the Witdoeke to oust some of the most stubborn Crossroads residents and force them to move to Khayelitsha by destroying their homes.

But the government barred the residents displaced by the fighting last month from returning to Crossroads and rebuilding their shanties. It cleared that ground of rubble, surrounded it with barbed wire and put a 24-hour-a-day military guard on it.

The government insists that all those displaced by the fighting must move to Khayelitsha—"our new home" in the Xhosa language used by most Crossroads residents—where they will be given temporary housing in tents and allowed to rebuild their shacks on sites with water and sanitary facilities.

Only 4,000 have so far gone to Khayelitsha. The rest, finding it too far from their jobs or fearing new attacks from vigilantes there, moved into other sections of Crossroads, including KTC or were taken in by residents of surrounding black townships. Some, like the Tembas, were housed in a Red Cross tent city that the Witdoeke vigilantes burned to the ground Monday, making them refugees for the second time this month.

In the view of many white relief workers, the government appears to be trying to force more to go to Khayelitsha by providing a minimum of shelter, food, clothing and medical care for the refugees. The Red Cross, churches, charitable groups and even foreign embassies—the U.S. Embassy donated $35,000—have given more aid to the refugees than the central government has.

J. Christiaan Heunis, the minister of constitutional development and planning, who has jurisdiction over Crossroads, told Parliament that although 35,000 people were made homeless in the fighting, the government saw no reason to declare an emergency or disaster area here because everyone could be accommodated at Khayelitsha.

The government's critics accuse it of trying to take advantage of the refugees' misery and forcing them into a move they had fought for so many years.

The Rev. Allan Boesak, a founder of the United Democratic Front, said on a visit to Crossroads that the government's actions there amounted to "a mass, forced removal of 35,000 people, and there should be no doubt about that."

Heunis replied that the security forces, whatever power they might appear to have been in other circumstances, could not protect the refugees from the Witdoeke vigilantes if they returned to their old camp areas in Crossroads.

But Colin Appleton, regional director of the Urban Foundation said that the government's decision not to allow the displaced residents to return and rebuild could itself bring further violence if they attempt to reclaim the land.

The decision also rewarded the Witdoeke for their violence, Appleton said. The Urban Foundation has withdrawn from a $12-million project to upgrade the squatter settlement.

The Progressive Federal Party's Van der Merwe sees the battle for Crossroads as a dangerous new development in the country's civil strife.

"If even half the allegations are true, then we are into a new ball game where the government is prepared to exploit divisions within the community ruthlessly and to support the bad elements to achieve its own political ends," he said. "This divide-and-rule strategy is very dangerous because it could become uncontrollable. . . . What it is doing is pushing us all the faster down the road to civil war."

SIMON, MARY, FATIMAH: VANISHING S. AFRICANS

JUNE 24, 1986

BY MICHAEL PARKS

JOHANNESBURG, South Africa—Simon M., Mary D., Nazareth M., Fatimah S., Fikile M.—where are they?

Simon, a 15-year-old schoolboy, was sent to the store near his home in Soweto, outside Johannesburg, last Wednesday evening for bread, milk and jam. He has not returned. His parents are frantic with worry.

Mary, 20, a student leader in Soweto, told her mother on June 15 that she would be spending two nights at a girlfriend's house and would be back last Tuesday morning. She has not come home yet.

Nazareth, 17, an altar boy at a Roman Catholic church outside Port Elizabeth, went to serve Mass on June 15 and was last seen being taken away from the church by three men.

Fatimah, an insurance clerk in her early 20s, went to a meeting on that weekend of an Indian cultural organization to which she belongs near Durban and did not return.

Fikile, a truck driver in his 40s, left for work on the morning of June 17 but, according to his Cape Town employers, never arrived, although he has a "superior attendance record." Neither his foreman nor the company lawyer has been able to locate him despite checks with police, local hospitals, the mortuary and all his known friends.

These five are among the hundreds, perhaps thousands, of South Africans who, according to the opposition Progressive Federal Party, have "disappeared" since President Pieter W. Botha imposed a national state of emergency June 12 and gave the police and army the authority to detain anyone without charge and hold him or her indefinitely.

"Security police are picking people up at their homes, places of work and off the street, and their next of kin are not being informed of their whereabouts," Ray Swart, a Progressive Federal Party member of Parliament, charged last week.

He said there have been "thousands of disappearances" under the state of emergency and that they are continuing.

Families of the five all have been to the police in search of their relatives but in each case the police did not say they were officially detained and offered no other answers. In the cases of Nazareth and Fatimah, they even took down details as they might for any "missing persons" case.

(Nevertheless, although the five have not been officially declared to be among the detainees, their last names have been withheld by The Times to comply with the South African government rules prohibiting publication of the names of detainees.)

The Progressive Federal Party established a "missing persons bureau" last week in Cape Town. It received more than 500 calls the first day and is now working on an around-the-clock basis, using computers to keep track of the multiplying reports.

To publicize the situation, the party's members of Parliament are using the privileged legislative forum to demand information on people who have been detained or are simply listed as missing.

LIST OF 1,034

Peter Soal, another Progressive Federal Party member of Parliament, cited a list of 1,034 persons believed detained, but he said the party's reports suggest that this was probably not even half of those held by the police under the state of emergency.

That list, compiled at the middle of last week by the Detainees' Parents Support Committee, which monitors detentions and advises the families of prisoners, includes the names of 255 political and community leaders, 115 students and teachers, 65 union officials, 44 clergymen and church workers, 12 journalists and about the same number of lawyers.

Three members of the Progressive Federal Party's "unrest monitoring team" were detained but released after strong complaints from the party that the government had infringed upon legal activities of a recognized political party.

An analysis by the Detainees' Parents Support Committee of the presumed but not confirmed detentions shows that more organizations were affected now than during the partial state of emergency imposed last July. It also shows that this crackdown reaches to many more outlying communities and rural areas to which the unrest has recently spread and that more lower-level activists, such as shop stewards and street committee chairmen, are being held.

The authorities appear to have worked from carefully compiled lists of anti-apartheid activists in the first detentions after the state of emergency was declared and are still seeking many people that they have missed. The Progressive Federal Party's Graham McIntosh says they also seem to be involved "in a massive trawling exercise." McIntosh, a member of Parliament, is in charge of the "missing persons bureau."

"They take everything in the fish pond and throw back the ones they don't want." McIntosh said. "This way they hope to get the guys they are looking for."

In one case over the weekend of June 14–15, everyone present at a Cape Town church prayer service was detained after the police said that the service was really an anti-government political meeting and thus prohibited.

The government information bureau, after first denying knowledge of the incident, said that 189 people were being held. On Sunday, the information bureau announced that about 150 had been released during the previous three days.

Another case cited by a Progressive Federal Party member of the President's Council as that of a 17-year-old Cape Town high school student, Helene Thornton, who was arrested June 16 at a church service commemorating the 575 people killed in the "Soweto uprising"—11 months of intermittent black riots that began June 16, 1976.

The police found a copy of a magazine published by the anti-apartheid United Democratic Front in her schoolbag and detained her, Progressive Federal member Robin J. Carlisle told the council. "This is a perfectly legal magazine, and I subscribe to it myself," Carlisle said. "Does this mean that I am going to be arrested too?"

Estimates last week by Amnesty International in London and international church groups in Geneva and New York put the number of detainees at more than 3,000. Calls are made from abroad almost daily demanding the release of prominent detainees, but emergency regulations prevent reporters here from reporting the names of any of those being held.

The government has refused either to identify those detained or even to say how many it is holding, declaring that "it is not in the state's interest to do so." After dismissing as "grossly exaggerated" reports that as many as 4,000 or 4,500 people have been detained, spokesmen now refuse to comment.

The government has also prohibited any news reports on policy activities beyond those announced by the government information bureau.

But Louis Nel, deputy minister in charge of information, assured Parliament that the police would inform the families of all those held under the emergency regulations. The government may also disclose the total number of detainees sometime in the future, he said.

The detentions are necessary, Nel said last week, to remove anti-apartheid activists from a "superheated situation," to let political passions cool in the black community and to ensure that political moderates, which the government hopes to bring into negotiations on political reforms, will not be intimidated by militant blacks.

'OTHER REASONS'

Even if the state of emergency were to be lifted, the detentions would likely continue, government ministers have told Parliament. The ruling National Party pushed through legislation last Friday that would enable the police, without a declaration of a state of emergency, to detain for up to six months anyone believed involved in civil unrest or likely to become involved.

Nel told journalists that, for the most part, the security police were acting on information of anti-government activities that they had long been gathering.

"No one has been arrested because he is a trade union leader," Nel said in reply to widespread allegations abroad of a crackdown on black labor unions. "That is not the reason he has been arrested. If a trade union leader has been arrested, then it is for other reasons."

Nel objected strongly, in Parliament and in talking to journalists, to the Progressive Federal Party's charges that the "disappearances"— as the Progressive Federal Party's Swart termed them—amount to a wave of terror intended to decimate anti-apartheid groups, whose leaders have reportedly been detained in large numbers, and to intimidate ordinary citizens.

Nel said that not only would families of detainees be advised of their whereabouts so that they could bring them clothing and spending money but that prisons and jails where they are held would be regularly inspected by judges and that medical care would be assured.

"The trouble is that almost nobody we have talked with has been officially informed that their relatives have been detained or told where they are being held," Audrey Coleman of the Detainees' Parents Support Committee said. "Because people have been given this assurance that they will be informed when a person has been detained, those families with missing persons who hear nothing from the authorities become all the more concerned. . . .

"Where are their sons and daughters, their husbands and wives? They don't know. What has happened to them? Are they detained, are they safe, have they been hurt, are they alive? They don't know, and when a person is missing in these circumstances it is very, very difficult to find out."

Another factor, Coleman said, is that many activists are "in hiding, on the run, not sleeping at home or going to work," and this "adds an element of uncertainty for their families, who don't know whether a missed phone call means detention or simply that the callbox wasn't working."

Simon's father, Petrus, a shipping clerk, went to the homes of all his son's friends, then to local hospitals and clinics, then with reluctance to nearby police stations and, finally, with dread to the morturary. No one knew his son's whereabouts.

NO INFORMATION

"I was told to go home and wait and that if my son had been detained I would be informed," he said. "We are still waiting, and not knowing is very, very hard."

When Nazareth did not return from church, his mother and three older brothers went looking for him and found fellow parishioners who said they had seen three men, apparently armed, put him and several other youths into a white van and drive off.

With this information, they went to the authorities but were told that no information was available on the incident, his brother Michael said.

"Our mother is so scared that he has been killed that I think she would be almost relieved if she were told Nazareth has been detained," Michael added.

Coleman, whose own activist sons have been detained in the past, commented: "When a person is missing, detention is only one possibility. There are (pro-government) vigilante groups that have been attacking activists in the (black) townships. There are criminals who may kill in the course of ordinary crime. There is also the possibility of accidents, and all the other things any parent worries might happen to a child."

U.S. FIRMS IN SOUTH AFRICA UNDER GROWING PRESSURE

AUGUST 10, 1986

BY MICHAEL PARKS

PORT ELIZABETH, South Africa—For nearly a decade, General Motors Corp. has been battling apartheid, becoming, along with other American companies, a major force for reform in South Africa. But now the giant auto maker is wondering what chance it has of winning that fight and whether it can even stay on here.

One of the first 12 American companies to sign the Sullivan Principles, a code promoting fair labor practices and equal employment opportunities in South Africa, GM desegregated its own facilities, hired more blacks and trained them for promotion, and every year pumped hundreds of thousands of dollars into programs to improve local schools, housing and health care.

In recent years, GM has joined with other American companies operating in South Africa to push for broader reforms and an eventual end to rule by the white-led government, an effort that has encouraged many South African businessmen to press for faster and more sweeping changes.

But GM is finding that it is near the limit of what it can do. Robert A. White, the company's managing director in South Africa, says he fears that its efforts and those of other American companies to promote change will not be enough—not enough to satisfy South Africa's restive black majority, not enough to satisfy the firms' critics in the United States, and perhaps not even enough to satisfy home offices debating the wisdom of remaining in such a politically turbulent environment.

Nor has GM satisfied its own workers. Even allowing for normal union-employer antagonisms, their view of GM is at times severe enough to call into question the company's claim that over the years it has been a force for change.

"GM b.s.'s the workers and it b.s.'s the public," said Norman

Erasmus, an overhead crane operator and a shop steward at the GM plant here.

Erasmus charges that the Sullivan Principles "protect the companies against criticism. They could say, 'We're living up to the Sullivan code,' and still avoid paying decent wages. . . ."

A 'DESPERATE SITUATION'

Other union officials complain of GM's poor record in advancing blacks, an area in which White concedes the company has much room for improvement.

All of which leads White to answer his own question—"Do we as American companies make a difference by staying in South Africa?"—pessimistically:

"Not as much as we want, that's for sure, and maybe not where it counts.

" The longer this crisis continues, the more desperate the situation will become," he said in an interview, "and the harder it will be for American companies to justify their presence in South Africa on an ability to effect change here.

"As a force for change, we are on a plateau," he added. "We have made considerable progress over the years, but it is hard to say how we are going to make more. We are not going to quit. We are committed to remain in South Africa as long as it makes business sense. But I admit that it's discouraging."

Discouragement is growing among the 260 American companies still operating here—55 have pulled out in the past 18 months—and American businessmen frankly acknowledge the need to justify their continued presence in South Africa, not only in terms of profits but in the ability to promote basic political change.

"Some American companies are frankly losing heart," said Lionel R.E. Grewan, a Citibank officer who serves as executive director of the Sullivan Signatory Assn., coordinating observance of the nine-year-old Sullivan Principles. "They are becoming discouraged about their ability to promote peaceful change. They are getting little encouragement from the South African government to stay. They are being told to leave by some segments of the black community, and they are taking a lot of heat back home for being here at all. . . .

TOOK COURAGE

"Over the years, however, American companies have . . . spent a lot of money on improving education for blacks, on creating decent housing and on other programs that showed the way forward. Today, desegregating their facilities may not seem like much, but when racial segregation was the law here, it took a lot of courage to go against it.

"There is no question that the American companies in the Sullivan program were the path breakers . . . and their activism encouraged South African companies to do the same," Grewan continued. "But those were soft targets, things we could achieve in our own plants and offices or could develop programs for and spend money on the outside.

"Now, we are into social justice and political change, and this is much, much harder. When we do achieve something, it is often not noticed immediately, almost impossible to claim credit for, and never, absolutely never, quick."

Many American businessmen say that their inability to promote broader, faster changes is an increasingly important factor in their firms' decisions on whether to continue operating in South Africa.

"Five years ago, no one even asked whether we should stay," the managing director of a large American food company's South African subsidiary said, asking, like many others, not to be quoted by name. "Then, we were both making money and promoting reforms.

"Today, the answer to whether we are an effective force for change is so finely balanced and our profits have been so greatly reduced by all this turmoil that I cannot say we will still be here at the end of the year."

The firms that have pulled out this year include General Electric, GTE, Bell & Howell, Ashland Oil, Phillips Petroleum, CBS, Eaton Corp. and Kidder Peabody. Although most cited South Africa's depressed economy and their own losses for their decisions, the growing divestiture campaign in the United States was clearly a major factor.

But even some of the American and European companies that are strongly and publicly committed to remaining and working for peaceful change are now drawing up contingency plans for leaving if they are required to do so by their governments.

"It would be stupid and irresponsible if we did not have contingency plans," said David English, local managing director of Rank

Xerox Ltd., which is looking into the possibilities of selling all or part of its South African subsidiary to local interests. "The future may not be in our hands."

At GM, which is in its 60th year in South Africa and is one of the largest American employers in the country, the future is further clouded by economics.

HARDEST HIT

The local auto industry is among the hardest hit by the recession of the past two years. Ford Motor Co. has merged its operations with a South African company and two European auto makers have pulled out entirely. Sales were down about 25% last year compared to 1984. The industry as a whole is not using even half of its single-shift capacity. Employment by the auto companies and then suppliers has been cut by more than a third since 1984.

"No one is making money—not last year and probably not this, and the future is uncertain," White said of the South African auto industry.

GM has reduced its work force over the past year and a half to 3,100 from 4,380. It has also increased the proportion of components that it buys from contractors, and is looking for a South African partner to help increase its share of the market—not 11%—which would enable it to borrow more money locally.

"The sheer economics of the business today limit what we can do," White said. "When you are reducing your work force, you can't promote as many people as you want, or hire more. When you are not making money, it is hard to put more funds into social action programs. And when you are focused on ensuring your survival in this very depressed market and protecting the jobs of more than 3,000 people, you can't do as much as you want on other fronts."

INITIATED REFORMS

Like most large American companies in South Africa, GM is "looking for ways to make a bigger difference here," said George Stegmann, the firm's acting personnel director.

"Even before we signed the Sullivan Principles," he said, "GM was initiating programs to upgrade the quality of life of its black and other nonwhite employees . . . and to implement fair labor practices and equal job opportunities. We desegregated all our facilities, we opened our apprenticeship programs to blacks, and we recognized black trade unions and provided dues checkoffs—all before the law allowed."

The Sullivan Principles, drafted in 1977 by the Rev. Leon Sullivan, a black minister from Philadelphia and a member of the GM board of directors in Detroit, called on American companies to adhere to such principles as equal pay for equal work, to provide training for black workers and promote them on merit, and to involve themselves in their local communities.

American businesses in South Africa now have a lengthy list of good deeds to their credit—millions of dollars in gifts to black schools, university scholarships, construction of clinics, contributions to rural relief programs, urban housing projects, development of black-owned companies—and President Reagan frequently cites the American companies as a major force for reform here.

But Stegmann, although proud of GM's record, acknowledged that "events have largely overtaken most of these programs and initiatives."

"The real issue, the priority issue, today must be the dismantling of apartheid," said Stegmann, a white South African. "That means entering into negotiations with credible black leaders in South Africa in order to take the necessary steps for a new South Africa, a South Africa beyond apartheid. This, of course, is a political issue, and it is difficult for a company, a foreign-owned company especially, to move to the core from lobbying government and from developing programs, however worthwhile, around the periphery."

White put it bluntly: "Today, blacks want Bob White and GM to get them their political rights. They say, 'Thanks for all GM has done, but we need political rights to change this country, top to bottom, and we want you to help us.' My question is, how?"

He rejects calls, by Sullivan and others, for a campaign of civil disobedience by American firms, of not complying with any apartheid laws or regulations, as well as demands that the companies withdraw from South Africa to protest continuation of the system of racial separation and minority white-led government.

"Civil disobedience—what's that going to do for anyone?" White said. "Given this government, that is not a strategy that will have much success here."

White and other American businessmen are following with rising apprehension the moves in the United States, Western Europe and Japan to impose economic sanctions on South Africa to try to force the government into negotiations with the country's black leaders.

A bill passed by the House of Representatives in Washington would require U.S. companies to pull out of South Africa within 180 days and to cut all their trade ties with this country.

Legislation pending before the Senate is less stringent, as are the proposals to the European Communities.

"I don't think we are going to be forced to leave, but some of the so-called compromise measures could make it very difficult to continue operating here," the managing director of an American-owned electronics company said. "If there is a ban on new investment, how do we bring in new products, which are the lifeblood of our industry?"

Even if their firms are not hit directly by the American or European measures, the executives at many foreign-owned companies fear that sanctions, such as boycotts of South African steel, iron and coal, will, if effective, further weaken the country's economy and make it less profitable for them to stay.

A second concern is a growing resentment of foreigners among whites, a situation evident in the government's determination to defy world demands for faster and broader reforms and in jingoistic assertions each day that South Africa can indeed go it alone and that the investment and expertise of foreign firms are not needed.

"Who gets hurt by sanctions depends on what kind of sanctions are eventually imposed," another American executive said, "but to my mind, South Africa is becoming both a politically and an economically hostile environment for our company and many other foreign firms. . . . People may decide to get out simply because it is not worth the pain—the agony, actually—of staying in a less and less profitable market."

American businessmen also question the underlying strategy of sanctions, doubting whether it is possible as one said "to hurt these Boers enough to make them give up what they've got here. It seems to me that what little we can do will only enrage them."

Views among South African blacks are as diverse as their politics. But even those who call for sanctions and for the withdrawal of foreign companies from the country and a total trade embargo do so more from the belief that every tactic must be tried rather than from the conviction that sanctions will end apartheid.

"Sanctions, disinvestment, boycotts—those are really American issues," said a politically active black executive at a U.S. computer company. "They are well-intentioned moves, and maybe they might shake up these people in [the] white Establishment. But we blacks know that our problems will have to be solved here, on the ground in South Africa, and while we are grateful for international support, we know that apartheid will have to be beaten here and by us."

At GM, the company's black employees believe the firm should stay and, as one shop steward put it, "really do all these things they say they believe in."

"GM leaving South Africa isn't going to end apartheid," Elliot Mtwa, another shop steward, commented, "but GM staying isn't going to end it either."

Fred Sauls, general secretary of the National Automobile & Allied Workers Union, which represents most of GM's 2,100 nonwhite workers, said: "When you are losing jobs the way we are, disinvestment just compounds the problem.

"Of course, we want GM to stay and expand and provide more jobs and pay better—much better—wages. We also want to live up to all this rhetoric—equal opportunity, affirmative action, social justice— that it uses to cover up what we see as its exploitation of black workers."

'WIFE AND 5 KIDS'

Erasmus, the GM crane operator and shop steward, is Colored, as persons of mixed-race are officially classified. He says that one form exploitation takes is poor wages. "For me to buy a loaf of bread, I must work a quarter of an hour," he said. "In other words, I have to build two cars to put a loaf of bread on the table. To buy a suit, I have to work two weeks. I have a wife and five kids, so how long do I have to work to clothe my family?"

Erasmus said he does not believe that GM is not making money in South Africa.

"The profits may not show up on the books here, but look in Germany, where we get a lot of our parts . . . GM may not like apartheid, but it sure seems to like the low wages that apartheid brings," he said.

Wages currently range from the equivalent of $1.28 an hour for unskilled workers to about $3.25 an hour for craftsmen. Blacks working at non-union factories in the Port Elizabeth area are paid as little as 60 cents an hour.

"What we wonder," Erasmus said, "is where the money goes if a car costs about the same here as in the United States but we only get paid a fraction of what American workers earn."

Union members are also bitter about the limited advancement of black workers despite GM's stated commitment to equal employment opportunity. Although blacks and Coloreds hold a number of supervisory positions as foremen and general foremen at GM, there are no blacks at the management level and only two, a physician and a data processing specialist, are in professional or executive positions. Blacks and Coloreds constitute 62% of the work force.

"We have an all-white management at GM that won't promote a black guy if a cousin or a friend won't get the job as a result," Sauls said. "This stems from our whole social situation in South Africa, not to mention the political-economic situation. You have to have a very strong guy politically to implement true equal opportunities. No one at GM is prepared for a real challenge to the system."

White, who came to Port Elizabeth from GM headquarters in Detroit a year ago, commented: "It's a failing I am determined to correct. There are reasons for it, among them our very substantial reductions [in staff], but we also still have white managers who give only lip service to upward mobility for blacks."

GM HAS HIGH RANKING

GM nevertheless has held a ranking in the top category—"making good progress"—of Sullivan companies for the past six years.

According to evaluations carried out by Arthur D. Little Inc., the Boston-based management consultant, 36 firms were in the top category, 89 were in the second—"making progress"—and 21 were in the third category—"needs to become more active." Some American companies, apparently unwilling to risk getting a low ranking, have refused to participate in the Sullivan program, and a few have pulled out.

The Sullivan program itself is often criticized by blacks here who say that their views have not been considered, that it encourages "paper compliance" and not real changes in company policies, and that many of the projects undertaken by American companies, such as the "adopt-a-school" program, unintentionally reinforce apartheid.

As criticism increases in the United States of companies that have continued to operate in South Africa, more firms have signed the Sullivan Principles, and the code itself has been strengthened to include a commitment to political action to end apartheid.

ADVERTISING CAMPAIGN

Over the past year, the 195 Sullivan companies have increased their private lobbying with government ministers and pressed publicly for political reforms with bold newspaper advertisements declaring, for example, "There Is a Better Way."

The latest advertisement, published in early August by Mobil, calls on the government to allow black and white leaders around the country "to negotiate new regional and metropolitan forms of government that respond to the wishes of the people living there."

"The time has come to build a new non-racial democracy from the regions up," Mobil says in the quarter-page ad. For a restoration of business confidence, "we want a vision of South Africa without apartheid, a land where people can freely participate in politics regardless of race," the ad states.

GM's White found himself in the middle of a nationwide controversy in January when, angered by the hesitancy of Port Elizabeth's city council to integrate the municipal beaches, he announced that the company would pay the legal costs of any of its employees charged with violating whites-only restrictions. The council, as a result, voted to drop enforcement of the regulations and asked provincial authorities to desegregate the beaches.

GM is now under fire, however, from the National Automobile & Allied Workers Union for refusing to pay the wages of two workers who were detained without charge under the two-month-old state of emergency. Stegmann said the company has kept both men's names on the payroll, continued their medical insurance and other benefits and will assist their families through local relief organizations but feels it cannot continue their pay in view of current layoffs of other workers.

"These are difficult times, and they require difficult decisions," Stegmann said. "Wherever our sympathies lie, we always seem to be caught in the middle."

The Sullivan companies have recently undertaken a number of "social justice" projects aimed, as one businessman puts it, at "dismantling whatever bits of apartheid we can and building a non-racial South Africa in its place."

U.S. companies have helped set up and pay for a network of legal aid centers and neighborhood clinics around the country, not only to help blacks with their day-to-day legal problems but to challenge such government measures as the nationwide state of emergency imposed June 12.

They are working to desegregate at least portions of the main Johannesburg hospital as well as some suburban medical facilities. They are promoting the incorporation of the black township of Alexandra and an Indian neighborhood into Johannesburg's wealthy white suburb of Sandton. And they are planning the quiet integration of some whites-only residential areas and the establishment next year of three housing developments that will not be racially segregated.

"These projects are intended to produce results that help dismantle apartheid, and some may prove quite dramatic in South African terms if they succeed," said Grewan, the Citibank officer who is classified by South African law as a Colored. "Of course, whatever we do will not be enough as long as anything remains of apartheid."

S. AFRICA'S JOBLESS WHITES OUT OF LUCK, OPPORTUNITY

DECEMBER 7, 1986

BY MICHAEL PARKS

JOHANNESBURG, South Africa—Gideon Beukes' luck ran out six months ago. The steel engineering company where he worked as a welder laid him off. The owner of the small agricultural plot on which he lived east of Johannesburg evicted him, his wife and four children because he could not pay the rent.

Beukes, 41, now has only odd jobs and small government welfare checks to feed his family, which has moved into an empty garage.

Each week, he pedals a battered bicycle more than 400 miles around the Johannesburg area, looking for work while saving bus fare. He often travels 50 or 60 miles on the bike to apply for a job he has heard about, only to find that it has already been filled, usually with a black worker who is paid half the $3.15 an hour that an experienced white welder would get.

Beukes' daughter Maria, 15, who is more used to the sheltered life of Sundra, the small town where the family once lived, "has fallen in with a fast crowd of these city kids for whom booze, drugs and sex are big," Beukes said the other day. She has run away from home, and her parents are heartsick with worry. Beukes has spent days searching Johannesburg for his daughter.

"I feel like my life has fallen apart, and I can't seem to put it back together," he said. "I've always been willing to try my luck and make a go of it, but my luck seems to have run out. I try not to be angry and bitter about it all, but it's difficult, very difficult."

His may seem to be "just another hard-luck story," as Beukes says with a self-deprecating smile and a slight shrug, but it is one that is heard with increasing frequency and growing bitterness around South Africa's major cities, where thousands of white workers have lost their jobs in the ecomomic recession.

Soup kitchens, not seen in white communities here since the days

369

of the Great Depression of the 1930s, are feeding hundreds of unemployed whites and their families every day around Johannesburg, Pretoria, Port Elizabeth and other major cities.

HIGH UNEMPLOYMENT

Long lines of job-seekers, mostly semiskilled workers from the construction industry, form daily outside the government's manpower offices. The men hope for at least temporary jobs, but most go away disappointed. The lines are even longer on the days that unemployment benefits are distributed, and there are angry arguments when the benefits run out. To the surprise of officials, municipal governments have had scores of whites taking some of the $2.25-a-day jobs as manual laborers that were created to ease black unemployment.

Evicted from their homes, many poverty-stricken white families have moved, like the Beukeses, into empty garages, houses waiting for demolition and even abandoned buses and trucks. Just opposite Johannesburg's municipal building, a dozen families are living in empty offices. Banks and other mortgage-holders are foreclosing on the homes of many unemployed whites, and applications for low-income municipal housing exceed vacancies by 15 to 1 in some cities.

Barefoot, flaxen-haired children of the unemployed go begging around the shopping centers of the working-class suburbs where they live, hoping for a can or two of food from shoppers or a few cents with which they can buy bread. Some come into downtown areas, shocking passers-by used to blacks begging but not whites.

Burglaries have increased markedly in many suburbs in recent months. Food is taken even more frequently than valuables. Supermarket managers tell of finding hungry children hidden in corners of the store, eating food taken from the shelves.

"We are in an economic, social and political crisis of alarming proportions as a result of this large-scale and rapidly growing white unemployment," said Clive Derby-Lewis, director of the Johannesburg-based Stallard Foundation, a conservative study institute.

"We have hundreds, literally hundreds, of men losing their jobs every day, and we have poverty among whites now of the scope that we have not seen since the Great Depression more than 50 years ago. This is a horrific situation, and we can say, without exaggeration, that it threatens what is left of the country's political and social stability, that it is not simply an economic problem. . . .

SEES A HIDDEN CRISIS

"So far, this crisis is largely a hidden crisis, because the government is embarrassed by its failure to manage the economy well and because it knows that its own continued existence in office is threatened."

The political implications of such widespread white poverty clearly transcend the suffering of the individual families.

The soup kitchens, unemployment lines and begging children painfully recall, particularly for the country's Dutch-descended Afrikaners, the problem of "poor whites" in the 1920s and 1930s, when a commission sponsored by the Carnegie Corp. found that 17.5% of the white population, about 300,000 people, were "very poor."

Many aspects of South Africa's system of apartheid were intended to protect the "poor whites," mostly Afrikaners who had been driven off their farms and into the cities where they had trouble competing for jobs. One of the National Party's proudest boasts over the years has been its resolution of this problem.

"With the abandonment of almost everything that it once stood for, the National Party is recreating the problem of white poverty on a scale that never existed before," said Louis Stofberg, a member of Parliament from the ultra-right Reconstituted National Party. The party wants a return to apartheid's strict racial separation as well as its assertion of minority white rule with Afrikaner dominance.

"We are heading for an economic disaster under this government, a catastrophe way beyond the Great Depression. . . . Since the war, South Africa has not had such white unemployment as we have now, and the poverty we have begun to see is worse than anything in our history," Stofberg said.

The withdrawal of dozens of American and West European companies from South Africa in recent months under mounting political pressure at home is certain to hasten this economic cataclysm, Stofberg argued, by depriving many key firms here of much of their access to foreign capital, technology, managerial know-how and export markets.

"The American and European companies all say, 'Not to worry, all the jobs are safe,' and maybe they are," Stofberg said. "But saving today's jobs is just the first step in dealing with this unemployment problem—who's going to create tomorrow's jobs? To me, that's the real worry."

For Stofberg's party and other groups on the far right, the country's severe economic problems not only prove what they call "the total incompetence" of the Nationalist government, but offer an opportunity for major political gains—perhaps not enough to oust the National Party but probably enough to thwart President Pieter W. Botha's plans for modest but continuing reform of apartheid.

Unemployed whites already complain that blacks, who are paid a quarter to half of what white workers would earn, are hired by employers trying to keep costs down. They also resent the scrapping of government regulations that reserved certain jobs in most industries for whites. And they are angered that the government, for years the employer of last resort for whites, is not only trimming many positions to reduce the swollen bureaucracy but is hiring blacks, Indians and Coloreds (persons of mixed race) for jobs whites once held.

COMPETING WITH BLACKS

"It is getting harder and harder for the white man to compete against the black in this country," complained Sharon Denicker, whose husband has been out of work for a year. "The black will work for a fraction of what the white man requires because his housing costs are only a tenth of what ours are, because he pays no taxes, because he has subsidized transport and subsidized food. . . . The supermarkets, for example, will take on a black girl as a cashier rather than a woman like me who needs the job to feed her kids. This is just not fair."

Blacks, for their part, resent unemployed whites taking the low-paid jobs, such as manual labor on public works projects, that they have come to regard as theirs. They also resent the substantially higher unemployment and welfare benefits whites get when out of work.

According to government employment statistics, there were fewer than 30,000 unemployed out of a white labor force of nearly 2 million in July, the last month for which figures have been released. But the Manpower Department in Pretoria reported that, a few months earlier, 188,000 whites were actively looking for work.

FIGURES ARE RISING

Both figures have risen significantly, according to recent government statements, and applications for unemployment insurance benefits are reportedly coming in at a rate of 45,000 a month. New statistics will not be out for several months, and government officials refused requests for interviews on the growth of white unemployment and efforts to deal with it.

Whatever its true proportions, unemployment for whites is just a fraction of what it is for blacks, more than 2 million of whom—about 30% of the black labor force nationwide—are without jobs and only rarely receive unemployment compensation.

A better indication of the scope of white unemployment and its growth is the establishment over the last year of dozens of local welfare programs, particularly the soup kitchens that have sprung up around the industrial centers where unemployment is greatest.

"We only help the really hard up, and I am feeding, plus or minus, 240 children, 120 pensioners and maybe another 100 adults a day," said Johanna Swanepoel, who runs a soup kitchen out of her small home in the hard-hit Jan Hofmeyr neighborhood on Johannesburg's near west side.

"A family with five kids can get 500 or 600 rand (about $225 to $270) from welfare for the month, but at today's prices that does not go very far at all," she said.

The Dutch Reformed Church, to which most of the Afrikaners belong, says it is feeding 900 children a day in the Johannesburg area alone. The Pinkster Evangelical Church, which has parishes in several blue-collar suburbs around Johannesburg, estimates that it is feeding about 1,000 people in its soup kitchens as well as delivering food to 150 families.

In working-class suburbs on the city's east side, the Jimmy O'Connor Welfare Service is directly helping 107 families and running a lunch program to feed children at 13 schools. State-run schools provide pupils in depressed areas around Transvaal province with free lunches, but government officials said the size of the program is secret and refused to give any information about it.

"We began our assistance after we heard stories about children at school fainting or falling over because they had not had breakfast or whose families have no food in their homes at all," said Ronnie West, chairman of the Jimmy O'Connor group.

The Afrikaner Resistance Movement, better known for its far-right politics than welfare activities, began collecting surplus produce from farmers three months ago and estimates that it has already provided more than 500,000 meals in the Johannesburg and Pretoria areas and expects to provide at least 5 million by July.

Giel Groenewald, head of the group's assistance efforts, said that many more whites, mostly Afrikaners, need help. "Some people are just too embarrassed or ashamed to ask for food," Groenewald said.

'SITUATION GETTING WORSE'

"The problem is huge, simply huge," said Rosa Hattingh, a relief coordinator for the Afrikaner Resistance Movement in Johannesburg's southern suburbs. "From family to family, the story is the same— they have lost their jobs because of the economic recession and they can't find another because the companies prefer to hire blacks for cheap labor. . . . So we have the bosses, big business and the banks exploiting both whites and blacks."

The situation around Cape Town, Port Elizabeth, Uitenhage and Durban, the country's other major industrial centers, is equally serious, according to welfare officials and relief groups there.

In the Cape Town area, for example, local governments are providing baskets of food to nearly 14,000 white families, probably about 80,000 people.

"People are really hurting, and the situation is getting worse," the Port Elizabeth church worker said, asking not to be quoted by name. "There has been less and less work, especially in the construction industry, the automotive industry, a lot of heavy industries, over the past year, and when there is a job going there are 50 or 60 white applicants and five times that many blacks for it."

A bitter envy of blacks, as well as an ignorance of their real circumstances, colors the conversation of the unemployed whites, who see blacks not only as rivals for scarce jobs but as being rewarded by the government for the country's continuing civil unrest.

"Blacks live fantastically, far better than we do," Sharon Denicker said in the sparsely furnished living room of her small but comfortable city-owned row house, which is perhaps twice the size of the average home in one of Johannesburg's black ghettos for a quarter the number of people at roughly the same price per square foot.

"The only blacks who've got problems are those who drink too much," she said. "The husbands get jobs as cheap labor, the women can work as maids and the whites subsidize everything."

Clive Derby-Lewis sees such rivalry "growing inevitably into serious racial conflict, with both sides using arms," unless the country is partitioned, as the Conservative Party and other groups on the far right advocate, into black and white homelands.

"The sheer numbers of the blacks in South Africa mean that this problem of white unemployment, and thus of white poverty, is just beginning," he said. "Blacks are pouring out of the rural areas in search of urban jobs. Big business and the banks are only too happy to exploit their cheap labor, and so the gulf between the super-rich and the poor is deepening and threatening any hope we have of re-establishing stability. . . . Even this government should realize that the solution to black poverty is not white poverty."

SEVEN

PEOPLE POWER IN THE PHILIPPINES

1987 WINNER IN THE SPOT NEWS PHOTOGRAPHY CATEGORY

"For a distinguished example of spot news photography in black and white or color . . . "

San Francisco Examiner
Kim Komenich

Ferdinand E. Marcos, a corrupt dictator but strong American ally, fell in disgrace as control of the islands he had headed for 20 years was wrenched away from him. Kim Komenich, armed with a camera, recorded the "people power" revolution that led to the election of President Corazon C. Aquino.

All the elements of a great news story were there. Philippines President Ferdinand E. Marcos, an ailing dictator with a long string of accusations of human rights abuses, was trying to salvage his credibility and hold on to power. He called a snap election for February 7, 1986, and faced the widow of a murdered rival as his opponent. The campaign promised to be bitter and, unfortunately, bloody.

It seemed the whole world was converging on Manila. The *San Francisco Examiner*'s coverage had begun in 1979 when reporter Phil Bronstein started writing about the Philippines from his base in San Francisco. After Bronstein returned from his first trip to Manila in 1983, we talked about the need for photographs as well as words and, during the next eight months, tried to convince our editors of the need to explain the growing unrest in the Philippines to our large Asian readership.

As things heated up in the Philippines, I made sure my passport and visas were in order. The final approval came four days before the one-year anniversary of the assassination of Benigno S. Aquino, in August 1984.

Our editors said, "Go, but stay together. Shoot travel section pictures whenever possible. Don't take unnecessary chances." They were not just polite words of concern: Of four photographers the *Examiner* had sent abroad in the past, only three had come back alive.

We spent a total of five months in the Philippines during the next two years. We covered stories important to our readers and left the rest to the wires. We worked well together, but we worked just as well apart. Bronstein would spend days on an investigative piece that I could cover well with photos in a few hours. I often used the spare time to seek out in-depth photo essays—subjects that he could write about in a short time.

This approach led to a strange blend of hard-hitting political investigative stories with photo essays exploring such unusual subjects as a cemetery where more than 200 impoverished families made their homes in opened crypts.

Some of Bronstein's investigations also led directly to subjects for my photo essays. His probe into Marcos's manipulation of the sugar industry, for instance, segued into my visual essay on the starving children of Negros Occidental, where poor sugar market conditions caused 70 percent unemployment.

And sometimes it worked the other way around. Another photo essay, on the Tala Leper Colony, led Bronstein to realize that one-third of the money destined for medicine and food for thousands of lepers was disappearing. The administrator of the colony was removed from office soon after President Aquino was elected.

Late in 1985, Marcos, responding to international criticism of his 20-year rule, called for a snap election while being interviewed on the TV program "This Week With David Brinkley." That was the beginning of the grand production that was Marcos's campaign.

Meanwhile, back in San Francisco, the financial outlook at the *Examiner* had changed. Our trip had exhausted half of the photo department's travel budget. In a meeting with Fran Ortiz, the new director of photography, and Frank McCullough, the managing editor, I was informed that part of the reason I had been sent to the Philippines was that the paper didn't want Bronstein there alone. McCullough, a former Saigon bureau chief for *Time* magazine, was a firm believer in two-person teams on overseas assignments. Despite the costs, they decided to send both of us back to the Philippines.

The mounting dangers of the job quickly became evident. Back in the Philippines only eight hours, Bronstein and I met with Lupita Kashiwahara, the sister of Benigno Aquino, in Capas, Tarac—the same day Aquino's campaign organizer, Jeremias DeJesus, and his driver were machine-gunned to death near the Capas town square.

To the people of Capas, we were not there merely to report the event. We were expected to document every grisly detail, as if our work were some sort of legal case they were building against Marcos.

I was brought to the embalming room, where the embalmer and I went to work while dozens of children looked on through a wire mesh window. I made some pictures for them, some pictures for me. Back and forth.

Bronstein and I had come to Marcos's snap election with about seven months of experience from three separate trips to the Philippines. Bronstein had interviewed Marcos and his wife, Imelda, twice in the palace, and he was on a first-name basis with everyone in the opposition. We had been allowed to attend private dinners with all of Benigno Aquino's former cellmates and their wives, as well as Mrs. Aquino.

In the Philippines, this kind of familiarity is an important way to gain access to the unstaged stories and pictures that make for something different.

However, it can also work at cross-purposes. On the advice of Evelio Javier, an Aquino campaign organizer with whom we had developed a close relationship, Bronstein and I traveled to the remote village of San Jose in Antique Province to cover the election. During a previous election, eight people had been shot to death there, and we were expecting another possible incident. We were playing the odds.

But absolutely nothing happened this time, and while photographers in Manila were taking photos of ballot-box stealing and street fighting, I was stuck 400 miles away from the capital.

Although Aquino won a majority of votes in the village, Javier was chased down like an animal a few days after the election and was shot 30 times in the town square.

Scattered atrocities like the death of Javier, coupled with a rigged vote-counting process that led to the mass resignation of government tabulators, fueled the "people power" revolt.

Things quieted down a week after the election. Opposition forces supported boycotts of Marcos-affiliated businesses. Each Sunday, Aquino supporters took to the streets with "indignation rallies." The church-sponsored radio station, Radio Veritas, urged Aquino backers to "love thine enemy."

Late on the night of February 22, 1986, the "people power" movement was born. Defense minister Juan Ponce Enrile and General Fidel Ramos, chief of the armed forces, announced the formation of an armed forces unit loyal to Corazon Aquino. They took over camps Crame and Aquinaldo, the Philippines "Pentagon."

I was in Mindanao, two hours away by jet. But the jets were the property of the government-owned airline, and there was no government. It was one of the longest nights I have ever spent—sitting next to my shortwave radio at the APO View Hotel in Davao City while listening to a revolution that I couldn't photograph.

I got back to Manila the next day to discover that Bronstein had spent the night filing story after story about the rebellion. I went immediately to the camps, where the rebels welcomed the media. I think the rebels figured Marcos wouldn't bomb the camps with foreigners in them.

The tension mounted during the next few days and we knew something had to happen, but where and when? We got an hour's sleep whenever we could. Our driver, Floro Arceta, spent much of the time listening to an AM radio tuned to the opposition station.

Millions of Manila residents crowded the streets to block the Marcos tanks and troops from moving about town. Many journalists who had left the city the previous week could not get back, because the airport had been closed. The human barricades made no exception for journalists, so what you covered depended on how well your driver knew the back roads.

I regretted my decision to develop and print my own film, as I brought back 25 rolls or so each night. The 16-hour time difference was perfect for our deadline—provided we never slept. The one-star edition deadline hit at about 10 P.M. Add two hours for each successive deadline and the four-star had us in bed by 4 A.M. sharp.

On February 25, Corazon Aquino was sworn in as president. An hour later, Marcos had himself sworn in. My most vivid memory of the day was of our car trip from Club Pilipino, where Mrs. Aquino's inauguration was held, to Malacanang Palace, where Marcos addressed his supporters after a private ceremony.

As we rounded a corner, seemingly on two wheels, we found ourselves heading right into a wall of a hundred thousand people. Floro stopped just feet away from the crowd and we backed up and tried another back road. Trees were burning, tires were burning and buses were stalled in the middle of intersections to stop Marcos's tanks.

In his last public appearance in the Philippines, Marcos told the crowd he was still their president and that he would protect them as Imelda sobbed quietly at his side.

Eight hours later, he was on his way to exile, and "people power" reclaimed Malacanang Palace.

During those eight hours, troops stormed the government television station. Somehow a Filipino TV crew and I got caught in the middle of an intersection as a firefight began. The crew ran from the intersection during the first lull in the fighting. Being a somewhat larger and slower target, I ducked behind some abandoned cars instead.

It was strange, covering an army fighting itself. The soldiers trying to kill one another were all wearing the same uniform and one side wasn't really very pleased to see foreign journalists like me hanging around.

As I scrambled toward a concrete outpost on one of the corners of the intersection, I passed a man calmly watching the battle. As I made my way toward a nearby compound out of the line of fire, I heard him moan. He had been hit in the head by a bullet.

He ran to me, and I wrapped his head with my bandanna. We made it to shelter safely. After getting him to a medic, I looked around and learned a very important lesson: Surrounding me were some of the best war photographers alive in good position to cover the conflict, and they had managed to avoid becoming part of it.

Aquino forces took control of the station just in time to pull the plug on Marcos's inaugural speech. Then Floro, who was still monitoring the radio, heard that Marcos's supporters were provoking a riot near the palace. This, he said, would be Marcos's chance to declare martial law and set in motion an intervention by government troops.

We arrived at the Mendiola gate, a palace entrance where dozens of opposition lives had been lost in anti-Marcos protests. People were cutting the barbed-wire barricades to shreds and forming from the scraps the pro-Aquino "L" sign for *laban*, the Tagalog word for fight.

On the palace side stood the remaining troops loyal to Marcos. It was their job to provoke Aquino supporters into charging the palace guard. Most of the Aquino supporters stood and watched. A few returned the rocks thrown by the loyalists. Many prayed, fingering rosary beads.

We covered the standoff until we realized the loyalists were as mad at journalists as they were at the Aquino supporters, so we headed back to the hotel to file.

I printed pictures as fast as possible while Bronstein filed his story. Word got to us that Marcos had fled the country and a mass of people was about to storm the palace. Bronstein was already back at the palace as I "moved" the next of eight pictures. I knew I was missing a key moment of the revolution, so I left the rest of my pictures with a hotel worker and told him how to transmit them.

Marcos's final defense, Bronstein wrote later, "was left to evil-spirited boys, paid $25 apiece to fire their guns and hurl rocks and obscenities under cover of darkness at the citizen force coming to reclaim its rights."

A few of the loyalists were caught. Many literally dropped to their knees and confessed that they had been hired to shoot at the wave of Aquino supporters.

Angry Aquino backers paraded captured loyalists down a street near the palace, punching and kicking them. Photographing such violence was a scary thing. I thought about intervening to save the loyalists until I understood the full extent of the crowd's anger.

The day after the revolution everyone slept. We made it down to the palace in the early afternoon and watched peanut vendors wheel their carts over the same ground that had been littered with tanks 24 hours before.

A few days later our request for an interview with President Aquino was approved, and we were ushered into her office in a guest house adjacent to the opulent palace that Marcos had lived in for 20 years. After the interview was over and we were on our way out, I saw the picture I had hoped for: the woman who was the symbol of a revolt against the government of Ferdinand and Imelda Marcos humbly at work forming a government of her own.

—Kim Komenich
San Francisco Examiner

1987 WINNER IN THE SPOT NEWS PHOTOGRAPHY CATEGORY

PEOPLE POWER IN THE PHILIPPINES

BY KIM KOMENICH

SAN FRANCISCO EXAMINER

Joselito Enriquez has worked the same rice field north of Manila for nearly 40 years. He is among millions of Filipinos who had to choose between Ferdinand Marcos and Corazon Aquino in the February 1986 election. He says he wanted to vote for Aquino, but his brother, a vice mayor in a nearby town, asked him to support Marcos.

Catholic nuns form the first line of defense against Marcos's troops at a staging area two miles from the headquarters of the soldiers who revolted against Marcos. The nuns were a major part of the "people power" uprising that brought Marcos down.

A young Aquino supporter flashes the *laban* ("fight") sign at a rally in Basilan, south of Mindanao. Laban was one of two opposition parties united against Marcos in the February 7 election.

P resident Marcos, his hand bandaged, wipes his brow during a campaign stop in Mindoro. His bandaged hand—he said he was wounded by overzealous supporters—and the state of his health were issues in the campaign.

After his own private inauguration ceremony, Marcos addresses a crowd of supporters from the balcony of the presidential palace. His wife, Imelda, is on the verge of tears. A few hours later, they fled the Philippines.

President Corazon Aquino reads in the guest house adjacent to the presidential palace a few days after the revolution.

1987 WINNER IN THE FEATURE PHOTOGRAPHY CATEGORY

SHATTERED DREAMS

BY DAVID PETERSON

THE DES MOINES REGISTER

The white cross had become a symbol of suffering and loss in the Iowa countryside. Some families, like Pat and Elmer Steffes, planted wooden crosses in their yards as constant reminders that their dreams had died with the loss of their farms. This photograph was taken shortly after the Steffeses' foreclosure.

This photograph unmasks the federal government's benign approach to the farm crisis. Pat and Elmer Steffes met with John Eichhorn, a lawyer for the Small Business Administration, to discuss options for paying back an overdue loan that they had taken out several years ago to keep their farm operation afloat. I started taking photos of the Steffeses, who had invited me to the meeting over the objections of the SBA officials. Then I noticed Eichhorn's body language. I moved around the conference table until I was in a position to focus on him.

Marathon, a community of 400 in northwest Iowa, looked like a modern-day ghost town. Half of the businesses on Main Street were boarded up, and there wasn't a single parked car in sight. I made arrangements to photograph one morning from the grain elevator at the north end of town. I wanted to show Main Street, devoid of life. Shortly after I began shooting, I heard the grinding sound of a tractor engine in the distance. The final element fell into place: a lone tractor traveling down a deserted Main Street—a town and country link that was weakening with the loss of each farm and each business.

Tears well up in the eyes of United Auto Workers union member Harold Lanning of Marshalltown, Iowa, at a farm-labor rally in Waterloo. Lanning was listening to a fellow union member tell of being furloughed at a John Deere plant that was scaling back in response to low demand for farm equipment.

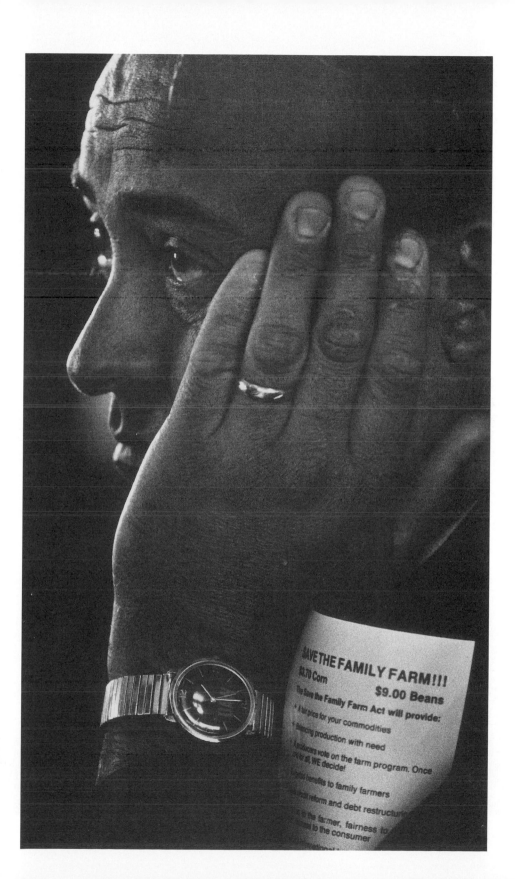

Frank Cordaro, an activist priest angered by the liquidation of farms, has pounded one wooden cross into the lawn of the Harrison County Courthouse for every farm forced to sell during the Reagan Administration—75 in all. "I just keep putting crosses in the courthouse yard and saying, 'Folks, when are you going to put up a fight?' "

With farms going under by the hundreds, the auctioneer's work load has been heavy—and profitable. One of those who has benefited from the farm crisis is auctioneer Larry Sharar of Dows, Iowa. "I don't want to be looked at as an undertaker," says Sharar. "People worth their salt in this business are sympathetic to these families facing trauma."

On a Sunday morning, Phil Fetter took his shotgun to the toolshed and waited for his family to return from church. His six-year-old son found him first while looking for a fishing pole. Moments later his wife, Norma Jean Fetter, was standing at her husband's side, begging him to move the gun away from his chest. Her hand was on Phil's shoulder when he pulled the trigger. Phil Fetter was conservative when it came to borrowing money, and he had an excellent credit rating. He was the kind of person others in the community looked to for support. But a series of events—low hog prices, high interest rates and a run of bad weather—eroded his financial base. "Phil just couldn't take it anymore—his mind snapped," Mrs. Fetter said. He left behind his wife, pictured visiting his grave site, and 10 children.

EIGHT

SHATTERED DREAMS

1987 WINNER IN THE FEATURE PHOTOGRAPHY CATEGORY

"For a distinguished example of feature photography in black and white or color . . ."

The Des Moines Register
David Peterson

From the cornfields and towns of rural Iowa, David Peterson depicts in a moving photographic essay the suffering and the struggles of Americans caught in an economic crisis that has shattered dreams across the nation's farmlands.

It was mid-winter of 1986. Soon the bleakness would give way to Iowa's glorious growing season. Fields of green would slowly shift to golden brown. Combines would roll and yet another crop would be ready to harvest. But masked behind this picturesque rural setting, farmers would live through yet another year of gut-wrenching financial woes. The previous year had reinforced the spreading belief that the current farm crisis marked the most difficult period since the Depression. A string of disturbing, sometimes tragic, events throughout the countryside gave little hope for an end to the long, costly skid.

I remember feeling a strange mixture of joy and apprehension when I learned a project that I had proposed—to document the troubles of rural Iowa—had been selected for the National Press Photographers Association–Nikon Sabbatical grant. I would get a chance to do something that I had always wanted to do: work independently on a long-term project. But with that came a responsibility to deliver the goods. I wasn't sure that I could.

The rural crisis in Iowa had been an ongoing story at *The Register* for several years. My job as a staff photographer had put me in the thick of it.

But while our writers were doing a masterful and thorough job of reporting, the photo staff was playing a minor role, providing the usual environmental portraits and record shots to accompany the stories. Many of the photos were assigned and shot after the stories had already been written.

In my travels throughout Iowa, I had seen the boarded up stores on Main Street, the weedy lots of defunct farm equipment dealers and abandoned farm houses that dotted the landscape. These artifacts stood in testimony to a steady erosion of a rural economy.

But what about the erosion of the spirit? That would be the photographic challenge: to show tragedy in the faces and postures of the people—a people that for years had believed in the values of citizenship and hard work.

As a journalist, my conscience was being tapped. This was easily the most important and far-reaching story that I had covered during my 10 years at *The Register*. The sabbatical gave me a chance to make a record of what I already knew existed.

To launch the project, I needed to devise a workable, yet simple plan. I chose to use only black-and-white film. It is still, in my opinion, the tool of documentary photojournalism. I decided to work within the borders of Iowa. Three months of leave time was generous but not enough to crisscross the Middle West in a car. I felt that the problems in neighboring states were similar to Iowa's. Moreover, in working with *Register* reporters, I had met many troubled farmers and other key people. To establish such contacts in another state would have taken weeks.

I also decided to break the sabbatical into three monthlong segments, one each in the spring, summer and autumn. This gave me a chance to follow farmers' growing cycle and would allow more time for the story to develop.

A progressive order began to take shape as the rural crisis spread doom and gloom. First, the farm families felt the weight of the economic collapse, which later spread to the small towns. Economists call this the trickle effect. I saw it as a way to structure my photo essay and sought a farm family and a small town that symbolized the problems rural Iowa was facing.

After interviewing families in the western part of the state, which had some of the best land and most of the rural activism, I selected Pat and Elmer Steffes. The Steffes family was the only one of those I interviewed that I had photographed before. I had covered their foreclosure the previous fall. They were in the process of putting their lives back together and agreed to let me document their struggle. I literally moved in with them, staying over many nights in an upstairs bedroom.

After driving through some 200 small towns in Iowa, I finally found Marathon, in the northwest part of the state. Many of the others could have served as a model of rural decline, but enough of the fighting spirit was left in Marathon to keep the small-town dream alive. A billboard at the edge of town with the message "Town and Country Working Together" belied what was happening there.

I still vividly remember my first drive down Main Street. It was around noon on a weekday and not a single parked car was in sight. More than half of the storefronts were empty shells. The only sign of life was around the grain elevator on the edge of town and few pickup trucks parked in front of a small grocery store. Inside the store, a handmade sign encouraged residents to pull together and support the few local businesses that remained. Marathon had become, in essence, a bedroom community for a couple of larger towns about 25 miles away.

When not in Marathon or with the Steffeses, I spent some of my first month following up on leads about foreclosures, sheriff sales, auctions, religious retreats—anything that related to the rural crisis.

Because some of these pictures were among my strongest, another aspect of the project began to take shape. I called it the face of rural Iowa—a portrait of a state in trouble. The first month was my most productive shooting month on the project, and I was relieved.

The Register's top editors were excited about what I had gathered and began actively planning for publication of the photos. They wanted a staff writer to accompany me, and assigned Sherry Ricchiardi to the job.

She was a good choice. Sherry and I had worked together on hundreds of stories during the last 10 years, many of which have been related to rural topics. Her caring and compassionate nature carried over to her writing. The result was a sensitive mixture of words and photographs.

It is my hope that our work will draw attention to the values and beliefs this nation treasures, especially as exemplified by farming as a way of life—being one's own boss, working outdoors, enjoying individual freedom.

My biggest fear is that, as the rural crisis wears on and we as a society become weary of the bleak statistics, we will become insensitive and callous to the human suffering. Others have said we should judge a society by how it responds to those in need. The tradition of rural America certainly has been one of self-help and volunteerism. If ever there was a time to encourage unity and esprit de corps in rural America and agriculture, surely it is now.

(The photographs appear in the photo insert that follows page 384.)

—David Peterson
The Des Moines Register

NINE

SUNRISE ON THE BORDER

1987 WINNER IN THE EDITORIAL WRITING CATEGORY

"For distinguished editorial writing, the test of excellence being clearness of style, moral purpose, sound reasoning, and power to influence public opinion in what the writer conceives to be the right direction . . ."

The Tribune *of San Diego*
Jonathan Freedman

Capping a five-year editorial page campaign to reform the nation's immigration laws, Jonathan Freedman reported, analyzed, argued, cajoled, criticized, lambasted, pleaded and finally cheered for passage of a bill that was left for dead in committee a week before it was brought back to life and passed.*

The story was buried in the morning newspapers. Three Mexicans were run over by a Border Patrol van on Easter Sunday. I thought I was inured to the suffering and carnage on the border, but the detail that they had been run over as they slept in the flowers on the day of their Lord's resurrection made my body hurt. I had been writing editorials calling for immigration reform for the past four years, and after two bills were defeated, the sum result was zero. Congress had killed border reform because of concerns about potential discrimination, while illegal aliens were being hunted like animals.

I went to the hospital. One man was fighting for his life in the intensive care unit. Another had left. A third, whose legs had been run over, was being released. Another reporter was already interviewing him. I remember thinking the reporter is going to tell the story of these men, but I have to do something more than that to change the reality on the border. I had to tell the story of millions of people through these three men.

The young Mexican with a wounded look in his soft brown eyes told me about his family in Mexico and why he had come to escape the poverty. He shared his hopes and his despair, because after being released on limping feet, he would be deported. Then he told me about the accident. How they had crossed in the night and lain down to rest for a little while and had fallen asleep. I tried to imagine the truck running over them, but I couldn't see or feel or hear the Border Patrol van. If I couldn't feel the hurt, there would be no way to make Congress wake up to the fact that these men were human beings, not aliens from another planet.

* From nominating letter to Pulitzer Prize Board written by Neil Morgan, editor of *The Tribune*

I went to the border. It was spring and wildflowers were blooming by the fence—yellow waves of flowers blowing in the ocean breeze. The Border Patrol took me to a crushed place in the flowers. There we found pieces of torn clothing; imprints of the tires and bodies were visible in the dust. As the agent explained that it was an accident— no one could have seen them sleeping in the predawn obscurity beneath the waist-high flowers—I saw a torn shirt blowing on the fence. The tattered sleeves looked almost like the outstretched arms of crucifixes in the churches of Mexico—the suffering Christ with dark wounds and blood.

I returned to *The Tribune*'s editorial page office and told Ralph Bennett, my editor, about what I had seen. Ralph had conceived of the immigration reform series before he had hired me in 1981 as a novice editorial writer. He had told me he was incensed by the status quo of hypocrisy and suffering; he believed this was a local issue with national repercussions. We could make a difference, he felt, if we dealt with the issue in depth and made strong recommendations.

He first sent me to the border in 1982 to write about what I saw and to base the editorials on my reporting. Week after week, editorial after editorial, he sent me to the border, the strawberry fields, the union hall, the immigration office . . . finally even to Congress. Our collaborative efforts were nominated finalists for the Pulitzer Prize in 1983 and 1984. But ultimately, we had not made a difference. The border was still a terrain of nightmare and blood. Americans were still hiring illegal aliens and exploiting them, while the workers were subject to apprehension and deportation for breaking our laws.

My family was personally involved. When my wife, Maggie Locke, and I moved to San Diego with our baby daughter, we looked for a woman to take care of her while we wrote. The first woman to answer the ad had a son our daughter's age. She didn't speak English, but we had learned Spanish while living in Latin America. We didn't ask if she had papers. It never occurred to us, as it probably didn't occur to many other Americans.

Months after Rosa and Carlitos (not their real names) moved in with us, Ralph told me to begin the border series. I had no idea what recommendations we would make, or that I would violate them. But the personal conflict soon became evident. In Washington, Senator

Alan K. Simpson, the coauthor of immigration reform, told me: "These hypocrites want to throw out all the illegals. Then they ask me privately about their maid, Maria. 'Maria doesn't count, does she, Senator? You won't take Maria away?' "

I turned away, because I had my Rosa. But I went back to San Diego and wrote editorials condemning employers who exploited illegal aliens and advocating a law to punish them with criminal penalties. Ralph insisted on this position, which, in the beginning, I had trouble accepting. But I wanted amnesty and this was the only way to get it.

"What should we do about Rosa?" I asked my wife.

"Do you want to throw her out in the cold?" she said angrily.

We didn't have to. She was eventually caught by the immigration service and put across the border. When she returned, she was pregnant and Carlitos was sick. In 1983, I sent her and Carlitos to live with her sister. The last thing I saw was Carlitos's frightened eyes as he boarded the airplane.

The same tangled motives and allegiances twisted Congress into inaction. Politicians with high ideals, such as Walter Mondale, who had been a supporter of the commission that drew up the immigration bill, got caught up in the political whirlwind. When Hispanic delegates to the Democratic convention in San Francisco threatened to switch their votes to Gary Hart, I watched Mondale pledge to kill the bill. After his nomination, he succeeded, with the help of farm lobbyists who wanted cheap exploitable labor.

The bill passed both houses of Congress, only to be knifed in the conference committee. I personally was fed up with Congress, with myself, with American democracy. When the bill died, I privately vowed to get off the immigration bandwagon.

But the image of the men run over in the flower fields inflamed me. As I was writing about the flowers, I saw the cherry blossoms in Washington and railed about Congress being oblivious to the border. Then I came back to the Border Patrol van and realized that the driver was not one of the immigration agents: It was me and Congress, and all of us were guilty for this hypocrisy. And then the figure of the crucified Jesus surfaced in my mind. "Congress, remove our guilt," I wrote. "Halt the crucifixion of illegal aliens on the border."

The editorial changed nothing in Washington, but I was writing about the issue with renewed conviction. Soon after, I was in New York City. The United States had just bombed Libya and a drunk in a bar was shouting that we should deport all the illegal aliens. I returned to San Diego to hear the sheriff calling for U.S. troops to patrol the border. Then South Africa burst into the news with violent images from the townships. Everyone was appalled by the apartheid system far away in Africa. But in California the aliens who were growing the produce had no more right to live there than the blacks of Soweto had the right to own land in the townships. "The House of Representatives passes sanctions to cut off trade with South Africa because of apartheid," I editorialized. "But the House perpetuates the apartheid of illegal alien labor in America."

Washington was still deaf. Worse, Congress got fired up over a whole new cause—drugs. Suddenly, without lengthy hearings, an omnibus drug bill was passed. Immigration reform was left languishing in committee. Bitter, I compared America's dependence on cheap exploited labor to a drug addiction. "Kick the habit, America," I screamed.

I didn't think the paper would run it. Ralph had retired and I had a new editorial page editor, Joe Holley. But instead of toning the editorial down, Joe went ahead with it. Editor Neil Morgan, who had stood behind my controversial editorials before, ran it.

The anger was shared by other editorial pages. Indeed, the staunchest supporters of immigration reform were the editorial pages of American newspapers. In 1984, I polled newspapers across the country and found that a majority supported the immigration bill.

That support represented, I believe, a deep feeling among the American people that something had to be done. Not deportations. Not tanks on the borders. But something both tough on exploiters and humane for the exploited. Congress had been paralyzed by special interests. But the tide of public opinion pushing Congress to act was now overwhelming. After being left for dead, the immigration bill was brought out of committee, debated fully and passed.

The principle behind the struggle first had been explained to me by Ralph, who believed that the law need not be an instrument of repression, but that it could be an engine of social change. In his view, which I gradually absorbed in my bones, immigration reform played a civil rights role by punishing Americans for exploitation and offering amnesty to people in hiding. The bill was a political compromise, but despite the uncompromising tone of my editorials, my personal path through the barbed wire of this issue—hearing myself called a "Nazi" racist and, conversely, an "apologist" for illegal aliens—had taught me the value of compromise. The bill, refined over the years, didn't have as broad an amnesty as I had wished. But it was a more liberal and humane bill than first had been proposed, with stronger protections against discrimination.

All this washed over me as I sat down to write the victory editorial. But instead of exulting, I was overwhelmed by the responsibility for what had been done. The end of the immigration reform fight was the beginning of the struggle to implement the bill and bring people out of hiding. I tried to see the change, as I had once tried to visualize the men sleeping in the flowers. But it was invisible.

"The naked eye can't see the change made today," I wrote. "But it is there, replacing lawlessness and injustice with rights and responsibilities. The border between America and the rest of the world is no longer defined by barbed wire," the five-year series concluded. "It is distinguished by law.

After immigration reform became law, the story wasn't over for me. I still had to reveal my hypocritical role. "I'm writing this to vouch for this woman and her child," I said, in a personal column about Rosa and Carlitos. "And I'm writing it to show that it's all right for others to admit their mistakes and vouch for their undocumented employees. I have owed this explanation to readers and to Senator Simpson. I owe an apology to Carlitos. Rosa, soon you can come out of hiding."

Three weeks after the announcement that I had won the Pulitzer Prize, which Ralph Bennett deserves to share, amnesty for illegal aliens began on Cinco de Mayo—May 5, 1987. I still don't know if Rosa has come out of hiding or if amnesty will reach the millions of people who crossed through the fields stained with blood.

—Jonathan Freedman
The Tribune of San Diego

EASTER SUNRISE ON THE BORDER

THURSDAY, APRIL 3, 1986

BY JONATHAN FREEDMAN

The night before Easter, three compañeros crawled through a hole in the chain-link fence—into America. The border where they crossed is a no-man's-land. But in the spring, yellow flowers bloom waist-high beside the torn fence.

The compañeros stopped to rest. Tomorrow was Domingo Santo, the holy day when the crucified Jesús rose from his tomb.

They laid a blanket under the flowers near a dirt track. They lay down and nestled together.

In the darkness, the fence was silhouetted against the garish lights of the Zona Norte, the red light district of Tijuana. Pieces of clothing caught in the fence fluttered in the wind. As the moon crossed the heavens it was possible, perhaps, to imagine the fence was a cross. And the clothing was the body of the Señor, crying out, "Porque me olvidaste?"

But that was on Good Friday. This was Domingo Santo—the resurrection. Today was the promise of rebirth, a new life in this land of work, America.

Before he slept, one compañero closed his eyes and put his hands to his forehead.

"I prayed for my little mother and my brothers," he said later, lying in a hospital room. "I prayed for myself. I was afraid of bandidos who assault us."

As he prayed, he thought of his mother and father and eight brothers back in Guanajuato. Their home was roofed with tin, and the floor was dirt. His father, a cobbler, earned 6,000 pesos ($12) a week: "Not enough to pay for the light and water and for schooling. There were times when we went hungry. I'm the oldest brother, so I came here to work."

It was the second time. Last year he dug ditches to build a road in Encinitas. He worked for an American. "His name was hard to pronounce. But he paid me $250 a week."

He slept in a van during the rains in Encinitas. He was better off than many illegal aliens in the North County, who shivered in ravines and in spider holes.

"I wanted to go back to work for the man in Encinitas," he said.

But after the long journey from Guanajuato he fell asleep in the flowers. In the darkness came others from Mexico and Central America and other parts of the world, countless as the chain links in the fence. The Border Patrol driving Ramchargers chased them along the fence, down paths between the flowers, catching some and letting others escape to El Norte.

Sometime in the early morning, when sunrise services were going on in San Diego, one of the Ramchargers turned down the dirt path near the fence.

"I woke up screaming," the 20-year-old remembered, his eyes filling with tears in the hospital room, where he had no family or friends. "The Migra ran over us with the van. My compañero was crying."

The Border Patrol agent called for help. A Life Flight helicopter landed and carried the aliens to the trauma hospital.

One was released with minor injuries. The second suffered bruises on his legs and was released in a wheelchair, to be taken back to the border to be held for deportation. Two floors below the room where the second told his story, the third compañero lay unconscious in the trauma unit. He was surrounded by tubes. Doctors said he had a chance of recovering. But he had lost his spleen.

As the second youth was rolled away to the Border Patrol sedan in his tire-marked jeans and dirty sweatshirt, he asked: "Where is my money? Where are my shoes? How am I going to work?"

Far away from the border, it is cherry blossom time in Washington. There the House of Representatives is taking up immigration-law reform once again.

Immigration law, like the fence on the border, is riddled with holes. And each loophole in the law is defended by a lobbyist, paid to keep that loophole open. Business interests want to keep the aliens coming through the fence, to work for cheap wages. Organized labor wants to stop the illegal aliens, but it does not want to provide an organized program of guest workers. Those claiming to speak for the illegal aliens represent Hispanic Americans, who have their own suffering and fears of discrimination. Nativists, who want to stir up opposition to all immigration, exaggerate the danger of the illegal alien "invasion" of America.

As the factions in the House Judiciary Committee fight over the remnants of previous immigration reform bills, the harsh reality on the border is as hidden as the three compañeros sleeping under the flowers.

The courts must determine whether the Border Patrol agent who ran over the aliens was negligent.

But the truck that drove over their bodies was driven by us, the American people. We make the immigration laws, and we hire the aliens who must cross the border like hunted animals in order to build our roads, harvest our crops, clean our hotels and serve dinner to the politicians banqueting in Washington.

Congress, remove our guilt. Halt the crucifixion of illegal aliens on the border.

HALT BACKLASH AGAINST ALIENS

TUESDAY, MAY 6, 1986

BY JONATHAN FREEDMAN

An ugly backlash against aliens is brewing in America.

You can see it in rural San Diego County, where farmers who hire Mexican laborers, but let them sleep in ravines, sign a petition complaining of "a growing congregation of illegal aliens too close to our neighborhoods, making large amounts of garbage and unhealthy conditions from their bathroom habits."

You can hear it in New York City, where a bartender cheering the bombing of Tripoli says Libyan taxi drivers and bus boys should be deported.

You hear it from Sheriff John Duffy, who says the border should be patrolled by troops.

The aliens who make our hotel room beds and pick our strawberries and sew our clothes are being mistaken for terrorists who murder children and push cripples out of wheelchairs into the Mediterranean.

Illegal aliens are easy to single out.

"They have no right to be here," some Americans complain. "They broke our laws. What do they expect?"

So far, there have been no bloody riots against aliens in the barrios of California. But vicious backlashes against aliens are not new in the Golden State. San Francisco brewed riots against Chinese in the 19th century and Japanese-Americans were interned in camps during World War II.

The pressure pushing hungry aliens into this country is growing as Mexico reels from the oil collapse, Central America twists in civil war and the Third World suffers debt.

The attraction pulling aliens to work here in service, light manufacturing, construction and farm jobs is increasing, as U.S. industry competes with cheap labor abroad.

As the number of aliens being pushed and pulled into our country increases, so do the forces of resentment and jealousy.

Texas, which tolerated illegal aliens during its oil boom, is now brushing off the unwelcome mat for illegal aliens.

The labor movement, which opposes a legal guest worker program, has a growing membership of illegal aliens who pay dues but have no legal rights.

Nativist jokes are becoming fashionable. It's chic to ridicule aliens, while enjoying their services.

When private frustration and public anger grow in a democracy, the natural escape valve is Congress. Yet debate on the immigration reform bill has been delayed, once again, by intense political infighting among special interest groups.

The latest delay was caused by a group of Democrats in the House Judiciary Committee who asked Chairman Peter Rodino to put off hearings while they work out a supposed compromise. The delay threatens to prevent the bill from reaching the floor in time for debate and a vote.

The Simpson-Rodino Bill deals with the problems of both legal and illegal immigration through law—not violence. The bill is scarred and flawed. Its ideal combination of tough sanctions and generous amnesty has been whittled away. But it is the only law that would diminish the lure of jobs by punishing employers of illegal aliens and offer amnesty to longtime alien residents.

Yet the bill is singled out for attack. It has become the scapegoat for those wanting blindly to perpetuate the status quo. As if illegal immigration could continue unchecked without an outbreak of violence or a militarized border.

This immigration reform bill has been proposed during three Congresses. Each time it was supported by the majority—but killed by a small group of opponents. This third effort is, perhaps, the final time when reason and law can prevail.

Those who would kill this bill in the name of liberalism should realize that they are no longer playing with party politics. They are playing with a wave of hatred that will not stop at barrios, that will not ask for residence papers, that will sweep from the border of San Diego to the Statue of Liberty and demand a halt to *legal* immigration.

Congress must act before its paralysis unleashes an indiscriminate backlash against all aliens.

PAYING FOR ILLEGAL IMMIGRATION

MONDAY, JUNE 23, 1986

BY JONATHAN FREEDMAN

The poorest Americans are those most hurt by illegal immigration. They are the first to lose jobs to cheap, exploitable undocumented workers.

Poor people are also those most hurt by the cuts of the Reagan administration, which has failed to curb illegal immigration. The number of apprehensions by the Border Patrol is the highest ever on our southern border.

Poor people are also hurt by the refusal of Congress to deal with the issue of illegal immigration by enlightened reform. It is a tragic irony that those who claim to speak for poor minorities have worked to preserve the flow of illegal aliens, bound in de facto servitude, who take poor people's jobs. The House of Representatives passes sanctions to cut off trade with South Africa because of apartheid. But the House perpetuates the apartheid of illegal alien labor in America.

Poor people are also hurt by farmers and employers who refuse to hire them. "Why hire an American when I can pay an illegal and give him no benefits?" asks the employer. But when the alien falls sick in his fields, the employer who benefited from his cheap labor does not pay the hospital bill. No. He sends the alien to the public hospital for the county to pay for him. Those bills are mounting in San Diego, El Paso, Los Angeles and Chicago.

Poor Americans are hurt because local services are being strained by indigent aliens. The University of California at San Diego Medical Center has provided $16 million in emergency care for indigent aliens since 1980. Undocumented workers who pick our crops must never be turned away from our hospitals. They pay more taxes than they, as a group, get back in benefits. But the money goes into the federal government and doesn't come back to counties most affected by illegal aliens. On the contrary, San Diego County is getting less federal aid while getting more illegal aliens.

County Supervisor Susan Golding wants to help poor people get their fair share of social services by having the federal government pay its fair share of illegal-alein costs. She has proposed a plan to identify county services affected by illegal aliens and to request impact aid from the federal government. If legitimate requests are denied, there is potential for a suit against the federal government.

The federal government should pay counties like San Diego impact aid to counter the direct costs of illegal immigration. If a federal dam broke and San Diego was flooded, the federal government would give assistance. The same should be true when illegal aliens inundate our hospitals, courts, jails and community services.

Getting the feds to accept this responsibility, without accepting the greater responsibility of dealing with illegal immigration, is like asking a sadomasochist to pay for the right to whip himself.

Who should take responsibility then?

It would be nice if the county could pass on the hospital bill to the farmer who used the bracero's labor and then abandoned him.

It would be nice if the county could pass on the bill to the consumer, who ate the fruit of the bracero's labor.

It would be nice if the county could pass on the bill to the politicians who wave on illegal immigration with one hand while cutting social services with the other.

It's not fair that the poorest Americans should pay for this bill, while losing jobs to illegal aliens. But the poor are paying it. And Golding, who is defending the poor Americans most dependent on county services, is being vilified by some Hispanics because she also raised the alarm of illegal-alien crime. Golding is guilty of poor staff work and flawed statistics—not racism. She was insensitive in not recognizing that Hispanics can't be blamed for illegal-alien crime and she has apologized.

But she is right on the larger issue. The county Board of Supervisors should join her effort to get federal impact aid.

Those who selfishly benefit from illegal immigration refuse to take any responsibility for its tragic consequences. That is why the American people must take responsibility by demanding immigration reform. Enlightened reform must include tough employer sanctions and a far-reaching amnesty, which compensates local governments for its costs.

Until the federal government curbs the flood of illegal immigration, it should pay for the damage that hits poor Americans the hardest.

THE ILLEGAL ALIEN CONNECTION

SATURDAY, SEPTEMBER 27, 1986

BY JONATHAN FREEDMAN

Immigration reform is dying with a whimper, the victim of a hidden drug racket.

Western growers are addicted to illegal alien labor. It's a drug to them—an economic stimulant. They appear to care no more for undocumented workers doing the stoop labor in their fields than a heroin addict cares for Turkish peasants who grow poppies. Western growers use their foreign workers and throw them away like empty bags of heroin. But let reformers try to intervene in this process of ruthless exploitation and the growers will fight for their source of cheap farm labor like an addict robbing old ladies to pay for his heroin habit.

Congress is easy prey to the farm lobby. There are always politicians who need campaign contributions from special-interest lobbyists. They speak the language of civil liberties. They wave the banner of compassion. But their role is to do what is necessary to protect the growers' connection to illegal alien labor.

Congress just voted to spend billions to fight a war against drugs. But yesterday the House of Representatives couldn't even agree on a rule to debate an immigration bill to stem smuggling of illegal aliens. The bill is languishing in no-man's-land as the clock ticks out the last days of the session.

The president went on national television with the first lady to plead for drug legislation. But where was our president when the immigration bill went before the House?

We, on the border, have asked Congress to stem illegal immigration with employer sanctions—not tanks. We've supported amnesty for undocumented families who came into the country through the current loopholes in the law. We've even supported amendments to turn the illicit traffic in human beings into an aboveboard program of guest workers.

Three times Congress considered immigration law. Twice, it was killed. Once more, it is dying.

Fool us once and we'll try again. Fool us twice and we're wary, but we'll persevere. Fool us three times and we throw up our hands. If Congress won't act, who will?

We cannot countenance vigilantes patrolling our border with shotguns. We abhor a nativist backlash against immigrants. But we see both a rise in vigilantism and in anger against *all* immigrants.

Who is to blame? *We* are.

The western growers and their political representatives are only doing the bidding of a larger constituency, the American consumer. A vast majority of Americans demand defensible borders. But the same Americans buy fresh strawberries picked by illegal aliens. They stay in hotel rooms cleaned by illegal aliens. They wear clothing stitched by illegal aliens.

There is nothing wrong, per se, in foreigners doing our work. But there is something deeply wrong in requiring them to break our immigration laws in order to do our dirty jobs for us.

America is growing more dependent on the drug of illegal alien labor and Congress is powerless to kick the habit. The addiction of this nation on cheap, exploitable foreign labor is hurting domestic workers. It's creating an underworld of hunted human beings. It's supporting people smugglers who are as ruthless as drug smugglers. It's dooming children born into the *alien nation:* babies crippled at birth because their mothers were afraid to seek prenatal care, children not sent to hospitals because their illegal alien parents might be discovered, young people growing up to hate the country which boasts of freedom but denies it to six million illegal aliens.

"Immigration reform looks dead, but there may be a way to revive the corpse," Rep. Dan Lungren said yesterday.

Perhaps he sees something we don't.

We see America hooked on the drug of illegal alien labor. We see Congress getting the payoff for keeping the border open. We see a rising backlash that threatens the very principle of immigration.

Kick the habit, America.

BORDER OF LAW, NOT BARBED WIRE

THURSDAY, NOVEMBER 6, 1986

BY JONATHAN FREEDMAN

Immigration reform was signed into law today, with political fanfare. Illegal aliens praying for amnesty rejoiced privately. But on the border, the triumph of law over anarchy was seasoned with skepticism and anxiety.

Parents clutching babies prepared to make their way through the Canyon of the Dead, unaware of the new law. Undocumented workers labored in the fields and sweatshops, unsure of their status. Employers worried about going to jail and some panicked, firing Hispanic-American workers.

Already, opponents of reform were pointing the finger. The president signed immigration law—but nothing happened!

Yes, on the surface, little seemed to change. But beneath the barbed wire, the legal terrain has changed irrevocably for illegal aliens and employers. America's borders soon will be monitored by employers, as well as the Border Patrol.

"Should we come out of hiding?" aliens ask.

Not yet. Until the amnesty program is instituted, undocumented workers should not turn themselves in. But they should begin gathering papers to prove residence in this country.

"Should we fire aliens?" employers ask.

No. Firing current employees could violate civil rights. Employers can request documents from employees and wait for regulations.

The coming months will be a test of action for the Immigration and Naturalization Service. The INS must swiftly draft regulations. It must organize an unprecedented legalization campaign. And it must educate employers, undocumented workers and foreigners about the new law.

The cooperation of the American people and of private and religious institutions is vital. Churches and community groups should serve as good-faith intermediaries between undocumented workers and the INS. We hope Hispanic leaders who fought immigration reform will join the effort to legalize undocumented workers and their families. We hope they continue to speak out against injustice. But we must not confuse the outcry against past injustice with a cry of hope for the future.

Employers who resisted employer sanctions should obey the law and not take out their anger on minorities. The Justice Department must prosecute violators and protect civil rights.

Those who fought for immigration reform have a special obligation to fight for its just implementation. Congress did not approve a generous amnesty for the INS to take it away. Nor did it pass tough employer sanctions for the INS to look the other way. The battle for reform now moves to the workshop and the INS office.

The naked eye can't see the change made today. But it is there, replacing lawlessness and injustice with rights and responsibilities. The border between America and the rest of the world is no longer defined by barbed wire. It is distinguished by law.

TEN

CRITIC'S CHOICE

1987 WINNER IN THE CRITICISM CATEGORY

"For distinguished criticism . . . "

Los Angeles Times
Richard Eder

When Richard Eder learned that he had won the Pulitzer Prize, he told a *Los Angeles Times* reporter, "I am very pleased and temporarily without words. When you sit all day in a room reading books, it's lovely to have the outside world bursting in with good news." His book reviews, says *Times* book editor Jack Miles, show "an independence of spirit and precision and color in language that have attracted a growing following."

Richard Eder publishes two book reviews each week in the *Los Angeles Times*. The following selection of his reviews aims to exemplify his distinctive merits as a reviewer.

Eder reviews far more fiction than nonfiction for the *Times,* and two kinds of fiction in particular.

The first kind is early fiction by talented unknowns. Busy book editors—in this like most other readers—are prone simply to skip the unknowns. Eder seeks them out.

The second kind is fiction by the most established of writers, writers about whom another kind of quick action is likely; namely, speed via the borrowing of received opinions. Eder's opinions are never borrowed.

Richard Eder is not a critic who would ever seek to raise his profile by clever sarcasm, and yet in a less aggressive way he manages not to care too much whether the world agrees with him or not. He possesses an eloquence with just a touch of toughness, the combination winning him a following among readers who know just how rare that combination is.

—The editors
Los Angeles Times

MONKEYS

BY SUSAN MINOT

(E. P. DUTTON—SEYMOUR LAWRENCE)

MAY 7, 1986

BY RICHARD EDER

Cold is the most low-energy and featureless of conditions, but given the right weather, it casts highly organized and entirely individual snowflakes.

Susan Minot writes about the common and endlessly chewed-over pain of childhood: the invasion of its presumed eternity by the mortality of parents' decay. I can't explain why, but only report that Minot's engagement of language with feeling precipitates this ordinary grief into the high energy of nine stories as sharp and original as ice crystals.

"Monkeys" is about Augustus Paine Vincent and Rose Marie O'Dare Vincent, and their seven children. The family is a ship, afloat at the start, though in shallow water. Over 13 years, it runs aground, sticks fast and breaks up. Each of the nine stories is another cry from the leadsman's diminishing count.

The Vincents live on the North Shore above Boston, and spend summers in Maine. They have an up-and-down prosperity, owing more to crumbs from Augustus' inheritance than to his industry. He is a WASP, though perhaps not of the first flight; he played hockey at Harvard. She is middle-class Irish-American and went to Boston College.

Augustus is clenched and aloof. When he takes the children on an outing it is more strenuous than intimate. Rosie is warm-spirited and lavish, a beauty and a former figure skater. Augustus married her for her life, and lives on with her to extinguish it. He is an alcoholic, secret at first, and bit by bit losing control. Rosie fights, flags and eventually dies trying to keep up the belief that every family creates for itself. As she wanes, the children, growing older, try to assume it.

That is the story, more or less, but Minot never once tells it. She makes us tell it; through isolated parental eruptions that can be painful or comical or trivial, but mostly through the movement of the children. They trace the unaware but erratic paths of goldfish in a pond whose oxygen is dwindling. Gradually, their consciousness grows, but not their ability to conduct more than a fighting retreat.

The opening story, "Hiding," is a sunburst that illuminates the pain that will grow. The children are still small; Rosie keeps up the household bustle, like one hand clapping. They all go skating and Rosie, urged by the children, does a figure-three spin in the glow of their regard. All of their regard except Augustus'. "Dad is way off at the car, unlacing his skates on the tailgate but he doesn't turn."

When they get home, Augustus goes off on an errand. Unlike Rosie, whose errands always involve a mob, he goes alone. Unlike Rosie, whose errands proliferate, he brings back the one thing he goes for. In his absence, Rosie and the children hide in a closet. Augustus will look for them, they will burst out, and the evening will lose its chill.

When Augustus returns, he calls out once; then settles down with the television, his bourbon and the potato chips he went out to buy for himself. The hiders come out, deflated; Rosie folds the linen they have disarranged. The children linger with her till she's through. "We don't want to go downstairs yet, where Dad is, without her."

The next few stories widen the desert. In "Thanksgiving," a family reunion is shattered by a venomous exchange between the usually decorous grandparents. Death, it seems, is hereditary. In "Allowance," the family goes on a Bermuda vacation. War rumors come from the parents' room while the children hang out in their own, at loose ends. Augustus' whiskey bottle is now gallon-size.

In "Wildflowers," we glimpse Rosie's dimly suggested romance with a rich friend. It is her last fling, and "The Navigator"—a brilliantly wrenching story—tells of her last hope.

On vacation in Maine, the older children, now almost grown, confront Augustus with his drinking; and he promises to stop. It is an unexpected victory that they all go on a picnic to celebrate.

They hear a sound. Minot compares it to a shot: but it is a hiss— the hiss of a beer tab being pulled off. Augustus is blandly off his wagon and betraying them once more. Minot gives us one of her final paragraphs which, with no sense of artificial theatrics, come like a trumpet perorating.

"Sometimes on still, black nights they had had throwing contests off the dock. They threw stones into the thorofare and listened to hear them land. Sometimes the darkness would swallow up a stone and they'd wait, but no sound would come. It seemed then as if the stone had gone into some further darkness, entered some other dimension where things went on falling and falling."

A year later, Rosie is dead; her car hit by a train as she was driving home, there is a suggestion of suicide. The next few stories tell of the silence that comes over things. The girls take turns caring for Augustus, shattered but still remote, and of the younger children.

One of the boys has a near-breakdown. An attempt to celebrate Christmas is clogged with desolation. Late at night, Augustus wanders downstairs, naked, and mutters his way back up to bed. The boys are off smoking pot. The daughters huddle by the Christmas decorations.

"Mum had had a certain way of cocking her wrist, with a finger out dangling the ornament while she decided where it should go. This year, decorating the tree themsleves, it was as if they had Mum's hands. The tree was approached by hundreds of Mum's hands."

A final story provides a touch of deliverance. The family goes out on their boat to scatter Rosie's ashes in the Maine waters. The ceremony uplifts them briefly and when they disembark they walk, for a moment, in a kind of procession. "No one with the slightest idea, when they raised their heads and looked around, of where to go next," Minot adds.

With its use of children to refract adult loss, "Monkeys" may remind us of Christina Stead's "The Man Who Loved Children," or, more immediately, of J. D. Salinger's Glass family. But the Glasses were golden-tongued prodigies whose sensibility magnified the pain. Minot's children are ordinary, even tongue-tied. This makes it all the more remarkable that the pain they summon up is equally piercing.

"Monkeys" is brief, unencumbered and unforgettable. Reading it, I kept thinking of Ravel's "Pavane for a Dead Princess." It has the quiet, the varied and purposeful reiterations, the touch of brass. It is a pavane for a dead childhood.

WINTER IN JERUSALEM

BY BLANCHE D'ALPUGET

(S I M O N & S C H U S T E R)

M A Y 1 8 , 1 9 8 6

B Y R I C H A R D E D E R

Every nation that I can think of, except one, has defined itself by virtue of existing. Israel is the exception; it exists by virtue of defining itself.

The distinctive national characters of Britain, France, Russia, China and so on have formed out of particular amalgams of geography and history. Their respective ideas of themselves were formulated as they went along. We may sometimes think of the United States as initiated by an idea—freedom from the Old World order—but mainly it is a country whose character has been assembled by letting itself happen to itself. Our Founding Fathers were great great grandsons, at least.

Existence, to use the old philosophical formula, preceded essence. In Israel, on the other hand, essence preceded existence. Raison d'être preceded *Raison d'état.* Israel had a reason for being before it had a being.

Which is why these last years have been so wrenching. There was the shadowing of the old Labor tradition by more purely nationalistic political currents, the rise of Begin and Sharon, the Lebanese invasion, the growth of religion and settler extremisms. These things have shaken, if they have not yet dislodged, the old assumptions of a bristly but humane social democracy where moral argument may not have always prevailed, but was always taken into account.

When Israel questions its essence, it questions its existence. And this is the theme of "Winter in Jerusalem," an impetuous and provocative novel by the Australian writer, Blanche d'Alpuget.

D'Alpuget's Jerusalem is a place where everything is in painful flux, and lives and assumptions have been turned upside down. Even the weather is subversive. The truth is that Jerusalem has its winters, and they can be cold. But the city, like the rest of the country, works on an assumption of heat and blue skies.

The Promised Land was promised sun and oranges. Jerusalem houses rarely, if ever, have central heating; people improvise as if winter each year were an annual string of daily exceptions. D'Alpuget uses a piercing wind and the emptiness of the streets on an icy night to say something about a society whose Utopian energy forged its own reality for a while, and which finds reality turning intractable once again.

Through these streets, in unsuitable Rodeo Drive boots, she dispatches Danielle Green, a high-strung, successful screenwriter who is trying to put together a fractured sensibility and a bits-and-pieces life. Born of a mixed marriage and reared in Jerusalem, she and her mother emigrated to Australia at the start of the independence fighting. Her father had kicked them out. The killing of Danielle's brother by an Arab sniper turned this urbane and sophisticated man into a religious and political fanatic with no use for a frivolous Gentile wife.

Now, in her late 30s, Danielle returns to write a script and to scout locations for a film to be made by a flamboyant Israeli-born Hollywood producer, Bennie Kidron. What she is really scouting is her past. She tries, with no success, to establish relations with her father, who has become an extremist leader bent on expelling the Arabs and rebuilding the Temple. She visits an old teacher, who has outlived her Zionist causes but not her idealism. She has a tormented affair with Bennie. And she is caught up, unwittingly, in a plot by a splinter group of homosexual Arab terrorists.

D'Alpuget, author of "Turtle Beach," is a gifted writer with an individual and powerful vision of the convulsions of our times. The hyperactive plot of "Winter in Jerusalem" serves to take us into the convulsions. On its own terms, though, it does not work very well. To get these assorted characters and their assorted purposes to move properly, you need cooler architecture than the author constructs. Her strength is to be hot and intuitive.

Some of her characters are shorthand for their own messages. The terrorists—one of them is an old schoolmate of Danielle—are repulsive, menacing and pathetic, but they are caricatures. The ambitious portrait of Bennie as a force of nature who is crass and sensitive at the same time, tries to be larger than life, but comes out simply as enlarged.

Danielle, the book's driving spirit, is flawed. When we have her churning over her love affairs and her brilliant career and her inner life, she is too crowded to be quite visible. Her emotions are over-dressed, as if the author had shirked selectiveness; a sculpture with too little chiseled out.

But to go on with these novelistic defects would be to miss the freshness and energy of the book's insights. Danielle's headlong and scattery probing produces extraordinary pictures of the pain of a creative and troubled society whose temperature, always above normal, has turned into serious fever.

Someone leaves a handbag on a bus. It proves to be nothing, but Danielle feels the reaction of her fellow passengers not as relief and solidarity after danger, but despair and withdrawal. Unable to find a taxi at night, she is picked up by a woman driving by. The driver pours out a torrent of talk about the situation. It is one of those electric Jerusalem conversations, full of that defiant fatalism and cynicism that masks love. Suddenly, the electricity stops. "Her frankness tipped upside down and became the opposite: inward brooding, resentment."

The portrait of the octogenarian teacher and former activist has a shining grace. She lives day by day, cheerfully and in the foreknowl-edge of tragedy. Undressed, she glances at her body, sticklike, in the mirror. "She was platinum and white, like an old moonbeam."

If there is a touch of contrivance in some of the characters and situations—the movie that Danielle and Bennie want to make is about the last stand of the Jewish Zealots at Masada—there is none in the portrait of Amos and his son, Gideon.

Amos, an old warrior and idealist, is bitter about the new Israel. He deplores the spirit of aggrandizement, the mood represented by Sharon and his followers, the loss of introspection. He wields his own foreboding that Israel will become "just another Middle Eastern state." He deplores the Lebanese invasion. Yet he can't accept Gid-eon's decision to face a court martial rather than return to the Lebanese front. And to these contradictions, a third one is added. The idealistic

Gideon is killed by the terrorist bomb and Amos, getting the news, is all but literally torn apart.

D'Alpuget's tumultuous sensibility, if it makes her novel suffer through haste and awkwardness, shines through it. "Winter in Jerusalem" stumbles, but partly because its path is an impressive ascent.

ROGER'S VERSION

BY JOHN UPDIKE

(K N O P F)

S E P T E M B E R   1 4 ,   1 9 8 6

B Y   R I C H A R D   E D E R

Like Byron and Hemingway, John Updike stands not just for himself but for a generation. It is the generation of the Fifties; the time of
small causes, good taste, individual salvation through personal relationships and, for seasoning, a tablespoon of Kierkegaard poured over
a pudding-like stability and set ablaze.

The generation grew older, with a feeling that it was still holding
the reins while subsequent generations went off the track—the Sixties
—or returned so massively as to turn the track into a rut—the
Eighties. On the other hand, the reins were never attached to very
much.

Byron died of revolutionary fever at 36; Hemingway, of suicidal
depression at 62. Updike, who is 54 and clear-eyed about those empty
reins, simply grows darker. "Roger's Version" is as close to pure
misanthropy as anything he's done, though his other books have had
inklings.

Rabbit Angstrom turned melancholy as time runs out, but Updike
lengthened the light upon him into a kind of benediction. "The
Witches of Eastwick" seemed black to some readers—its petal-like
women transformed into middle-aged cactuses—but Updike was entranced with them, and it showed.

He is not entranced with Roger Lambert, the masculine counterpart
to Eastwick's witches; and that shows too. Updike's religious nimbus
curdles when he does clergymen, and Roger is an ex-minister and a
theologian. Packed so tight with self-knowledge that not a mite of
grace can get in, Roger is evil, though it is the evil of decay, not of
willfulness. Or perhaps, only of the willfulness that comes with decay.

Roger is assistant professor at a school of divinity that can only be

Harvard's; and he lives in an old house in a town that can only be Cambridge. Perhaps it suits Updike not to be specific, but he is our master of the details of place, and here he is so exact that the reticence seems ludicrous. It is as if, ordered into disguise, he had selected a mask that covered only the point of his chin, leaving in plain view his celebrated long nose and sad eyes.

Roger lives with his second wife, Esther, whom he married after the loving acrobatics of a typical Updikian adultery. The love has dwindled to exasperation. The same holds true for Roger's vocation. Adopting the Barth-like position that any worthwhile God must be unknowable, he is quite satisfied not to know Him. Instead, he specializes in medieval heresies.

Into these closed lives squeeze passion and challenge, in the form of two young people. By the end, Roger and Esther have squeezed them right back out again. The book has a number of themes, but perhaps the deepest and chilliest is that in the Reagan era, age is perfectly well able to prevail over youth.

One of the youths is Dale, a graceless computer scientist who comes to Roger for a grant to set up a computer program to demonstrate the existence of God. The second is Verna, the sexy daughter of Roger's stepsister. She is living in the slum end of Cambridge with an illegitimate baby by a black father; and she needs Roger's help.

Roger's battle with Dale is the philosophical heart of the most explicit novel of ideas that Updike has written. Dale is a creationist, though a sophisticated one. In a protracted series of arguments, he sets out the contemporary doubts that scientists have expressed about current cosmologies and evolutionary theories. Updike has done his homework—once in a while, it seems like just that—and expressed prefatory thanks to the likes of Robert Jastrow, Sir John Eccles, Fred Hoyle, Chandra Wickramasinghe and a number of others.

As dense as some of it is, though, Updike is a superb glosser. When Dale is speaking, the non-scientific reader finds extraordinarily plausible his arguments about the unlikely holes and coincidences needed to account for a universe without a God. But he finds equally convincing Roger's rebuttal that it is senseless to make God rush into every gap that science has so far failed to fill.

Finally—and this is no small triumph for the author—two alternatives come to seem equally unlikely: first, that such an unlikely beast as the giraffe should evolve by natural selection, and second, that God should trouble Himself to make one.

Of course, it is splendid irony for the scientist to be intent on proving God's existence, and the theologian on rejecting the possibility of such a proof. But Updike takes it beyond irony. It is perfectly natural. The theologian can't abide having his specialty—faith—made as commonplace as the physics of the seesaw. The scientist can't abide an enclave posted: "Faith—Keep Out."

But Dale is much more than an intellectual challenge. To Roger, he is the rival, the son threatening the father, the example of zeal that shames his cynicism. Specialist in heresies, Roger recognizes himself as the heavy hand of the Church suppressing youthful enthusiasms. "Jesus Christ, John the Baptist: Raggedy outsiders. Insiders tend to be villains, like me."

That is self-knowledge but not conversion. Roger, in a Machiavellian, back-handed way, sees that Dale gets his grant. And Dale all but destroys himself crunching numbers and hoping that God will fall out of them. Meanwhile, Esther conducts a passionate affair with the youth and emerges much refreshed; while he, double bamboozled, breaks his heart.

As for Verna, Roger helps her and, eventually, himself. The exploitation is mutual and rather chilly, but there is a lot of savor to it. Updike is extraordinarily skillful at writing about male arousal, particularly when it is middle-aged and reluctant. The quarrels and cross-purposes of Roger and Verna are a knowing comedy of manners between generations. She is tough and naive; he is gentle and concerned and really much tougher.

When finally, considerably relieved, he dispatches her back to her family in Cleveland, he gives her $300 from his bank's cash machine. "Do you wish any more transactions?" it asks. And Roger punches the "no" button.

That must be the first fictional love affair with an epitaph by cash machine, and it is unreasonably clever. Throughout "Roger's Version," in fact, Updike's cleverness is prodigious. His capacity to interrogate every moment and get surprising answers, his ability to encapsulate, skewer or celebrate in a phrase; all these are as remarkable as ever. He is master of a sheer elegance of form that shows itself time and again.

It can be too much. He keeps interrupting himself. When he stops Roger in the act of fetching cranberry juice in order to tell you why cranberry juice depresses him, it is brilliant. But is it necessary? Sometimes you feel that this radiant rightness of detail, repeatedly exercised, is exercised in the hope that it will attach to the larger dimensions of the writing.

The brilliancies of "Roger's Version" often make its darkness palatable, but I think ultimately the darkness is a defect. It is more a state of weariness than an act of negative affirmation. There is a heaviness about it; it is perhaps his only novel without a sympathetic major character.

In the title, Updike presumably intends to distance himself from Roger. It is inevitable, though, that to some degree and on some occasions, he appears as Updike's alter ego. To the degree that he does, the author might almost be writing of his own as well as his character's despair. For the theologian, despair is the ultimate sin against the Holy Ghost. For the novelist, it need not be. But it makes you worry about the next book.

PACO'S STORY

BY LARRY HEINEMANN

(FARRAR, STRAUS & GIROUX)

DECEMBER 7, 1986

BY RICHARD EDER

The most profound social distinction is the one between the living and the dead. Ghosts have fallen into the lower classes. They are as invisible as Ralph Ellison's Invisible Man, as the Hispanic busboy in a high-priced restaurant, or as the Suffolk laborers in "Akenfield" who patterned their work schedules so that estate owners would not be troubled by the sight of them.

Like others who have written fiction about the Vietnam War in recent years, Larry Heinemann is haunted by its present invisibility only a dozen years after it ended. Hundreds of thousands of veterans, tens of thousands of them dead, fall under that dark American shadow: to be out of fashion, not hot, off of prime time.

"Paco's Story," brief and with a remarkable intensity, presses the social claims of those who died literally, and those who survived but whose history, for all the place it has today, might as well be dead. Using the simplest of stories—a grievously wounded veteran gets off a bus in a small Texas town, finds work, stays a while and moves on—Heinemann writes of the two universes that coexist in our country: the large one that can't remember, the small one that can't forget.

Heinemann foreshortens the remembering and forgetting. Paco Sullivan's brief passage through Boone, Tex., takes place not now but while the fighting was still going on, or perhaps recently over.

Even then, the line between those who are at peace and those who are at war is brutally drawn.

Paco's Spanish name and Irish surname make no special point except to declare him a kind of unprivileged Everyman. He is the sole survivor of Alpha Company. It was destroyed, in a single moment, by a barrage of "supporting" fire while defending its outpost against a Viet Cong attack.

And Paco himself was so badly hurt that the word *survivor* scarcely applies. That is the book's theme. It is also the inspired device that makes Paco's encounters such a glowing metaphor for this theme.

Heinemann puts the narration of Paco's sojourn in Boone in the mouths of his dead companions. "Paco's Story" seems to be told by ghosts. I don't think the author means these ghosts literally, although this is purposely ambiguous.

More likely, Paco feels himself to be one of the dead as well, and tells his story on their behalf. He speaks of himself in the third person, as if the living Paco were an accidental surviving limb of his own essentially dead self. It is the way you might speak of an amputated appendix. Not "I was removed," but "My appendix was removed."

The horror that Heinemann wants to rescue from oblivion is expressed in the notion that it is not death that amputates the victim from the survivor, but life that has amputated the survivor from the company of the dead.

The ghostly voice, which by turns is colloquial, brutal, obscene and remarkably cheerful, and which, throughout the book, addresses an imaginary listener named James—I haven't the slightest idea who he is—begins by assuming that most people won't want to hear its story. It is aware of its own low social standing.

Then it goes on to relate tersely and vividly the ordinary hell of Alpha Company's existence, and the special hell of its destruction. It tells of the discovery of Paco's shattered body among the minute fragments of his companions' corpses; and of his slow and painful mending in a hospital. It is a recovery as precarious and unlikely as Lazarus'.

The narration moves forward to tell of Paco arriving in Boone— simply a matter of giving all his money to the bus driver to go as far as it was good for—and of his time there. Continually, it reverts to the war days. It is as if only the terrible past were believable, and as if the everyday life in Boone were an invention too fanstatic to sustain.

Paco, crisscrossed with scars, limping and in continual pain, goes from door to door looking for a job. It is a stunning chain of vignettes. He visits an antique shop whose owner, a refugee from the concentration camps, hallucinates that he is his dead son; and to a barbershop where the townspeople look at him as if he were from another planet. Finally, the owner of the local diner, a World War II veteran, hires him as a dishwasher and, without listening to Paco's story, tells him his own story about the bloody days in the Pacific.

Paco tries to hold on to this life, as strange to him as a grafted organ. (Heinemann conveys the effort with a minute description, lasting an audacious and oddly gripping six pages, of just how Paco gathers up, washes and replaces the diner's dishes and pans.) But the graft doesn't take.

Paco, and the larger phenomenon he represents, is not real to the townspeople; they are not real to him. They are two entirely different aquatic species, swimming side by side in the same aquarium.

He is attracted to a young woman who lives next door in his broken-down hotel; and she is aroused by him and his scars. But on her side, it is a peripheral fantasy she indulges in while making noisy love with her boyfriend. Paco listens sleeplessly to the lovemaking and is seized by desire. But desire leads him away, and back to the real world of memory. It is a memory, told in dreadful detail, of the rape-killing by Alpha Company of a Viet Cong woman prisoner.

Paco's young neighbor comes close to him only in a dream. She dreams of making love, in the course of which she peels off his hundreds of scars and lays them gently upon her. The image could be grotesque; but it is delicate and heartbreaking.

Dreams are the closest we come, Heinemann is saying in his deeply original and affecting book, to bridging the gulf between our lives and our snubbed, dead history.

ELEVEN

POLITICAL PRESCRIPTIONS

1987 WINNER IN THE COMMENTARY CATEGORY

"For distinguished commentary . . ."

The Washington Post
Charles Krauthammer

Charles Krauthammer gave up a career as a medical doctor to write prescriptions for the nation's social and political ills in a syndicated column. His commentary carries weight both inside and outside the Washington beltway.

In less than two years on the nation's editorial pages, Charles Krauthammer's syndicated once-weekly column has attracted attention for its clarity of thought and elegance of style. His voice quickly became nationally recognized as influencing our perception of major news events.

On October 17, Krauthammer's analysis of the Reykjavik summit helped shift the center of the debate about what happened at those negotiations. Others concentrated on the stalemate over the Strategic Defense Initiative. But Krauthammer, as did Senator Sam Nunn, pointed out early that it was Reagan's offer to eliminate ballistic missiles to save SDI that was newsworthy. And had the offer been accepted, the allied defense system would have been turned on its end. Similar commentary came after Krauthammer's.

He wrote on November 7 one of the first syndicated columns on the Iran scandal. Two days after a Lebanese magazine published the story of U.S. arms shipments to Iran and before the administration confirmed it, Krauthammer wrote of the dangers of allowing foreign policy to become an instrument of the plight of individual citizens. His judgment was continually cited in the debate that followed.

With convincing humor and independence of mind, Charles Krauthammer brought into sharp focus a spectrum of issues—affirmative action, Gramm-Rudman, AIDS in the workplace. A physician before he became a journalist, he has added a fresh intellect to public policy discussion that newspaper readers depend upon to form their own opinions.

—Anna Karavangelos, associate editor
Washington Post Writers Group

IN PRAISE OF GRAMM-RUDMAN

IT'S ALREADY WORKING

FRIDAY, JANUARY 24, 1986

BY CHARLES KRAUTHAMMER

When the recidivist dieter decides he can't go on any longer, one more Twinkie and he'll explode, he does this: he locks the refrigerator door and mails the key to his uncle in Yuma.

The strategy is, of course, illogical. If he has the willpower to resist the call of the pilot light, he doesn't have to go through these shenanigans. And if he doesn't have the willpower, he can still fly to Yuma, pick up the key, come home and open the refrigerator. What's the point?

The point is that it is a long way to Yuma. People don't always have the will to do what they know they have to do, so they invent little stratagems to make the alternatives unpalatable.

Welcome to the world of Gramm-Rudman. If Congress and the president cannot agree on a budget that cuts the deficit by a reasonable amount (one-fifth) every year for the next five, automatic cuts go into effect. An agent of the president (director of the Office of Management and Budget) and an agent of Congress (director of the Congressional Budget Office) agree on the amount of the shortfall. A referee (comptroller general of the General Accounting Office) then resolves discrepancies.

The three uncles calculate the projected deficit and the required across-the-board cuts to meet Gramm-Rudman targets. The cuts then automatically go into effect. Unless, that is, the threat moves Congress and the president to reason—i.e., judicious, non-automatic defense and domestic cuts and a tax hike.

From the anguished cries of critics, you'd have thought representative government as we know it had come to an end. Twelve House members are asking the courts to rule unconstitutional this transfer of power from the elected branches to the unelected.

But it is the elected branches that created the formula that governs the cuts. The formula—calculate the shortfall, divide by X, add Y, and multiply by the number of cowards in Congress—is in the Gramm-Rudman bill. And being a bill, it was passed not by the Supreme Soviet but by Congress, and signed by the president, also elected.

How can one seriously talk of excessive delegation during the reign of an imperial Federal Reserve? Who elected Paul Volcker? What the CBO and the OMB and finally the GAO do is no more than, as we used to say in grade school, plug in the values. Theirs is not a political decision but a determination of numbers, something the elected branches delegate to unelected folk all the time. Census Bureau calculations determine huge shifts in the allocation of federal monies, even of congressional seats. Who elected its chief?

So, line of attack number 2: Gramm-Rudman allows no choices. And to govern is to choose, said John Kennedy, an insight recently rediscovered by The New York Times and Sen. Daniel Moynihan, among other critics.

If to govern is to choose, the United States has been in anarchy for some time now. Last month, faced with a reconciliation bill cutting $75 billion over three years (out of a three year deficit maybe eight times that size) the 99th Congress boldly chose to adjourn.

True, Gramm-Rudman has no priority list. But neither does Congress. At least Gramm-Rudman has three classes of program: those subject to full automatic cuts, those subject to partial automatic cuts, and those exempt. Call it the modified flat cut, the budgetary equivalent (but enjoying none of the vogue) of that hot political property, the modified flat tax.

Now, if nothing happens other than Gramm-Rudman, the results will be absolutely intolerable—soon. Soon no FBI. Soon no Coast Guard. Soon national parks paved over to pay their way as parking lots.

In short, a disaster, and a man-made one at that. But the deficit (dignified by the adjective "structural" to make it sound inherent to the natural order of things) is equally man-made, and threatens a worse disaster. What awaits us in 1991 if we accumulate $1 trillion more debt is far more serious than asphalt in Yellowstone—the debt will pave over the whole economy—but far less tangible.

And that is the genius of, and sole justification for, Gramm-Rudman: nothing but a threat this palpable will concentrate the mind of Congress and the president on cuts and compromise.

It is only January and the assumption is proved. In Washington today, political talk starts and ends with Gramm-Rudman. Everything is driven by Gramm-Rudman. That is, driven by the deficit. Except that the term "Gramm-Rudman" has the law behind it and a buzz-saw ahead of it. "Deficit" is mush.

In Congress, says Rep. Les AuCoin, "people are looking at this [coming session] with real dread." Already, words of hope.

Says Senate Majority Leader Robert Dole: "There's likely to be a lot of china broken around here before it's over." A nation awaits the first blessed sound.

The elected branches, incapable of choosing and aware of the incapacity, have undertaken an act of reckless wisdom and daring cowardice. They mailed the key to Yuma.

Sure it is a trick, the worst trick around except for all the others.

NEEEEE-KAHH-*RAAAHH*-GWAHH?

FRIDAY, JULY 11, 1986

BY CHARLES KRAUTHAMMER

When I was a kid, movie Indians said things like "me no like-um pale-face." No one ever explained the origins of the peculiar "-um" declension, but no matter. Logic was not expected of Indians, and the same held for other native peoples in other movies from "Tarzan" on up.

Things have changed. The dignity of language has been restored to movie Indians (well, PBS Indians—there are none left in the movies). They speak in their own tongue now, and the subtitles report them saying lyrical things like, "The cry of night pierces the soul of my darkness."

This process of language decolonization follows the general political decolonization of the last 30 years. It also follows modern recognition of the dignity and complexity of native cultures. That is all to the good. It even makes more fictional sense for Indians to be speaking something other than a bizarre variant of Ellis Island English.

The trend, however, has not stopped there. It never does. Linguistic emancipation, it seems, is for everyone. Even, say, cavemen. Twenty years ago, the Hollywood Neanderthal communicated with a pound on the chest and a wield of the club. It is hard to see one today for whom some consultant anthropologist has not invented a language as elaborate as it is bogus. And honored, like the highest German, with subtitles. Thankfully, the movement to subtitle dolphins is stalled.

I find these good intentions strained but tolerable. Less tolerable is the direction of another wing of the language decolonization movement, the school of Militant Anti-Colonials—MACs for short. MACs insist that whenever, in conversation, you cross an international border, you must turn in your English and go native. A MAC is the guy (English-speaking) who, in the middle of a discourse (in English) about Central America, tells you that you totally misunderstand the situation in Neeeee-Kahh-RAAAHH-gwahhh.

Neeeee-kahh-RAAAHH-gwahhh? Pronouncing Nicaragua the

Spanish way is perhaps a sign of sophistication, but it is also an advertisement of one's raised consciousness. More annoying still is the ringingly rococo "elll-sahl-vahh-DOHRRRRR," all liquid l's and rolling r's, climaxed in the triumphantly accented last syllable. All this to signify hopes for a liberated El Salvador and, some day, a liberated listener.

MACs can easily be picked out of a crowd even before their conversation has wandered south. A MAC is anyone who carefully and aggressively says "North America" to mean "United States" (as in "North American aggression") to demonstrate that he has transcended the imperial (North) American tendency to appropriate for one country the name of two continents.

I can take this oblique swipe at the Monroe Doctrine. What I cannot take is the follow-up reference to, say, the drug problem in "Kohl-LOHHHHM-bia." My habit now is to respond with the observation that the problem is seen very differently in Paa-RRREEEE, is ignored totally in Mohs-KVA, though it has provoked street demonstrations in KUE-bin-hah-ven (DAN-mark).

Not that such an anti-MAC attack ever satisfies. But it does make the point that what drives English speaking MACs is not a sense of linguistic authenticity but merely a bad colonial conscience. They would never think of assaulting you with "Mahhh-DRRREEED." We never sent a Marine there.

In my calmer moments I do admit the existence of a real dilemma here. It is a problem: how *do* you pronounce a foreign-language word when speaking English?

My answer: when in Rome, speak Roman, when in America (what some call the United States), speak English. Drop the umlauts, the aigues and graves, and give foreign words their most mundane English rendering.

About the use of fancy accents in mundane situations, I speak from experience. When I was five, my family moved to Montreal, in part because it was French-speaking (my mother being Belgian, my father French). But our French was not the kind spoken in Quebec. Ours was what Montrealers called "Parisian" French, the language of Quebec's upper class (ie., snobs, such as Pierre Elliott Trudeau, who once dismissed Robert Bourassa, the current Quebec premier and of work-

437

ing class origins, as "a hot dog eater"). This bit of local sociology was unknown to me the first time I got on a bus and asked, in my Parisian French, for directions. The bus driver did not take kindly to being linguistically patronized by a creature four feet tall and wearing short pants. I learned my lesson. From then on I used only English in public.

But one can't totally avoid foreign words, even when speaking English. I still did not know what to do with French words that pop up in everyday English. For years, I doggedly, and self-consciously, pronounced "deja vu" precisely as my folks insisted at home, with sharps and flats and lips pursed ("vuh") as if to whistle.

Then came "Deja Vu," the album. It's been "vooo" ever since. One does not discuss Crosby, Stills, Nash and Young in an Inspector Clouseau accent. The gig was up. Time to learn to embrace English, jettison flatulent foreignness, and say ciao to all that. So how about it, guys? Ni-cuh-rag-wa.

TEEN-AGE SEX: THE BATTLE IS LOST

FRIDAY, DECEMBER 5, 1986

BY CHARLES KRAUTHAMMER

The latest outrage of American life: The pill goes to school. There are now 72 "comprehensive health clinics" in or near the nation's public high schools. Very comprehensive. More than a quarter dispense and more than half prescribe birth control devices. When the New York City Board of Education found out that two of its clinics were in the dispensing business, it ordered them to cease and desist.

Secretary of Education William Bennett has waxed eloquent on the subject. He is surely right that birth control in the schools legitimates sexual activity and represents an "abdication of moral authority." Clinics are not only an admission by adults that they cannot control teenage sexuality, but also tacit consent, despite the "just say no" rhetoric.

Unfortunately, there are two problems: not just sex, but pregnancy. As in all social policy, there is a choice to be made. Is it worth risking the implicit message that sex is okay in order to decrease pregnancies? (Clinic opponents sometimes argue that birth control dispensaries do not decrease the number of pregnancies, a claim that defies both intuition and the evidence.)

Bennett is right about the nature of the message. But he vastly overestimates its practical effect. Kids do not learn their morals at school. (Which is why the vogue for in-school drug education will prove an expensive failure.) They learn at home. Or they used to. Now they learn from the culture, most notably from the mass media. Your four-eyed biology teacher and your pigeon-toed principal say don't. The Pointer Sisters say do. To whom are you going to listen?

My authority for the image of the grotesque teacher and moronic principal is "Porky's," the wildly popular teen sex flick that has spawned imitators and sequels. My authority for the fact that teen-age sex-control is an anachronism is Madonna. "Papa don't preach," she sings. "I'm gonna keep my baby." She is months—nine months, to be precise—beyond the question of sex. Her mind's already on motherhood.

Kids are immersed in a mass culture that relentlessly says yes. A squeak from the schools saying no, or a tacit signal saying maybe, is not going to make any difference. To pretend otherwise is grossly to misread what shapes popular attitudes. What a school can credibly tell kids depends a lot on whether they grew up on the Pillsbury Doughboy or on a grappling group of half-nudes spaced out on Obsession.

Time to face facts. Yes, birth control clinics are a kind of surrender. But at Little Big Horn surrender is the only sound strategy. Sex oozes from every pore of the culture, and there's not a kid in the world who can avoid it. To shut down school birth control clinics in order to imply the contrary is a high-minded but very costly exercise in message sending. Costly because the message from the general culture will prevail anyway, and sex without contraception means babies.

The sex battle is lost. The front-line issue is pregnancy. Some situations are too far gone to be reversed. They can only be contained. Containment here means trying at least to prevent some of the personal agony and social pathology that invariably issue from teen-age pregnancy.

Not that the sexual revolution can never be reversed. It can, in principle. In our time, the vehicle might be AIDS. The association of sex and sin elicits giggles. The association of sex and death elicits terror. Nevertheless, the coming counterrevolution, like all cultural revolutions, will not be made in the schools. It will happen outside— in movies and the newsmagazines, on the soaps and MTV—and then trickle down to the schools. As usual, they will be the last to find out.

I am no more pleased than the next parent to think that in 10 years' time my child's path to math class will be adorned with a tasteful display of condoms in the school clinic window. But by then it will be old hat. The very word condom has just this week broken through into the national consciousness, i.e., network TV. It was uttered Monday for the first time ever on a prime-time entertainment show ("Cagney and Lacey," so I am informed by USA Today). Condoms will now find their place beside bulimia, suicide, incest and spouse murder in every child's mental world.

If the schools ignore that world, it will not change a thing. Neglect will make things worse. In a sex-soaked culture, school is no shelter from the storm. Only a monastery is, if it doesn't have cable.

TWELVE

MEDITERRANEAN PATROL

1987 WINNER IN THE FEATURE WRITING CATEGORY

"For a distinguished example of feature writing giving prime consideration to high literary quality and originality . . ."

The Philadelphia Inquirer
Steve Twomey

"Catapulting off a carrier, which subjects [flight crews] to a jolt seven or eight times the force of gravity 'is a lifetime E-ticket at Disneyland,' " a pilot explained to Steve Twomey, who had never before been aboard an aircraft carrier. The ride might be a thrill, but the mission of the carrier fleet is always deadly serious.

The ramp in the plane's tail slammed shut. We were now in twilight in the belly of a COD, short for Carrier On-board Delivery, an ugly propeller-driven baby transport that would shuttle us back to Sicily. They strapped us in and showed us how to cross our arms. They showed us how to angle our heads. They showed us how to brace our legs so they would not escape at launch and strike the seats in front of us—and break. There was no need to repeat the lessons. The nervous audience complied in seconds. With that, the COD lumbered forward on the flight deck, bound for catapult No. 1 on the starboard bow of the U.S.S. *America,* an aircraft carrier.

Mike Mally, a photographer for *The Philadelphia Inquirer,* and I had arrived two days earlier steeped in the theory of the *America* and its 13 supercarrier sisters—the backbone of the United States Navy. Now, the COD was about to take home notes and photos of a carrier's reality. It was about to take home two thrilled, frightened and confused visitors, too—thrilled and frightened because they had never catapulted off a carrier before, confused because their story had changed in the midst of the Mediterranean Sea.

By the late spring of 1986, the time of our journey, United States aircraft carriers had become an evening news staple. They had supported marines hunkered down in Beirut in 1983 and 1984. Their planes had forced down the hijackers of the Italian cruise ship *Achille Lauro* in October 1985. They had bombed Libya in April 1986. They were being used to keep open the Persian Gulf during the Iraq-Iran war. The moment seemed opportune to raise an issue often debated in military circles but rarely in family newspapers: whether these warships—the largest in the world—are still the right ones to have in the age of cheap, supersonic, deadly missiles and ever more quiet submarines.

The Falklands War had shown what missiles and submarines can do. Yet the Navy was not only standing by its big carriers, it wanted more, even though each one costs taxpayers more than any other single weapon. The stakes for the nation, in short, were high.

But there was another, perhaps less noble reason to write a story about carriers: There was a certain *Inquirer* reporter who had always wanted to be on one. Our story would be about naval theory, but to tell it intelligently, I reasoned, the reporter ought to visit a carrier, preferably in the Mediterranean, the scene of much of the carrier activity. The *Inquirer*'s magazine editors agreed to my fantasy. They even agreed to send Mally to shoot color photos.

The Navy's permission was swift. It is proud of its carriers. And it knows how they can seduce skeptics. Based in Paris as a correspondent for the newspaper, I worked with the Navy's European office in London to fix the date and length of our trip. Though willing to arrange one, Navy public relations officers did not want us to remain long aboard a carrier, largely because they fear civilians can easily stumble into a jet intake, given enough chance. Bad for the Navy's image. So they suggested a single day. I suggested seven. They agreed to two.

Twice dates were set, twice they were canceled as tensions rose in the Mediterranean. Finally, in June 1986, Mally and I found ourselves boarding a COD at Sigonella, Sicily, for a one-hour flight out to the *America,* cruising with its escorts. To our dismay, the approach offered no dramatic vistas of the carrier because the COD has only two portholes high in its hold. Strapped in, we couldn't see out. Thus, landing came abruptly: a bump and a grind, followed by a tremendous shove against the seat as the plane's belly-hook grabbed an arresting wire, bringing the COD to a halt. The rear ramp swung down—and there was Captain Richard C. Allen, his hand extended in greeting.

Throughout, the *America*'s hospitality was impeccable, though there were some rules. We could not go to the Combat Information Center. Top Secret. We had to have a baby-sitter, the public relations officer who went where we did. And the captain kept wanting us to do or see things that, given the short time we had, we didn't want to do. Participating in a nuclear attack drill for two hours, for example. But we did it, right down to the gas masks.

Within an hour of our arrival, we went aloft in a helicopter so Mally could take photos of *America* as it was underway. It was then, as we hovered abeam while jets were slung into the sky or recovered, that the story began to change shape. It could no longer be just about carrier strategy and theory, with a little on-board color for leavening. It had to be about this machine and what it did as well. As journalists, we were enthralled by this slice of the real world. We assumed readers would be also—an assumption I think is always safe.

But that made the task one largely of writing, not reporting. We catapulted off *America* on the COD, a far dicier experience than landing. By the time I reached Paris, I had no idea how to marry the feel of the flight deck with the grand strategy questions. The paralysis lasted a week. There seemed to be no storytelling relationship, for example, between the skill of landing an F-14 fighter and the issue of a carrier's vulnerability to Soviet submarines. What was the connection between the beauty of whining jets bathed in catapult steam and the Navy's new "forward strategy" for using carriers? And if there was a connection, how to write it gracefully?

Not writing at all wasn't an option an editor would accept, of course, so a solution was eventually found out of professional fear. Going through notes and research material over and over, I realized that certain scenes I had witnessed aboard *America,* or had been told about while there, opened the door to discussing the big-picture issues that were the genesis of the assignment. We had been tailed by a Soviet ship, for example, which could lead into a discussion of Soviet capabilities in tracking U.S. carriers. The symbols of *America*'s size— its two television stations, for example—were grist for discussing the advantages of bigness.

I decided to organize the piece in digestible chunks. Call them chapters, though they are not so labeled. They are delineated only by abrupt transition. And though I find it almost impossible to discuss my style—it just comes out this way—sentences seem to have gotten simpler and punchier over the years, the adjectives and adverbs fewer. That seems reflected in the carrier piece.

When it was finished, the article did not exude greatness to its author. Certainly, the last thing he expected was that it would win a Pulitzer Prize.

—Steve Twomey
The Philadelphia Inquirer

HOW SUPER ARE OUR SUPERCARRIERS?

O C T O B E R   5 ,   1 9 8 6

B Y   S T E V E   T W O M E Y

Air boss looked aft. Through the haze of a June morning off Sicily, an F-14A Tomcat fighter was already banking in low over America's wake, a couple of miles out and coming home to the Bird Farm. Air Boss looked down. Damn. Still no place to put the thing.

On the flight deck below, opposite Air Boss's perch in the control tower, an A-7E Corsair II bomber sat astride the No. 4 steam catapult amidships. By now, the A-7 should have been flying with the rest of the day's second mission. Nobody would be landing while it straddled America's only available runway.

"What's taking 'em so long down there?" Air Boss growled. He had left his leather armchair in his glass booth in America's superstructure. He was standing up for a better look, which he always does when the flight deck crunch is on.

The ship's 79,724 tons suddenly shuddered. Steam billowed from No. 4. The A-7 had vanished, rudely flung out over the Mediterranean by the "cat stroke," like a rock from a slingshot. Finally.

"Launch complete, sir!" said Mini Boss, his assistant.

"Clear decks!" Air Boss boomed into the radio to his launch crews. It would be close, maybe too close. "Secure the waist cat! Prepare to recover aircraft! Hubba, hubba!"

The F-14 was closing at 150 miles per hour. A mile out now. On the deck, crews were frantically stowing launch gear. They had to seal the long slit down which the catapult arm—the "shuttle"—races as it yanks a plane along the deck and flips it heavenward. They had to shut hatches and make them flush with the deck. America had to become seamless for its bird.

"Commmme on, commmme on," said Air Boss. His eyes flitted from the looming F-14 to his crews working below. The plane's variable wings were swept wide for landing, 64 feet tip to tip. Its wheels were down, its twin tail jets were spewing heat waves. It was a pterodactyl about to prey on the carrier.

"We're not going to make it!" said Air Boss.

"We'll make it!" said Mini Boss.

Unless they made it, the F-14 would have to be waved off, sent around for another approach. In peacetime, that is not fatal. It costs fuel—266 gallons a minute for an F-14, $1,100 an hour—but no more. In war, a carrier's ability to cycle its jets in seconds—to launch them, land them, rearm them, refuel them, launch them again—could mean victory or defeat. America is not at war now. But America trains as if it is.

"We're not going to make it!" Air Boss said again.

"We'll make it!" said Mini.

Catapult crews had almost finished. The F-14 was just off the stern and plunging, a long hook dangling from its belly that would, it was hoped, catch one of four cables laid across the rear flight deck to stop the plane cold. It was time to decide: Wave it off or land it. The last of the crew was scampering out of the landing area.

"They made it!" said Mini.

Over the stern, down, down.

Bam.

Fifty-six thousand pounds of F-14 slammed home. Simultaneously, the pilot pushed to full throttle. Heat blasted down the aft flight deck. If the hook missed all the cables, the pilot would simply keep going, over the now-dormant site of the No. 4 catapult, flying off and coming around again. But he was no "bolter." He snagged a wire for a clean trap. Time from the last launch to the first landing: 45 seconds.

Air Boss grinned.

Mini Boss grinned.

Hubba, hubba.

It is hard not to love the dance of the carrier deck—the skill, beauty and sheer guts of men launching and landing warplanes on a 1,000-foot slab on the sea.

Seventy-five times on an average day, up to 400 times during crises such as Libya, America's crew members dodge sucking jet intakes and whirring props to hitch aircraft to the catapults and send them flying. That many times, they help them home and snare them and park them. They can launch planes a minute apart. They can launch and land at the same time. They can do it in the dark or in the rain. Their average age is 19½.

Engines whine, then race—and a plane disappears from the deck in 2.5 seconds. Its exhaust heat bathes launch crews. The air reeks of jet fuel. Steam seeps from the catapult track. The next plane is already moving forward to take the "cat stroke," and there's another behind it. Noise overwhelms the deck. All the while, the carrier slices through the blue.

"There's no way to describe it," said an A-7 pilot aboard America. "There's no way to see it in a movie. You've got to come out here and smell it and see it. It's too dynamic. The whole thing's like a ballet."

In all, the United States' carriers number 14, no other nation has more than four. They are the largest engines of war; no one else's are half as big. They bear the names of battles won, Coral Sea, Midway and Saratoga; of leaders gone, Eisenhower, Forrestal, Kennedy, Nimitz and Vinson, and of Revolutionary War vessels, Constellation, Enterprise, Independence and Ranger. One evokes the place where man first flew, Kitty Hawk. And one is called America.

With their pride of escorts, the 14 carriers and 878 carrier-based fighters and bombers are the most tangible sign of U.S. power that most people around the world ever see. They are the heart of the nation's maritime defense, its glamour boys. They are the costliest items in the military budget, the price of one carrier and its escorts equaling the bill for 250 MX ballistic missiles.

Yet, for all their impressiveness and for all the importance the Pentagon attaches to the vessels, many congressmen and defense analysts argue that the supercarriers' day is history. The critics fear they are now unnecessary, too expensive, and, worse, easy marks. Some of the doubters are even Navy men: Stansfield Turner, a retired admiral and the former director of the Central Intelligence Agency; Elmo Zumwalt, the retired Chief of Naval Operations, and Eugene J. Carroll Jr., a retired admiral who once commanded Nimitz.

"Like the battleship the carrier replaced, its magnificence cannot nullify basic changes in the nature of war at sea," Sen. Gary Hart, the Colorado Democrat, writes in a new book on U.S defense, *America Can Win.* "The day of the large aircraft carrier . . . has passed."

Today, all surface ships are highly vulnerable to two things—missiles and submarines. A British frigate was sunk in the 1982 Falklands War by a single Exocet missile fired from an Argentine jet it never saw. The Soviet Union has 304 attack submarines, enough to dispatch 21 to hunt each U.S. aircraft carrier. By opting for 14 big carriers—a 15th, the 91,487-ton Theodore Roosevelt, will join the fleet soon—the United States could lose, perhaps fatally, a very large portion of naval power in a very short time from a very few Soviet missiles and torpedo hits.

In short, it might have the wrong navy for the late 20th century. "When you concentrate your total offensive capability into 15 platforms, the targeting system of the adversary becomes very focused," said Carroll, the ex-carrier captain, who is now deputy director of the Center for Defense Information, a private Washington research group.

No one doubts that the United States ought to have carriers. They have uses. The answer to vulnerability, critics say, is to have more of them, to spread the risk. The big ones, however, cost big bucks. Roosevelt and two other new, huge, nuclear-powered carriers authorized by Congress, the Abraham Lincoln and the George Washington, will cost $3.5 billion apiece. Without planes. Add those and add the cruisers and frigates that must escort any carrier—the Navy concedes they need protection—and it costs $17 billion to put a carrier group to sea. That is 10 times the 1986 Philadelphia city budget. The cost of the three carrier groups combined would be enough to pay for all city services—police, fire, sanitation, everything—for 30 years without any resident paying any taxes.

That is money that cannot be spent on other military items. And most of that money goes for "the purpose of protecting this goddamn carrier," said Robert Komer, who was an undersecretary of Defense for policy during the Carter administration. Even most of the carrier's planes are there to protect it.

Instead, many critics say, it's time to think small. Overhauling the big carriers at the Philadelphia Naval Shipyard—Independence is there now, under the Service Life Extension Program—is merely fixing up the past. The nation should have smaller, cheaper carriers. They can do the job. And the nation could then afford more carriers, and more would cut the impact of losing any given one if war comes.

Of course, to speak of cutting losses in any war seems surreal. Only the Soviet Union could really challenge the U.S. Navy. But any sea battle with the Soviets would trigger nuclear war, many analysts say. In that case, it wouldn't much matter if the United States had 15 supercarriers or 30 medium ones. The game would be over. Still, the Pentagon plans for old-fashioned conflict. Its theory is that because nuclear war is final, no nation would start one. But the Soviets might be willing to start a regular war, so it's vital to have good conventional armed forces. In that context, debating what kind of navy to have does make sense.

And the U.S. Navy has no doubt that it wants big carriers. It would even like seven or eight more, up to 22 or 23. In fact, the Reagan administration, under Navy Secretary John. F. Lehman Jr., has made big carriers the key to a strategy that would take them right into the teeth of Soviet defenses in wartime. That is how much confidence it has in carriers' ability to survive today. Critics, said Adm. Henry H. Mauz, commander of America's battle group, "are well-meaning people, I'm sure. But they're wrong."

Lehman even said in testimony before Congress last fall that to build small is communistic, to build big is American. "Should carriers be bigger or smaller? There is no absolute answer to that question," he said. " . . . [But] our tremendous edge in technology is a permanent edge built into the nature of our culture and economic system, compared to the Soviets. It is to that advantage we must always build, not to go to cheaper, smaller, less capable ships in large numbers. That is an area in which a totalitarian, centralized, planned economy excels."

Big is beautiful.

America's crew sometimes gets lost. There are so many decks and passageways that sailors don't know where they are. "I get fouled-up all the time," said an officer who was consulting a deck plan on a bulkhead.

Crew members can ask someone for help, though it'll often be a stranger. With 4,950 men—there is not one woman—who work different hours on different decks, most don't know each other, even after spending six months at sea on the same ship. Usually they learn about a fellow crew member by reading about him in the ship's daily newspaper or seeing him on one of two television stations that beam live news and old movies and TV shows. (The most popular fare is a raunchy movie about a riot in a women's prison, one aired repeatedly and so bad that the crew says it's great.)

Many days, there is no sensation of being at sea. Unless they stand on the flight deck or work in the "island"—the starboard-side command structure that rises above the flight deck—crew members can't see the ocean. There are no portholes. And America is so massive, it is often unaffected by the water's roll. Being belowdecks can feel like being in a building.

When it left Norfolk, Va., on March 10 for a Mediterranean patrol, America took $9 million in cash because at sea it becomes its own economy. The crew gets paid. The crew buys things at the ship's stores. The proceeds are then used to pay the crew. Eighteen thousand meals are fixed a day, 280,000 gallons of sea water is distilled. The Navy loves to boast that there is a barber shop, a bakery, a photo lab, a post office, a printing plant, a tailor, and a public relations staff. In other words, much of the crew has nothing to do with weapons or war. They are service-sector Navy.

The bigness does have an objective, of course: to fly a lot of planes and carry fuel and bombs for them. A U.S. carrier has 80 to 90 planes, more than all four Soviet mini-carriers combined. America has eight types of planes, more types than either the three British or two French carriers can hold.

Besides 24 F-14s and 34 A-6 and A-7 bombers, America has four planes to refuel its planes in the air, four to detect enemy planes, four to jam enemy electronic equipment, 10 to hunt for submarines, and six helicopters to find downed pilots and to hunt for submarines. All told, there are 86 aircraft, which together can deliver 480,000 pounds of bombs, as much as 10 World War II-era aircraft carriers. When they're not flying, the planes can be stored and repaired on the hangar deck, which runs almost from bow to stern below the flight deck.

The aircraft fly off a deck that is 1,047.5 feet long, not the biggest in the Navy, an honor that belongs to Enterprise at about 1,100 feet. But if stood on end, America's flight deck would be almost twice as high as William Penn's hat on City Hall. It is 252 feet wide. All told, the deck covers 4.6 acres, an expanse coated with black, coarse, nonskid paint. The crew has plenty of straightaway to jog in the hot sun when the planes aren't flying. Five lengths is a mile.

The flight deck is so big, America can launch four planes almost at once, two from bow catapults and two from catapults amidships, on an extention of the flight deck that angles left. The angle enables the ship to launch and land simultaneously in some cases. While a plane is launched forward, another lands on the angle. If it misses all the arresting cables, it keeps going left, thereby avoiding the bow catapults.

Despite its weight, America, which is 22 years old, can glide through the water at 30 knots. The power is not nuclear but conventional boilers that drive four 22-foot-high propellers. In fuel for the ship and planes, in crew pay and in food and supplies, each hour of patrol costs taxpayers $22,917. That is $550,000 a day. That is $99 million for the normal six-month cruise—not counting the bills that its escorts run up.

Overall, America exudes seductive and expensive power, a sense magnified by the stateroom of Capt. Richard C. Allen. There, in the bowels of a ship designed for war, is an elegant living room with coffee table, sofa and wing chairs. The carpeting is bulkhead-to-bulkhead. The dining table can seat at least 10. Several lamps lend a soft light to the room.

Its occupant is a serious man who was born 46 years ago in Wisconsin and flew carrier jets until his eyes went bad. He wears wire-rims now; they give his soft and narrow face the look of a teacher. Allen, who has commanded America since July 1985, seemed perplexed by a suggestion that his ship might be at risk or should be anything but the size it is.

Two carriers half as big, for example, would mean two of everything. Allen said, two engine rooms, two sets of catapults, two bridges. Thus, two small carriers would be more than the cost of one big one. But neither would be as stable in rough seas, hampering flight operations, and neither would have so many planes able to do so many things. Even with the advances in missile and submarine warfare, he would much rather command a carrier now than during World War II. Besides, because America is big, it can take many bomb hits. And it is much harder to find than an airfield ashore.

"It's mobile, it's moving, it's never in the same place," the captain said. "Like right now. You're on it. Do you know exactly where we are? I'll share with you: We're southwest of Sicily. Tonight, we'll go north of Malta. This morning, we were east of Sardinia. The carrier moves. As a result, the targeting problem against a carrier is very complex . . .

"It's extremely remote a carrier would ever be totally put out of—I mean, *sunk.* I think it's just something beyond imagination as I see it, by any threat that we see today or in the near future. This is a very capable piece of machinery."

Libya. They were actually going to hit Libya. Night had fallen. It was April 14, 1986. Allen looked down from the bridge at a dimly lighted flight deck jammed with aircraft, bombs and bullets bound for Benghazi. It was no drill. "I don't believe we're really doing this," he thought. "It's just unbelievable."

The crew had manned battle stations in record time. "All you have to do is tell somebody, 'We're going to go kill something,' and the level of interest goes up logarithmically. I mean, people become— they're *motivated.*"

Thirty-eight planes from America would go. Somewhere in the darkness of the Mediterranean, the scene was being repeated on the Coral Sea. One by one, planes roared away. The most beautiful were the F-14s because, in order to get extra lift, they always flipped on their afterburners just before the "cat stroke," sending twin cones of flame 20 feet down the flight deck and lighting up the dark sea.

He was proud, Allen said, "to watch the complexity of the carrier pull together and to watch the thing take shape, until *boom,* there you are at night, and the cats start firing, and things happen just as they were planned."

And in the early hours of April 15, as the planes began coming back, crew members belowdecks watched the closed-circuit television shot of the flight deck to see whether the bombers had bombs under their wings. They didn't. And all 38 planes returned. The crew cheered wildly. (Fearing terrorist reprisals against the crew's families in the United States because of the carrier's role in the raid, the Navy requested that no crew member's name be used in this article, except Allen's, and it told crew members not to discuss Libya.)

"I just never thought the national decision would be to engage," Allen said. "I'm extremely proud of the President for having had the guts to do what he did."

Whatever its merit or morality, the U.S. raid on Libya to counter terrorism showed what carriers do best. They can sail to remote places and deal with Third World crises. They can, as the Navy puts it, "project power." Virtually every day of 1985, four U.S. carriers were somewhere at sea on patrol. Not the same four, of course, but a rotation that enables crews to avoid prolonged periods away from home. No other nation can deliver so much airpower wherever it wants. It is this ability to pop up anywhere swiftly that even critics of big carriers say makes carriers worth having.

It was carrier planes that forced down the civilian jet bearing the four hijackers of the cruise ship Achille Lauro. Carriers stood off Grenada and Lebanon during land operations in 1983. It is carriers that would be called on to reopen the Strait of Hormuz should Iran ever carry out its threat to cut oil lanes in its war with Iraq. Often, the mere arrival of the carrier is enough; none of its jets has to fire a shot.

"The carrier is an enormous politico-military capability," said Rear Adm. Jeremy J. Black, assistant chief of the Royal Navy Staff. "It is evident power. As you approach the thing, it emanates power. And wherever it will be, it will be a symbol of *American* power. That in itself is so significant."

"The aircraft carrier," said Norman Polmar, a noted U.S. defense analyst, "has demonstrated that it can move to the troubled area. It can remain offshore, in international waters, for days or weeks or months. . . . You're going to see many more low-level conflicts and confrontations, and aircraft will be necessary for us to observe, deter and, if necessary, fight."

Used this way, carriers are not at much risk. Grenada or Libya do not have the military skill to mount a serious threat. Or so the Navy thinks. Carriers stood off North Vietnam for years, launching air strikes but never taking one in return. The Navy has plans for big carriers, however, that would put them at risk.

Imagine: On May 30, 1987, Soviet tanks and infantry swarm across central Europe. For the moment, the conflict is conventional. The European Allies are barely holding on, and they need troops from the United States. Convoys are pieced together, civilian 747s commandeered. And carriers flood the Atlantic to baby these sea and air fleets across to Europe. They are to sink submarines and shoot planes. They are to sweep Soviet surface ships out of the sea lanes linking Old World and New.

That has been part of U.S. strategy for years. Navy Secretary Lehman has added a twist, however. After carriers make the oceans safe for passage, he wants to send them on aggressive forays close to the Soviet Union to finish off the Soviet navy and then bomb land targets. Carriers would sail near the Kola Peninsula, off the Soviet Union's far north coast. They would sweep into the Baltic Sea. They would cruise off the Soviet's Pacific coast. By crushing the Soviets on their Flanks with carrier power, Lehman argues, the United States would take pressure off the war in central Europe.

This "forward strategy" fuels a push by Lehman for a 600-ship Navy. The number of warships had slipped to 479 after Vietnam, and the Carter administration had decided not to build carriers to succeed the aging Coral Sea and Midway, which were both due to be retired. It thought big ships were too vulnerable and expensive. The number of carriers was set at 12.

But Lehman sought—and got—congressional approval during the first Reagan term for three giant nuclear-powered carriers and all their escorts, which together will consume 41 percent of Navy construction costs from now to the year 2000—$60 billion. Two of the carriers will replace Midway and Coral Sea, and the third will represent a net gain. So, the number of big carriers will actually rise to 15.

Lehman says the fleet expansion centered on big carriers is crucial to the "forward strategy." The United States must get the enemy in his lair, and only big carriers can do it. But it's not the same enemy as it used to be.

"Captain said to tell you we got a Udaloy coming in."

Churning on an opposite course in the twilight, the sleek visitor whipped past on America's port side, swerved across its wake and pulled up off the starboard side about 1,000 yards away. Its speed and course now matched the carrier's. From the flight deck, a few crew members gave a look, but they had seen one before.

The Udaloy is a new class of Soviet destroyer. Each has 64 surface-to-air missiles, eight torpedo tubes, eight antisubmarine missiles and two helicopters. The ships steam at 32 knots. America's crew calls them "tattletales."

Soviet destroyers and frigates routinely weave in and out among U.S. battle groups. The high seas belong to no one; the Soviets have every right to sail wherever they want. The encounters are always courteous. Both sides follow the rules of the road. What the Soviets are doing is taking notes. They watch the pattern of flight operations and the types of exercises. They see how the task force moves. They watch how different planes perform.

"The Soviets? Oh yeah, they'll come right off the quarter, 1,000 yards, 500 yards, follow us around, back and forth," Allen said the next day as the Udaloy hovered. "Whatever we do, they do. If we turn, they turn. . . . They take pictures. They pick up garbage. They do weird things. Usually they just follow you around."

Such open-ocean presence reflects the new Soviet Navy. Russia had never been a sea power, under the czars or under communism. Just 20 years ago, Soviet ships spent a fleet total of 5,700 days at sea, according to U.S. estimates. Last year, they spent 57,000. The Soviets now have the world's largest navy, with 283 major surface ships and 381 submarines, split between 77 ballistic missile-launching submarines (for delivering nuclear warheads to the United States) and 304 attack submarines (for sinking ships, such as U.S. ballistic missile-firing submarines or the carriers). That is 664 warships, compared to the 541 the United States has at the moment. That is three times the total of U.S. attack submarines, the kind needed to find Soviet attack submarines before they find U.S. carriers.

Assigned to the Soviet navy are 1,625 aircraft, mainly operating from land. Their job, too, is to sink U.S. ships. Most formidable, perhaps, is the new Backfire bomber, which can fly at 1,100 knots for 3,400 miles without refueling, bearing big air-to-surface missiles. At the end of 1985, there were 120 Backfires, with more being added each year.

Some Soviet planes are even at sea. Four modest aircraft carriers have been built, and each has 13 planes and 19 helicopters. Like British "jump jets," the planes take off and land by moving vertically. Last year, the Soviet Union launched an American-size carrier of at least 65,000 tons and designed for 60 planes and helicopters. It will not be operational for several years, however, because the Soviets must first master the dance of launching and landing so many aircraft.

Though the Soviet navy is large, there is disagreement about how much of a threat it is, at least away from its coastal waters. In a study last year, the Center for Defense Information said that 145 of the Soviets' surface ships were too small, less then 2,000 tons, to venture into the open sea for long. It said the Soviets have a limited ability to resupply ships at sea, which America does very well. (It has to: A battle group gulps 10,000 barrels of fuel a day.) Nor do the Soviets have as many anchorages in other countries as the United States has. And while the Soviets now have carriers, no one argues that the vessels are any match for U.S. carriers.

Nonetheless, Lehman and other Navy officials tout the Soviets as a huge, aggressive force, plying waters they never did before with power they never had before. They point to the Gulf of Mexico, where major Soviet naval forces sailed twice last year. "In many areas of the world, the Hammer and Sickle now overshadows the Stars and Stripes," the unabashedly pro-Navy magazine Sea Power intoned last fall.

Much of this gloom-and-doom, of course, is to justify the need for 600 very expensive ships: The Pentagon must face a worthy foe. And even the Center for Defense Information, in its study, said the Soviets would be very tough adversaries close to home if Lehman's "forward strategy" were ever tried. And farther out to sea, Soviet attack submarines and Backfire bombers could, indeed, threaten convoys and their carrier escorts.

Yet even while highlighting Soviet power, the Navy says, in effect, no problem. It's got a system.

Much of the time, America seems alone in the Mediterranean, free of Soviet tattletales and steaming toward an empty horizon. Not even fishermen chug by. But the Small Boys are never far away.

There are 10 sprinkled in a circle around America, two cruisers, four destroyers and four frigates, sometimes moving in close, sometimes sailing out of sight. One or two U.S. attack submarines are often there as well, but because they are underwater, it's hard to be sure; Allen said only that they are not there all the time.

America never leaves home without the Small Boys, whose crews say that they are the true sailors and that the carrier is just the Bird Farm. Battle groups are the key to what the Navy calls defense-in-depth. The idea is to keep the $3.5 billion airfield at the center from being sunk.

The first sentry is not a ship, however. It is a plane, one that does not carry any weapons and cannot fly fast. The E-2C Hawkeye looks like a small AWACs plane, the Air Force's Airborne Warning and Control aircraft that seem to have a giant mushroom on their backs. The mushroom has radar.

Often the first plane to leave the carrier during launches, the E-2's job is to park in the sky and see what else is up there. Its radar can scan 100,000 feet up and in an arc 250 miles around America. If it identified enemy planes, the E-2 would call in what deck crews call the Super Hot Fighter Pilots, only they use a more descriptive word than *super*.

The men who fly the $38.7 million F-14 fighters are just about as smug and smooth as *Top Gun* portrays them. America's pilots haven't seen the movie because they have been at sea. But they've seen the Kenny Loggins video clip, featuring shots of twisting, blasting F-14s. It was flown out to the ship. They love it.

"Yeah, that's us," said a 28-year-old pilot from Drexel Hill. We're *cool*. We're *fighter pilots.*"

Most are in their late 20s or early 30s. Handsomeness seems to be a job requirement. Catapulting off a carrier, which subjects them to a jolt seven or eight times the force of gravity, "is a lifetime E-ticket at Disneyland," said the Drexel Hill pilot.

"To be sitting in that machine and to know that 300 feet later you'll be going 200 miles per hour and the whole thing takes 2½ seconds—well, the level of concentration in sports or whatever has never reached *that* adrenaline high," said a 42-year-old pilot from Philadelphia, who has done it 1,250 times.

Their job is to hunt down enemy planes and destroy them before they can launch missiles at America. Or, as Adm. Mauz, the battle group commander, put it, "We want to shoot the archer rather than the arrow."

F-14s, which can fly at more than twice the speed of sound, have Phoenix missiles with a range of 120 miles, as well as shorter-range Sidewinder and Sparrow missiles. The F-14s would be helped by four EA-6B Prowlers from the carrier, planes whose task is to scramble the radar of attacking enemy planes and baffle their missile guidance systems. Needless to say, the fighter pilots don't think anyone will get past them. What a silly suggestion; without the carrier, they would get wet.

"This is home," said the air wing commander, 40, who is in charge of all the pilots of all the various types of planes. "This is where dinner is. This is where the stereo is."

If attacking planes did skirt the F-14s and fire missiles, the next line would take over, the Small Boys. They would rely on Aegis, a defensive system just entering service aboard a new line of cruisers and destroyers; America's battle group has one of the new ships, the cruiser Ticonderoga. The Aegis is designed to find and track dozens of hostile missiles at once—the exact number is classified—and launch shipboard missiles to destroy them. It can coordinate not only the cruiser's reply missiles, but also those of all the ships in the battle group, automatically. An attack would be swatted out of the skies. In theory.

If that fails, and missiles are still boring in, America has a modern Gatling gun called Phalanx. Mounted at three points on the edge of the flight deck, the computer-directed gun has six barrels that together fire 3,000 rounds a minute. That is supposed to shred any missiles. Judging by a test one day on America, the gun's noise alone might destroy them.

Soviet submarines would be found by America's 10 S-3A Viking planes. Their electronics can look down through the water and spot a submarine. The plane then drops a depth charge or torpedo. The battle group also scours with sonar and can fire an array of weapons at submarines.

Actually, Navy officials hate to talk about all this defense. They say outsiders spend too much time worrying about how vulnerable carriers are. The ships are for offense, first. "It's sort of like your house," said the air wing commander. "You take steps to protect it, but you don't go around protecting it all the time. I'm not worried every day my stereo's going to be stolen. I'd rather go bomb something."

• • •

It came out of the west just after launch, skimming 10 feet above the South Atlantic at 680 miles per hour. On the bridge of Sheffield, a British frigate, Lts. Peter Walpole and Brian Leyshon had seen a puff of smoke on the horizon but didn't know what it meant and hadn't seen the Argentine Super Etendard fighter. One mile out, they both recognized what was coming their way.

"My God," they said simultaneously, "it's a missile."

Four seconds later, the Exocet hit starboard amidships, above the water line, and veered down into the engine room, where its 363 pounds of high explosive detonated. In an instant, Sheffield lost electrical power and communications. Fires broke out. The edge of the hole in the ship's side glowed red from the blazes, but there was no water pressure to put them out. As flames crept toward the magazine, where ammunition is stored, the crew abandoned Sheffield.

A new, $50 million ship had been destroyed—and 20 of its crew killed—by a single, small computer-guided missile costing one one-hundredth as much.

What happened that Tuesday, May 4, 1982, during the Falklands War was the most stunning example in history of the power of the anti-ship missile. These weapons can strike from much greater distances than naval guns and, unlike shells, can be guided to their targets. Photos of Sheffield, listing and burning, depict the critics' nightmare of what will happen to carriers.

There is little chance, certainly, that one, two or even three Exocets could sink a U.S. carrier. It is just too big. And the Navy accurately says that the British had less ability to detect, track and destroy enemy planes than a U.S. battle group has. Britain's two Falkland carriers had no planes like Hawkeyes to spot the Super Etendards. They had far fewer fighters to attack them. No British ship had Aegis. Polmar, the military analyst, says a U.S. carrier force would have destroyed the Argentine air force "in two days."

But there are missiles that could threaten a carrier—cruise missiles. They are flying torpedoes with large warheads, launched up to 350 miles from their targets and often moving at supersonic speed. Backfire bombers can carry them. About 30 Soviet surface ships can carry them. And so do 62 Soviet submarines, including the new Oscar class. Each Oscar has 24 cruise missiles. Two are at sea now, with another joining the fleet every two years.

"We do not have an adequate defense for cruise missiles," said Adm. Carroll of the Center for Defense Information. "It's been the bete noire of naval strategy for some time now. We've made progress. We've got Phalanx and such. But I'll guarantee you that if you take those carriers in range of Soviet land-based aircraft and cruise missiles, there will be enough cruise missiles coming through the defense to hit the ships. I don't know how many will get through, but say it's one out of five. And if one out of five hits our ships? It's all over."

Aegis is supposed to deal with cruise missiles, but its performance has not been flawless. Initially, it knocked down only four of 15 attacking missiles in tests. Later, that rose to 10 of 11, but doubts remain. Moreover, a missile doesn't have to sink a carrier to render it useless. Each carrier has four very weak points—its catapults. Without them, planes don't fly. The Navy thinks it is highly unlikely that any enemy will get so lucky as to put all four out of action at once. But then, naval history is replete with lucky moments.

A carrier's greatest foe, however, is not in the air. It is the enemy it never sees. Gary Hart calls them the kings of the sea. And the Soviets have more of them than anyone. In March 1984, a Soviet nuclear-powered attack submarine rose up under Kitty Hawk in the Sea of Japan, bumping it and damaging both ships. It was an accident, not an attack. But the battle group had not detected the sub, even though at least five Small Boy's were around Kitty Hawk.

Because it was peacetime, it was possible the escorts weren't "pinging" with sonar to find subs. The incident, however, illustrates how stealthy subs can be. They are a threat not only from their cruise missiles, but from their torpedoes. While the Navy believes its detection skills are good, they are not perfect. "We don't always know where they are," said Capt. Allen, "so we don't know whether we're being followed or not all the time."

Oddly, Allen has never been on a submarine at sea, despite being in the Navy for 27 years. Critics say that would be an excellent way for carrier captains to learn how their underwater adversaries work and think.

Given the air and sea threats to carriers, Lehman's "forward strategy" could end in the destruction of the heart of the Navy. It would be going right where the defenses are thickest. Stripped of even a few of its carriers, the Navy might then be unable to do its more important job, protecting the sea lanes. That, in turn, would jeopardize a war in central Europe.

"If we sail into battle against the Soviets depending on just 15 ships, we will, like the Spanish Armada, sail in expectation of a miracle," Hart writes in *America Can Win.* "Perhaps we will get one, although the precedent is not encouraging. Perhaps the opponent, despite numerous submarines and aircraft, will prove incompetent. But our survival, as a navy and a nation, would depend . . . on massive incompetence, not on our strength."

Even if the strategy worked and the carriers sank huge portions of the Soviet navy, the cornered Soviets might shift first to tactical and then strategic nuclear weapons to stave off surrender. In that case, the carriers' size wouldn't matter.

Astern of America, they formed a necklace of lights in the night sky, 15 planes strung out in a row. They had lined up to take their turns coming home. It was 11:30 p.m.

On a catwalk hanging over the side of the flight deck, four landing-signals officers stood peering into the dark. LSOs can tell just by looking at wing lights, if a returning pilot is on the right glide path, dropping 100 feet for each quarter mile to the ship.

"You're high, high," an LSO said softly into his radio to the first inbound plane. It was too dark to see what kind it was.

No task in all of aviation is more difficult than landing on a carrier at night. While modern jets can all but fly themselves and the carrier has runway lights, pilots have none of the usual reference points, such as the lights of a city. The sky is black, the water is black. They cannot tell where one stops and the other starts. All they can see is a short line of light. They cannot even see the ship, let alone the deck. No matter what instruments can say and computers can do, that is frightening.

The first plane drew nearer. It crossed the stern. Sparks shot from the flight deck as the arresting hook hit first, searching for one of the four cables. It found one, yanking an A-7 to a halt in 350 feet, one-tenth of the distance a plane needs on land. The lights of the next plane grew larger.

"Foul deck! Foul deck!" said two LSOs.

Until the A-7 could be unhooked and moved aside, until the arresting cables were back in position, until deck crews had moved, the LSOs would keep telling the next pilot his runway was blocked. If necessary, they would wave him off. On this night, they would not have to; the crews were perfect.

Sparks flew, engines roared. In 16 minutes, all the planes were down. The ship grew quiet for the night, sailing on.

"Sometimes," said an LSO, "I can't believe what we do out here."

THIRTEEN

ALTERED FATES

1987 WINNER IN THE EXPLANATORY JOURNALISM CATEGORY

"For a distinguished example of explanatory journalism that illuminates significant and complex issues . . ."

Chicago Tribune
Jeff Lyon
Peter Gorner

More than 12 million Americans are afflicted by the cruelest of all diseases—killers and cripplers that are inherited. Five years ago, there was no hope for the victims of genetic disease. Now there is. Peter Gorner and Jeff Lyon explain the progress in gene therapy and the barriers yet to be overcome.*

The *Tribune*'s series, "Altered Fates: The Promise of Gene Therapy" ** came about because we and our editors were convinced that society is standing at the threshold of a medical revolution unparalleled in human history.

We both are feature writers with substantial experience with medical topics. Earlier series for the newspaper had brought each of us to the outer borders of molecular medicine. Here was an even bigger story: Science, for the first time, has mounted a credible assault on some of the most horrible of all diseases—killers and cripplers that are inherited.

It was time for the *Chicago Tribune* to go after this story, to alert readers to the issues, and to try to explain the complex and endlessly fascinating worlds of molecular biology and molecular genetics.

Genetic disorders afflict about 12 million Americans and cost society billions of dollars each year, accounting for nearly half of all pediatric hospital admissions, for a fifth of all infant deaths, half of all miscarriages, and up to 80 percent of all mental retardation.

Society in the past has done little more than shrug at children who lose in nature's lottery. Few things are as final—or as cruel—as being born with a genetic disease. There are nearly 4,000 of them, all incurable. They cause immeasurable pain and guilt because they are passed on by unsuspecting parents to their young.

Down syndrome, muscular dystrophy, cystic fibrosis, sickle-cell anemia, hemophilia, Tay-Sachs, Huntington's chorea—the dismal litany goes on and on. Because genetic screening will be here long before

---

* From nominating letter written by Colleen Dishon, associate editor, *Chicago Tribune*.
** Six of the *Chicago Tribune*'s eight prize-winning articles are reprinted here.

any gene therapy for most of these illnesses, society will be forced to face some hard issues, including privacy and increased abortions.

Moreover, bad genes also are being increasingly implicated in the biggest health problems plaguing Americans—heart disease, stroke, cancer, diabetes, multiple sclerosis, arthritis, Alzheimer's, schizophrenia and other mental illnesses.

As we embarked on an odyssey that took us into the field for several months and covered more than 12,000 miles, we found the laboratories of molecular medicine to be pervaded by feelings of exhilaration and heightened urgency.

Because of recombinant DNA technology, scientists suddenly find themselves racing to make fundamental finds, to be first to understand such diseases and attack them at their very source. For medical science to actually cure human genetic disease—to alter fates—would fulfill one of mankind's most cherished dreams.

Painstaking basic research has led to one triumphant accouncement after another—genes for diabetes and heart disease; the historic genetic marker for Huntington's chorea; the recent pinpointing of the genes responsible for the dreaded killers cystic fibrosis and muscular dystrophy; identification of genes suspiciously involved in manic depression, Alzheimer's, and retinal and bone cancer, to name but a few.

Finding the culprit genes is merely the first step in eradicating these scourges, but it's a crucial step, and this hopeful list is growing by the week.

The biggest problem facing us as reporters was the complexity of the material. In the labs, there is nothing to see or touch, and little to describe. Everything revolves around strange machines, petri dishes and computer printouts—the sagas of viruses and bacteria into which human genes have been spliced; life forms so unimaginably tiny they often must be sensed by intuition.

We began our research at the Northwestern University medical library in Chicago and asked the computer for anything dealing with molecular medicine. We were given a list of more than 500 technical papers written in just the last two years. We culled as many as we could, but found them incomprehensible; utter gobbledygook. It took us months to understand the jargon so that we could discern the important papers from the inconsequential.

The next stop was the National Institutes of Health in Bethesda, Maryland, where the head of the Office of Recombinant DNA Activities—the federal agency that will regulate gene therapy—gave an overview of the contenders and the rules they would have to follow.

Accordingly, a series of trips were planned: to Texas, to survey the teams at Baylor University; to California, for the teams at City of Hope, Cal-Tech, the University of California at San Diego and the Salk Institute for Biological Studies; to Boston, for the teams at Harvard, the Massachusetts Institute of Technology, Boston Children's Hospital and Massachusetts General.

Eventually, we taped and transcribed in-depth interviews with more than 60 scientists, each working on a different piece of the puzzle, plus dozens of ethicists, other experts and many families. Other institutions that assisted us in our story included the University of Chicago, the University of Wisconsin, Johns Hopkins, Yale, the University of California at San Francisco, the University of Utah, Columbia University, the University of Pennsylvania, Georgetown University and the National Cancer Institute.

As we divided up the labor, each of us writing whole parts, every word and every image was weighed by our editors for clarity. Graphics and artwork were used extensively, both to aid comprehension and, importantly, to set moods. "Altered Fates" would never become simply a dry scientific explanation. From the start, we were determined never to lose sight of both the great adventure and the human dimension. This is a series in which lonely battles are being fought by very brave people. Numerous journalistic ethical decisions had to be made.

The leading candidate for the first gene therapy experiment, for instance, is the so-called "Bubble Boy" disease, a rare disorder known as ADA—the deficiency of the enzyme adenosine deaminase, which is crucial to the formation of white blood cells. Children born with ADA deficiency have no immune systems. The flu can kill them.

Despite the rarity of the disease, we found three cases. Two of the children died in the course of our research and the other was fighting for her life. We never considered exploiting their families. The series was postponed repeatedly. The grief was shared.

The *Tribune* devoted its entire Tempo section to the 50,000-word series, which ran for seven days in March and April of 1986. Not a word was trimmed. We couldn't begin to guess how the series would be received—it was very long and covered a lot of ground. We began to suspect that we had perhaps done our jobs when all our sources and the institutions we had visited immediately requested copies of the articles. Next, the *Tribune*'s reprints sold out quickly. Then the National Institutes of Health asked to reissue the series.

As we repeatedly cautioned our readers, gene therapy is not here yet. But it is coming, and the explosion in genetics research offers hope to millions of people who formerly had no hope. The work may ultimately affect everyone in the world.

—Peter Gorner and Jeff Lyon
Chicago Tribune

GENE THERAPY
RESHAPING OUR FUTURE

SUNDAY, MARCH 2, 1986

BY JEFF LYON AND PETER GORNER

BETHESDA, Md.—In a laboratory here on the sprawling campus of the National Institutes of Health, an experiment is under way that could change the face of medicine forever.

Reduced to its barest details, the experiment sounds hardly momentous, and possibly eccentric, or even cruel. Since early September, researchers have been drawing bone marrow from rhesus monkeys, deliberately infecting it with cancer virus and injecting it back into the monkeys' bloodstreams.

But the goal is not to give the monkeys cancer. In fact, the virus has been altered so that it will not cause tumors. The goal is to alleviate human disease—and do it with a power that has heretofore been reserved for the gods.

If the research leader, W. French Anderson, gets the results he hopes for, then sometime in the coming months he will apply for permission to try the same experiment on a different kind of test subject: a human child.

The procedure would represent a scientific milestone of incalculable magnitude. It would mark the first authorized attempt at human gene therapy—a bold attack on inherited disease at its very source.

In an extraordinary coming together of the latest discoveries in biology and genetics, researchers are gearing up to undertake something that would have seemed like science fiction less than five years ago. They hope to break into a patient's cells and replace a malfunctioning gene.

In all probability, the initial experiment will be aimed at a rare genetic defect called ADA deficiency, the disease that led to the death of Houston's famous "Bubble Boy" and that destroys a child's immune system.

But if successful, the technology ultimately may be applied to a

471

vast array of hereditary diseases that exact a huge toll in human suffering and economic dislocation.

Many genetic researchers foresee a day when such inherited killers and disablers as cystic fibrosis, muscular dystrophy, hemophilia, sickle-cell anemia, beta thalassemia, Tay-Sachs disease, phenylketonuria [PKU], Huntington's chorea and neurofibramatosis [Elephant Man's disease] may be treated and cured by gene therapy.

Such disorders, all caused by an error in just one of the thousands of genes that each of us carries in our cells, have remained stubbornly resistant to the progress made in other areas of modern medicine.

Gene therapy may also be enlisted one day in the fight against a number of other human ills, including heart disease, cancer and even schizophrenia.

Nevertheless, researchers caution that gene therapy is in its embryonic stages and will require many more years of research before it comes of age. In the meantime, molecular technology will introduce far more sophisticated tools for detecting and treating inherited flaws, in both the born and the unborn.

And the maturation of genetic medicine will be played out against a backdrop of ethical and political questions that will fuel fierce debates.

Genetic diseases cause a fifth of all infant deaths, half of all miscarriages and up to 80 percent of all mental retardation. They are responsible for 40 percent of pediatric admissions to hospitals and 13 percent of adult admissions.

Apart from the human suffering, such diseases exact a substantial economic toll. Some 1.2 million people are hospitalized in the United States annually for congenital illnesses, at a cost of $2.35 billion, and several million others are in institutions, each at a cost of up to $30,000 a year.

Individually, most inherited diseases are rare. But tallied together, they are surprisingly common. Five percent of children are born with genetic disorders, including such chromosomal abnormalities as Down syndrome. And if disorders that appear later in life are counted, such as diabetes and schizophrenia, as much as 15 percent of the population suffers from seriously handicapping conditions related to flawed genes.

Even that understates the problem. Millions of people suffer from diseases that, although once thought to be environmental in origin, are now believed to have a substantial genetic component.

These include some forms of heart disease, as well as cancer, diabetes, multiple sclerosis, arthritis and such neuropsychiatric disorders as Alzheimer's disease, manic depression, schizophrenia, clinical depression and alcoholism.

Since the beginning of time, hapless souls have suffered horribly and died young because of gene mistakes often unwittingly passed along to them by their parents. These mistakes can stem from spontaneous changes, or mutations, in a parent's genes, or they can be the legacy of ancestors from time out of mind. One's genetic fate hinges on an inflexible lottery whose outcome is determined at the instant of conception—to wit, by which sperm fertilizes which egg.

Now, after years of learning how to cut, glue, mix, zap and otherwise manipulate the genetic material of everything from fruit flies and tobacco to mice, sheep and Pacific salmon, scientists are on the verge of taking the first step in trying to alter the genes of man.

The biological sciences are at a threshold comparable to the one that confronted the physical sciences just before the dawn of the age of space exploration.

Rehearsals of gene therapy, using mice and rhesus monkeys as stand-ins, are going on not only at the National Institutes of Health [NIH] but at a host of other institutions, including the University of California at San Diego, the Massachusetts Institute of Technology, Harvard University, Baylor College of Medicine, Yale University and Johns Hopkins University.

All is part of the countdown for the human experiment soon to come.

"We anticipate we'll be receiving a gene therapy proposal within six months or a year," says William J. Gartland Jr., executive secretary of NIH's Recombinant DNA Advisory Committee. Because NIH bankrolls virtually all biomedical research in the United States, "The RAC," as the committee is jocularly called, must grant approval before a laboratory may attempt the procedure.

"Until recently," says Gartland, "researchers lacked enough scientific data to justify trying gene therapy in a patient. But now, I think they're approaching the point that it's reasonable to proceed."

The idea behind gene therapy is simple, though the techniques involved are exceedingly complex. "It's basically a transplant," says Stuart Orkin, a physician and molecular researcher at Harvard.

What sets the procedure apart from implanting a new heart or kidney, however, is that the body parts to be installed—the genes— are molecules only a few hundred thousand atoms in size, far too small to be seen under even the most powerful microscopes.

An identical set of 50,000 to 100,000 genes is stored in every cell of our bodies, strung, something like beads, along sinuous structures called chromosomes.

Both genes and chromosomes are composed of deoxyribonucleic acid, or DNA, an astonishing and versatile substance that is the very essence and common denominator of all life.

DNA is in the cells of every living thing, controlling growth and vital functions, supervising mental activity and enabling reproduction.

It is when the DNA in a gene supplies biochemically incorrect information that one of these important body processes can go awry.

To repair such genetic defects through gene therapy, two hurdles must be overcome. Scientists must first isolate particular genes that need correction and decipher their biochemistry. To date, they have made some spectacular progress.

For example, researchers in Boston and Toronto recently located the apparent site of the gene responsible for the most common form of muscular dystrophy, a fatal muscle-wasting disease that strikes 1 in every 4,000 male children.

And on Thanksgiving Day, a consortium of three laboratories announced they had found a gene they believe is "just a stone's throw away" from the gene responsibile for cystic fibrosis, the most common lethal genetic disorder in the Western world. They are now zeroing in on the CF gene itself.

"The technology that has developed for finding genes is going at blinding speed," observes Robert Dresing, national chairman of the board of the Cystic Fibrosis Foundation, who describes it as "awesome."

The pace is so dizzying that merely to visit a laboratory often is to learn of a new gene that the lab has just discovered. For example, the week that a Tribune reporter interviewed researcher Savio Woo at Baylor, Woo's lab assistant discovered a gene mutation at fault in PKU, a metabolic disorder that has caused mental retardation in generations of children.

Victor McKusick, the official archivist of human genetic disease, says that the number of genes that have been "mapped" to particular chromosomes is on the order of 900. "The field is just racing along," says McKusick, director of medicine at Johns Hopkins and author of an exhaustive textbook listing everything known about hereditary disease in man.

An indicator of how fast things are going is this: McKusick's book had 344 pages when first published in 1966; today's edition is 1,378 pages long.

But merely locating defective genes and identifying their biochemistry will not cure disease. It is only the first step in the process.

Equally important is the question of how to get "healthy" versions of those genes into a patient's body—and in sufficient quantities to do the patient some good. One can't just rub genes into the skin or take them in pill form. Genes must enter the body at the cellular level, where they will be absorbed by the chromosomes.

Nor is it enough to get them into a few cells. You must insert them into whole legions.

Science is trying to solve this problem by using one of mankind's most ancient enemies: the virus.

Viruses are a natural gene-delivery system that scientists are just beginning to harness. It is the stock-in-trade of a virus to invade cells, which it commandeers by inserting its own genes into leadership positions in the host's DNA.

The trick that virologists have mastered is to crack open viruses like walnuts, remove the genes that make the virus dangerous and fill the gap with the gene they wish to insert in a patient. The virus then becomes a beast of burden; getting the gene into the desired cells as it carries out its invasion.

Or so the theory goes. It remains to be seen whether what has worked in mice and in human cells in a laboratory dish will work in a living, breathing human being.

Gene therapy will not come into the world without serious labor pains. Not only the RAC but a host of regulatory agencies must approve the first human trial. No event in medical history will have undergone such intense scrutiny before being given the go-ahead.

This is because of serious ethical concerns that surround the procedure. These concerns stem in part from two previous attempts at human gene therapy conducted without official sanction over the last 20 years. Both experiments, deemed vastly premature, failed, and the researchers were severely censured.

Furthermore, some people worry that the technology will someday be used to modify genes other than those associated with disease, that it will be used, instead, to modify those pertaining to intelligence, behavior, physical appearance and so on. They envision a nightmarish world in which genetic "perfection" becomes the norm, to the detriment of human diversity and frailty, perhaps even to the exclusion of certain racial and ethnic types. Those who believe in such scenarios argue that all new technologies are eventually abused.

Others discount this view. They contend that modifying such traits would be impossibly complex, because most human traits such as intelligence apparently involve the interplay of dozens of genes.

Contributing to the ethical reservations are huge and very basic question marks. Gartland himself concedes that gene tinkering is still a "black box"—nobody knows for sure what will happen when you put a new gene into a person's body.

Moreover, substantial technical problems remain to be solved before the procedure is to have widespread medical value. Researchers have almost no idea how to "target" a gene to the desired organ or chromosome.

Nevertheless, if gene therapy survives its birth and ultimately proves successful, it will at last lift the curse from a population whose destiny has heretofore been sealed: those who suffer from one of the nearly 4,000 known diseases of genetic origin.

But long before gene therapy becomes routine, what scientists learn about our genes will have tremendous diagnostic application.

Every gene has a unique biochemical sequence that, in its way, is as recognizable as a face. Once that sequence becomes known, scientists can prepare matching radioactive probes that will home right in on the gene as it lies hidden in the haystack of the patient's chromosomes.

Thus, if you want to test a person for the presence of a bad gene—or a normal one, for that matter—all you need is a sample of that person's DNA on which to set the probe loose.

In fact, you need not even be able to recognize the "face" of the gene itself. It is sufficient to know the identity of a gene that is very close to a disease gene on a chromosome, because when genes are that intimately situated, they tend to be inherited together. Such telltale bits of DNA are known as "markers."

One application of this diagnostic legerdemain is prenatal testing for hereditary disease. A sample of genetic material from a fetus is obtained through amniocentesis—or a newer technique, called chorionic villi sampling, that can be used much earlier in pregnancy—and is subjected to a probe for whatever disease one is worried about.

This will allow millions of Americans the option of terminating a pregnancy, should a test come back positive.

Similarly, blood samples from children can reveal whether they harbor underlying hereditary disorders—useful in identifying such frequently misdiagnosed maladies as cystic fibrosis. And adults can learn if they are "carriers"—that is, whether they carry certain deleterious genes that could be passed along—before deciding to have children.

Perhaps most fascinating is that it is increasingly possible to test individuals for their underlying propensity to cancers, cardiovascular disease, even their susceptibility to certain environmental toxins.

Armed with knowledge of their physical vulnerabilities, people can dramatically alter their lifestyles and avoid things that, interacting with their genes, could cause them serious harm.

For example, a person who learns that his genes make him vulnerable to lung cancer no longer need play the odds. He has an extremely powerful motivation to stop smoking. Another person, upon being told that he has an elevated sensitivity to certain chemicals in the marketplace, might switch occupations.

Overshadowing all research, however, is the fear among scientists that the first experiment with human genetic therapy might fail. Given the large amount of publicity the experiment is likely to attract, this not only would be personally embarrassing, it could give the entire discipline a black eye.

Hence, it is considered extremely important that scientists be ready before doctors carry out the first human experiment. And there is great wariness about going out on a limb.

"Everyone wants to be first," says Douglas Jolly, a molecular biologist at the University of California at San Diego. "But nobody wants to be first by very much."

A BRAVE GIRL WAITS FOR A MIRACLE CURE

SUNDAY, MARCH 2, 1986

BY JEFF LYON AND PETER GORNER

LAGUNA HILLS, Calif.—Entering Alison Ashcraft's bedroom, you get the feeling that you are being watched. Stuffed animals are everywhere. More than 200 of them fix visitors with a glassy stare from all corners of the room.

Girlish excess? No, good parental psychology. Each button-eyed, felt-tongued rabbit, tiger, and bear represents a time in the last five years that doctors have had to draw Alison's blood.

For Alison, common colds and flu are a calamity. Chicken pox is a deadly scourge. She has had pneumonia no fewer than 18 times.

At 12, she is the oldest known survivor of a devastating genetic disorder called adenosine deaminase [ADA] deficiency, which has decimated her natural immune system. The disease, whose most famous victim was David, the now-deceased "Bubble Boy," is rare, striking only once in every 150,000 births. Few afflicted children live beyond the age of 3.

The only cure, a bone marrow transplant, would be extremely risky for Alison. But hope may be on the horizon. ADA deficiency is expected to be the first disease treated by a startling new medical procedure called gene therapy.

Gene therapy draws on technological breakthroughs achieved in just the last three years. It is designed to strike inherited disease at its very core: the genes. If the procedure works—and there are many ifs involved—it may one day revolutionize the treatment of hundreds, perhaps thousands, of human ills, ranging from the rarest of childhood killers to such commonplace evils as cancer and heart disease.

Most people have been conditioned to think of genes as too small or elusive to deal with medically. But scientists now believe it possible to enter the fortress of the human cell and actually correct a genetic flaw.

479

Researchers will call on an unlikely ally in their attempt to deliver a healthy gene to people whom nature has shortchanged. The ally is the rascal of the microscopic world, the virus.

Viruses love to invade foreign cells and stick their own genes into the host's genetic material, thereby creating a kind of puppet government in which the virus is in control.

What scientists have learned to do is remove the nasty viral genes and replace them with the healthy genes they want to insert in a patient. When the virus is subsequently allowed to do what comes naturally—infect cells by the millions upon millions—it puts a healthy gene into each one, and does it without causing disease.

Researchers have already tried the technique successfully on mice and on human cells cultured in a laboratory dish. Soon—perhaps within this year or next—they may be ready to try it on the first human test subject, someone like Alison.

"The doctors have told us that the best opportunity for a cure would be gene therapy," says her father, Aaron Ashcraft. "They explained it would take anywhere from one to five years to develop it, but it could resolve Alison's problems."

That would be welcome news, not only for Alison, but also for millions of other victims of genetic diseases whose afflictions might be cured by gene therapy. Conquering ADA deficiency is only a stepping-stone, explains W. French Anderson, a physician and molecular researcher at the National Institutes of Health, who some consider the front-runner in the race to be first to try gene therapy.

"ADA deficiency," says Anderson, "is just a breakwater to answer the question: Will gene therapy work in ideal circumstances? Can you put a gene into a human being and cure a disease? If so, all kinds of other diseases are down the road."

Nearly 4,000 medical conditions can be attributed to the influence of defective genes. They range from diseases of childhood, such as cystic fibrosis and muscular dystrophy, to those associated more with advanced age, such as cancer and cardiovascular illness, and from single-gene disorders, such as sickle-cell anemia and hemophilia, to polygenic disorders—those caused by genes acting in concert with the environment—such as diabetes, spina bifida, and multiple sclerosis.

The list does not end there. It also includes mental disorders such as schizophrenia, manic depression, and clinical depression, and is even believed to extend to Alzheimer's disease, alcoholism and learning disabilities.

In theory, any of these could one day be treatable by gene therapy —although enormous technical obstacles still stand in the way.

These obstacles are currently hindering efforts by Anderson, and his counterparts at several competing research centers, to bring gene therapy off the drawing boards and into clinical practice.

Nevertheless, the vast potential of genetic medicine has allowed Alison Ashcraft and her family to finally see some light at the end of the tunnel.

Alison was 7 years old before she was diagnosed, although she had been plagued by inexplicable ill health almost from birth.

"She was sick frequently," recalls Corinne Ashcraft, Alison's mother. "Ear aches. Nose and upper respiratory infections. Pneumonias. And she didn't get over things quite as quickly as she should. Usually with kids one dose of medicine is enough to take care of it, but with Alison we'd have to go back for a second round."

As the Ashcrafts moved from city to city, following the demands of Aaron's career as an automobile sales executive, they sought explanations from a string of pediatricians, first in Walnut Creek, Calif., then in Denver and Detroit.

"No one could tell us why this child was sick so often," Corinne recalls of that frustrating, anxious time.

Alison's troubles mounted. For one thing, she was remarkably small. Her bone age was only half her chronological age. Doctors attributed it to the effects of her constant illnesses.

"She was iron deficient," notes Aaron. "Her eating habits would fall off every time she got sick and she'd become anemic. All she wanted to do was sleep. She'd sleep up to 22 hours a day."

Out of any given year, Alison was sick 8 to 10 times, each time for as long as a month.

"When she was in second grade, out of nine months of school she missed five full months," says Corinne.

Only once in their years of searching did the Ashcrafts come close to finding an answer for Alison's health problems. A doctor in Detroit hospitalized her and, after taking extensive blood samples, told the family that Alison had "very strange" T cells—immune cells whose job it is to fight cancer and foreign invaders.

"But then he forgot about it and decided she had cystic fibrosis," says Aaron ruefully. "He ran a CF test on her three times and each time it came back negative. And still he wanted to do the test some more."

The vexation continued until the Ashcrafts were transferred back to Walnut Creek in the summer of 1980. There, Corinne sought out the same pediatrician she had used when Alison was born.

The second week in Walnut Creek, Alison got very ill. On examining her, the pediatrician told Corinne that the child had pneumonia. "So what's new?" said Corinne wearily. "What color medicine are we going to now?"

Two pneumonias later, the doctor finally threw up his hands. "This isn't normal," he said, telling Aaron and Corinne what they already knew. But now he suggested something that would ultimately lead to an answer. He thought Alison should be tested by an allergist.

The allergist, Dr. David Cook, performed 36 scratch tests on Alison's back. He tested her for a variety of different foods, grasses and animal hairs. When the testing was finished, he shook his head quizzically and said: "This is very puzzling. She doesn't show a positive reaction to anything. Everybody gets a small reaction to something."

What the allergist had stumbled on was Alison's inability to muster antibodies to anything at all.

Providentially, Dr. Cook also happened to be an immunologist. He immediately asked if he could take a large sample of Alison's blood for study. Corinne and Aaron readily agreed.

A few days later the doctor called back. The Ashcrafts will never forget the day. It was a Friday in late May of 1981, and they were about to take Alison, and her brother, David, then 11, to Yosemite National Park for the weekend.

"Please come to my office immediately," Dr. Cook demanded.

The doctor sat them both down and said, "I think I have found Alison's problem. She has an immunodeficiency in her blood."

The doctor recommended that she be seen at the University of California, San Francisco, whose immunology department is world renowned. Two weeks later, Alison entered the hospital in San Francisco, where a team of 20 physicians, led by Doctors Arthur J. Ammann and Morton Cowan, went over her with a fine tooth comb.

"It was their unanimous opinion that she had ADA deficiency," says Aaron.

"We were totally panicked," puts in Corinne. "After so many years without an answer, all of a sudden we were inundated with information we didn't understand."

But there was a curious sense of relief, as well. And a vigorous desire to prevent Alison from becoming some sort of hothouse flower.

"The prognosis at the time was that she was in very severe danger," recalls Aaron, "and they said we'd have to be very careful with her. But we also decided at that time that the quality of her life had to count for something, too. The child had gone for seven years with this problem without us knowing it and had somehow survived. So we just decided we'd go ahead and try to live a normal life."

And so they have. Alison's condition has been more or less stabilized with monthly, three-hour infusions of immune globulin, a blood extract rich in antibodies, which provides her some temporary immunity. Her diminutive size—which was subsequently discovered to stem from a thyroid insufficiency—is being handled with doses of thyroid medicine.

An intelligent, pretty, blond girl, Alison leads as full a life as her illness will allow. She attends public school, has many friends, and pals around with her brother David, now 16, who is quite supportive. She attends rock concerts, goes camping and has taken modeling and ballet. She swims, skis and has a black standard poodle named Schroeder.

But she has to wear a Medic Alert bracelet specifying that in case of accident, she must only receive blood that has been irradiated to kill all virus. And she still gets sick. Last Thanksgiving a flu turned into pneumonia and it stuck around until after Christmas. It was a reminder that her medical condition remains fragile and could destabilize at any time.

Though Alison aspires to be a model someday, she knows in her heart that science is going to have to buy her that someday.

One recent Friday afternoon, she sat discussing her present and future with a visitor. She nodded soberly when her father said, "We are going to have to attack her underlying problem at some point."

What might her options be? she was asked.

"The doctor says I could get a gene transplant," she said.

How do you feel about that?

"Well, I don't really want to. I don't like operations. But if it would make me better, I'd do it. I'd like to be cured."

In order to understand what gene therapy is all about, it is necessary to know what genes do. Very simply, they tell the tiny factories within each cell how to make proteins, the basic materials required for growth and maintenance of the body. Each gene contains a code for a specific protein, a code consisting of a distinctive sequence of chemical subunits called nucleotides.

There are only four of these basic chemicals, but they can occur in an endless variety of combinations.

In each of the 100 trillion cells in our bodies there is an identical set of genes, half of which come from our mothers, the other half from our fathers. These genes are strung onto long structures called chromosomes that coil up tightly in the cell like miniature Slinky toys.

Both genes and chromosomes are composed of a remarkable substance called deoxyribonucleic acid, or DNA.

DNA is so flexible that nature can compress six feet of it into every human cell; there is enough in the average person to stretch from Earth to Pluto 1,600 times. But it is so durable, it is virtually immortal. In every human being are remnants of the original piece of DNA that gave rise to all life eons ago.

DNA is interchangeable among species. You cannot distinguish between the chemical composition of mushroom DNA and beetle DNA, or horse DNA and human DNA. The difference between a mushroom and a horse lies simply in the sequence, or order, of the chemical subunits.

Think of a gene as two strands of DNA wound together like a twisted rope ladder whose rungs consist of two nucleotides joined together. Nucleotides don't pair off indiscriminately. Each one of the four will bond with only one other kind.

• • •

Because nucleotides show such preferences, molecular biologists are able to cut genes apart and glue them together—including ones from different species. They do this by making the ends of a gene "sticky," that is, they leave one nucleotide unattached so that it "trolls" for its matching nucleotide.

This ability to recombine genes in ways unintended by nature is called recombinant DNA technology, or genetic engineering. Developed only in the last 15 years, it allows scientists to do a number of fascinating things.

They can make multiple copies, or clones, of genes by putting them into bacteria, which duplicate the genes over and over as they reproduce.

They can fashion exotic creatures, as did two researchers in 1982 when they injected the gene for rat growth hormone into mice embryos and harvested "supermice" that were double normal size.

They can design probes, sequences of nucleotides that will attract —in effect fish out—genes from a sample of DNA. Such probes are proving immensely useful, not only in identifying new genes but in diagnosing genetic disease. A probe can detect the presence of a particular disease gene in a patient's DNA.

And most intriguing, from a medical perspective, scientists can insert a "healthy" gene into the DNA of a virus, which they have engineered to deliver the gene to a sick human being.

How would this new gene cure a patient? By simply assuming the function of the patient's own defective gene. When a gene is faulty, it cannot make its accustomed protein. If a tissue protein is involved, then some physical structure—an organ, perhaps—may not get made properly. If two other kinds of protein, called enzymes or hormones, are involved, then some chemical process—the metabolism of a kind of food, for example—may not occur the way it ought to.

Should an important enough process be short-circuited, the result will be disease or death.

ADA deficiency, Alison Ashcraft's illness, is caused by a flaw so obscure that it strains the mind to contemplate it. Buried deep inside each of our cells—within the nucleus, a command center no larger than 1/12,000th of an inch—are 23 pairs of chromosomes.

In this infinitesimal world, on the 20th chromosome, is a gene containing a complex recipe that normally tells the body how to make adenosine deaminase, an enzyme whose job it is to convert certain natural compounds into other ones, preventing a toxic buildup. At any given moment, the body is streaming with thousands of such enzymes, each controlling a vital biochemical reaction.

But in Alison, the recipe for ADA contains a misprint, or mutation. A single item is incorrect out of a list of thousands of ingredients. As a result of this minuscule error, her body cannot make sufficient ADA and the compounds don't get converted as they should.

When a child can't make ADA, one of these unneutralized compounds starts rattling around the body like a loose cannon. It combines with phosphorous to form something called deoxyadenosine ATP, a deadly poison to immune cells. It ends up wiping out a child's immune system.

Most children with ADA deficiency die in infancy. Victims lack defense against the simplest infections. Chicken pox will kill them. So will a yeast infection. Their risk of cancer, especially leukemia, is 10,000 times greater than in normal people. In its action, the disease strongly resembles AIDS, although the cause is genetic, not acquired, and it cannot infect others.

Alison has survived because her body produces a trace of the ADA enzyme—2 to 3 percent of normal—and because every month, she receives an infusion of immune globulin.

Despite its rarity, ADA deficiency is an excellent model on which to try the principles of gene therapy. For one thing, it is a disease of the bone marrow, and at the moment, the only tissue into which scientists know how to put new genes is bone marrow. For another, the condition is so devastating that a chance of curing it justifies almost any experimental risk.

The most-publicized research leader, the NIH's Anderson, says he has so far succeeded in getting a human ADA gene to make its protein in monkeys. Unfortunately, the level of production is less than one percent of normal, still far too low to justify experimenting on humans. Twenty percent is considered to be the threshold for good health, and Anderson says he won't feel confident until the monkeys are turning out at least 10 percent.

Working with the monkeys satisfies Anderson's secondary objective: to smooth out kinks in the actual gene therapy procedure. The operation goes like this:

First, bone marrow is extracted from the hipbone of a patient—in this case, a rhesus monkey. Then the marrow is placed in a lab dish and exposed to Anderson's test virus into which has been spliced the human ADA gene.

The game plan calls for the virus to do what it does best: infect huge numbers of the patient's marrow cells. In so doing, Anderson hopes, the virus will insert enough ADA genes into the patient's DNA to take up the slack for his or her own defective gene.

The altered marrow cells are then returned to the patient's body. If enough of the new genes subsequently start turning out ADA, the treatment will have brought about a cure.

Gene therapy will at first be limited to diseases that can be treated via the bone marrow. Marrow, which is the factory where red and white blood cells are made, has several attractive features for the molecular researcher. It is relatively easy to obtain, easy to work with in the laboratory, and offers a way to treat any malady associated with the bloodstream.

Because of this, it was assumed for a while that the first attempt at gene therapy would be made on one of the inherited blood disorders, notably sickle-cell anemia, a disease of blacks in which red cells become sickle-shaped and obstruct blood flow, or beta thalassemia, a disease of Mediterranean and Far Eastern peoples in which red cells are too fragile and die prematurely.

Both diseases are caused by defective genes for hemoglobin, the oxygen-carrying protein in blood. These genes were among the first to be isolated by scientists, and can rather easily be put into bone marrow "stem" cells—cells that operate like sour-dough bread starter, manufacturing other blood cells by the trillions. Each descendant of an altered stem cell would presumably carry the newly implanted gene for good hemoglobin.

However, it was soon learned from experiments in tissue culture that although hemoglobin genes can be implanted with little difficulty, researchers cannot yet regulate how much hemoglobin they make and when. They tend to make too little to reverse disease, and at the wrong times.

"The regulation of hemoglobin is very complex," says William Gartland, Jr., director of NIH's Office of Recombinant DNA Activities. "It's so complex that it now seems unlikely a hemoglobin disease will be among the first tried."

Next, everyone thought that a cruel disorder called Lesch-Nyhan syndrome would be the subject of the first trial. Because of a defective gene, victims lack an emzyme called HGPRT, resulting in a mysterious array of terrifying symptoms, including cerebral palsy, retardation, kidney damage, and an uncontrollable compulsion to mutilate oneself.

But Lesch-Nyhan's worst ravages are manifest in the brain. Early evidence indicates that putting the HGPRT gene in bone marrow will not have any impact on neurological symptoms. To reverse those, one must presumably get the new gene into brain tissue, and as yet there is no way to do that.

The kind of virus that researchers are currently using in experiments is admirably suited for getting genes into something extractable, like bone marrow, but it is not very good at hauling genes to tissues that cannot be removed from the body. This creates a major problem where diseases such as Lesch-Nyhan or muscular dystrophy are concerned, for they involve brain and muscle tissues that must stay intact.

The solution may turn out to be the use of viruses that show a distinct preference for certain parts of the body. Herpes viruses, for example, flock to nerve tissue, offering a way to get neurological genes into the central nervous system. If this sounds dangerous, keep in mind that gene therapists presumably engineer the virus to be harmless to the patient.

Why is it so necessary to target a particular gene to a particular body site? The answer lies in something called cell differentiation. While every cell of every organ in the body contains the same set of genes, only those genes required for a particular organ's function are switched on. All others are supposed to stay permanently switched off.

For example, the only genes that should be working in a pancreas cell are genes needed by the pancreas. It does you no good to put a brain gene or a bone gene into a pancreas cell, and it might even be harmful.

But getting the new gene to the right part of the body is only half the battle. Ideally, you also want the gene to be delivered to precisely the right point on the proper chromosome; in other words, the spot occupied by the defective gene.

Every gene has its customary address on the chromosomes. When it feels at home, it will happily make its protein all the livelong day. But if it is dumped off in a strange place, it often rebels and won't work a lick.

Unfortunately, viruses tend to slap genes on the chromosomes randomly. Genes end up everywhere, without rhyme or reason. This creates two problems. First, the new gene may be finicky and not produce any protein. And even worse, by landing haphazardly there is always the chance it might disrupt the function of some vital, unrelated gene—or trigger one of the cancer genes we all have lurking in our cells.

The good news is that scientists are working out ways to airmail genes to precise chromosomal addresses, and they've had some encouraging success.

In an ingenious experiment concluded last summer, researcher Oliver Smithies, of the University of Wisconsin, and Raju Kucherlapati, of the University of Illinois College of Medicine, dropped a hemoglobin gene right where they wanted it—onto the hemoglobin site on chromosome 11. They were able to do this by making their gene "sticky"—that is, they exaggerated the natural magnetism that causes like genes to attract one another.

Smithies admits he only got one gene in a thousand to go to the right spot, but points out that that's three million times better than chance. "We've got a long way to go," he says, "but that's what makes science fun."

Thomas Maniatis, chairman of molecular biology at Harvard University, one of the world's leading experts on gene regulation, notes that the next step will be to "kick out the bad copy of the gene, leaving only the good copy.

"That's the ultimate objective of gene therapy," says Maniatis, "to not disrupt in any way, to just go in and cleanly, surgically alter a gene."

The attraction of ADA deficiency for genetic therapists is that none of these regulation and targeting difficulties appears important. Regulation of ADA production is not essential. Even a small amount of the enzyme will prevent the destruction of enough immune cells to improve the child's health. Nor is targeting a worry. In contrast to Lesch-Nyhan syndrome, bone marrow is exactly the place one wants the new gene to go.

If gene replacement works in ADA deficiency, it will quickly replace bone marrow transplants as the treatment of choice.

Such a transplant is very risky for someone like Alison Ashcraft, because neither her parents, nor her brother David, 16, are a tissue match. Thus Alison's own bone marrow must be destroyed chemically to keep it from rejecting the donor marrow—a step that could be fatal if the transplant fails to take.

If somebody overtakes W. French Anderson in the race to perform the first experiment on a human, it is likely to be Richard Mulligan, a virologist at Massachusetts Institute of Technology, who is also studying ADA deficiency.

Right now a disagreement exists between Anderson and Mulligan over how close the first gene therapy experiment actually is. Anderson says nearly enough work has been done to justify a human trial. Mulligan says not by a long shot.

The dispute boils down to this: Mulligan believes Anderson leapt prematurely into working with monkeys, before ever getting a human ADA gene to make its protein in mice. He feels another year of mouse studies will demonstrate whether the gene delivery system that both have put their faith in actually works.

Anderson responds that he has all the proof he needs of the delivery system's effectiveness, and that he wants to try it on animals that are the closest physiologically to man. He says he is "only a few months away" from making an application to NIH's Recombinant DNA Advisory Committee, which must approve any human gene therapy experiment before it is tried.

The dispute highlights the classic tug of war in medicine between the clinician and the pure researcher. The clinician—as embodied by Anderson, an M.D. specializing in blood disorders—threats sick patients on a regular basis and tends to be so affected by the human misery he sees that he wants to bring new treatments on line as soon as possible. The pure researcher—exemplified by Ph.D. Mulligan—tends to be personally insulated from patients and can be more cautious in certifying that a treatment is safe and effective before releasing it to the market.

It is unclear who is more on track, Anderson or Mulligan. The level of ADA production Anderson has been able to wrest from his monkeys —less than 1 percent—is termed "negligible" by Mulligan. And it falls well short of what Anderson himself says is necessary.

Even Mulligan agrees, however, that the first gene therapy experiment is just a matter of time. "I think these are technical difficulties, the kind we can probably solve."

Clearly, many knotty problems remain to be solved before gene therapy becomes commonplace. Future generations will almost certainly look back on today's tentative research with the same tolerant amusement with which we view the first efforts of the Wright Brothers to fly at Kitty Hawk.

"There are still technical impasses which make even the first demonstration projects an uncertain distance in the future," notes David Baltimore, Nobel Prize-winning cancer biologist at M.I.T.

Baltimore is a spectator rather than a participant. But even some directly involved in the gene therapy sweepstakes share his doubts. Harvard's Stuart Orkin, Mulligan's physician-partner in the race to cure ADA, describes the initial gene therapy experiment as "something of a stunt" that will have only limited medical application for some time to come.

Baylor University's C. Thomas Caskey, on the other hand, is impatient with such negativism. "This field is just going to do nothing but explode," says Caskey, a pioneering molecular geneticist and biochemist who is pursuing both ADA deficiency and Lesch-Nyhan syndrome. "It is well worth the effort to give gene therapy the full shot, because if it does work, the payoff will be big."

And others echo the haunting view of David Nathan, chief physician at Boston Children's Hospital, who believes the prospect of ending the heartbreak of genetic disease impels medicine to lean on the throttle in pursuing gene therapy.

Nathan is one of the world's leading specialists in childhood blood diseases and cancers. He says: "Once you have taken care of patients and had to say to their families, 'I have basically nothing to offer you in the way of treatment,' then you understand why we're so grateful for progress. If you've had to do that enough, then by God, when you see a little opening, you run through it like a pro halfback through a line."

On the outskirts of this swirl of words are Alison Ashcraft and the other victims of inherited disease, who are waiting for gene therapy to come of age.

The Ashcrafts have become astute health care consumers since Alison's condition was diagnosed in 1981. Before then, they had no idea what immunodeficiency was. Now, they have become founders of the Immune Deficiency Foundation of California, affiliated with the National Immune Deficiency Foundation headquartered in Baltimore. As such, they are tireless promoters of new kinds of treatment, particularly genetic therapy.

Nevertheless, Alison's father, Aaron, confides that he and his wife still have some reservations about gene therapy that have to be overcome.

"We are worried because they use a virus to transport the recombinant DNA," he says. "If something went wrong with the virus, if it infected Alison somehow, she couldn't survive."

To which W. French Anderson, still patiently testing and retesting his monkeys at NIH, replies that his research team will not seek permission to try the first experiment "until we are convinced we're ready."

Says he, "When we have good results in monkeys, when we could sit down with our own sister and say, 'Trust me with your child, we are ready to do gene therapy,' only at that point will we move ahead."

TO LOOSEN THE BINDS OF A HIDEOUS DISEASE

MONDAY, MARCH 3, 1986

BY PETER GORNER AND JEFF LYON

SAN DIEGO—Imagine the subtle urge that sometimes makes you chew your fingernails. Amplify that feeling a million fold and you have a sense of the bizarre compulsion for self-destruction identified 24 years ago by pediatrician and geneticist William Nyhan.

Ever since, Nyhan has been struggling futilely to conquer the appalling hereditary sickness of childhood to which he lent his name.

"An utter nightmare," Nyhan calls the Lesch-Nyhan syndrome. "Absolutely the worst disease I treat. These kids act as if they're possessed."

As many as 2,000 American families must live day-to-day with sons, never daughters, suffering from an enzyme deficiency that has crushed their bodies and their minds.

Although born apparently normal, they inexorably grow mentally retarded, violently spastic, utterly helpless. Even worse, they constantly must be kept tied up—their hands and feet strapped in restraints—lest they attack and bite themselves and others.

"Each family feels like they're visited by a special plague," says Nyhan, 59, a lanky, friendly man. "I've tried to bring families together for mutual support, but they decline. I think it's because each of these kids has awful behavior. But they're all different. And the mothers figure that if their son got together with another Lesch-Nyhan kid, he'd pick up something else that was even *more* awful.

Nyhan is totally committed to gene therapy, the revolutionary experimental technique that offers the only hope for Lesch-Nyhan youngsters. They, in turn, represent millions of victims of nearly 4,000 known genetic diseases.

The number of ailments recognized has been dramatically increasing as science develops keener methods of genetic analysis.

Individually, most genetic diseases are rare. But scarcely a week goes by without genetic abnormalities being linked more closely to such major health problems as cardiovascular disease and heart attacks, diabetes, arthritis and degenerative disorders, aspects of aging, schizophrenia and other mental disorders, and forms of cancer.

Among the 4,000 genetic disorders, 1,637 are known to be caused by just one mutant gene among the 50,000 to 100,000 genes that all humans have. These so-called "single-gene defects" will be the first targets of gene therapy.

Genes have been studied with awe for a century, but now boldness has begun to replace the awe. Largely because of gene splicing, scientists now are able to home in on the deepest, molecular levels of life. Genes have become things for manipulation and modification.

By cleverly tinkering with the genes of the simpler forms of life [viruses, bacteria, pink bread molds, fruit flies], biologists have learned to read the chemical messages encoded in all genes. Scientists now have the technical facility to clone any gene of any organism, from a mushroom to a man, and to determine its complete structure.

This explosion of knowledge in biology has brought medicine bobbing in its wake. Gene therapy eventually may prove to be a medical innovation that dwarfs even the landmark discovery of antibiotics. The ramifications may ultimately affect everyone in the world.

Model systems are being developed that will teach doctors how to aim things at bad genes, how to add new parts to the messages genes contain, how to change genes or remove them, how to modify their activity.

The rare and pitiful disease known as the Lesch-Nyhan syndrome, which affects only one child in 100,000, would seemingly belong in the backwaters of such research. But Lesch-Nyhan has become what biologists call an experimental battlefield for gene therapy, a prototype for other researchers battling to follow.

The renegade gene responsible for Lesch-Nyhan syndrome has been captured. It has been torn apart in the laboratory and studied. Corrected versions have been created.

Months ago, the good genes seemed ready to go, ready to be placed into a youngster in hopes of repopulating millions of his cells and curing him. Lesch-Nyhan is so hideous that victims and their families will try anything.

But then this syndrome, perhaps the most mysterious in medicine, revealed even deeper mysteries that the Nyhan team is working to solve.

A biochemist as well as a physician, Nyhan has earned a reputation as one of the world's greatest genetic sleuths. As chairman of pediatrics at the University of California at San Diego [UCSD], he has helped transform a lovely oceanside campus into one of medicine's busiest genetic research and treatment facilities.

Most people have never heard of the cruel diseases that he has made his specialty. Many pediatricians have never even *seen* the mystifying sicknesses that Nyhan routinely diagnoses and challenges, rare inherited sicknesses that always strike children, many of whom he was the first to treat, and all of whom he calls heart-rending.

"We're at a very exciting time now," Nyhan says. "The children I treat—in addition to those with the Lesch-Nyhan syndrome—have a terribly tenuous lease on life and yet they *ought* to be cured.

"Never before could I make a statement like that. But because of gene therapy, we're on the verge of being able to take what's wrong and possibly fix it. To me, the idea seems magical."

Parents whose youngsters have lost in nature's lottery routinely move to California to be near Bill Nyhan. Physicians worldwide, confused and frustrated, send him puzzling children. Despite his renown, Nyhan remains the kind of pediatrician frantic parents roust from sleep at three in the morning. At such times Nyhan often feels like them—alone and bewildered. It's as if he were the last doctor on earth who can help. Sometimes he truly is.

His specialties have jawbreaking or vividly descriptive names: Argininosuccinic aciduria, cystinuria, citrullinemia, ornithine transcarbamylase deficiency, propionic acidemia, maple syrup urine disease— these are but a few.

In all such disorders, a malfunctioning gene permits toxins to accumulate in the bloodstream and the brain, causing physical and mental devastation. Formerly fatal within days, if not hours, such diseases often may be controlled by vigilant tightrope-walking regimens of diet, vitamin therapy and antibiotics.

But such children, to Nyhan, are "walking time bombs." Only good new genes would truly cure them.

The Lesch-Nyhan syndrome is unwittingly passed from mothers to sons. One gene gone haywire causes almost unimaginable havoc. But Lesch-Nyhan, which affects victims mentally as well as physically, is a model for scientists to study how genes affect intelligence and behavior.

Diseases such as Lesch-Nyhan result from the lack of an enzyme, an enormous class of protein molecules that operate as catalysts, controlling the tens of thousands of chemical reactions in the body. Enzymes help do everything from transmitting nerve impulses to assembling genes. Life cannot exist without them.

Lesch-Nyhan syndrome stems from what is called a "housekeeping gene" that makes an enzyme with the formidable name hypoxanthine guanine phosphoribosyl transferase [HGPRT]. The enzyme is crucial to the complex biochemical chain of events in every cell of the body that clears the body of uric acid.

Although every cell of the body produces some HGPRT, the genes in the brain produce 50 times more than those anywhere else. With too little HGPRT, the buildup of insoluble wastes can cause arthritis and kidney damage. A total absence of the enzyme results in the Lesch-Nyhan Syndrome.

Afflicted infants appear normal at birth, but by eight months their arms and legs become flaccid and weak. Movements grow spastic. Mental growth can just stop. Agonizing arthritis and kidney stones are common.

Then come the night terrors, as infants are swept by strange new feelings that force them to bite themselves, to lash out at those who love them.

Nyhan spotted the disorder in 1962. He and one of his medical students, Dr. Michael Lesch, were then at the Johns Hopkins School of Medicine. A retarded, palsied, spastic boy was brought to the emergency room.

"His name was Michael and he was four years old," Nyhan recounts. "His immediate problem was blood in his urine. But we were struck by something else. He had a badly mutilated lip and fingers. He had done it himself, and it was the first self-mutilation I had ever seen in my life.

"This, as it has turned out, is an absolutely uncontrollable compulsion," says Nyhan, his rising voice emphasizing his frustration. "These kids are ferocious and quick the way they do this.

"You must keep them in physical restraints—hands and feet tied —all the time. A Lesch-Nyhan kid gets loose and he might amputate a finger—he'll chew his fingers to pieces. Let him loose for just a short time and there's blood everywhere."

Unlike other severely mentally retarded youngsters who may injure themselves and seem oblivious to pain, children with the Lesch-Nyhan syndrome are spared no such peaceful oblivion.

"These kids *hurt*. They scream in pain while they bite themselves. It's just terrible. They really are happy only when protected from themselves by restraints. As babies, these children scream all night until their parents are taught how to restrain them securely in bed."

When they're tied down, an incredible change occurs. As Nyhan described it for the scientific journals: "All these children have bright, understanding eyes. They relate unusually well to people and they are usually felt by those closest to them to understand everything that is said to them."

The behavioral change is bizarre. "They are unusually engaging children while they are restrained," Nyhan says. "They all have a good sense of humor and smile and laugh easily."

They remind Nyhan of the principal character in the ballet "Petroushka," with their tragicomic air, exaggerated posturing and mitten-like protective coverings on their hands.

"The nightmare," he says, "is that some of these children even have normal intelligence, and lots of them are *not that* retarded. They *know* their plight. And it obviously puts a complete limitation on their lives.

"I had one kid who learned to use crayons and pencils. And then, all of a sudden, he learned he could put his pencil in his eye. He missed, the first time. But it scared the hell out of him, and out of me. And now, he's deleted all that handwork from his life."

• • •

Nyhan marvels at the ingenuity these children display in hurting themselves when unloosed from their bonds. Placed in a wheelchair, some youngsters find they can jam their fingers into the spokes of wheels. Braces prescribed for cerebral palsy are turned into weapons. Children may find hot water faucets and scald themselves. They vomit compulsively—and sometimes voluntarily, Nyhan believes—and are prone to wrecking family gatherings, such as birthday parties.

"They will suddenly strike anyone who comes near them," Nyhan says. "They kick, hit, and break the eyeglasses of nurses and doctors who care for them. They sometimes develop such disconcerting habits as pinching the breasts of their mothers or nurses or grabbing for genitals.

"I remember we had a boy here for several months, and his mother came from out of state to visit him at Christmas. Somebody had given him a toy fire truck as a gift. She walked into the room and he hit her with it.

"On the other hand, they are just as often remorseful about having produced injury.

"As they get older and learn to speak, they become verbally aggressive as well. They love to swear, to scream, to shock."

When Nyhan examined that first child 24 years ago, he found the boy's urine teeming with microscopic uric acid crystals—a sure sign of gout. Fascinated, Nyhan knew that gout seldom occurs in children.

Since the 1960s, gout has been effectively treated through drugs, such as allopurinol, that controls the formation of uric acid. This has meant that Lesch-Nyhan boys now are living into their 20s, rather than dying early in childhood. But drugs have no effect on the disastrous brain malfunction.

In studying that first child, Nyhan learned that the boy had an elder brother who had been institutionalized with the same complex problems. That meant the syndrome probably was genetic. Nyhan and Lesch dropped all other research and studied the boys for a year. The boys were producing 10 times more uric acid than any other patient ever had.

When Nyhan reported his findings, doctors with patients responded from all over the world. The pattern of inheritance became plain. In one extended family alone, Nyhan found 15 males with the disease. No female victims have ever been discovered.

In the 1960s, scientists learned how to locate genes on individual chromosomes by fusing human cells with mouse cells in a test tube.

Selectively bred mice were used because the animal and its cells were known quantities to laboratory researchers. Because of the willingness of mice cells to fuse with human cells, human chemicals that are present can be isolated. This leads scientists to the specific genes that made those chemicals.

In 1967, the HGPRT enzyme deficiency in Lesch-Nyhan children was discovered by Nyhan's UCSD colleague, Dr. J. Edwin Seegmiller. HGPRT quickly became one of the most studied enzymes in science.

But it wasn't until 1982 that new genetic engineering techniques allowed the scientists at UCSD [and another group at Baylor University] to isolate the HGPRT gene from the surrounding chromosomal material.

The UCSD team, led by pediatrician-geneticist Theodore Friedmann, cloned the gene by using chemistry that selected it out of DNA —the master molecule of life. The scientists were ingenious. They put human DNA into mouse cells and asked the mouse cells to make the human enzyme.

Mouse cells, which had been engineered to contain no HGPRT, were fused with human cells containing the gene, and placed in a petri dish. The dish held a culture medium called HAT. Cells lacking HGPRT cannot survive in HAT.

A small fraction of the fused cells had eaten bits of human DNA, some of which contained the HGPRT gene. Those cells that could put the gene to work churning out HGPRT survived and multiplied.

The next step was to retrieve the human gene from the mouse DNA. After some virtuosic maneuvering, Friedmann managed to get a piece of the gene.

Then the Friedmann team used this piece to pull out a whole HGPRT gene from chopped-up human DNA. By cloning the gene, Friedmann had an unlimited supply for study. The plan was to mix the gene with white blood cells from a Lesch-Nyhan patient in tissue culture and see if the cells would start producing HGPRT.

But no matter what they did, the genes stubbornly refused to enter the human cells.

Team members, however, had been working with virologist Inder

Verma, at the nearby Salk Institute for Biological Studies. Verma is a world renowned pioneer in the use of viruses to ferry genes into new cells.

To get the correct DNA into cells, Verma and other scientists have spent years engineering viruses to infect cells but not damage them. Verma does this, in effect, by castrating the virus—biochemically snipping out the genes that give the virus the ability to reproduce. Then he stitches in the human gene and the signals that regulate it.

Using Verma's viruses, the team in 1984 was able to put healthy HGPRT genes into new cells. By taking bone marrow from a mouse, they showed they could infect the marrow with human HGPRT genes. The animal would carry that gene and sometimes make the enzyme.

This was the first time a foreign gene was successfully placed in bone marrow using a virus.

Then, last November, the Friedmann team was able to design a virus that successfully implanted the HGPRT gene into human bone marrow cells in culture. This is important because marrow cells make red and white blood cells that potentially could carry replacement genes to many organs in the body.

All this work has been leading to an attempt to inject the genes in the bone marrow of a Lesch-Nyhan victim and see what happens.

But the Lesch-Nyhan syndrome poses a crucial scientific problem. The disease occurs when there is an absence of HGPRT in all cells, yet the worst symptoms are blamed on the disruption of normal brain functions.

Upon autopsy, however, no brain defect has ever been found. Lesch-Nyhan brains look normal.

This has given rise to the hope that perhaps the retardation, the palsy, the spasms, the gout, the kidney stones and the insane behavior are not permanent. Perhaps they could be reversed.

The notion has aroused considerable skepticism among other scientists.

It is true that bone marrow replenishes itself constantly, making new blood. Bone marrow is readily accessible, and transplantation is a practiced art. If all went well, the new HGPRT gene would send the enzyme coursing through the victim's blood.

As the gene replicated, it would produce HGPRT, more and more of it, like a gushing faucet. Many genes are delicately tuned, and switch themselves on and off. The laboratory sophistication required to mimic this has eluded scientists so far. But the added HGPRT gene would stay switched on.

All this seems like an elegant solution to the Lesch-Nyhan syndrome—except for one thing: There is yet no way to get new genes to the brain.

The brain presents huge problems for gene therapy. Brain cells, whose impaired function afflicts Lesch-Nyhan patients, do not proliferate as bone marrow cells do after they mature. Genetic material introduced into the brain cell will not be spread to others by cell division.

Moreover, the brain has a highly selective mechanism—the blood-brain barrier—that filters substances that enter from the bloodstream. Genes being transmitted by recombinant viruses probably would be screened out. Correction of a defect elsewhere in the body thus may have no effect on the brain.

No one knows, however, which brain defects may be corrected by modifying other body cells. So along with the laboratory research, Friedmann and Nyhan also schemed to find another way to determine if gene therapy might have a chance.

"We're painfully aware of the warts in this model. We don't know the nature of the brain defect," admits Friedmann, a slight, bearded man who is recognized as one of the pioneers of gene therapy.

"Maybe there's a defect in a peripheral organ, an organ like the liver, that leads to the accumulation of uric acid, or the failure to elaborate something that the brain needs.

"There are many diseases that masquerade as central nervous system diseases that are really diseases of the liver. PKU [phenylketonuria] is such a disease. It's not a brain disease at all, yet it shows up as a brain disorder. So with Lesch-Nyhan there's no assurance the defect is in the brain."

[PKU, to which Friedmann refers, is the well-known inherited metabolic disorder, discovered in 1934, in which an inability to metabolize the amino acid phenylalanine, a common ingredient present in all food protein, can lead to serious mental retardation. The disease may be treated by dramatically restricted diets. All American newborns are tested for PKU before being allowed to leave the hospital.]

Moreover, Friedmann says, cells do talk to one another. There is evidence that they help cure each other. Perhaps if doctors helped the bone marrow, the brain might get the word. Nobody really knew. There was only one way to find out, and that was by trying a routine bone marrow transplant in a Lesch-Nyhan victim; in effect, giving him new HGPRT genes donated by a sibling and seeing if they helped.

Last year, bone marrow transplant techniques had improved sufficiently for Nyhan to propose the idea to a Lesch-Nyhan victim and his family. The patient, 22, had a normal sibling whose tissues matched.

The family readily consented to the experiment. They lived on the East Coast and came to California where doctors performed the transplant, giving the patient healthy bone marrow from the sibling which, of course, contained normal HGPRT genes.

The results were tantalizing at first. The victim's body accepted the bone marrow from his brother and soon was producing the missing enzyme. For a few days after the transplant, the recipient asked for his restraints to be taken off. He was able to sleep without them. He began to feed himself. He stopped vomiting—one of his major neurological symptoms.

Then the roof fell in.

"He seemed improved for about a week," Nyhan says. "Then he developed a kidney stone. The urologist tried to handle it without surgery—they instrumented him from below, which, as you can imagine, is painful at best. At worst, it didn't work. So he finally went into surgery and had the stone removed. In the course of that, the vomiting returned, and he went back into restraints."

Even though he had received new HGPRT genes, they didn't seem to make any real difference. This was devastating news, though many scientists were not surprised.

"The California people have a problem: They tried a bone marrow transplant and the patient didn't rise like Lazarus," says Dr. Stuart Orkin, a Harvard Medical School researcher working on an immune disease called adenosine deaminase deficiency [ADA], the other illness frequently mentioned as a candidate for gene therapy.

In fact, since the Lesch-Nyhan marrow transplant failed, ADA has become the leading candidate. "Lesch-Nyhan doesn't look like a good model," insists Orkin.

• • •

The Nyhan team disagrees. Despite the setback, team members view the experiment as just that, although Friedmann gets prickly when pressed: "An experiment doesn't fail," he insists. "An experiment tells you something."

Was the temporary improvement wishful thinking? Friedmann doesn't know, nor does Nyhan. The young man had been so miserable, the family so hopeful.

"I have mixed feelings about the transplant," Nyhan says. "Before we did the experiment, I took the hypothetical position that if we put the enzyme in the marrow and let it circulate in the blood, it ought to be able to fix the head.

"Like Ted [Friedmann], I keep thinking about PKU," he says. "You and I don't have PKU because we have the necessary chemical in the liver, and that keeps our head normal. The kids who don't have it become mentally retarded. And if I came along and transplanted a liver at age 20, they'd still be retarded. But if I transplanted it at 2 weeks, I'd fix them.

"Also, if you're as intelligent as our patient is, and you spend your life mutilating yourself, and even if now you've got a little enzyme that would normally protect you, it might be that these patterns of behavior are so ingrained that you're never going to get rid of them.

"Another thing, if we're asking this marrow to populate the brain with glial [connective tissue] cells, we wouldn't expect it to happen quickly. It could take a few years. So there still may be some beneficial effect in our patient."

The next step for the San Diego team would be to get the genes in earlier—to perform a regular bone marrow transplant in an infant suffering from the Lesch-Nyhan syndrome and see, once and for all, if there is reason to think that planting a gene in the bone marrow will affect the brain.

"Now, you're talking," Nyhan agrees. "Asking the transplant to prevent the disease is a smaller request than asking to cure it.

"There's a definite window. These babies appear to be normal. And they develop normally for six to eight months. What I would dearly love would be to do this in somebody who was in that window."

Although the symptoms are not yet evident, doctors can identify Lesch-Nyhan youngsters by their lack of the HGPRT enzyme. The deficiency shows up in amniocentesis, for example. Otherwise finding such a child is not easy, Nyhan admits.

"If the disease has struck once in a family, we do prenatal diagnosis, and when there's an affected fetus, the family generally chooses an abortion. But that certainly is not the case 100 percent of the time. Some people are so opposed to abortion they wouldn't consider it under any circumstances.

"So that's where we stand now," Nyhan says.

"The lab research is progressing, and we're looking for a baby. We truly are. Maybe if we could get the genes in *before* the damage shows up, we could do something. Maybe we could stop this horrible thing once and for all."

A DESPERATE RACE AGAINST A DEADLY LEGACY

WEDNESDAY, MARCH 5, 1986

BY PETER GORNER AND JEFF LYON

BOSTON—James Gusella's congested lab here at Harvard's historic Massachusetts General Hospital seems a far cry from the fishing villages that dot the steamy shores of Venezuela's Lake Maracaibo. That far cry actually is an unremitting wail of despair.

It haunts Gusella, a molecular geneticist whose laboratory, jammed to the gills with equipment and workers, is studying blood from a thousand Venezuelans. Their fates are shared by thousands of American families accursed for generations by a fatal flaw. *El mal,* the villagers call the horrifying thing that has lurked in their midst for 150 years: the sickness.

And it haunts Nancy Wexler, a vivacious 40-year-old New York clinical psychologist who has devoted her life to solving the mystery of hereditary disorders.

As with the Venezuelans, Wexler has a family history that means she may carry the fatal flaw herself. She has teamed up with Gusella and other researchers in a partnership that has galvanized science.

For the first time, a killer gene has been mapped to its home chromosome without anyone having a clue beforehand where the gene was, or what it did. The feat opens the door to ways to detect genetic flaws that give rise to almost any disease, and years before trouble shows up. As science races ahead, this ability to tell the future will cause ethical quandaries, political debates and painful personal dilemmas.

El mal is short for *El mal de San Vito*—what the Venezuelan villagers call the deadly dance of St. Vitus—an apt description for a brain in agony as it slowly dies.

The medical term is Huntington's chorea, known to most people as the savage brain disease that killed folksinger Woody Guthrie. The term harks back to Dr. George Huntington, the young American physician who identified the disorder in 1872.

Huntington grew up near a Long Island family suffering from the strange illness he called hereditary chorea, from the same Greek root as choreography. In the disease, it refers to the uncontrollably fierce twitching of the extemities typically produced in victims.

Huntington's disease, a term that incorporates the progressive dementia also caused by the disorder, is now preferred by medical scientists.

Only 21 years old when he contributed his sole paper to science, Huntington correctly attributed the disease to inheritance, passed directly from parent to child:

"It is confined to certain and fortunately few families," he wrote, "and has been transmitted to them, an heirloom from generations way back in the past."

An heirloom particularly cruel, the fatal Huntington's gene rarely blazes into action until the third or fourth decade of life. By then, unsuspecting victims have married and started families.

Because children receive half their genetic legacy from each parent, the offspring in Huntington's families have a 50-50 chance of inheriting the disease if one parent carries the dominant gene that produces it.

Sometimes, the offspring already have had children of their own before the disease strikes the parent. Three generations are suddenly at risk. The gene, by hiding out for 35 or 45 years, ensures its own perpetuity.

In 1979, Wexler and Gusella joined forces to find the gene that causes Huntington's disease. As president of the California-based Hereditary Disease Foundation, Wexler has led five landmark expeditions to Venezuela where blood samples were taken from more than a thousand inhabitants of three villages with the highest rate of Huntington's in the world.

In 1983, after analyzing the blood and the ancestry of 3,000 Venezuelan clansmen, Gusella was able to discover a piece of genetic material [DNA] that, while not the actual Huntington's gene, is so close to it that its presence strongly indicates that someone will develop the disease years later.

"The story," says Wexler, "is a combination of absolutely sophisticated molecular biology, and people and families—the lowest tech there is.

"When we started out supporting the idea of using recombinant DNA techniques to find genes, there was a lot of skepticism in the field. On paper it looked good, but what a total long shot. Nobody had any idea where the Huntington's gene was. It could have been anywhere on the 46 human chromosomes.

"We went to the biologists who were developing budding technologies and said. 'Why don't you cure a fatal disease while you're thinking? We'll give you the tissues to study and the money to get started, and put post-doctoral hands in your labs.'

"They got very excited about using Huntington's as a model," Wexler says. "First, it's absolutely horrendous, but scientifically it's a good disease to work with. If the gene is present, it always switches on. So if there's a good family history, diagnosis is relatively easy

"Also, Huntington's most likely hinges on just one bad gene. And the disease appears in mid-life. Why does it wait? These are interesting issues to a scientist.

"High-tech labs, though, lack the families to trace the gene through generations—the key to finding a marker. The Venezuelans had lots of families. So we went down there to explore this monster-sized family.

"We did it, basically, by winning their trust, taking their blood, and working backward—trying to find out who their relatives were. The family itself was so powerful, genetically, that it permitted Jim Gusella to find the linkage right away."

Before the discovery, genetic markers were located only by slow and laborious processes that probably would be useful for very few diseases. In order for these tests to work, scientists first had to find the gene and learn what it does—a major undertaking. In prenatal tests, for example, the presence or absence of enzymes in the fetal cells tells doctors about the conditions of the genes that made them.

The Gusella team showed that science now has the ability to jump directly to the bottom line—the DNA itself—and use a system of rapidly locating genes for disease that won't show up for decades.

With more than 12 million Americans being affected by genetic disorders—there are nearly 4,000 identified so far—Nancy Wexler believes that the Huntington's story may even serve as a model for finding the genes that cause most of them.

The potent technique that Gusella has established will allow scientists to hunt genes believed responsible for sicknesses that also may be inherited and affect all aspects of body and mind—among them muscular dystrophy, cystic fibrosis, and perhaps Parkinson's, Alzheimer's, schizophrenia, epilepsy, and manic depression.

When the Huntington's gene itself is finally found—and it could happen tomorrow, or, guesses Gusella, within five years—scientists may be able to determine what the horrible gene does. Perhaps doctors can find a treatment that HD patients need. If biologists find the gene, there's always that chance.

But discovery of the marker already has spurred scientific interest in a disease that most doctors have considered hopeless.

And because of the discovery, Gusella's lab is working on a test to determine if someone carries the gene for Huntington's disease. He estimates that a pilot program will be available within two years for people with extensive family histories. It will be the first of many tests for genetic diseases that will become available long before the treatment.

Would you take Gusella's test?

"What we've done is to create a way to predict a fatal disease when there's yet no treatment," Gusella says. "That's a real quandary, let me tell you.

"We've created a situation where people who seem perfectly healthy today will know that in 30 years they're going to look like their sick parent, and there's no hope.

"That gives us incredible momentum to find the gene. If we can learn what's wrong with it, we may be able to do something. That's no guarantee, but a possibility."

Twenty thousand Americans suffer from Huntington's disease; 100,000 more are at risk. Some are unaware of their peril—misdiagnoses, mistreatments and misinformation have surrounded the disease for years.

Thousands of others live under the sword. They have witnessed the death of a parent and know full well what having the gene means. There is no escape from the killer gene, no cure. No gene is more potent than the one Gusella seeks. When present it is implacable. The outcome is inevitable.

Death sneaks in covertly, insidiously, and takes a long, long time. Its presence is meekly announced. A dropped glass, a stumble— they may mean nothing, or may signal the beginning of the nightmare.

A victim may start forgetting things, can't seem to balance a check-book or recall a phone number. Odd and inexplicable outbursts of fury are common. So are other personality changes. With these first telltale signs, the body gradually begins to act as if it were working by remote control.

It starts to move.

Normal movement may slow down and twist, forcing the trunk to shuffle and arms to writhe as a victim tries to walk. Often, the trunk and limbs begin to flail—accelerating faster and faster, involuntarily in jerks, constantly twitching, fighting off all attempts at control. The victim feels like a puppet on a string.

As the disease attacks relevant brain centers, speech often grows indistinct; a repeated grimace or tic may progress to a frenzy of facial movements: eyes roll, the tongue darts in and out, the palate jumps, the eyebrows glide up and down.

The entire body may become a horror of grotesque, uncontrollable movements. This is chorea.

In the 20 years it generally takes Huntington's to reach full cry, some bedridden victims stiffen up like boards and lose the ability to talk and to swallow. Sometimes, especially in younger victims, the violently awkward movements overwhelm with relentless vengeance, making the entire body a convulsion.

Huntington's kills the brain. No one knows why, or how. One theory is that certain brain cells are made of defective proteins that wear out abnormally fast. Yet many victims actually die of malnutrition: They cannot be fed because the movements are so fierce. Others accidentally inhale food and eventually succumb to pneumonia.

The long downward course often produces profound depression, which may lead to schizophrenic patterns, suicide or criminal behavior. About 12 percent of victims take their own lives, but research indicates that as many as 30 percent say they are prepared to when the time comes.

Victims in the early stages typically are arrested for drunkenness, as happened to folk balladeer Woody Guthrie because of his staggering gait and slurred speech.

Guthrie had been a teenager when his mother died of a mysterious malady that seized her mind. As he reached the prime of life, Guthrie also started showing the signs.

By 1952, Guthrie's inexplicable rages forced his family to hospitalize him. Misdiagnosed as schizophrenic for years afterward, he lost his coordination and ability to make music as his brain slowly but relentlessly deteriorated.

Only because of the persistent skepticism of his wife, Marjorie, was a correct diagnosis ultimately made. But that came too late for Guthrie to understand what had happened to him. In his last years, he lay in his bed paralyzed, able to communicate only by opening and closing his eyes. He died in 1967 at age 55.

Marjorie Guthrie, who organized the Huntington's Disease Foundation of America to battle the stigma and shame that often accompany the disease, died two years ago without knowing what would happen to their children. Arlo Guthrie, star of the 1970 film "Alice's Restaurant," and his brother and sister remain at risk. According to published accounts, Arlo has said that he will not take the test for the genetic marker.

In order to find the marker, Gusella embarked on a search that was, in molecular terms, awesome. It spanned 46 chromosomes, about 100,000 genes and a total of 3 billion chemical subunits of DNA [deoxyribonucleic acid], the fundamental genetic material of all living things.

This mass of material is packed in the nucleus of a human cell, a package so incredibly small that its outlines only can be seen with difficulty under a microscope.

The marker for Huntington's, which Gusella pinpointed to one place on Chromosome 4, is only 17,600 subunits long. The chromosome has a total of 200 million subunits.

"It's a big chromosome, and we're still a long way from the gene itself," Gusella cautions.

"Think of it this way: When we started out, the gene could have been anywhere on the 46 chromosomes.

"It's as if we were peering out at an ocean, and there were 3 billion barrels bobbing in the water. The gene is inside one of the barrels. We cut the search down to 200 million barrels by finding out it was somewhere on Chromosome 4.

"Next we narrowed it further to 10 or 20 million barrels by learning that it's somewhere out in the tip of the short arm [top half] of the chromosome.

"We're still about 5 million barrels away. But we're closing in."

Those who choose to be tested for the marker will bet their lives on the result, although Gusella stresses to add that his test is not yet perfect.

Even if the test detects the marker, there is a 5 percent chance that the lethal gene is not nearby. As he works to make the test nearly 100 percent accurate, Gusella is looking for a flanking marker—a marker that sits on the other side of the killer gene—so he can home in on the gene.

According to Dr. Susan Folstein, a psychiatrist and Huntington's specialist at Johns Hopkins University: "The idea of telling a perfectly healthy person that they carry a gene which will definitely express itself in a fatal genetic disorder is a unique situation in human history.

"There is no way to predict how people will handle this, or if they will be able to handle it at all."

Nowhere is the Huntington's "heirloom" more evident than in the impoverished Venezuelan fishing villages along Lake Maracaibo. The poor have big families—12 or 14 children are common—and everyone seems related to everyone else. With this has come *el mal*.

In the 25-square-block barrio of San Luis, for instance, the Huntington's rate is 700 times higher than normal. About 150 of the 3,000 villagers currently are living with the disease, and 2,000 others are at risk.

In the little isolated village of Lagunetas, just 21 tin shacks built on stilts over the water and accessible only by boat, many of the 200 residents are descended from or related to one husband and wife, both of whom are Huntington's victims and still alive. As many as 25 percent of the villagers are doomed.

These huge clusters of victims were discovered in the 1950s by a physician, Dr. Americo Negrette, who had been assigned rural duty.

When Negrette walked into San Luis, he noticed that people looked strange.

"Why is everybody drunk?" he asked. "They're not drunk," he was told. "They're sick."

Negrette was flabbergasted. By 1952, he had diagnosed the San Luis plague as Huntington's but was scoffed at by colleagues. Such a high incidence was unheard of.

Negrette and his medical student, Avila Giron, though, methodically compiled a family pedigree of 200 residents that later became the foundation on which researchers could trace the pattern of the inherited disease, the key in finding a genetic marker.

Negrette also speculated—correctly, researchers say—that all the families must have inherited the common gene 150 years ago from a single ancestor, perhaps a Spanish sailor who had brought it to the New World.

Negrette paved the way for Nancy Wexler in 1979, when she made her first scientific expedition to Venezuela.

Wexler organized and served as project officer for the study while on staff at the National Institute of Neurological and Communicative Disorders and Stroke.

Wexler shares a special bond with the Venezuelans, who call her *La Catira,* the blond. In 1968, she and her sister, Alice, had been carefree college students when their father, psychoanalyst Milton Wexler, summoned them home to Los Angeles for a family meeting. They learned that their mother, Leonore Wexler, then 53, had been diagnosed with Huntington's.

"We were stunned," Nancy recalls. "She had never mentioned that she might carry the gene. She had believed that only men got HD. Her father died from it, we learned, as did her three brothers. By the time she found out that she could be a carrier, my sister and I had been born. So she was hopeful that she had escaped."

Milton Wexler started the foundation in order to try to help his wife and others. The family purpose: "To get the disease before it gets us." Leonore Wexler died 10 painful years later.

Both sisters, who earned their doctorates [Alice in history, Nancy in clinical psychology], decided not to marry and to remain childless.

The foundation solicits public money, sponsors scientific workshops, which have become highly respected, and awards grants.

After a scouting trip to Venezuela in 1979, Wexler led her first expedition. Doctors and nurses drew blood and interviewed families. Psychologists administered tests to detect early signs of impairment. Neurologists gave physical exams, checking for deterioration.

Blood samples were drawn from those Venezuelans closely related to a Huntington's victim, a complicated matter because so many people have the same names. Such days were always chaotic, Wexler says.

"It was always hot and humid—about 100 degrees. And, of course, there was no air-conditioning. Many people had never given blood before and were afraid to lose their fluids. Men were more recalcitrant than women. Some men believed they couldn't drink if they gave blood and they didn't want their drinking interrupted. So we had to resort on occasion to drawing blood from one arm and giving them a beer in the other.

"The hardest people to collect from were the old and healthy. They had escaped the illness. They were scared because we wanted their blood, too. What did that mean?"

The scientists took special interest in those villagers who had inherited a double dose of the gene. One Lagunetas husband and wife had 14 children, each of whom had a 75 percent chance of developing Huntington's. Furthermore, these 14 had produced 62 grandchildren and great-grandchildren. Their risks vary from 25 to 100 percent.

As the study progressed, a crucial family tree was laboriously and meticulously compiled. The result was a computer printout that stretches more than 100 feet and holds the family history of more than 5,000 people, more than 4,000 of whom are still alive. Scientists believe that all these people were related to one woman who died of Huntington's more than a century ago.

Each year that Wexler has returned, the neurologists silently study *her* for the earliest, soft signs of the disease. She doesn't let it bother her.

"I try to be as counter-phobic as possible. It seems better to me to know what the truth is going to be and try to do something about it, rather than not take a step for fear of what's ahead."

For the scientists, the work has been heartbreaking.

"We were in tears a lot," Wexler admits. "We feel a fantastic sense of urgency and desperation. Each year we go back, the people want to know if we've found a cure. The disease usually has a mid-life onset, but it sometimes does strike children. We estimate that about 500 village kids who have the gene will die in the next 10 to 30 years. It's a very young population down there.

"These are closed communities. Outside their towns, the people are ostracized; so they have to stay together. They still intermarry. When we went in, we had Dr. Negrette's blessing, which helped a lot. The people thought the disease was unique to them. They hadn't a clue that anybody else had it.

"The men, the heads of households, get knocked out early. They become uncoordinated and fall off the fishing boats. Then they can't support their families and may commit suicide because of that.

"There currently are about 100 patients with Huntington's— brothers, sisters, uncles, aunts, cousins. These numbers are extraordinary for a dominant fatal disease. Some 2,000 people are still at risk."

The scientists were impressed by how well victims have been integrated into village society.

"It's incredibly dramatic to find a Venezuelan woman lying in her deathbed," Wexler says, "and her family is all around her taking care of her.

"They know absolutely that some of them will get this disease and, indeed, some already are starting to show signs. So they're looking at their future mirror image, while they're giving her water and changing her."

But even some of the children are running out of time.

"There's one little girl who's absolutely stunning. When we first went down there, she looked perfectly fine. Suddenly, now, as they say in Venezuela, 'she's lost.' People kept telling us she was lost to the disease.

"On our last trip, we looked at her, and oh, my God, something *was* going on. She just clung to my neck and started sobbing and saying 'Don't go,' and 'Take me with you.' That just rips you apart. You're trying desperately to find something that's going to stop this thing. You're trying to turn back history. It's like trying to stop a tidal wave."

A thousand carefully labeled vials of blood were gingerly transported 2,000 miles to Gusella's lab within 48 hours after being collected.

Gusella, a member of the Harvard Medical School faculty and of the neurology department at Massachusetts General, set to work extracting the DNA and looking for differences. He was trying to determine if there was anything special in the DNA of Huntington's victims that normal people didn't have.

Gusella had expected to spend at least a decade looking for the marker among those three billion pairs of the four basic chemicals that compose chromosomes of a single cell.

To narrow the search, he first whittled down this mass of molecular material to manageable size, using enzymes that will slice DNA in particular places.

A DNA sample cut by these enzymes may result in fragments of different lengths, called polymorphisms. They can be used like fingerprints. They represent the minute chemical differences that make each of us unique. But those from Huntington's victims, as Gusella would discover, have a pattern of fragments in common.

Just as no two personalities are identical, we all differ slightly in our biochemical constitution. Our blood groups, blood pressures, metabolisms, etc, are individual. We also vary as to the number of sites we have in our genetic material where enzymes can cut, and the number and length of fragments produced when exposed to enzymes.

These patterns can be inherited like any other trait. Scientists in the lab can use your pattern to analyze your gene structure. They also may use the distinctive patterns as genetic markers.

By studying large Huntington's families over many generations, Gusella found that a particular pattern was the constant partner of the gene and could indicate its presence or absence.

If a pattern type is the next-door neighbor to a gene, the pattern can serve as a signpost for the presence of the gene. Within a family, all the Huntington's patients will have the same pattern type, and their unaffected relatives will have a different pattern.

To find the marker, Gusella took from an established library of human DNA fragments short stretches called probes. The probes have the amazing ability to home in on very specific sections of chromosomes. When mixed with fragmented genetic material from a cell, a probe will seek out and bind to its complementary sequence of chemical subunits like a magnet.

Scientists engineer probes to be radioactive, and a radioactive probe shoots off a tiny flare when it connects: It makes a black spot on X-ray film. The spot shows where on the chromosomes the complementary DNA lies.

Gusella expected to try some 800 probes before finding a pattern that would always travel with the Huntington's gene. "Brute force," is the whimsical term for such scientific tedium.

But he hit pay dirt after only 11 tries. He found a marker for the killer, to which he gave the benign name "G-8," that he believed could distinguish among those people who carry the gene for Huntington's and their relatives who have been spared.

Dr. P. Michael Conneally of Indiana University analyzed the data and determined that the marker could be used to indicate the presence of the gene. Conneally had computerized the Venezuelan pedigree and collected comparison tissues from an American family through the National Huntington's Disease Research Roster, of which he is director.

He even had run sophisticated new paternity tests on the Venezuelan blood samples to prove that fathers listed on the family tree were, in fact, the real fathers.

Finally, Gusella and Dr. Susan Naylor of Roswell Memorial Park Institute, Buffalo, N.Y., determined that the marker is on Chromosome 4.

Gusella knows that the marker is near the faulty gene because the Venezuelan pedigree enabled him to watch it travel down through generations. This is where the low-tech tools of classical genetics—family pedigrees—team up with the high-tech tricks of genetic engineering.

The pattern of inheritance allows Gusella to calculate that the marker, of unknown function, lies about 5 million chemical subunits from the gene. The stretch is large enough to include several hundred genes, yet so small that it constitutes only a tiny portion of the chromosome.

Each day, though, Gusella continues to "walk" along the fourth chromosome, stalking the gene itself. It probably represents less than 1 percent of the total 5-million-unit DNA region Gusella identified. Finding this unknown piece of DNA by existing techniques is an enormous task.

"We're throwing more probes at it, seeking a flanking marker. But this time, we know where to look," he says.

Surveys indicate that 75 percent of the 100,000 Americans at risk for Huntington's say they would want to know if they carry the marker. But once the test is available, many people may refuse it. "A lot of them," Wexler notes, "are starting to believe that a 50-50 risk isn't all that bad."

For those who will choose to take the test and learn they probably have the fatal gene, awaiting the subtle first signs could be torture. When will they come and what will they be like?

The raw terror alone can make people listless or explosive, depressed or hypersensitive, clumsy, forgetful.

Just like Huntington's disease.

Wexler has made her own decision about whether to take the test, but is keeping her decision to herself. Privacy, in fact, is a critical and potentially volatile issue in all this, she says.

Huntington's patients often require custodial care that can cost $25,000 a year, Wexler says. Once the test becomes available, insurance companies may refuse to cover afflicted families unless members prove their risk is minimal. When the test is no longer experimental, employers may insist that all family members take it.

The possibilities worry Wexler and Gusella. "On the other hand," Gusella says, "can we ethically hide this information from those who want to know? I believe they have a right to it. The knowledge may well determine how they lead their lives."

Wives or husbands of people from Huntington's families may also have a right to know what their futures hold, but their at-risk spouse may choose not to know. Divorce and possible suicide in patients with a high risk are a real danger.

Regardless of conflicting rights, curiosity over the test results would obviously be intense. Silence from doctors, or delays to recheck results, might be unbearable.

There are five people at risk for every one who develops Huntington's disease. Those at risk range from very young children to people in their 80s and 90s who still feel some sense of jeopardy, Wexler says. Because of the wide age range, two-thirds of them could be freed by the test. The genetic chain will be broken. But what about the others?

"There definitely must be counseling programs," Wexler says. "All researchers agree. We'll need psychiatric therapy, hotlines, crisis intervention—all of it.

"We must never forget, after all, that we can offer some hope," she emphasizes. "Due to the late onset of the disease, there's always the possibility that a cure will be found before the gene switches on."

Gusella will even be able to diagnose the presence of the Huntington gene before birth. This prenatal test would be like no other, however. If a fetus is shown to carry the gene, it could only have come from one place.

"With a dominant disease, if the fetus is affected, the parent is affected as well," Wexler says.

"You can be a carrier for muscular dystrophy and still be safe. But with Huntington's the loss of a baby presages the loss of your own life. The blow is double.

"This test will be able to predict the future," she says. "And we as a society had better become prepared to deal with these issues.

"Prenatal and carrier tests will be coming soon for almost all the genetic diseases. Huntington's is a dramatic example. But we'll be able to diagnose many diseases long before there's any gene therapy for them.

"An awful lot of people will be in this painful hiatus."

Wexler should know, even though her health is fine so far.

"I've got good genes," she says, with a smile.

"Most of 'em, anyway."

GLOSSARY

CHROMOSOMES   the filament-like structures in a cell's nucleus that contain genes and store and transmit genetic information. Chromosomes are composed of DNA and protein, the genes being duplicated whenever cells divide. Each species has a characteristic number of chromosomes; humans have 46.

DNA [DEOXYRIBONUCLEIC ACID]   the material of genes. All inherited traits have their origins somewhere in the code of each individual's DNA.

ENZYME   a protein that facilitates a chemical reaction. Enzymes control the rate by which the body breaks down food.

GENE   the fundamental unit of heredity. A specific sequence of the four basic DNA chemicals comprising a segment of a chromosome. Genes express given traits by assembling amino acids to build specific proteins that determine life functions. Humans have as many as 100,000 genes, complete sets of which are found in every cell of the body.

GENE THERAPY   introducing normal genes into cells where abnormal genes have caused disease.

MARKER   a genetic signpost near a disease-causing gene, often inherited together. Markers can be used to predict the presence of the disease-causing genes.

NUCLEOTIDES   the chemical subunits of DNA. They come in four kinds: thymine [T], adenine [A], cytosine [C] and guanine [G]. Genetic material of all plants and animals consists of long chains of these four basic chemicals in specific order.

WHEN DOES GENE DOCTORING GO TOO FAR?

FRIDAY, MARCH 7, 1986

BY PETER GORNER AND JEFF LYON

The true fathers of gene therapy most likely will never win Nobel prizes. Their reputations have been badly damaged by what many view as premature, and thus unethical, attempts to cure fatal disease by giving patients new genes.

But the brouhaha stirred up by past attempts cannot compare with the maelstrom of controversy yet to come. Egos and expertise will clash like cymbals as the technology of gene splicing keeps racing along so fast that it laps ethical debates about what it all means.

The first pioneer to tangle with taboos over tinkering with genes was American virologist Stanfield Rogers, who in 1969 was studying a benign virus that produces warts in rabbits.

Rogers was fascinated by a phenomenon he discovered by accident: the virus, the Shope papilloma virus, somehow lowered the level of the amino acid arginine in the blood of laboratory workers who had been inadvertently infected.

Other than that, the workers suffered no ill effects. Hence, Rogers reasoned that anybody who happened to have too much arginine in his blood could theoretically be cured by the virus. However, he knew of no such people.

"We had uncovered a therapeutic agent in search of a disease," Rogers was to say later.

One day, though, Rogers was reading an account in a British medical journal that told of two young German sisters, aged 18 months and 5 years, who were desperately ill with seizures, palsy, and severe retardation—all because of too much arginine in their blood.

What would happen, Rogers wondered, if the papilloma virus were injected into the sisters' bodies?

In 1971, after having received permission from the girls' family and their physician, Rogers flew to Germany with a vial of virus. He had no idea how much the girls should be given and he and colleagues proceeded with caution. Too much caution, perhaps: "The dose of virus first used was about one-twentieth of that which we had previously found harmless to mice," Rogers later said.

"As might be expected from this tiny dose, no effect whatever was found in the condition of the children."

Subsequent attempts using slightly more virus were inconclusive. But before he could proceed any further, Rogers was capsized by a wave of professional criticism from colleagues who labeled his work rash and irresponsible. His funding dwindled, and chastened, he turned to studying viruses in plants.

No further experiments were tried for nine years. Then in 1980, Martin Cline, chairman of hematology at the University of California at Los Angeles, ignored the lesson that Rogers had so painfully learned.

Cline wanted to put healthy hemoglobin genes into patients suffering from beta thalassemia, a progressively fatal blood disorder. Without waiting for approval from his home university's human testing review committee, he flew to Israel and Italy, where he had already obtained permission to treat two young women.

Cline's results were similarly inconclusive, but while he was abroad, UCLA rejected his application, saying more animal work was needed before any human experiments were tried.

More trouble followed after the National Institutes of Health [NIH] found Cline in violation of federal guidelines as well, stripped him of $190,000 in grants [half his federal funding], and let him know he was on bad paper.

The furor was so great that Cline resigned as chairman of his department at UCLA.

The stories of Rogers and Cline underscore the ethical quandaries posed by the prospect of human gene therapy. Scientists no less than churchmen and politicians are troubled by our newfound ability to manipulate the genes of human beings and other organisms.

The controversies are many. A litany of agonizing issues must be resolved by society in coming years.

Among them are these:

• Safety. No one knows for sure what will happen when a new gene is put into a person. Premature experimentation runs the risk of unleashing something dangerous and irreversible into the human gene pool.

• Abortion. Medicine's enhanced ability to detect genetic diseases before birth will almost certainly lead to more abortions and political wrangling. In Illinois, for example, a controversial new law might forbid the most sophisticated prenatal testing unless it can be shown to be beneficial to the fetus.

• Body cell versus sex cell therapy. Body cell [or somatic] therapy affects only the patient whose disease is being treated. Sex-cell [or germline] therapy involves changes in the patient's sperm or egg cells that would be passed on to future generations and could cause cataclysmic changes in the species. The distinction has been called the Maginot Line of genetics.

• Eugenics. The ability to manipulate genes for medical purposes might prompt broader applications such as the intentional "improvement" of the human species. A variety of traits, ranging from intelligence and physical prowess to character and even ethnic type could conceivably be altered some day.

• Genetic screening. It will be possible to test children and adults for their inherited vulnerabilities to environmental hazards and diseases. This will have obvious benefits in terms of people being able to alter their lifestyle, but the benefits carry risks: If the information gets out to employers and insurance companies, serious civil rights issues could ensue.

"Gene therapy is not just a medical question," says Jeremy Rifkin, a Washington attorney who is the most vocal critic of genetic engineering.

Rifkin is scared silly by the ramifications of technologies that are about to leave the laboratory and enter the everyday world.

"Where do we draw the line?" asks Rifkin. "We'll want to eliminate Tay-Sachs disease, an early childhood killer. Heart disease can kill you at 20, emphysema at 60 and Alzheimer's at 80. All may be genetically induced. Would you say no to curing any of them? Probably not. But what about myopia [near-sightedness], a genetic trait? How about acne? At what point do we move from trying to cure horrible genetic diseases to trying to enhance genetic traits?

In Rifkin's mind, we are in quixotic quest of perfection.

"Immortality, that's what it is. We're trying to perfect our gene structure over the long run so that we never die. Do we really want to perfect ourselves in that way? That gets us into the area of eugenics and civilization, a very troubling possibility. That's the most impressive social question the human family has ever had to deal with, excepting the dropping of a nuclear bomb."

The mechanisms have been put in place for discussing these issues, believes Leroy Walters, a prominent Georgetown University ethicist who has been an active consultant to the federal government in creating the guidelines for the first gene therapy experiments.

"Gene therapy is a very promising approach, and initial applications to try it in humans will go through a public national review process," Walters says. "I think the most reasonable application will be to cure intractable diseases. What's important is that we protect individual freedoms and engage in public debate."

Basic safety concerns are paramount to Inder Verma, a renowned virologist at the Salk Institute for Biological Studies in La Jolla, Calif. Verma worries that the use of engineered viruses to ferry new genes into sick bodies raises the specter of runaway viruses. As the scientist who has helped design most of these delivery systems, Verma's fear is that a doctor may prematurely use the viruses to try to save a dying child.

"The viruses we make are innocuous, but not totally inert," Verma says.

The engineered virus itself probably would cause no trouble: "By itself, it can't do it," Verma says. "But let's imagine that there's another virus in the body. Could the two of them combine and spread to other tissues? I don't know. We need more animal testing to find out."

The revolutionary and perhaps perilous nature of the new therapy is being soft-pedaled to the public, some ethicists believe.

Says NIH bioethicist John Fletcher, who stresses that he is speaking for himself, not NIH: "The feeling is that we should try gene therapy and see if it will work. Because in essence it's not different from other kinds of new drug trials, or the use of human products [such as blood transfusions] for the first time. DNA [basic genetic material] is just another human product—so the thinking goes."

Such thinking is flawed, Fletcher says.

In fact, says bioethicist Mark Lappé, it's "short-sighted, unimaginative, and straight-out wrong."

Medicine, Fletcher and Lappé emphasize, has never treated genes before.

"There really is no assurance," says Lappé, "that the gene being replaced can be sufficiently targeted to go into the cell nucleus at just the right site so as to correct the defect in an ideal way. We don't know what will be the effect of putting novel genes in our chromosomes. They may inadvertently activate neighboring genes. They may set off oncogenes and cause cancer.

"So I see a dearth of imagination on the part of the bioethics community and researchers to fully anticipate all the ramifications for making this technique available for the first time. Instead the discussions have focused on minutiae and consent procedures for kids suffering from ADA [adenosine deaminase deficiency] or Lesch-Nyhan syndrome. Everyone is totally missing the really revolutionary nature of this therapy. They're trivializing it. Minimizing its impact."

But, predicts Lappé, "we'll probably just go ahead and try it anyway. We'll just make our mistakes as we attempt to find out if some of these tragic diseases can be miraculously cured."

Fletcher points out that "genetic burdens are among the most significant burdens that human beings have. The promise of treatment is absolutely thrilling to everyone in the field. There is a very strong consensus in virtually every quarter of ethics and religion that somatic cell gene therapy is ethically acceptable. At the same time, the power and control over a hitherto undisclosed area of life is foreboding—at least to people like me. It makes me very cautious."

What happened to Martin Cline and Stanfield Rogers, though, apparently could never happen again. No medical event will have been so carefully scrutinized as the first attempts at gene therapy.

Anyone who applies to try the procedure must follow federal guidelines, as well as the rules of the institution at which the experiment will be performed.

The thinking embodied in the guidelines and likely to be applied by those reviewing applications for experiments is straightforward:
• Only a life-threatening or horribly debilitating illness should be a

candidate for body-cell [somatic] gene therapy. The patient must have no other option.

• Doctors should fully understand the disease under consideration. They should be able to identify the specific genetic defect, as well as the course of biochemical events that make people sick.

• Adequate animal work must indicate the therapy is safe. The new gene must be deposited in the right target cells, and stay there. The gene also should make proper amounts of its product to do no harm to any cells.

• The experiment must be planned in such a way that even if results are not successful, scientists should have a good idea of why the failure occurred. Shots in the dark should not be tried.

Few, if any, controls exist, however, for a spin-off technology—prenatal diagnosis by means of fetal DNA testing. Anti-abortion activists fear that large-scale screening of the unborn for inherited illnesses will necessarily result in a greater number of abortions, which already total 1.5 million per year, the overwhelming majority of them for reasons other than genetic defects.

Scientists and doctors agree about the potential for broader prenatal diagnosis, but most don't fear the possibility. Nobel Prize-winning biologist David Baltimore, director of the Whitehead Institute, affiliated with the Massachusetts Institute of Technology, warns that society will soon have big choices to make.

"The real question is to what extent are we going to want to have children born with genetic diseases," Baltimore says.

"Within the next few years we will be able to identify nearly all children who are the potential recipients of deleterious genes in utero early enough to abort them."

Except for the perspective of those who are opposed to abortion, Baltimore believes, "it would be cheaper, more effective, and cause less pain and suffering to abort most cases of genetic lesions, rather than allow them to come to term, and then try to deal with their disease."

In the near future, Baltimore says, only families that are alert for individual genetic problems probably will avail themselves of the new tests.

"But eventually, we'll be able to survey the whole population. Because, increasingly, people are going to want to know whatever they can know about their inheritance when they have a child.

"When we find the genes responsible for cystic fibrosis, for example, I can imagine a desire to screen the entire adult population to see if they're carriers. Then, individuals would know whether it's worthwhile having amniocentesis done to check their children. It's solely a matter of how much money we're willing to spend once we've got those genes. And getting the genes is a technical problem, not a theoretical one."

In Illinois, legislators may have cast a shadow on the ability of geneticists to perform state-of-the-art prenatal diagnosis. Both Illinois houses recently overrode Gov. Thompson's veto of a bill that says: "No person shall sell or experiment upon a fetus . . . unless such experimentation is therapeutic to the fetus."

The law specifically says that it is "not intended to inhibit the performance of in-vitro fertilization," the laboratory mating of sperm and egg.

But Charles Strom, a University of Chicago physician and molecular researcher, says the bill's real effect may be to "severely cripple our ability to do genetics in this state." Strom serves as president of the Genetics Task Force of Illinois, mandated by the state "to foster the development and delivery of genetic services and research in Illinois."

Strom, women's groups and the American Civil Liberties Union believe that the new law may forbid prenatal diagnosis by a new—and experimental—technique called chorionic villus sampling [CVS].

With CVS, a bit of fetal genetic material is suctioned out of the mother within the first 10 weeks of pregnancy. The material can then be exposed to a variety of DNA probes to detect inherited diseases in time for a first trimester abortion.

"It's an incredibly vague law," Strom says. "What's experimental? CVS is an experimental procedure, of no benefit to the fetus."

If the fetus is defective, Strom asks, isn't the likely outcome an abortion?

"They've made it a right-to-life issue. I see it as an issue over whether the state is going to interfere with the right of geneticists to practice modern genetics."

One of the bill's sponsors, Rep. John O'Connell [D., Western

Springs] denies this was his intention. O'Connell, in fact, says he never heard of CVS.

He sponsored legislation, he said, after anti-abortion groups told him of reports that doctors in other states were doing laboratory experiments on human embryos ostensibly resulting from in-vitro fertilization.

O'Connell says he knows of no such experimentation going on in Illinois. Moreover, he says his bill was not designed to interfere with prenatal testing.

"Prenatal diagnois is not experimenting in my definition," O'Connell says. "That's a device used to ascertain the status of the child. As the law exists now, the mother has the option to either proceed or abort. It was not my intent that prenatal testing would be included under the term 'experimentation.' "

Lawyers for the ACLU are expected to challenge the constitutionality of the new law. Its effect on CVS remains to be determined.

So far, all talk of gene therapy involves body cells. If the technique works, though, a powerful impetus will exist to extend it to reproductive cells as well.

The day may come, for instance, when victims of fatal blood diseases can, through manipulation of their genetic material, be enabled to produce normal blood. But because the treatment would be aimed solely at their bone marrow cells [those that make blood] it presumably would not alter genes in their sperm or ova. The defect could still be passed along to descendants.

Should gene treatment stop at curing the patients? Or should patients have the right to ask that their children yet unborn be freed from the danger as well?

Conceivably, there are two major ways by which science may some day alter the sex cells in the body, or perform germline therapy, as it's called.

One way would be to selectively alter sex cells in an adult by somehow constructing a gene delivery system with an affinity for the sex glands.

The other would be a shotgun approach, altering all the cells at once. But the only way to do that would be to catch an individual very early—shortly after fertilization, when he was only a cluster of say, four or five embryonic cells. The altered cells would proceed to divide normally and eventually become a baby carrying the change in each of its cells.

Germline therapy, at least at the adult level, is a "straw man," says David Comings, a well-known geneticist at the City of Hope in Duarte, Calif.

"There's no rationale to try it," he says. "It would make sense to do it only on those people who have a 100 percent risk of having a child born with a genetic disease.

"Who runs such a risk? Only parents who are both victims of the same recessive disease."

Such parents would each have two defective genes, four of them between them. The child would have no chance of inheriting a healthy gene.

"But what recessive diseases are there that would allow victims to grow to adulthood and want to have children?" asks Comings. "Obviously, extraordinarily mild ones."

The other contemplated technique—germline therapy in a human embryo—makes no sense either, at least to virologist Inder Verma:

"In a body cell transplant, we're dealing with hundreds of like cells. If the new gene hits one of those genes that's making insulin, say, 99 others are still okay. But supposing we accidentally hit the insulin gene in a single-celled embryo. If we screw up that cell, everything that comes from it is screwed up."

Moreover, with current methods, the amount of invasion necessary to evaluate the condition of a newly fertilized egg would presumably destroy it, scientists say.

It may be possible some day to go into an embryo consisting of only a few cells and surgically alter individual genes. But to Verma and others, that day is very distant.

A thoughtful man, Verma often ponders the irony of the work that has made him a principal figure in the race to perform gene therapy:

"In these days when we have a million kids dying of malnutrition, it becomes a different ethic. I must say, coming from India, that I cannot be totally insensitive to these issues. Children in India die from lack of water. And here we are talking about bone marrow therapy and other exotic things."

Often overlooked in the body cell versus germline debate, says Mark

Lappé, is the possibility that bone marrow cells may also affect the germline.

"It's often forgotten that bone marrow is the home for many traditional cells for many organ systems, not just blood. It's possible that engineered bone marrow cells may find their way to the germline," Lappé says.

In his opinion, there is nothing essentially wrong with the idea of individual couples someday opting for germline therapy to erase a bad gene from a family: "Both somatic [body cell] and germline pose risks. What I object to is the head-in-the-sand attitude that flatly accepts one and rejects the other."

Perhaps the master of germline research in mammals is Ralph Brinster, a quiet biologist who works in the veterinary medicine college at the University of Pennsylvania in Philadelphia.

Brinster can put human genes into animals and get the genes to work. He does so by extracting the fertilized animal eggs and injecting engineered genes by using a tiny hollow glass needle less than the width of a human hair. Then he transplants the eggs into new mothers.

Most of his microinjection has been done with mice. The technique has been compared to being speared by a telephone pole, but Brinster's mouse eggs don't seem to mind.

In a typical experiment, after treating the eggs, he puts them into the uteri of ordinary mice, and babies are born 21 days later. The mouse pups look normal, but some of them will balloon to three times normal size. In every cell of their bodies, the gene for human growth hormone is doing its stuff.

Such "supermice" have brought great scientific fame to Brinster and his partner, Richard Palmiter of the University of Washington. The two have injected new genes, some of them human, into thousands of animals ranging from mice and rabbits, sheep, cows and pigs.

"Microinjection works best in mice." Brinster says. "Of the other species, the only animal we've done enough testing in is the pig, and it grows very little, if it grows at all."

Brinster insists that such gene transfers "are not a reasonable approach for humans in the forseeable future.

"On technical grounds alone I see no use for it—the genes don't work very often, only between 1 and 5 percent of the time. That's good enough for animal research, but you can't take 100 human eggs and expect to have only 1 or 5 survive with the gene.

"Moreover, it seems to me on the basis of past history that man has been very reluctant to tamper with his germline. Man has known for 2,000 years that he could breed good animals with good animals and make better ones but he hasn't done it to himself. He's known about artificial insemination for 40 years, but he hasn't used it to change any characteristics. Man in general is a lot smarter than a lot of people think he is."

In animals, though, the possibilities are awesome, Brinster says.

"It's true that you can learn things about genes in test tubes and by putting them into cells," Brinster says. "But you can only learn how a gene functions in *every* cell of the body by introducing it into the fertilized egg, and exposing it to all the developmental influences that occur over time.

"Microinjection lets us study how genes are controlled, and how to get them to work in a variety of tissues. By learning how the animal develops from the fertilized egg, we have a very powerful way to learn about cancer, for example."

It is suspected that cancer starts when an ordinarily dependable gene inexplicably goes awry.

"Now we have a system to put that gene, or little pieces of it, into animals and see how cancers develop," Brinster says. "I believe that someday everybody in the world will be affected by this kind of work."

The implications of Brinster's work, however, greatly concern Jeremy Rifkin. He once filed suit, in fact, to stop the federal government from using Brinster's techniques to try to genetically engineer pigs for faster growth.

"The question of changes in the code of life raises overwhelming long-term social issues," Rifkin insists. "You can't get around the question of eugenics. Nobody is suggesting the racial eugenics of Nazi Germany. The new eugenics is commercial—we want healthy babies. So it's not coming to us as a curse, but as a blessing.

"Moreover, there are no evil people involved. Nobody is trying to force us into any brave new world. Quite the contrary, I'd say. These scientists and doctors are trying to enhance our world and make a better one for us. They're a reflection of our culture. They're giving us what we want."

But, asks Rifkin, do we really know what we want? What criteria do we establish for perfect and imperfect genes?

"And which institution are we going to entrust with the ultimate authority to decide which genes should be engineered in, and which should be engineered out?"

Every animal breeder knows the value of hybrid vigor, Rifkin says.

"We each carry as many as 10 recessive traits for diseases that are essential in providing the viability of the species," Rifkin asserts. "If we begin to eliminate genetic diversity for short-term benefits, we do so at the expense of undermining the long-term vitality of the species. We become more efficient, but less fit. The reservoir of recessives is beneficial."

Sickle-cell anemia, he notes, is a recessive trait that also protects blacks against malaria. If one evolved in Africa, it was better to be anemic than to be dead.

Experts predict that the ability of medicine to compile genetic profiles to people also will kindle sparks.

Through computerized information bureaus, insurance companies and employers already are privy to private facts about our sex problems and family histories of epilepsy, heart disease and mental illness. A list of genetic vulnerabilities could easily go into the computer, too.

"Why should the company you work for groom you to be its president if you're going to get Alzheimer's disease at 60," says Rifkin.

"When screening becomes widespread, we'll see a nightmare," he predicts. "It will reshape our whole concept of constitutional rights and the relationship of the individual to the culture."

Rifkin's critics often accuse him of omitting people's common sense and good will from his doomsday scenarios.

Nobel laureate Paul Berg, for one, calls Rifkin, "a professional gadfly . . . with a commitment to prevent progress in genetic engineering."

Rifkin responds by noting that he does not oppose body-cell gene therapy, only germline: "Something very strange happens, though, whenever I try to raise these issues for debate. Scientists call me an alarmist because they can't yet do X, or Y, or Z. It's science fiction, they say. Forget it. Then a month later, the technology comes on line and I say let's debate it now. Then they say, 'You're too late. You can't put the genie back in the bottle.' There's never a magic moment when I can join this debate. I'm either too early or too late. It's weird. They won't let me play."

At least one recent precedent exists for society to have learned from overzealous mass genetic screening—that for sickle-cell anemia initiated by Congress and a number of states in the early 1970s.

Some states require blacks to be screened before they could get married or attend public schools. Many programs were not confidential and failed to educate people about the crucial difference between actually having the disease [0.3 per cent of blacks] and being a carrier of the sickle-cell trait [8 to 13 per cent].

Carriers generally are unaffected by the recessive disease. Only when two carriers have a child does that child stand one chance in four of getting sickle cell anemia.

Great confusion and fear occurred among many blacks, both about the disease itself and the motivations of whites who seemed so eager to help detect it and limit black reproduction.

However, about 750 children a year continue to be born with this devastating disease. Despite the sordid history of genetic screening, voluntary programs are likely to expand.

The reason for them has been eloquently stated by Ola Mae Huntley, of Los Angeles, whose words have resounded through genetics research. Huntley has five children, three of whom have sickle-cell anemia.

"At the time my husband and I married, we had never heard of sickle-cell anemia," she has said. "There were no tests to determine who were carriers of the genetic trait for sickling cells, and there was no genetic counseling."

For more than 25 years, Huntley watched doctors repeat the same procedures, same drugs, same promises of temporary relief from the life of misery her children have endured.

"Very little has changed," she said. "The current state of medical art is to treat the symptoms, but little has been done about treating the cause."

Huntley has expressed anger "at those well-meaning theologians and politicians who wish to curtail genetic engineering research.

"To them I would like to say: 'Until you have had intimate contact with those who have suffered or have yourself experienced the pain, strokes, seizures, and leg ulcers; the ridicule from peers, low self-esteem, desire to die, and diminishing hope for the future associated with sickle-cell anemia, do not deny me the right to decide for myself and my children whether to try the procedures.'

"So long as the proper guidelines are in place, the research should proceed. The possibility of an improved quality of life is worth the clinical trials."

GLOSSARY

AMNIOCENTESIS a technique for detecting genetic defects before birth. Fluid is withdrawn from the uterus during the 16th week of pregnancy. The fluid contains cast-off fetal cells that are grown in tissue culture for weeks, then analyzed.

CARRIER OF GENETIC DISEASE a person who possesses one defective gene for a trait together with its normal partner. Although the product of the defective gene may not be detectable, the gene can be transmitted to a carrier's children. Genetic disease will occur if the children also inherit a copy of the same recessive gene from the other parent.

CHORIONIC VILLUS SAMPLING a new method of prenatal diagnosis that allows detection of many fetal genetic defects as early as the 9th week of pregnancy, many weeks sooner than amniocentesis.

GENETIC ENGINEERING altering genetic material for the study of genetic processes, to correct defects, or to make hormones.

SICKLE-CELL ANEMIA a severe blood disease affecting blacks almost exclusively. It is caused by the mutation of a single chemical in the gene for beta-globin, one of the components of hemoglobin. Red blood cells containing abnormal hemoglobin become deformed into sickle shapes, blocking blood vessels and causing anemia, pain, leg ulcers, and even death.

THALASSEMIA a chronic and often lethal anemia found among people of Italian, Greek, or other Mediterranean descent.

AND SOON, THE FRUITS OF GENETIC MEDICINE

SUNDAY, MARCH 9, 1986

BY JEFF LYON AND PETER GORNER

Robert Ledley's latest invention looks like a Rube Goldberg device, what with its Geiger counter, plastic trays, robot arm and microwave oven, but in fact it is a technological marvel that is on the cutting edge of human genetics.

What biophysicist Ledley has wrought, in his workshop at Georgetown University Medical Center in Washington, D.C., is nothing less than the world's first Automatic Genetic Analyzer.

The AGA, as it's called, fills up half a room. Entirely automated, it can test a patient's DNA, or genetic material, for the presence of eight inherited diseases at once and do it ten times faster than a laboratory technician.

A diagnosis that would take months manually—such as whether a person is genetically susceptible to any of 100 different hereditary ailments or environmental hazards—can be done by the AGA in little more than a week. The cost would be only a few hundred dollars. The rewards in terms of prevention and peace of mind could be immeasurable.

Diagnostic tools like the AGA—and more sophisticated models to follow—are just one dividend of the molecular revolution in medicine that is going to transform the delivery of health care in the United States within the next several years.

The revolution, which has been ebulliently described by Arthur Riggs, chairman of the biology division of the City of Hope research hospital in Duarte, Calif., as "molecular paths to a disease-free society," is no figment, nor does it represent a sudden breakthrough.

It is the logical culmination of more than 30 years of dedicated tinkering with particles of nature so minute they resist observation by even the most sophisticated electron microscope, but which are so powerful that they control the destiny of all living things, be they protozoa or prime ministers.

These particles, the genes, are actually long chains of DNA. The key elements in the chain are four chemical subunits of DNA, called nucleotides, which may occur in an endless variety of combinations. Each gene contains a precise order, or sequence, of these nucleotides, which is, in essence, a code telling the cell how to make a particular protein. Proteins are the family of substances needed by the body for health and function.

When the fruit of this gene research is brought soon into general clinical use, the sick will find themselves wandering through a bazaar of exotic techniques and therapies for which they have been poorly prepared.

Perhaps the most dazzling will be gene therapy, the total cure of formerly irreversible genetic diseases by the insertion of new genes. But gene repair is just one of these awesome prospects. Others include:
• Cancer diagnosis and treatment by means of so-called "magic bullets," tiny laboratory products called monoclonal antibodies that seek and destroy tumors with the single-minded tenacity of a Royal Canadian mountie.
• Improvement of existing natural enzymes and hormones by "protein engineering," in which substitutions are made in an enzyme's amino acid building blocks that actually streamline its physiological performance. Similarly, enzymes may one day be invented that do not even exist in nature. The result, for patients whose genes produce deficient proteins, may be cures that actually go nature one better.
• The increased use of genetic engineering to turn common bacteria into miniature factories cranking out gobs of such scarce drugs as interferon, insulin, growth hormone, and TPA, a substance that dissolves the blood clots that cause heart attacks. The hope is that manufacturing costs can be lowered dramatically. New vaccines will also be mass-produced in this manner.

Among the first of these bold new technologies to confront the average person will be medicine's advanced capacity to screen people for genetically-based ills.

Machines like Robert Ledley's will greatly improve doctors' ability to test the unborn for the presence of rare inherited disorders, such as cystic fibrosis, phenylketonuria [PKU], muscular dystrophy and others.

Prenatal tests already exist for some 300 inherited or congenital disorders. The tests make use of samples of fetal cells and enzymes obtained via amniocentesis, in which a needle is inserted into an expectant mother's uterus, through her abdomen, and amniotic fluid is withdrawn.

The problem with current methods is that amniocentesis cannot be done before the 16th week of pregnancy, when enough amniotic fluid begins to accumulate. To make matters worse, the yield of fetal cells is generally small, hence there is another four-week wait while the cells multiply in culture.

By the time researchers have a large enough cell sample to work with, there are only a few weeks left in which the pregnancy can be terminated safely, should serious abnormalities be found in the fetus. Thus, there is not enough time to screen a fetus for more than a few genetic disorders. Manual DNA testing is labor intensive and quite slow.

Automated gene analysis, on the other hand, can subject fetal DNA to dozens of tests in rapid succession, and have the results back in a week.

If the technique is combined with a newer retrieval method, called chorionic villi sampling, which yields a large sample of fetal cells as early as the eighth week of pregnancy, a fetus can be screened for an entire battery of diseases in sufficient time for a first trimester abortion, if the parents so choose. It promises to be an inexpensive and efficient way to relieve much of the anxiety of pregnancy, for those without philosophical objections to abortion.

With the development of even newer and cheaper methods of obtaining fetal cells, such as extracting them from maternal blood, the door would be opened to routine mass screening of every fetus for serious inherited abnormalities.

Mass prenatal screening for beta thalassemia, the most common single-gene disorder in the world, is currently being carried out by the Italian government on the island of Sardinia, which has the highest incidence of the disease on earth.

But even more intriguing than prenatal screening is the potential for testing children and adults for future susceptibility to a host of common, genetically influenced conditions, including cancer, heart disease, diabetes, and neurological illness.

They can even be tested for their vulnerability to specific environmental toxins, such as asbestos, benzopyrene, naphthalene, and cyanide. The genes that enable us to detoxify many dangerous chemicals are being identified at an accelerating pace. A defect in one of these genes can be fatal.

For example, one in 15 asbestos workers has a genetic predisposition to asbestos-related cancer. His fellow employees are relatively safe. Similarly, there are people who are genetically susceptible to benzopyrene, common in the air in many factories. They are 26 times as likely to get lung cancer from it as others. Naphthalene, present in mothballs, is harmless to most people but causes severe anemia in a small percentage of blacks, Jews and Orientals. And atmospheric cyanide, prevalent in modern-day, polluted air, causes terrible symptoms in a percentage of the population genetically unable to tolerate it.

"Genetic screening has fantastic possibilities for giving people information about themselves," says Ledley, one of the nation's leading medical instrument designers, who also is responsible for developing the whole-body CAT scanner [which produces a three-dimensional X-ray].

Imagine this scenario. A young man comes in and has a small skin or blood sample taken. From this, his DNA is easily extracted. The DNA contains all of his 100,000 genes.

An automated gene analyzer like Ledley's then exposes the DNA to an extensive series of clinical "probes"—pieces of synthetic DNA that zero in on DNA segments of matching biochemical structure. Each probe has been designed to correspond to a gene associated with a particular disease.

Within a matter of days, an elaborate profile of the man's genetic endowment will be returned to his physician. The man might learn, for example, that he has a tendency to heart disease, arthritis, gout, and lung and bladder cancer; also that he is particularly susceptible to pesticides.

His physician would then be in a position to recommend major changes in the patient's lifestyle to minimize the man's chances of developing disease. Dietary restrictions and prohibition on smoking would be good places to start. The man would also be urged to stay away from employment, such as farm work, in which he would be exposed to pesticides.

"We are going to see a new emphasis on preventive medicine that will be very powerful," says Theodore Friedmann of the University of California, San Diego.

Most authorities stress, however, that patients' genetic profiles must be kept strictly confidential to avoid abuses that might occur if employers or insurance companies acquire the information.

Ledley's machine is also sensitive enough to reveal whether a person has only one bad copy of a disease gene. Where so-called recessive ailments are concerned, two bad copies must be inherited for the disorder to manifest itself. If only one is present, then the good version will manufacture enough of the vital protein to protect against disease.

However, the bad copy can still be passed along to one's children —and if one has had the misfortune of marrying somebody with the same bad gene, the child may inherit two copies and become a disease victim.

Thus, another valuable use of automated gene analysis will be to tell people whether they are silent carriers of certain diseases. Our hypothetical patient, for example, might learn that he carries the genes for cystic fibrosis and Hurler's syndrome, a disease marked by skeletal deformities, "gargoyle" facial features, severe retardation and early death. But a similar test on his wife might reveal that she carries neither gene, so there would be no reason to worry that their children might end up with either disease.

Ledley developed the automatic gene analyzer for An-Con Genetics, Inc., of Melville, N. Y., which began marketing the $100,000 device last year. As yet, not a single one has been sold, although at least one biotechnology firm, Collaborative Research Inc., of Boston, has expressed serious interest.

Collaborative hopes to be the first in the industry to offer a large-scale, nationwide DNA testing service for a variety of genetic diseases.

• • •

To offer such a service, however, Collaborative and similar firms will require a sizable bank of disease probes.

"The problem is we're a little ahead of the probes," admits Ledley. "A lot of genes have been found, so the probes exist, but they are still experimental. For actual clinical use, some company is going to have to manufacture them on a commercial basis. That's about a year away."

With the hardware now in hand for mass genetic screening, the software—probe technology—obviously becomes paramount. The more genes that can be uncovered that lead to disabling conditions, the better diagnosis will become.

As of this writing, only a few hundred disease genes are already in hand. But, according to gene archivist Victor McKusick of Johns Hopkins University, 1,500 more gene villains have been tentatively "mapped" to particular chromosomes, and it is just a matter of time before their sequences are determined.

Two areas of great progress involve genes that relate to heart disease and cancer. Answers to the mystery of both of these illnesses will ultimately be found at the molecular level—and such answers are tantalizingly close.

But genes that may be at fault in other tragic human ailments, including diabetes and various neurological and psychiatric disorders, are also the focus of an intensive search by dozens of laboratories worldwide. A review of progress in each of these areas is in accompanying stories.

It will be a number of years before the full shape of molecular medicine becomes apparent. The complete menu of therapeutic and diagnostic tools that will ultimately be available can only be guessed at.

Nevertheless, with science learning ever more about manipulating our genes and their respective proteins, it is clear that a medical revolution of monumental proportions is underway.

"I've lived through a miracle, I really have," says David Nathan, physician-in-chief at Boston Children's Hospital. "Is it a fast miracle? No. But we're doing things that I think are amazing compared to my internship in 1955 when absolutely none of these things were available.

"The field moves along. The experiments are being done by some terrific people, and my patients are going to be the beneficiaries of it. I'm absolutely certain of that. We're going to win. I don't know quite when, but we're going to win."

FOURTEEN

THE FALL OF THE HOUSE OF BINGHAM

1987 WINNER IN THE SPECIALIZED JOURNALISM CATEGORY

"For a distinguished example of reporting on such specialized subjects as sports, business, science, education, or religion . . ."

The New York Times
Alex S. Jones

One of the nation's great newspaper enterprises, led by Barry Bingham Sr., split up after seven decades amid feuding among Bingham family members. They presented their rigid positions to one another, and later they recounted them to Alex S. Jones. The result is a dramatic saga written, as Mr. Bingham described the articles later, "with sensitivity and understanding."

Trouble in the Bingham family—owners of the Louisville *Courier-Journal* and *The Louisville Times*—became a story for me a year before the final breakup and sale of the companies in January 1986.

A friend had alerted me to rumors that Sallie Bingham, the oldest Bingham daughter, was so angry with her brother and with the family in general that she was going to sell her holding of approximately 15 percent, and she didn't much care whether it was to the family or to an outsider.

Sallie confirmed this, and welcomed the chance to spread the news via *The New York Times,* complete with detailed balance sheet information.

During the winter and spring of 1985, I met with Sallie in New York and Louisville on a couple of occasions, and she would describe her frustration with what she regarded as the family's sexist treatment of her, and her hopes that she would be able to sell her interest for a very handsome price.

That all the family enterprises would be sold seemed extremely unlikely. Sallie had been unable to persuade her younger sister, Eleanor, to also put her shares on the market, and the other family members had united in a voting trust.

Sallie seemed not to know what the other members of the family were up to, and they weren't talking to the press. But from the outside, the likely outcome seemed to be that the family would put a few more dollars on the table than an outsider would bid, Sallie would eventually be bought out and the stout Bingham ship would sail on.

In a stunning turn, that scenario proved to be all wrong.

Although I had an afternoon deadline on a story about journalists riding on an upcoming space shuttle, I went to lunch with a friend on Thursday, January 9, 1986. I returned to the newsroom about 2 P.M. and was pecking away at my word processor when I received a phone call from a friend who had connections in Louisville.

"Jesus Christ," he said. "The Binghams are selling out!"

That set in motion a frantic afternoon of phone calls and hurried writing that lasted well into the evening. The *Courier-Journal* and *The Louisville Times* were such celebrated newspapers, and the family such a famous one, that Abe Rosenthal, then executive editor of *The Times*, and other editors decided to place the story on the front page in Friday's edition.

Along with the story, *The Times* published the texts of the poignant announcements by Barry Bingham Sr. and Barry Bingham Jr.—father and son—that had been posted side-by-side at the papers.

Barry Sr.'s statement said, with regret, that the family businesses were to be sold, and that part of the reason for the decision was disagreement within the family.

Barry Jr., who had been running the businesses for the family since 1971, was much more blunt, and clearly devastated. He said that his father's decision was irrational and a betrayal, and he resigned.

The next morning, I caught the first plane out of New York bound for Louisville. My mission was to do a piece for Monday about the impact on Louisville of a change in ownership of such distinguished papers after so many years.

When I called my office to check in about noon, I was told that the editors of the Sunday Business section also wanted a long, in-depth article for the following week that would tell in detail what had led to the sale of the companies. I was told by Fred Andrews, the business editor, to write and write and write.

I had never met any of the Binghams except Sallie, but I immediately recognized Barry Jr. from photographs I had seen of him. His heavily waxed regimental moustache was in place when I walked into his office about 1 P.M., but his eyes were red, apparently from strain and lack of sleep. He was not a man to weep.

We spoke for an hour or so. He was very courteous and correct but eager for his anger and point of view to be understood. He then excused himself to go to a meeting of the staffs of the two newspapers that had gathered in the company cafeteria. It was to be the first such gathering since the announcements were put up the day before.

He left me, and I wandered down the hall, then joined the morose and frightened people heading for the cafeteria.

It was packed, and the staff meeting became such an emotional moment that I described it in the lead of the article I wrote for the Sunday Business section. After the speeches ended and the applause died, I lingered to talk with the employees who seemed thunderstruck at the notion of a *Courier-Journal* and *Louisville Times* that were not Bingham-owned.

Later, I drifted back to the executive floor, where Barry Bingham Sr. had his office just down the corridor from his son's.

Looking tired, Barry Sr. received me warmly. He also seemed eager to explain what had happened.

For the next six days, I interviewed and wrote almost nonstop. I was holed up in an increasingly chaotic room at the Hyatt Hotel, where I had a computer and a phone.

That weekend I wrote the piece about the sale's impact on Louisville and also finished the shuttle article that I had underway when I learned of the sale. Then I turned to the big piece.

At first, most of the time was spent rushing out to interviews, talking to Binghams and members of the staffs of the companies until they wouldn't sit still any longer, and contacting by phone other people who I thought could shed light on the story. My practice is to take notes on yellow pads, and my room quickly filled up with stacks of stapled paper. Across the top of the first sheet, I wrote the name of the person I had interviewed, and as the week wore on, I had to number the piles to indicate which of the sometimes multiple interviews with the same person the stapled sheets represented.

On Monday night, I began to write.

That night I wrote the first draft of the introductory section of the article. My writing method was to sit in front of the computer, surrounded by cigarette butts, paper and trays of half-eaten food, and try to concentrate. Hours pass quickly in such a state.

The days were used for interviewing, the nights reserved for writing. On Tuesday night, I wrote the final section of the story that began with the return to Louisville of the Bingham sisters in the late 1970s.

On Wednesday night, I wrote the heart of the story—about the family. That took all night, and I was consuming cigarettes and iced tea furiously, much to the confusion of the bell clerks, who by then were delivering such supplies by the trayful.

When I tried to sleep, I would get only short spurts of rest because I was frequently waking up to write notes to myself about things to check, questions to ask, words to change.

Finally, at about 5 A.M. on Thursday, I finished the article, which was then about 8,000 words, roughly twice what my editor had given me as an upper limit.

With a satisfaction perhaps only another journalist could understand, I called my wife, Susan Tifft, who is also a journalist in New York, to tell her that I didn't know what anyone else thought, but I was sure I had just finished the best thing I had ever written. She was kind enough to stifle her yawns and listen to me roll on and on.

On Thursday morning, I sent the whole package to New York, caught a plane home and slept for about 14 hours.

I arrived at *The Times* Friday morning to find that the Sunday Business staff was as excited about the piece as I had been and was scrambling to make more space available. Lou Uchitelle and Soma Golden, the editors, decided to eliminate a graph illustration and to kill an advertisement to make more room.

At 6 P.M., the deadline for the Sunday Business section, we all went to the composing room to watch the story being pasted up on the pages.

It was too long, despite the added space and cuts that had brought the piece to 6,500 words. We trimmed a photograph, shortened a headline, but it was still too long. A paragraph came out here. One there. Finally it was finished, and the section closed.

I went to dinner with my wife that night. We planned to fly early the next morning to visit my family in Tennessee, a family like the Binghams in that it was Southern and, after many generations, still in the newspaper business. The Binghams' story was a nightmare to newspaper families such as mine, and for that reason its telling was all the more intensely important to me.

On the way home from the restaurant, I stopped by *The Times* and picked up a couple of freshly printed copies of that Sunday's Business section—something to read on the flight to Tennessee.

—Alex S. Jones
The New York Times

THE FALL OF THE HOUSE OF BINGHAM

SUNDAY, JANUARY 19, 1986

BY ALEX S. JONES

LOUISVILLE—"It's a sad day for all of us," said Paul Janensch, executive editor of the Courier-Journal and The Louisville Times, hoarsely addressing several hundred somber co-workers who had jammed the company cafeteria to consider their uncertain future. It was 3 P.M. on Friday, Jan. 10, the day after the abrupt announcement that the Bingham family, the glamorous and tortured clan that had owned the newspapers for almost 70 years, was selling out.

The decision to sell was a shock, but not a surprise. For two years the staff had watched as the Binghams warred with each other over the family holdings. Finally, in desperation, Barry Bingham Sr., the 79-year-old patriarch, decided to sell, hoping that his decision would somehow bring a semblance of peace to the family. What it brought initially was a blistering accusation of betrayal from Barry Bingham Jr., the son who has run the family companies since the early 1970's.

Barry Jr. resigned in anger and was in the cafeteria to speak. "In my proprietorship here," he said, "I've tried to operate these companies so that none of you would be ashamed of the man you work for."

When he had finished, the employees rose as one in a standing ovation. Many wept. But the applause was not entirely for Barry Jr., it was also for his stand against selling. And the tears were for themselves, for the uncertain future of the newspapers, for the tragedy of the Binghams and for the passing of an era.

News of the sale prompted a flood of expressions of grief, mostly from Kentuckians, mourning the end of the Bingham stewardship. Under the Binghams, the Courier-Journal won eight Pulitzer Prizes, establishing the newspaper as one of the finest in America.

For large families struggling with the problems of multi-generational ownership of a business, the saga of the Binghams and their failure to hold together was particularly poignant. And for the dwindling number of families still operating their own newspapers, the news from Louisville was chilling.

For the proud Binghams—a clan of southern patricians who are often compared to the Kennedys because they share a history of tragic death and enormous wealth—the pain of selling was redoubled because it may have been avoidable. It is not financial duress forcing the sale, but implacable family strife, as ancient as the struggle between Cain and Abel.

A week of interviews with the key family members, with many of their employees and with their friends has revealed the details of the Bingham family feud. From the interviews comes a portrait of a family both hugely blessed and critically flawed, a family caught in a dispute that it was unable to resolve.

"It became increasingly clear that there was just no way out of the emotional tangle we'd fallen into," Barry Sr. said. "In bringing up my children, I somehow did not get across to them that people have to make compromises."

In the drama, there is no single villain, nor a hero or healer who might have bridged the gulf of distrust and anger. In the end, a powerful gridlock developed among the three Bingham children— Barry Jr., Sallie and Eleanor. Their parents, convinced that no amicable way could be found to keep the business in the family, elected to sell all the holdings. It was a decision that Barry Sr. said he made now so that he and his 81-year-old wife could face the trauma together.

In part, the roots of the crisis may lie in the family's enormous wealth that allowed the Bingham children to grow up in what Sallie calls a "golden dream," creating a generation of Binghams used to their own way. The parents' insistence on unruffled family relations and their distaste for overt emotion left Barry Jr. and his sisters without the need to forge deep relationships with each other as children— relationships they might have called upon to resolve their impasse as adults.

Running through the Binghams' story are the devastating deaths of two sons. The death of Worth Bingham, the first-born, haunted Barry Jr., who eventually took over stewardship of the newspapers, the role intended for his older brother. In recent years, Barry Jr.'s devastating sense that he was losing the family's confidence seemed to make him dig in his heels so rigidly that he invited the decision to sell—perhaps, as Sallie says, in an unconscious wish to be delivered of his burden.

Sallie, now a determined feminist, emerged as a chief protagonist in the saga. Her resistence to Barry Jr.'s decision to remove her from the boards of the family businesses set in motion what became the final crisis.

At the end, even Eleanor, the younger and more conventional sister, who had tried to maintain her family ties, opposed her brother—as implacable in her way as the others.

Now that the decision to sell has been made, a number of media companies are competing to buy the Bingham properties—The Courier-Journal and Louisville Times Company, WHAS Inc., which includes a television station and two radio stations, and Standard Gravure, a commercial printing operation. They are expected to bring about $400 million, with the families of each of Barry Sr.'s children likely to receive about $40 million (see box).

But the family peace that Barry Bingham Sr. and his wife, Mary, hoped for seems far, far away.

THE HISTORY

"Scale the characters down, and it's definitely Faulknerian," said Robert Bingham, the 19-year-old grandson of Barry Sr., comparing his family to the tortured Mississippi delta families of William Faulkner's novels.

Just as Faulkner's fictional characters plumb the past seeking explanations for the pain of the present, the Binghams tend to look far back to pick up the threads of their undoing.

The Binghams, like the Kennedys, started poor, certainly in comparison with their present great wealth. Barry Sr.'s great-great-grandfather, a Scotch-Irish immigrant, founded the Bingham School, a secondary school, in North Carolina shortly after the American Revolution. Barry Sr.'s great-grandfather was also a teacher; so was his grandfather, Robert Bingham, a Confederate soldier, who returned to North Carolina after the Civil War and worked at educating freed slaves.

But Robert's son, Robert Worth Bingham, became a lawyer and moved to Louisville in 1896, at the age of 25, eventually becoming the city's mayor and a circuit court judge. He lost his first wife in 1913 when a car in which she was riding was hit by a train. Barry Sr.

was seven years old when his mother died; his brother and sister not much older.

Three years later, Judge Bingham, as he was then and forever after known, married Mary Kenan Flagler, the widow of an oil tycoon with a $100 million estate. Judge Bingham signed a pre-nuptial agreement stating that, upon her death, he would receive $5 million from her estate. As Barry Sr. tells the story in a memo to his children, Judge Bingham insisted on the pre-nuptial agreement, even though without it he would have been entitled to half his wife's fortune.

Eight months after their wedding, the new Mrs. Bingham died, apparently of cardiac arrest. But her brothers accused Judge Bingham and her doctors of conspiring to poison her and the body was exhumed. An autopsy revealed that the cause of death was, indeed, cardiac arrest, and her brothers dropped the charges.

In 1918, Judge Bingham bought, for $1 million, a majority interest in the Courier-Journal and The Times, which even then were Kentucky's premier newspapers. He also acquired a 40-acre estate overlooking the Ohio River, a few miles outside Louisville, and on it a huge red-brick Georgian mansion where Barry Jr. now lives. Judge Bingham christened the estate "Melcombe," after an estate in Dorset, England, where Binghams had lived since the 12th century. The judge had another house built on the estate, which, though generous, was smaller than the mansion and came to be called the "Little House." Barry Sr. and his wife Mary live there today.

The judge was an ardent Democrat and a supporter of the League of Nations, and his newspapers reflected his views. In the 1930's, he backed the New Deal and President Roosevelt rewarded him in 1933 with the ambassadorship to the Court of St. James. Judge Bingham died in London in 1937 and the next ambassador was Joseph Kennedy.

By then, Judge Bingham's younger son, Barry Sr., a magna cum laude graduate of Harvard, was deeply immersed in the family business, which had grown to include WHAS Inc.—then an AM radio station—and Standard Gravure. He alone had moved back to Louisville; his brother and sister spent most of their lives in England and Barry Sr. soon bought them out.

He was 32 years old when his father died, a handsome, garrulous and charming man with a cello voice, and he had married Mary

Clifford Caperton, a Richmond girl whom he had met while he was at Harvard and she at Radcliffe. The two are very close. Barry Sr. says that he decided to sell the family companies now rather than later so that he and his wife, who is 81 years old, could face the ordeal together. "It would have been almost impossible alone," he says.

In fact, Barry Sr. says that his successful marriage and the extremely close relationship with his wife somehow contributed to what he says was his clear failure to communicate effectively with his children.

Under Barry Sr., known simply as "Senior" to his employees, the family business flourished as Louisville boomed with new industry in the post-war years and Kentucky prospered as a coal mining and tobacco center. But the Courier-Journal and The Times, in the Southern liberal political tradition, frequently supported positions that put the papers in conflict with their more conservative readers. In their columns, labor unions found strong support and strip miners were blasted for not restoring the land.

But it was the strong stand in favor of civil rights that drew the most controversy. Barry Sr. says that one of his proudest accomplishments was that Louisville had the South's first integrated school system, a victory won largely without violence—but at a price.

"I came to Louisville in 1964," said Mr. Janensch, the papers' executive editor, "and Senior was not a beloved figure then. The Binghams were considered the liberal elite. The papers were despised as Communist. And the image of the Binghams was that they were not at all concerned with common people. Patronizing." It was only in recent years that Barry Sr. emerged in Louisville as a popular elder statesman.

THE CHILDREN

For his children, life was very easy. The Binghams, Sallie recalls, had five servants, including a particularly beloved nurse called Nursie by Sallie and her two older brothers, Worth and Barry Jr.

"There was no other family like it," says Sallie, who adds that she remembers a family sense of being liberals under attack; of being somehow "much better looking" than other people, and of being free of the burden of "time wasted on petty boring details." These were handled by the servants and company managers. It was a family, Sallie says, in which the highest priority was placed on an absence of friction and conflict, where troublesome details of day-to-day living simply were taken care of "like magic."

She now blames what she calls the family's "smoothness" for producing a generation of children who did not have to depend on each other, and, in the case of Sallie, Barry Jr., and the youngest child, Eleanor, never created the close ties that often come with the give-and-take of childhood.

"We all seem to have some inhibitions about each other; it's very hard to express to each other the way we feel sometimes," Barry Sr. says, somewhat ruefully. The Binghams, he says, might have been "much better off if we'd been a more Latin-type family with a lot of outbursts, tears, screams and reconciliations. But that has not been the way any of us operates."

The first-born of this special family was Robert Worth Bingham 3d, as handsome and garrulous as his father and clearly heir to the top spot in the family kingdom. Barry Sr. describes Worth, who was born in 1932, as a natural athlete, a natural newspaperman, a natural leader who loved mixing with politicians and other powerful figures.

He was also a reckless, profane and overbearing personality, according to Sallie and others who were close to him. He loved to take risks, as though the family's seamless lifestyle had cheated him of being tested. As a young man he delighted in fast driving and in trips to Las Vegas, where his losses sometimes forced him to make urgent calls to the non-family executives who managed the Bingham holdings, asking them to replenish his bank account and not tell his parents. He was one of the Louisville businessmen who originally syndicated Muhammad Ali, then a young Louisville boxer named Cassius Clay.

Worth's younger brother by 16 months was Barry Jr., a very different, less daredevil personality. Barry Sr. remembers his second son as having been "a merry little boy," thoroughly devoted to his older brother, as Barry Jr. himself confirms. Despite Barry Jr.'s near adoration, Worth teased his brother relentlessly. For instance, Barry Jr. was overweight until he went to college, and Worth delighted in introducing him as "Belly," rather than Barry.

Even so, Barry Jr. says that he was quite content to grow up in Worth's shadow. Explaining Barry Jr.'s yearningly tender feelings for his brother, Sallie says that Nursie once told her of a time when Worth and Barry were quite small and were gazing together at the night sky at Melcombe. "You can have the moon and all the other stars," Barry told his older brother, "but just let me have the evening star."

Sarah Bingham, whom the family called Sallie, was born in 1937 and was quickly recognized as the writer in the family, sending poems to her father during World War II and carefully printing them in a red leather book that he sent to her from London and that she still has.

Sallie says she always considered herself to be an outsider, a person apart from Worth and Barry, who were nearly inseparable. It was only later, she said, that she came to realize—and to resent—that she had been groomed by her parents for a supportive, woman's role, in contrast to her brothers, for whom management positions in the family business were assumed.

But as a child she grew particularly close to her father, and he to her, in part because she did not go away to prep school, as did her brothers. Night after night, Barry Sr. would read to her from the works of Dickens and Mark Twain. As a writer, "she was always very productive," he says. "She's a strong person and her feelings have been strongly expressed through the years."

The two other children, Jonathan, born in 1942, and Eleanor, in 1946, were raised almost as a second generation of children within the family. "Jonathan was probably the most brilliant intellectually of all," Barry Sr. says. A quiet child, he seemed drawn to science and medicine, while Eleanor was active, outgoing and gregarious. "She's never been the lonely, artistic person that Sallie was almost from the beginning," the father says.

In the Bingham tradition, Worth and Barry graduated from Harvard, and Sallie from Radcliffe, magna cum laude. Eleanor graduated from the University of Sussex, drawn to England as her aunt and uncle had been.

At college, Sallie had unusual success as a writer, and by 21 she had a three-book contract with Houghton-Mifflin. A novel, "After Such Knowledge," was published in 1959. In 1960, one of her short stories was selected for a collection of "Forty Best Stories From Mademoiselle," and she seemed headed for a successful writing career. She married and moved to New York, with no intention of involving herself in the family business or returning to Louisville.

Worth and Barry Jr. also were on their way. By the early 1960's, Worth was working at the newspapers. Barry Jr., who had slimmed down as a rower at Harvard and in the Marines, had developed a taste for broadcasting. He had worked as a broadcast journalist for CBS and NBC, then returned to Louisville at his father's urging to work at WHAS.

Jonathan had dropped out of Harvard and soon after, in 1964, tragedy struck—the first of the Bingham family misfortunes that draw comparisons with the Kennedy clan. Living in Louisville again, Jonathan climbed a utility pole to tap electricity into a barn at Melcombe; his intent was to illuminate a reunion of the members of his boyhood Cub Scout troop. When he tried to make the connection, he was electrocuted. He was 22.

Two years later, Worth, age 34, was driving a rented car with his wife, Joan, and their two children early one morning during a vacation in Nantucket. To accommodate a surfboard, the windows of the car had been rolled down and the long surfboard protruded from both sides of the car. When Worth drove too close to a parked car, the right end of the surfboard struck the car. The surfboard, in a snapping pivot, broke Worth's neck, killing him with a sort of karate chop.

For Mary Bingham and Barry Sr., whose brother and sister had passed away in the two years between Jonathan's and Worth's deaths, the tragedies were incalculable. "There were times that I wondered if I would be able to keep on," Barry Sr. says. "Nature helps, and I drew great strength from the church." As always, he depended heart and soul on his wife.

But no one was more devastated by Worth's death than Barry Jr., Sallie says. "He sobbed and cried at Worth's funeral; it was absolutely heart breaking."

Until Worth's death, the assumption was that he would eventually take over the newspapers, while Barry Jr. would operate the broadcast and printing companies. But at his father's invitation, Barry Jr. moved to the newspapers and in 1971, when his father retired his operating control and became chairman, Barry assumed the titles of editor and publisher, and took operating command of WHAS and Standard Gravure.

That same year, 1971, Barry Jr. learned that he had Hodgkin's disease, a form of lymph cancer that had killed his grandfather, Judge Bingham. After months of chemotherapy, the cancer went into remission and has not reappeared.

But Barry Jr. was much changed from the merry boy the family knew as a child. Rail-thin and quite reserved, he became extremely cautious and, at times, rigidly inflexible—traits that played a decisive role at critical stages in the later crisis over the family holdings. He seemed to take great pleasure in the untroubled solitude of cutting wood on the family estate or in a hunting trip with a close friend.

Barry Jr., who is known to his employees as "Junior," acknowledges that he changed as a result of Worth's death and his own potentially fatal illness. But he says another reason for his austere, somewhat beleaguered manner was the burden of presiding over drooping newspaper and printing companies. "You have to have a certain personality to manage in decline," he says.

The Courier-Journal and The Louisville Times had a combined daily circulation of about 408,000 in 1973, their peak year. By last September that had fallen to 304,000, with advertising lineage down almost as dramatically. A flat Louisville economy and the steadily increasing cost of maintaining the Courier-Journal's statewide circulation—it is the only daily circulated in every Kentucky county—added to the difficulty. So did the trend of American newspapers away from costly Sunday magazines, which Standard Gravure specialized in printing.

Profits at the Bingham companies reached a low ebb in the 1970's, of below 10 percent of revenues, and though they have rebounded, to about 12.6 percent in 1984, according to figures compiled by Henry Ansbacher Inc., all of the companies are below industry profit margins.

But while fighting a defensive economic battle, Barry Jr. mounted an aggressive one in news coverage, winning, since 1971, three of the newspapers' eight Pulitzer Prizes, and maintaining at great expense the Courier-Journal's statewide reach.

Very much in the family's liberal tradition, Barry Jr. also took pride in the newspapers' support of court-ordered busing, a position that infuriated Louisville's other leaders. And he imposed rigid—some observers say too rigid—conflict-of-interest standards on his staff. He is a man who refuses to socialize with politicians, lest he be perceived as playing favorites or chilling his staff's reporting. As a result, he is considered to be somewhat isolated and aloof in Louisville. The tributes from people in Kentucky carried in the newspapers following the sale announcement spoke fondly of Barry Sr. None mentioned Barry Jr.

And Barry Jr. struggled to live up to his dead brother Worth. Barry Sr. says that his son is terribly burdened by the myth that has grown up around Worth, a myth that compares Barry Jr.'s performance as head of the family business with what Worth might have accomplished.

In Barry Jr.'s view, the heaviest burden has been to endure a sense that "the family was losing faith" in him. "The family becoming more critical and less supportive," he says, "that's the most debilitating experience."

His mother, Mary, says she may have been the source for a disproportionate share of Barry Jr.'s sense of being assailed by the family—because of her letters-to-the-editor opposing the paper's editorial positions and her defiance of Barry Jr.'s objection to her appointment to a state environmental commission. "I think I've been more outspoken about things I don't like," she says. "I have very positive ideas."

THE SISTERS RETURN

It was into this volatile atmosphere, overlaid with a veneer of Bingham smoothness, that Sallie and Eleanor returned to Louisville after many years away from home. With their arrival, the stage was set for the drama that led to the decision to sell the family business— a decision that might have been avoided if one of the family could have played the role of a healer. But, as Barry Sr. laments, there was not an effective healer among them.

Sallie came home from New York in 1977 "to be a little safer for a while," she says, after suffering "complete demoralization." She had three children, but her second marriage had broken up, and she was frustrated by a stalled writing career. "She needed some family support," Barry Jr. said, "and I certainly was willing to be part of the family to support her."

But Barry Jr. and his sister had never been close. In fact, they had barely seen each other in 25 years, and they continued to go their separate ways: Barry immersed in the struggle to reverse declining advertising revenue and circulation, and Sallie involved with her children, writing plays and teaching.

Eleanor came back in 1978, from California. In the decade since college, she had worked on a series of video documentaries, some financed by dividends that came each year to all family members. But a favorite project, a broadcast showing the inner workings of the Ku Klux Klan that was aired on public television, did not result in a network job, as she had hoped, and she returned to work at WHAS.

Barry Sr. made Sallie, then over 40 years old, and Eleanor, in her early 30's, voting members of the boards of the family's three companies. Sallie says they viewed the appointments with delight and terror, having always regarded the businesses with awe. Barry Sr. also made Barry Jr.'s wife, Edith, a board member.

For the businesses to survive under family ownership for another generation, Barry Sr. decided that his two daughters needed to be involved; otherwise they might lack an emotional commitment to preserve family ownership. Still, neither of the daughters was considered for management jobs by Barry Sr., who said they had never shown an interest in such roles. Sallie disagrees. She says she came to the bitter realization that the family was infused with an unspoken, perhaps even unconscious, assumption that management of the family businesses was men's work.

No one in the family can precisely date when relations between Sallie and Barry Jr. began to sour, but a frequently mentioned benchmark of bad feeling was publication in 1979 of an article in Louisville Today, a local magazine, headlined "The Bingham Black Sheep." In it, Sallie went public with some matters the family considered very private, including her resentments about the sexism she saw in the family and "the emotional distance separating both she and Eleanor" from Barry Jr.

Not long afterwards, Barry Sr. intervened to have Sallie made book editor, a job her mother had once filled. Barry Jr. says he had no objection to Sallie's becoming book editor, although he "disagreed on method." The woman who had held the job was moved to another post.

Tensions heightened when Sallie wrote a letter to the editor assailing Barry Jr.'s endorsement of a political candidate, and, according to Barry Sr., their relationship came to be one fundamentally of suspicion and lack of confidence. "The family has a way of making it difficult for each other," Barry Jr. says. "When your sister writes a letter to the editor denouncing the editor's endorsement, that doesn't make it any easier for you."

At board meetings, Sallie says that she asked questions—sometimes pointed ones about the poor performance of the family's printing operations—but she never cast a negative vote. Barry Jr., she said, "was completely silent at board meetings." Though there was no overt conflict, the tension between brother and sister was apparent to all.

Barry Jr.'s frustration finally surfaced a few days before Thanksgiving 1983 when Barry Sr. summoned his daughters to the Little House. He told them that Barry Jr. had issued an ultimatum: either the women family members left the boards of the three family companies or Barry Jr. could no longer go on managing them.

The elder Binghams, the sisters, Worth's widow, Joan, and the non-family management staff pleaded with Barry Jr. not to insist on his sisters' removal, fearing a catastrophe. But Barry Jr. was adamant. The women, he said, had to go to make room for experienced professionals. In addition, he said, the women family members were making no contribution.

"There were board meetings when my wife was doing needlepoint, one sister was addressing Christmas cards, and one sister didn't bother to attend," Barry Jr. says.

To Barry Sr. it seemed clear that Barry Jr.'s goal was to purge Sallie from the boards, not so much for what she had done, but for what Barry Jr. was convinced she would do. "He felt she would be very critical of him," Barry Sr. says. "He strongly suspected she would undermine him."

In this period, Barry Jr. also offered to turn over management of the companies to what came to be called "a regency" of non-family professional managers, but his father argued that the companies might as well be sold if the Binghams were not going to manage them.

"He just communicated desperation," Sallie says of Barry Jr. "He looked like someone pleading to be let off somehow," contributing to her feeling now that Barry Jr. unconsciously wanted to be relieved of his burden, but did not want to be the one to force a sale.

Barry Sr. and his wife decided that, like it or not, the women had to resign from the boards as a demonstration of support for Barry Jr., who bore the burden of management on their behalf. But Sallie, bolstered by a feminist assertiveness, refused to resign.

Sallie remembers her decision to resist as a turning point in her life. "My mother has a tongue that just will take your skin off," Sallie said, recalling a moment when she says her mother accused her of "trying to destroy your brother."

But Sallie did not back down. "She said," Sallie recalls, " 'Don't you care what we think about you?' and I finally was able to say, at 47, 'No, I really don't,' and mean it."

At the shareholders' meeting in March 1984, Eleanor, Mary and Barry Jr.'s wife, Edith, resigned. Sallie was voted off the boards, and remembers watching the votes being counted against her as a searing humiliation. Two or three days later, Sallie says her mother called her and suggested they go to a movie. Sallie says she responded that the two of them could not simply go on as before. Sallie and her mother have not spoken to each other since.

But Barry Sr. and top officials consider the removal to have been an extremely damaging tear to the family fabric that ultimately led to the sale.

Sallie made the first move, telling the family in July 1984 that she wished to sell to them all of her interest in the businesses. With her consent, the family asked Lehman Brothers, an investment banking firm, to appraise the companies to determine their market value and the value of her approximately 15 percent interest. Lehman Brothers finally established a value for her shares of between $22 million and $26.3 million.

Sallie considered the valuation too low, and announced publicly last January that she would consider selling to outsiders. She hired Henry Ansbacher Inc., a New York investment banking firm specializing in the sale of communications companies, to seek a buyer, and Ansbacher estimated the value of her holdings at more than $80 million.

Barry Jr., meanwhile, had begun to feel that he had lost the confidence of the rest of the family. He was suspicious of "the air of celebration" that accompanied his decision to go on a nine-month sabbatical in September 1984 to be with his wife while she completed courses for a degree from Smith College in Massachusetts. It turned out to be a relaxing interlude and he returned refreshed. "But almost immediately he stepped back into all the old pressures," his father says, "tightening up almost week-by-week."

Relations also began to sour between Barry Jr. and Eleanor, who remained friendly with Sallie while supporting her parents and brother. Last February, Eleanor sent Barry Jr. a letter in which, he says, she "told me she was disinterested in staying in any company with me as the head and her dependent on dividends."

The growing division between brother and sisters gave rise in March to a "stock swap" plan in which Barry Jr. would exchange his interest in WHAS for Eleanor's interest in the newspapers, leaving each with a property to run. Eleanor had said she wanted to own and operate something, and, if Sallie could be bought out, the struggle for control could end.

With the stock swap plan on the table, Barry Sr. tried to pressure his children into compromise by issuing what he titled the "13 commandments," a list of directions regarding the family business that had, as the last commandment, the edict that if Barry Jr. and Eleanor could not come to an agreement, the companies should be sold. "That is not a threat, it is a fact," the document said.

To Barry Jr., the 13th commandment put Eleanor in the driver's seat. By her simply not agreeing to a settlement with him, he said, a sale would become inevitable—and that was her real goal. But Barry Sr. and Eleanor maintain that Eleanor's real goal was to acquire WHAS. In the end, Eleanor agreed to the stock swap, but only if the family could reach agreement with Sallie on a buyout price. Otherwise, Eleanor wanted the family businesses sold.

Sallie, meanwhile, put a $42 million price on her shares, and the family turned it down, having made an offer of $25 million, which Sallie rejected. During the negotiations, she met with her father, who was increasingly in despair over the conflict.

"He told me that he loved me," Sallie says, adding that it was the first time she ever recalled him saying this. Barry Sr. says his daughter advised him that she did not want to have any more contact with her father until the sale question was settled, which created a break that hurt Barry Sr. terribly and colored his thinking when the breach seemed likely to persist indefinitely.

Sallie had lowered her asking price to $32 million, and Barry Jr. had reluctantly agreed to an increase in the family offer, to $26.3 million, the top value established by Lehman Brothers. Sallie spurned that offer in early December, saying that unless her price of $32 million was met, she would oppose in court a change in a family trust that was necessary for the stock swap to be accomplished.

But Barry Jr. adamantly refused to increase the $26.3 million offer. The result was a gridlock: Eleanor insisted that Sallie agree to a price before Eleanor would proceed with the stock swap. Sallie insisted on $32 million or she would fight revision of the trust, and Barry felt the company could not prudently afford to pay more than $26.3 million.

Barry Sr. and the professional staff pleaded with Barry Jr. at least to offer Sallie $28 milion, arguing that Sallie's top priority was getting money to endow a foundation that she had started for Kentucky women in the arts. But Barry Jr. was not to be moved, although the debt burden involved did not seem excessive to anyone but him.

Based on a 20 year projection that took all of the company's expenses into account, including a planned investment of $73 million in equipment, paying Sallie $28 million would mean a maximum debt of $45 million vs. a $40 million debt at the $26.3 million offer.

Barry Jr., in his own projection, predicted minimal increases in operating profits for the 20-year period, which the professional staff regarded as unrealistically conservative.

Even using Barry Jr.'s projections, the professional staff regarded the debt as manageable.

Barry Jr. says that, because he was considering the financial security of his children and, because he would be partners with Joan and Worth's children, he felt it would have been imprudent to offer Sallie more than $26.3 million. "I wanted a comfort factor," he says, noting that he could accept one year of a drop in credit rating that a $40 million debt would have prompted, but no longer.

But to his father and the professional staff, Barry Jr.'s attitude seemed to be based more on emotions than rational business judgment.

"I think he felt anything more would be a victory for Sallie and a defeat for him," Barry Sr. says.

Sallie also viewed it "very personally" and for her "it became a feminist issue of the men in the family over the women in the family," Barry Sr. says. Eleanor thought Sallie might accept $28 million, and urged such an offer.

Through it all, Barry Sr. struggled to reconcile his children. But he failed and the elder Binghams finally came to a reluctant decision, "in the small hours of the night, together," Barry Sr. says.

On Wednesday morning, Jan. 8, Eleanor and Barry Jr. were summoned to the Little House and told by their father of his decision to sell all the properties. Barry Sr. said that the stock-swap option appeared dead, and that another proposal, strongly urged by Barry Jr. involving the sale of WHAS and Standard Gravure and the buying out of Sallie and Eleanor, would leave the newspapers financially vulnerable and unlikely to be operated in the Bingham tradition. Profits from the two non-newspaper companies have been used to pay family members the approximately $300,000 in annual dividends they depended upon, while the newspapers' resources supported a generous— even excessive, to some—news operation. Barry Jr. had argued that buying his sisters out would leave the newspaper in no worse financial jeopardy than the stock-swap.

Barry Jr. reacted to his father's decision in fury, accusing his father of putting the wishes of Sallie and Eleanor above his own, the son who had devoted his working life to the family business. But he did not suggest reopening negotiations with Sallie by increasing the family's offer.

The decision to sell, Barry Sr. says, was "in desperate necessity to break through what had become impossible for all of us, and was best in the long run for all of us. Barry, Sallie, Eleanor and the nine grandchildren."

And with the decision, the Bingham tradition in Kentucky came to an end.

DIVIDING UP THE FAMILY FORTUNE

LOUISVILLE—When sale of the three Bingham properties is completed, all family members will receive generous, but not precisely equal, shares of the proceeds.

According to non-family managers of the family businesses who asked not to be named, each group owns a different percentage of each of the businesses, and will be paid accordingly.

Barry Bingham Sr. and his wife, Mary, will receive all of their money directly. The remainder will go to the three surviving children and nine grandchildren in a mixture of direct payments and payments to a maze of trusts. The two grandchildren over 21 years of age will receive some money directly, and others will do so when they reach that age.

John Morton, a communications analyst at Lynch, Jones & Ryan in Washington—who prepared a quick appraisal of the companies for Sallie Bingham a year ago—now says that the Bingham companies will bring in about $390 million. His estimates: $300 million for The Courier-Journal and Louisville Times Company; $50 million for WHAS-TV, a CBS affiliate; $10 million for the AM and FM radio stations, and $30 million for Standard Gravure, the printing company.

Based on these projections, Barry Bingham Sr. and his wife would receive about $106 million.

Barry Bingham Jr. and his wife, Edith, and two daughters, Emily, a 20-year-old college student, and Molly, 17 and also at college, would receive about $45.6 million.

Sallie Bingham and her three children would receive about $55.2 million. Her children include Barry Bingham Ellsworth, 24, an independent film maker whose father is A. Whitney Ellsworth, publisher of The New York Review of Books. By her second husband, Michael Iovenko, a Wall Street lawyer, she has two sons: Christopher, 18, and William, 15. She and Timothy Peters, a Louisville builder whom she married in 1983, have had no children together.

The family of Eleanor Bingham Miller would receive about $55.8 million. Mrs. Miller married Rowland Miller, a Louisville architect, in 1979, and they have two children: Rowland, 3, and Worth, born last year. The family of Joan Bingham, widow of Worth Bingham, would receive about $42.9 million. Worth's children are Clara, 22, now living in Hong Kong, and Robert, a 19-year-old college student.

About $84.5 million would go to Trust 9, a generation-skipping trust established by Barry Sr.'s father. Upon the deaths of the senior Binghams, Trust 9 will be dispersed in equal quarters, with Barry Jr., Sallie and Eleanor receiving one quarter each, and Worth's two children sharing a quarter.

Although the grandchildren have played largely an observer role in the family struggle, Worth and Barry Jr.'s children and Sallie's son Christopher had expressed some interest in going into the family business. Robert, Worth's son, said that he and his sister had appealed directly to Barry Jr. and Barry Sr. not to sell the businesses.

"I don't really feel cheated out of anything," Robert said. "I just feel a general sense of loss." He added that the family trauma of recent years had been "a strange binding force" on his generation of Bingham descendants, and that they do not share the bitterness of their parents' generation.

Christopher Iovenko, Sallie's son, said, "I feel sorry it had to fall to pieces, but it's better for my mom."

All of the grandchildren except for Robert and Christopher either could not be reached for comment or declined to do so.

—Alex S. Jones

THE BINGHAMS, AFTER THE FALL

DECEMBER 21, 1986

BY ALEX S. JONES

On the Bingham estate overlooking the Ohio River outside Louisville, Ky., Barry Bingham Sr. and Barry Bingham Jr. live in houses separated by a short walk across a tended lawn. But each rarely crosses that short space to visit the other's home. "It's like the green line in Beirut separating the Christians and the Moslems," said Joan Bingham, an in-law.

The father and his only living son have barely spoken since Barry Sr. announced last Jan. 9 his decision to sell the family's media empire, including the Courier-Journal and The Louisville Times, the Pulitzer Prize-winning newspapers that had been in the family for nearly 70 years. Barry Jr., who had managed the enterprises for the last 15 years, denounced the sale as "a betrayal" and, almost overnight, the Binghams became a public archetype of a family destroyed in a struggle over business.

The year since then has been a period of lingering bitterness, grief and unrepentance. Barry Jr. crossed the lawn on Thursday to bring Christmas presents to his parents, a gesture he described as "correct." The whole Bingham family has not gathered together for Christmas since 1983, and this year will be no exception.

For the Binghams, the question of what ultimately happens to such a family after its business is sold remains unresolved. But outwardly, at least, all of them have lost the pallid, pained look of last January. They take pleasure in giving away chunks of their separate shares of the $434 million that the sale brought in. They are all building new lives. "It's over. It's accepted. It's done," says Emily Bingham, Barry Jr.'s daughter and a student at Harvard.

The wounds, however, will undoubtedly be reopened next year when Sallie Bingham, the daughter whose decision to sell her minority ownership triggered the family crisis, publishes her memoirs of growing up a Bingham. The book is tentatively titled "Passion and Prejudice," and it is likely to reflect her scathing criticism of the family.

"I'm afraid after this book comes out, our relationship will be impossible," says her mother, who will be 82 on Christmas eve.

There have been moments when it looked as though the wounds were closing. There was November's benefit reading of "The Tempest," for one. On stage was 80-year-old Barry Sr. in a brilliant scarlet smoking jacket, playing the part of Prospero the magician who banished old hurts and made everything right again. And in the audience were his wife, Mary, and his two daughters, Sallie and Eleanor Bingham Miller. Robert Schulman, a lecturer at the University of Louisville who was there, especially remembers the moment when Sallie rose to greet her mother with a kiss.

But the suggestion of rapprochement was misleading. A few days before the performance, Barry Sr., his eyes tired, shook his head dismissively at the notion that, like Prospero, he could restore peace to his family by selling the business that had brought them to blows.

The family remains divided, the old hurts still fresh, the principal players still convinced that they were right. It is as though the Binghams ended their private civil war, only to enter into a period of angry reconstruction.

Joan Bingham, the widow of the Binghams' eldest son, Worth, who was killed in a 1966 accident, has moved to Paris. Eleanor, 40, the youngest daughter, who encouraged her parents to sell at the end, remains in Louisville and although she is close to her parents, has been unable to thaw the ice with Barry Jr. and his wife, Edie.

Sallie Bingham, 49, a published fiction writer, rarely sees any of her relatives. Since January, she has appeared in forums ranging from Ms. Magazine to the Louisville Rotary Club to denounce what she says was the sexist treatment she received in the family. Of her memoir she says, "My aim is to tell my story, as I remember it, as I see it. They will find things, certainly, to disagree with."

The unhappy Bingham saga has become a cautionary tale for other families, one that instructors use as a case history of what can go wrong in a family business. Milton H. Stern, a professional counselor to families in business, whose offer to help the Binghams was politely spurned by Barry Sr., says that, without dramatic moves, relations are now apt to become "more and more distant."

The sale itself is resolved. In mid-July, the Bingham newspapers were acquired by the Gannett Company Inc., one of the nation's largest newspaper chains. Earlier this month, the process was completed with the purchase of the remaining Bingham properties: WHAS Inc., a television station and AM and FM radio stations in Louisville, and Standard Gravure Inc., a printing company.

With the sale behind them, the elderly Binghams are weary and heartsick over their alienation from Barry Jr., his wife Edie, and from Sallie—but not apologetic, although Mary, whose criticism of some of her son's decisions created a lasting wound, has some second thoughts.

"I was very naïve," she says. "Barry Jr. was far more uncertain than I had realized and I never grasped that he was feeling this cumulative sense of persecution." But she adds: "I don't think, being the kind of person I am, that I could have not said what I thought."

For Barry Sr., his biggest concern is that the reputation of his father, Robert Worth Bingham, may be tarnished by upcoming books on the family. Robert Bingham's second wife was Mary Lily Kenan Flagler, one of the nation's richest women, who died in 1917 after eight months of marriage, amid rumors of possible foul play. Barry Sr. says the rumors were scurrilous. An autopsy was performed, no charges were ever filed, and the stories died, only to be resurrected when the sale focused attention on the family.

Barry Sr. has recently found documents that he says further exonerate his father, but he remains deeply anxious that the memory of a man he admired above all others could be damaged. Robert Bingham inherited $5 million of Mary Lily's approximately $100 million estate, and used the inheritance to purchase the papers in 1918, founding the family business.

But for the senior Binghams, life since the sale has not been all sadness and regrets. Their only contact with the papers is as interested readers, and the separation seems to have liberated them. With over $110 million from the sale to dispose of, they have not lacked attention. They have found giving away money to be great fun, and have already pledged nearly $10 million to a variety of causes.

They have underwritten high-culture performances in Louisville. Barry Sr. has pledged $4 million toward building a club for the faculty and staff of the University of Louisville. Mary has offered to invest $3.25 million in Open Court Publishing Company, a firm whose textbooks teach reading phonetically, reflecting her conviction that Barry Jr.'s slowness in reading as a child was created by non-phonetic reading instruction.

Their friends say they even see a sense of contentment in Barry Sr. and Mary. They have each other, the devoted attention of Eleanor, and they have taken pains to maintain ties with their nine grandchildren.

But Barry Bingham Jr. and Edie are far from content.

"I've really been burned in this relationship," says Barry Jr., who is 53 years old and rich now, but without the serious work that for years was the focus of his life.

Like his father Barry Jr. offers no apologies. For example, he would change little about how he conducted himself in the struggle with his sisters. Though the family gridlock at the end might have been broken if he had offered Sallie more money for her shares, he still insists that the company could not afford it.

Barry Jr. now rises for his daily jog at 6 A.M., an indulgence for him; his days as editor and publisher began at 5:15. He devotes most of his time to searching for a data-base information company or similar venture in which to invest the $24 million in cash that he received from the sale. Another $26 million went into trusts. His portion was somewhat less than his sisters' because most of his shares were in the less valuable broadcast companies.

"Damn right I miss it," he says of his role at the newspapers, "but it's like the death of a friend. You've got to go on."

Rebuilding family ties is not a priority for Barry Jr., despite the knowledge that the senior Binghams may be nearing death. In fact, if a new job demands it, he will leave Louisville without much regret, he says.

Barry Sr. still insists that the combination of inheritance taxes, the need to buy new presses, and loans incurred in keeping the papers would have left a legacy of debt for the children and grandchildren. Selling, he says, spared Barry Jr. the odious task of operating the newspapers without the open-pocketbook style that had been the Bingham tradition, and also avoided a possible battle over succession among the nine grandchildren.

"Inevitably the value and prestige of the papers would decline," Barry Sr. says. His son "would have stayed at the papers 24-hours-a-day. It would have been a terrible life for him and unfair to the grandchildren."

To Barry Jr., such sentiments represent an "incredible stack of failure-laden assumptions," rationalizations that mask a collapse of the parental will and confidence that had been the steely backbone of the family.

"This has gone from a can-do family to a can't-do family," he says. And, in a voice tinged with controlled anger, he describes the sale as "as tragedy; a bad decision on my father's part."

. Barry Sr. has tried not to be critical of his son. But his wife, Mary, who her children say possesses a devastating candor, speaks her mind. To her, Barry Jr. and his wife are acting as if they were martyrs, behavior for which she has little patience. "He's such a Marine," she says, "and Edie is as stiff-necked as Barry is."

The real family trouble probably began early in 1984 when Barry Jr. insisted that his mother, wife and two sisters leave the boards of the companies. Barry Jr. said he wanted a more professional board; his parents say he wanted to remove Sallie, who had become critical of Barry Jr.'s management. Sallie refused to resign and, in what she has described as a bitter humiliation, the other family members pushed her out.

Later that year, Sallie determined to break with the family and sell her approximately 15 percent interest. Soon after, Eleanor said that she wanted out as well, but vacillated between wanting to run WHAS and wanting to sell everything. No one could agree on terms. By the time Barry Sr. took matters into his own hands and sold the companies in January, the younger generation was in unbreakable deadlock.

Barry Jr. hoped that his father, who controlled 95 percent of the stock through a voting trust, would back the dutiful son who had operated the newspapers on behalf of the family for so many years. However, Barry Sr. and Mary elected to sell everything, creating a breach with their son that both parties say will be long, if ever, in healing.

For Barry Jr., the memory of his mother's criticisms are a source of resentment. "She's a very harsh person," he says of his mother, "a very damaging person."

While his feelings toward Sallie seem to be wary disinterest, the voices of both Barry Jr. and Edie turn cold when describing the roles of Eleanor and Rowland Miller, her husband, in the sale.

Eleanor, he says, "strung me along" by engaging in the long negotiations to swap her interest in the newspapers for WHAS Inc. According to Barry Jr., his relationship with Rowland, an architect, soured because Rowland interfered in management and editorial decisions. "He tries to tell you how to do your job," Barry Jr. says, adding that Rowland didn't like being criticized at cocktail parties for the papers' editorial positions. But both Barry Jr. and Edie are most angry at Rowland, because they say he pushed Eleanor to urge her parents to sell the businesses, and they say he did it because selling everything meant more money.

To Rowland, Barry Jr. was a bully who was trying to push his wife around. "It made me mad to see the way he treated Eleanor," Rowland says. Both Rowland and Eleanor say that Eleanor sincerely wanted to operate WHAS, and that her indecision came out of conflicts over taking on such a responsibility while caring for two small children.

"They think Rowland brainwashed me to be pro-sale and that I brainwashed my father," Eleanor says, "but Father makes his own decisions, with my mother's advice."

That decision, she says, was "absolutely the right thing."

Eleanor, who is 40 years old, says that she has tried to keep in contact with her nieces and nephews, including Barry Jr.'s two daughters. But of her relationship with Barry Jr., she says, "It's not something I miss and I don't guess he misses it either."

Though friendly, she and Sallie see each other infrequently.

In some respects, Eleanor has drawn even closer to her parents since the sale. In Barry Sr.'s new offices, which were designed by Rowland, Eleanor has a room next to her father's. She has started a video production company.

She received $62 million from the sale, and plans to donate some money to support such causes as farming using draft horses, which she describes as "low tech and less damaging" to the soil.

"There really hasn't been a revolution in our lives," she says. "We just bought a new pick-up truck."

The next visible public crisis for the Binghams could well be the publication of Sallie Bingham's book next year. Sallie knows her memoir is a potential minefield, but hopes that a successful book will rekindle interest in her other work, which includes four unpublished novels. She is best-known as a short-story writer.

Women who are part-owners of family businesses now frequently call her, and she advises them to get a woman lawyer, first thing. She has appeared on such television programs as the Phil Donahue show. "I enjoy the attention," she says.

Sallie, who has three children and has been married three times, received $62 million from the sale; like Eleanor, she got about $25 million to spend, with the rest in trust. She has given $1 million each to Ms. Magazine and to the American Place Theatre, a New York company that has produced some of her plays.

She has also spent $8.5 million to endow the Kentucky Foundation for Women, but created a storm of controversy in November when she dismissed four women on the staff because well over half the Foundation's income was going for administration.

As for the family, she says she is not angry now, as she was when she was kicked off the boards. Sallie has done little to forge a reconciliation with her parents that is more than polite. But that will get better "someday," she says.

FLYING HIGH–PILOTS ON DRUGS

THE PITTSBURGH PRESS

Andrew Schneider, 44, won his second Pulitzer Prize this year. His first, in 1986, was awarded for his work on stories about the international market in human kidneys used in transplants. Mr. Schneider has worked for *The Pittsburgh Press* for three years, where he has covered many other issues in public health, including stories about the lack of standards for emergency medical services in Pennsylvania.

Matthew Brelis, 29, is a general assignment reporter for *The Pittsburgh Press*. Mr. Brelis worked briefly as a reporter/trainee at *The Washington Star* before joining the regional news desk at *The Press* in 1981. He has reported on bidding irregularities at Pittsburgh's largest community college, a prison uprising in Moundsville, West Virginia, and the 1984 industrial disaster at Bhopal, India.

THE GOODYEAR WAR

AKRON BEACON JOURNAL

Doug Oplinger, 35, has been the business editor at the *Akron Beacon Journal* since early 1986. For eight years before that, he was assistant business editor and a business reporter, covering the rubber industry. Mr. Oplinger joined the paper in 1971 while attending the University of Akron. As the *Beacon Journal*'s business editor, Mr. Oplinger directed much of the daily coverage of the Goodyear story.

THE *AKRON BEACON JOURNAL* TEAM

The difficult problem with the newspaper winning an award of such importance is determining whom to recognize. Scores of newsroom employees were affected, either by being directly involved in the coverage or filling the gaps left by those who were shifted to cover the event.

The following were the primary reporters and writers in the Goodyear coverage:

Rick Reiff, 34, was one of the three reporters who covered the takeover on a daily basis and then worked on the special team at the end. He has been with the *Beacon Journal* since 1975, working the police, general assignment and City Hall beats before joining business in 1983.

Lawrence A. Pantages, 31, has been an employee at the *Beacon Journal* since 1972. He became a reporter in 1977 after graduating from Syracuse University. He transferred to business news in June 1985. Pantages was one of the three business reporters responsible for the daily coverage of the Goodyear takeover and was part of a special team to produce the eight-page reconstruction.

Greg Gardner, 35, joined the *Beacon Journal* business desk in July 1983 after working for the Columbus, Georgia, *Ledger-Enquirer* and the *Tullahoma* (Tennessee) *News*. He was one of the three business reporters responsible for the daily coverage of the six-week Goodyear takeover story.

Stuart Warner, 34, wrote frequently about Goodyear in his daily column and was the lead writer for the reconstruction. He is a native of Lexington, Kentucky, where he began with the Knight Ridder newspapers there at age 17. He came to the *Beacon Journal* as sports editor in 1979 and became a writer in 1983.

Melissa Johnson, 27, is a general assignment reporter on the metro desk and contributed two major stories during the takeover. She also participated in the reconstruction. Ms. Johnson worked for The Associated Press before joining the *Beacon Journal* in 1984.

Other major contributors were:

Ron Shinn, 40, assistant business editor. He has been at the *Beacon Journal* since 1977.

William Hershey, 42, *Beacon Journal* Washington correspondent.

He covered the legislative angle and coordinated our coverage of the hearing in which Goodyear and Goldsmith faced off. He has been with the *Beacon Journal* 14 years.

Glenn Proctor, 40, a business reporter. He has been at the *Beacon Journal* since 1981.

Katie Byard, 26, now a metro reporter, was on the business desk at the time. She came to the paper in 1983.

Our special eight-page reconstruction of the attempted takeover, a 10-day project, was headed by managing editor Larry Williams. Pantages, Reiff and Ms. Johnson and assistant managing editor John Greenman were the other contributors on that special effort, which allowed us to describe in colorful detail how the takeover unfolded. (Greenman and Williams also were responsible for day-to-day coverage.)

Others were: Francisco Badillo, Don Bandy, Kathleen Byland, Mark Calvey, William Canterbury, Jim Carney, Patrick Cole, Mark Dawidziak, Jim Dettling, Bob Dyer, Diane Paparone Evans, John Funk, Peter Geiger, Laura Haferd, Robert Hoiles, John Kostrzewa, E. L. Langer, Steve Love, Marcia Myers, Charlene Nevada, Terry Oblander, Bill Osinski, Mary Grace Poidomani, Yalinda Rhoden, Eric Sandstrom, Cristal Williams, Dennis Balogh, Chip Bok, Dennis Earlenbaugh, Dennis Haas, Art Krummel, Walt Neal, Ott Gangl, Susan Kirkman, Ron Kuner, Don Roese, Lew Stamp, Ed Suba Jr., Paul Tople and Robin Witek.

—Doug Oplinger, business editor
Akron Beacon Journal

EVIDENCE OF INNOCENCE

THE PHILADELPHIA INQUIRER

John Woestendiek, 33, has been a reporter with *The Philadelphia Inquirer* since 1981. He was assigned to the Bucks County bureau for one year and has covered prisons and mental institutions in Philadelphia for the last five years. Before coming to *The Inquirer,* he worked briefly as a reporter at *The Arizona Daily Star* in Tucson, and later as a reporter, assistant city editor and finally city editor at the *Lexington Leader* in Kentucky.

DISORDER IN THE COURT

THE PHILADELPHIA INQUIRER

Daniel R. Biddle, 33, joined the *Inquirer* staff in 1979. Mr. Biddle previously worked for three years as a reporter for the Cleveland *Plain Dealer.* At *The Inquirer,* he has covered Philadelphia City Hall and the Pennsylvania Supreme Court. After taking a year off in 1984 to teach journalism at the University of California at Berkeley, Mr. Biddle returned to *The Inquirer* as a general assignment reporter.

H. G. Bissinger, 32, was a nominated finalist for the Pulitzer Prize in feature writing in 1982 for an article on the near crash of a jetliner. Mr. Bissinger joined *The Inquirer* in 1981 after working on the staffs of *The Ledger-Star* in Norfolk, Virginia, and the *St. Paul Pioneer Press* in

Minnesota. He was a Nieman Fellow at Harvard University from 1985 to 1986.

Fredric N. Tulsky, 36, joined *The Inquirer* in 1979 as the paper's transportation reporter. His coverage included a series of articles in 1981 on safety hazards resulting from neglect of Philadelphia's transit system. Since 1982, Mr. Tulsky has covered City Hall. He worked previously at the *Los Angeles Herald-Examiner,* the Jackson *Clarion-Ledger* in Mississippi, and the Port Huron *Times Herald* and the *Saginaw News,* both in Michigan.

BLOOM COUNTY

T H E   W A S H I N T O N   P O S T

Berke Breathed, 29, created the "Bloom County" cartoon in 1980. Since then, it has evolved into one of the most popular cartoon strips in the country, appearing in some 1,000 daily, Sunday and college newspapers. While a student at the University of Texas at Austin, Mr. Breathed developed "The Academia Waltz," a cartoon that ran in *The Daily Texan* newspaper. More than two million copies of four collections of his comics have been sold.

THE CONTRA CONNECTION

T H E M I A M I H E R A L D

Alfonso Chardy, 35, has been a Washington correspondent for *The Miami Herald* since 1982. He was born in Mexico and has done extensive reporting from Latin America, working for several years as a staff reporter with *The Mexico City News,* four years as a correspondent in Mexico, Argentina and Colombia for The Associated Press, and two years in Nicaragua and Panama with United Press International. He joined *The Herald* in 1980.

Alexandra Dibble, 33, joined the *Herald* staff in 1981 as an intern. A native of Alexandria, Egypt, Ms. Dibble worked previously for *Al-Anba',* a Kuwaiti daily, and for United Press International in Mexico City. She has a bachelor's degree from the University of Utah and a master's degree in journalism from Columbia University.

Tim Golden, 27, a member of *The Herald*'s Latin America staff, is currently assigned to its San Salvador bureau. Before coming to *The Herald,* Mr. Golden worked for the *Los Angeles Times.* He is a graduate of Dartmouth College.

Sam Dillon, 35, has been a member of *The Herald*'s Latin America staff since 1982. A correspondent in San Salvador until 1983, Mr. Dillon is now based in Miami and reports frequently from Central America and the Caribbean. He worked previously at the *St. Paul Pioneer Press* in Minnesota and for The Associated Press in San Salvador.

Andres Oppenheimer, 35, joined the business news staff at *The Herald* in 1983. A native of Buenos Aires, Argentina, Mr. Oppenheimer previously worked for The Associated Press and for *Siete Dias* magazine in Buenos Aires. He holds a law degree from the University of Buenos Aires.

Jim McGee, 34, has been a reporter for *The Herald* since 1980. He worked for three years as a reporter at *The Fort Myers News-Press* in Florida. While at *The Herald,* Mr. McGee worked on a 1985 investigation of anti-Castro terrorism and stories about drug enforcement efforts in south Florida in 1981. He was a John S. Knight fellow at Stanford University for one year.

THE CHALLENGER EXPLOSION

THE NEW YORK TIMES

Philip M. Boffey, 51, was a member of *The Times*'s staff that won a Pulitzer Prize in 1986 for coverage of the Strategic Defense Initiative. He has been a Washington correspondent for *The Times* since 1982. Mr. Boffey joined the paper in 1977 as an editorial writer and later served as a science writer before being assigned to the Washington bureau.

William J. Broad, 36, was a member of the team that won a Pulitzer Prize in 1986 for its coverage of the Strategic Defense Initiative. He joined *The Times* in 1983 as a science reporter. Before coming to *The Times,* Mr. Broad held several reporting and teaching positions in science fields.

Richard Witkin, 68, has been transportation editor of *The Times* since 1968. He joined the paper in 1954 as an aviation specialist and became aerospace news editor in 1963. Mr. Witkin began his newspaper career in 1940 at the *Detroit Free Press* and was a news writer for a wire service before coming to *The Times.*

David E. Sanger, 26, has been a reporter for *The New York Times* since 1983. Based in *The Times*'s Business Day section, Mr. Sanger covers a wide range of issues relating to high technology, including developments in computer design, software and microelectronics. He has also written extensively about defense contractors, the Strategic Defense Initiative and national security.

John Noble Wilford, 53, won a Pulitzer Prize in 1984 in the National Reporting category for his writing about space exploration. He joined *The Times* in 1965 in the science section and directed science news coverage from 1975 to 1979. Since he joined the paper, Mr. Wilford has covered all the major space missions. From 1973 through 1974, he worked as an assistant national news editor.

Stuart Diamond, 38, has been covering issues in technology, energy and the environment since 1984 as a reporter in the Business Day section. Before that he worked for 11 years as a reporter for *Newsday* in New York, and from 1969 to 1973, for *The Daily Home News* in New Brunswick, New Jersey.

Richard Flaste, 44, has been director of the science news section since 1982 and was deputy director for nearly three years before that. He joined *The Times* in 1962 as an office aide and held a number of editorial jobs, including that of assistant style editor, before being assigned to the science section.

William E. Schmidt, 40, has been the Atlanta bureau chief since 1983. He joined *The Times* in 1981 and was made the Denver bureau chief that year. Before coming to *The Times,* Mr. Schmidt worked for *Newsweek* for eight years, holding assignments in Miami, Chicago, Cairo and Moscow.

Holcomb B. Noble, 53, deputy metropolitan editor, served as deputy director of science news from 1982 to 1987. He won a Pulitzer Prize in 1986 as part of the team that covered the Strategic Defense Initiative. Before his assignment to the science section, Mr. Noble worked for 10 years as a copy editor and acquisitions editor for *The New York Times Magazine.*

CENSORED IN SOUTH AFRICA
L O S   A N G E L E S   T I M E S

Michael Parks, 43, has been the Johannesburg bureau chief for the *Los Angeles Times* since 1984. He previously served as bureau chief in Beijing for four years. Before joining the *Times,* Mr. Parks worked for 11 years for the Baltimore *Sun,* where he served in a number of foreign posts. He was previously assistant city editor of *The Suffolk Sun* on Long Island and a reporter for *The Detroit News.*

PEOPLE POWER IN THE PHILIPPINES
S A N   F R A N C I S C O   E X A M I N E R

Kim Komenich, 30, has worked for the *San Francisco Examiner* for five years. A general assignment photographer, he has covered local, national and international news and produced a feature photo essay about a burn victim. Before joining the *Examiner,* Mr. Komenich was a photographer for the *Contra Costa Times* in California.

SUNRISE ON THE BORDER

THE TRIBUNE OF SAN DIEGO

Jonathan Freedman, 37, has been a Pulitzer prize nominated finalist twice, in 1983 and 1984, before winning this year in editorial writing. Mr. Freedman joined *The Tribune* of San Diego in 1981 as an editorial writer. He previously worked for The Associated Press and as a free-lance writer.

CRITIC'S CHOICE

LOS ANGELES TIMES

Richard Eder, 54, has been a book critic for the *Los Angeles Times* since 1982. Before that, Mr. Eder had a long career at *The New York Times,* starting as a copyboy in 1954 and serving in a range of positions, including that of police reporter, State Department correspondent, and drama critic; he also held several European assignments, and from 1980 to 1982 was the paper's Paris bureau chief.

POLITICAL PRESCRIPTIONS

THE WASHINGTON POST

Charles Krauthammer, 36, began writing a weekly column for *The Washington Post* in 1985. Mr. Krauthammer practiced psychiatry at Massachusetts General Hospital for three years before coming to Washington in 1978 to direct planning in psychiatric research for the Carter Administration. He later served as a speech writer to Vice President Walter Mondale during the 1980 presidential campaign. After the campaign, he joined *The New Republic* as an editor and writer.

MEDITERRANEAN PATROL

THE PHILADELPHIA INQUIRER

Steve Twomey, 35, has worked in a number of positions at *The Philadelphia Inquirer* since 1973. He started as a general assignment reporter, later was assigned to a suburban political beat and then became the paper's education writer, labor reporter and Los Angeles-based West Coast correspondent. In 1983, Mr. Twomey was appointed Paris correspondent. He recently returned to Philadelphia from that post.

SHATTERED DREAMS

THE DES MOINES REGISTER

David Peterson, 37, has been a staff photographer for *The Des Moines Register* for 10 years. He has won numerous honors for his photographs and is a four-time recipient of the Iowa Photographer of the Year award. Before coming to *The Register,* Mr. Peterson worked for two years at the *Topeka Capital-Journal* in Kansas.

ALTERED FATES

CHICAGO TRIBUNE

Jeff Lyon, 43, joined the *Chicago Tribune* as a reporter in 1974. He wrote a column for five years until he was assigned, in 1981, to the features department. Before coming to the *Tribune,* Mr. Lyon worked at the City News Bureau in Chicago, *The Miami Herald* and at *Chicago's American* and its successor, *Chicago Today.*

Peter Gorner, 44, has been a critic, editor and feature writer at the *Tribune* since 1967. He has covered a wide range of issues, including diabetes research and topics in the arts and sciences. He also worked on an investigation of the divorce system in Chicago. Mr. Gorner began his journalism career in 1959 as a reporter for the City News Bureau in Chicago.

THE FALL OF THE HOUSE OF BINGHAM

T H E   N E W   Y O R K   T I M E S

Alex S. Jones, 40, joined *The New York Times* business section in 1983 and was later transferred to the metropolitan staff. Before coming to *The Times,* Mr. Jones was the editor of *The Greeneville Sun* in Tennessee for five years. He worked previously as an aide in Tom Wiseman's gubernatorial campaign in Tennessee and as a reporter and managing editor at *The Daily Post-Athenian* in Athens, Tennessee.

ABOUT THE EDITOR

Kendall J. Wills is assistant editor of the Op-Ed Page at *The New York Times*. He joined the paper in 1982 and worked for the business and foreign desks before being assigned to the Op-Ed section. Mr. Wills earned a bachelor's degree at Columbia College and a master's degree from the School of International and Public Affairs at Columbia University. A native of Milwaukee, Mr. Wills lives in New York City.